Charles Sanders Peirce

Charles S. Peirce in Berlin in 1875.

Charles Sanders Peirce

A Life

JOSEPH BRENT

Indiana University Press / BLOOMINGTON AND INDIANAPOLIS

The paper used in this publication meets the minimum requirements of American National Standard for Information Sciences—Permanence of Paper for Printed Library Materials, ANSI Z39.48-1984.

TM

Manufactured in the United States of America

Library of Congress Cataloging-in-Publication Data

Brent, Joseph
    Charles Sanders Peirce : a life / Joseph Brent.
        p.   cm.
    Includes bibliographical references and index.
    ISBN 0-253-31267-1 (cloth)
        1. Peirce, Charles S. (Charles Sanders), 1839–1914.
    2. Philosophers—United States—Biography.   I. Title.
    B945.P44B73   1993
    191—dc20
    [B]   92-19888

    1 2 3 4 5 97 96 95 94 93

To
Thomas A. Sebeok
and in memory of
Duncan Brent

Contents

FOREWORD

I was an undergraduate at Cambridge in 1936, just mastering English, when I first encountered Charles Sanders Peirce, in the appendix of *The Meaning of Meaning* by C. K. Ogden and I. A. Richards. There, pressed between a consideration of Baldwin at one end and "a little fable concerning Amoeba" at the other, a discussion of Peirce's thinking, especially of a seminal paper of his dated May 14, 1867, took up about twelve pages. The efforts of Peirce, identified as an "American logician . . . from whom William James took the idea and the term Pragmatism, and whose Algebra of Dyadic Relations was developed by [Ernst] Schroeder," were further characterized as by "far the most elaborate and determined attempts to give an account of signs and their meaning. . . . "

Those of us in England who troubled to read these passages on and by Peirce mispronounced his name (which is correctly pronounced "purse"). Worse, we were put off from pursuing his writings because Ogden, alluding to a letter of 1908 from Peirce to Lady Welby, felt compelled to add that, "unfortunately," Peirce's "terminology was so formidable that few have been willing to devote time to its mastery, and the work was never completed." Only at the outset of the 1940s, in the second of Charles Morris's University of Chicago seminars on "semiotic," did I hear Peirce's name uttered correctly. Too, it was there that I came eventually to realize that Morris was propelling me toward the same lofty intellect Ogden and Richards had ephemerally ushered in to their readership. Thereafter, at the instigation of Morris but later strongly abetted by the illustrious Russian philologist Roman Jakobson—who time and again insisted that, after the 1940s, Peirce was his "most powerful source of inspiration"—I embarked with determination and ever-escalating awe on my studies of Peirce's "semeiotic." That Peirce's reputation for turgidity was unjustifiably overstated by Ogden and others, at least as concerns semiotic studies, became apparent to me only after decades of attentive study.

Collaterally, I began to wonder about this prodigious thinker, to whom Ernest Nagel still felt compelled to refer in a 1959 *Scientific American* review as a "little known American philosopher." There were, to be sure, occasional sightings highlighting this or that aspect of Peirce's life or character—just its "glassy" overall shape, never the jagged details. For instance, according to a sharply etched cameo by Joseph Jastrow, Peirce's former pupil and sometime collaborator, Peirce's personality

> was affected by a superficial reticence often associated with the scientific temperament. He readily gave the impression of being unsocial, possibly cold, more truly retiring. At bottom the trait was in the nature of a refined shyness, an embarrassment in the presence of small talk and introductory salutations intruded by convention to start one's mind. His nature was generously hospitable; he was an intellectual host. In that respect he was eminently fitted to become the leader of a select band of disciples.

"Under more fortunate circumstances," Jastrow had intimated but never made plain, "his academic usefulness might have been vastly extended. For he had the pedagogic gift to an unusual degree, had it by dower of nature, as some men handle a pencil and others the bow of a violin."

Jastrow went on to comment, not on the actual or possible causes but on the deplorable implications of Peirce's presumptive shortcomings and misadventures in Baltimore: "It may be an inevitable result of the conventional system of education, but it is none the less a sad one, that his type of ability does not flourish readily in an institutionalized atmosphere than had Johns Hopkins in those days." He then proceeded to formulate this laudable yet nebulous moral: "Systems must give way to personalities, if the best talents of the best men are to be available. . . . An educational policy that makes it possible to find a place for such men as Peirce on their faculties of the great universities is a worthy ambition for those who control the educational future of America." The antecedent of the head pronoun "It" must have remained irksomely opaque to all but Peirce's best-informed contemporaries, as it certainly did to me. To be sure, Peirce's years at the Johns Hopkins were reinvestigated by Max H. Fisch and set forth in 1952, but again they were reported on so allusively that the Cheshire cat almost within view once again evanesced into the woods. Some years afterwards, when I asked Jakobson, by then himself an acclaimed professor at Harvard, what he thought about this sort of equivocation, he gave me this Delphic answer: "I think that Peirce was much too good for Harvard."

Indeed, Peirce's close friend William James characterized him, in a vain plea to Harvard's President Eliot to secure the fifty-six-year-old American master even a temporary academic appointment, as a "name of mysterious greatness." His stature was palpable to discriminating contemporaries such as James and, after his *Collected Papers* began to appear in the 1930s, to a host of devoted followers, but his manifestly quirky personality continued to perplex. I grew increasingly curious about the man concealed behind the philosophical, mathematical, and scientific opulence. But other than a handful of perfunctory, curtailed portraits and a couple of shallow, derivative biographies composed by some of Peirce's deepest misinterpreters, there was precious little to go by.

In 1968, there did appear a useful book by Paul K. Conkin, titled *Puritans and Pragmatists: Eight Eminent American Thinkers*, the sixth chapter of which was devoted to Peirce. Fourteen pages or so dealt with his "life," the rest (sixty pages) with some of his ideas. I dipped into Conkin's book with zest in the late 1980s (mainly for the chapter on Emerson) but found myself wondering uneasily where Conkin had gotten the data for his succinct biographical sketch of Peirce. He provides no references, only a short "reading guide" at the end of his collection, where he divulges that "more than any other major American philosopher, the life of Peirce is hidden from lay readers. There have been," he confirmed, "no full biographies, nor even very helpful intellectual portraits." Then his "guide" casually reveals: "of greatest assistance to me . . . was Joseph Lancaster Brent, III's unpublished Ph.D. dissertation, 'A Study of the Life of Charles Sanders Peirce' (University of California at Los Angeles, May 1960)." In his preface, he acknowledges that Dr. Brent provided him with "indispensable insights and knowledge about Peirce."

When I later chanced across a footnote in a book about Emerson which credited the same dissertation for incidental data about Peirce, I decided that the time had come for me to search directly in what was undoubtedly the fountainhead: Brent's manuscript. But first I needed to make sure that I had not overlooked a version, or at least an excerpt, published in the intervening thirty years. Although Brent's dissertation was listed in Christian J. W. Kloesel's and Joseph M. Ransdell's bibliography of "secondary studies" on Peirce, and again in Beverley Kent's "selected bibliography" to her study of Peirce's logic and classification of the sciences, I was unable to find any other citation in the by now massive literature of Peirceiana, not even among the writings of Fisch.

I obtained Brent's dissertation via interlibrary loan and read it in January 1990. I was greatly impressed. The first surprise was that it was written by a professional American intellectual historian, not a philosopher, let alone a semiotician. On February 7, I contacted the (then) chairman of UCLA's Department of History to ask, "If Dr. Brent is alive, can you tell me his whereabouts? And if he is deceased, do you know who his heirs or executors are? Or at least his attorney?" In due course, UCLA sent me a form, dated June 4, 1959, marked "Last known info," giving a California address which turned out to be a dead end.

In the meantime, however, I learned from the front matter of the dissertation that Brent was an alumnus of my graduate alma mater, Princeton University. So I called our Alumni Office hoping to locate him. A month later, I at last contacted the elusive Dr. Brent in Washington, D.C. I subsequently invited him—with the enthusiastic concurrence of the director of Indiana University Press—to submit his original and still unique biography of Peirce for publication. Brent soon agreed, his manuscript having languished for more than thirty years, to thoroughly revise, document, check and recheck, and much expand his embryonic 1960 version. The issue of his backbreaking labors is, at long last but luckily not too late, available here for all to enjoy.

Brent's account of Peirce is scrupulously searched and researched, conservatively empirical in documentation, superbly written, and compulsively readable. His sense of the concrete is enhanced throughout by the powers of his imagination. Biographies, being preeminently social constructions, depend on the way biographers ask the key questions. As, from time to time, all superior historians must, Brent does not hesitate to allow himself the intuitive surge of a creative intellect, grounding his speculations in the context of Peirce's immediate temporal and spatial circumstances. He sweeps cant away with compelling discernment as well as with a rare dramatic flair.

Note especially his Chapter 6, aptly titled "The Wasp in the Bottle." This section constitutes the culmination of Brent's strange *Bildungsroman*. With overtones of a softly familiar myth, he demonstrates how perverse it would be to dispute that the canon of this immensely complex polymath—deprived during so much of his career of simple human decencies as well as the healthy ambient noise of peers and students, and so frustrated, as he was to the end, in his pecuniary ambitions—mirrors, or at the very least can illuminate, his progressively lamentable life.

To me, this book finally reads like a tragicomic thriller. (As a bonus, perhaps Brent's accomplished tapestry could provide the basis for an entertaining movie "treatment," a suspenseful American film noir.) It delicately intermingles catastrophe with farce while revealing a seamy side to American academic polity, its sometime brutality and mendacity, and the often cruelly corrupt machinations of higher political authority. These actions worked their calamitous effects on this most finely honed, yet in some ways so sadly unworldly, of American intellects, and ultimately wore Peirce out.

As Peirce scholarship tends to take a perhaps excessively and uncritically laudatory view of Peirce (he has lately become something of a cult figure, with his bearded portrait occasionally decorating T-shirts), even the simplest sketches of the life of this profoundest of philosophers have been beclouded by the cult of his imagined personality. Brent's unique account is therefore bound to raise many questions—and eyebrows. Why did it remain shrouded, not just from the lay public but from entitled academics, for more than three decades? Why couldn't Brent find a publisher thirty years ago? Was his work suppressed? Why? And by whom? Was Peirce's life, its triumphs and disasters, too sordid for delicate contemporary and posthumous sensibilities? Did Brent really receive a long-distance call past one midnight from a famous lady in New York City claiming that Peirce (who died in 1914) had appeared to her in a dream to instruct her to phone Brent at once and inform him that he does not wish, transcendentally, to ever have this biography published? Stay tuned . . .

Floyd Merrell, one of our strongest semioticians, recently remarked on the fact that "semiotics, Peircean semiotics, continues to survive, even though at certain times and places it lies at the periphery or the underworld of academia." Yet his outlook is, I think, unduly modest. Don't doubt that Peirce lives (and his semiotics along with him). But Brent's book will be the decisive one in keeping body and soul together in and for the times ahead.

Thomas A. Sebeok

Charles Peirce has been a constant companion in my thinking life since I discovered him in 1957 in Perry Miller's perceptive anthology, *American Thought: Civil War to World War I*. The first book I bought containing significant work by Peirce was a secondhand first edition of Morris Raphael Cohen's collection (published in 1923, nine years after Peirce's death) called *Chance, Love and Logic*, and subtitled *philosophical essays by the late Charles S. Peirce, the founder of pragmatism*. The idea that it was Peirce rather than William James who originated pragmatism denied what was then the accepted attribution, and I decided to pursue the earlier Cohen version in the face of Ralph Barton Perry's well-known 1935 biography of James. Three years of research in various manuscript and document collections produced over three thousand pages of notes, which were the basis of a dissertation biography in History at UCLA in 1960. It was my intention to revise it for publication over five years, but this proved impossible. The Harvard University Department of Philosophy, which owned the Peirce papers, while it granted me access to all but four boxes of biographical material restricted from consultation, declined to allow me to quote its large collection of letters and other material essential for a Peirce biography. I am very grateful to Israel Scheffler and the other members of the present department who gave me the permission I desired in late 1991, with the consequence that this study appears—at long last—thirty-two years after the dissertation from which it derives.

The reader will find that I have included lengthy Peirce quotations. My purpose has been to give a strong sense of Peirce's presence. Contrary to the usual scholarly practice, I have often used these passages as part of an argument, rather than as support for it. On occasion, I have included relevant material that I have not commented on in the text, leaving it to the reader to follow out Peirce's thinking about the subject. Because knowledge of the chronological development of Peirce's ideas is so important for understanding his thought, I have included at many points in the narrative my and, wherever possible, Peirce's description of what he was working on at the time.

Peirce wrote more than one version of almost everything he believed important. This was as much true of his correspondence as of his philosophical and scientific writings. It was often impossible to decide which version of a letter (and sometimes there are many) he sent, or if he sent it at all. I have used any version I judged useful in illuminating his life and thought, regardless of its disposition. Indeed, it is often in unsent versions, or in letters he merely considered sending, that the most useful information appears, especially in touches and nuances of intent and feeling which fill out the larger elements of his life and thinking. There is a risk in this practice of giving improper weight to statements which Peirce put forward tentatively. To reduce the danger, I have been careful to use the test of consistency with other evidence bearing on the matter at issue.

Peirce was a polymath, at home in the physical sciences, especially chemistry, geodesy, metrology, and astronomy. He was the first experimental psychologist in the United States, a mathematical economist, a master of logic and mathematics, an inventor of the field of semeiotics, a dramatist, actor, and book reviewer. In philosophy he was one of the most original thinkers and system builders of any time, and certainly the greatest philosopher the United States has ever seen. I have been forced, both because of the limits of my knowledge and because of the sheer breadth and depth of Peirce's competence, to concentrate on a few of Peirce's interests, only mentioning the rest along the way. My greatest interest (and it is more than enough in itself) is his architectonic—his unparalleled system of philosophy—which, from his middle twenties, he was convinced had the power to include all knowledge within its vantage. My main purpose in this study has been to present the outline of the chronological development of this system along with the major developments of his life as interrelated and interdependent facets of a complex and fascinating man.

Much of what I have written about Peirce is controversial, because much of Peirce's life was itself controversial in the extreme. He was profoundly confused about himself, a fact which makes understanding him particularly difficult. I have done my best to be true to Peirce, for whom I have a deep affection, and this has led me to propose a number of hypotheses about his life and thought for which the evidence I have is not incontestable. I point out in the text where I do so. My reason for proceeding in this way is appropriately contained in Peirce's description of the logic of inquiry, which requires that the risk of hypothetic inference or guessing (which he called abduction) be the first step toward knowledge, a step always subject to inductive test by the community of inquirers. I present my findings in the spirit of what Peirce called "contrite fallibilism."

ACKNOWLEDGMENTS

Two people made it possible for me to write this book. One is my wife, Ann Garfinkle the lawyer, who thought so highly of my dissertation that she never allowed me to forget my long and deeply held desire to expand it into a full-fledged biography of Peirce. She persuaded me lovingly and at length to complete an earlier version, which became the basis of this one.

The other is Thomas A. Sebeok, the distinguished semiotician and Peirce scholar and for many years the chairman of the Research Center for Language and Semiotic Studies at Indiana University. Tom's great interest in Peirce's life led him to the discovery of my dissertation and to push for its publication in revised form by Indiana University Press. This unimagined happening has been the happiest surprise of my professional life. Through Tom's persuasion, John Gallman, the director at the Press, became convinced of the value of the project. John's many arguments with me over my approach to my subject were always fruitful. He supported and encouraged me, no matter the drain on his time and resources, generously providing me with an advance which made it possible for me to pay for unexpected but necessary editorial work. It was through John that Nathan Houser, associate editor of the Peirce Edition Project at Indiana University–Purdue University at Indianapolis, became interested in the book. He read the many revisions critically with great care and made recommendations which, with his excellent knowledge of Peirce's life and thought, improved the book substantially in ways that would not have occurred to me, especially by his friendly exposition of my errors, both philosophical and factual. Nathan also brought me up to date on recent Peirce scholarship, his own being some of the most useful to me, and went out of his way to provide me with a number of important Peirce manuscripts unknown to me. Cathy Clark, editorial associate at the Project, privately, with the assistance of John Hirschman, helped me recheck notes and bibliography, made sure that the Peirce quotations were accurate, and found appropriate photographs. Their dedication and assistance were invaluable. Jane Lyle, manuscript editor at Indiana University Press, devoted extra time and care to the manuscript. Her knowledge, experience, and skill made it much clearer and better, at the same time that she taught me by her example to write better myself.

My former wife, Barbara Warden, did half the original research, shared with me her sharp insights into Peirce and his world, and typed the dissertation manuscript. Kimball C. Elkins, long since retired as archivist of the Widener Library at Harvard University, was especially helpful in finding sources, many of them known only to him, which helped to explain aspects of Peirce's life. Norman Lehde, editor of the *Pike County Dispatch* in Milford, Pennsylvania, enabled me through his knowledge and connections to better understand Peirce's life there, as did Cornelia Bryce Pinchot, Gifford Pinchot's widow. Norman's widow Elise, Barbara Buchanan, and the other members of the Pike County Historical Society kindly gave me permission to use Peirce's deathbed photograph. At considerable inconvenience to themselves, my colleagues in the Department of Criminal Justice at the University of the District of Columbia arranged a writer's class schedule for me.

I remember gratefully the assistance given me more than thirty years ago by the staffs of the Library of Congress Manuscript Division, the National Archives, the Smithsonian Institution Archives, the Carnegie Institution of Washington, the Sidney Lanier Room at the Johns Hopkins University, and the Massachusetts Historical Society.

I would also like to express my appreciation to the following persons, libraries, and archives:

Rare Book and Manuscript Library, Columbia University;

Houghton Library and University Archives, Harvard University;

Special Collections, Johns Hopkins University;

Beinecke Rare Book Room and Manuscript Library, Yale University;

Cornelia Bryce Pinchot, for permission to quote from the Gifford Pinchot Papers;

Henry Cabot Lodge, Jr., for permission to quote from the Henry Cabot Lodge Papers;

Sylvia Wright Mitarachi, for permission to quote from her collection of Harriet Melusina Fay Peirce manuscripts;

Katherine Abbot Wells, for permission to quote from the Francis Ellingwood Abbot Papers;

Alexander James, for permission to quote from the William James Papers;

Paul Weiss, for permission to quote a letter from Edwin Bidwell Wilson.

Photographs courtesy of the Library of Congress, the National Oceanic and Atmospheric Administration, the Harvard University Archives and Houghton Library, the Pike County Historical Society, the Museum of the City of New York, the Peirce Edition Project, and Betsy Peirce Prince.

Charles Sanders Peirce

Facets of the Puzzle

> [I intend] to make a philosophy like that of
> Aristotle, that is to say, to outline a theory so
> comprehensive that, for a long time to come, the
> entire work of human reason, in philosophy of
> every school and kind, in mathematics, in
> psychology, in physical science, in history, in
> sociology, and in whatever other department there
> may be, shall appear as the filling up of its details.
>
> CSP, "A Guess at the Riddle," 1887

The past is a city in ruins—melancholy debris of the feast. The past haunts us with vague recognitions and inspires in us a musing curiosity about our seamless continuity with it. We guess at the riddle it embodies as we wander its vast reach lost in concepts, hunting for clues, inquiring of our ancestors about the signs of their times, and uncovering symptoms of our own malaise. We are pierced by time's barbed arrow, and from that irresistible outward clash we know that our universe is irreversible. The beauty of the past arises from its permanence, from the impossibility of changing what was done. It is this forgiving permanence, suffusing even folly and tragedy with melancholy beauty, that transforms the brilliant, bitter, humiliating, and above all tragic life of the American philosopher Charles Sanders Peirce into an odyssey of spirit which is at once fascinating, saddening, and compelling. Peirce died at the age of seventy-four in the spring of 1914, five months before the guns of August thundered abroad the beginnings of the First World War and the end of an age whose dominant values he despised.

In 1934, the philosopher Paul Weiss, in his brief account of Peirce's life in the *Dictionary of American Biography*, called him "the most original and versatile of American philosophers and America's greatest logician," but outside the philosophic community his name and work are even now little known. Even among philosophers, he is usually mentioned only in passing as the founder of pragmatism, and his work is seldom studied or discussed. Three years before Weiss's article, in the epigraph to the book he called *Brown Decades* to characterize a people sobered by the deep-set horror of the Civil War, the cultural historian and critic of the arts Lewis Mumford named a number of forgotten Americans who he believed had created a revolution in thought in the 1870s. Among them were the painters Thomas Eakins and Albert Pinkham Ryder, the designer and builder of the Brooklyn Bridge John August Roebling, the architects Henry Hobson Richardson and Louis Sullivan, the pioneering ecologist George Perkins Marsh, the physicist Josiah Willard Gibbs, and the historian and writer Henry Adams; "the procession of American civilization divided and walked around these men": and the first name on the list was that of Charles Peirce.[1] In an earlier essay in which he deplored the fact that Peirce's philosophical work had not been published (an undertaking that had a difficult birth in 1931, seventeen years after his death), Mumford placed Peirce in very great company indeed:

> The mere failure to publish the greater parts of Peirce's thought has obscured the fact that, in the very dregs of the Gilded Age, a large and universal mind quietly fulfilled itself, a mind whose depth and impact have still to be felt and fathomed. If one is to condemn the Gilded Age for Peirce's lack of influence, one must equally condemn the glorious thirteenth century for the comparative obscurity of Roger Bacon, or the sixteenth century for not publishing the notes of Leonardo da Vinci. Doubtless the condemnation would be deserved, but the glory of their positive achievements still remains.[2]

Max H. Fisch, who spent fifty years in the dedicated study of Peirce's life and thought, offered a far more knowledgeable and even grander judgment of Peirce's achievements:

> Who is the most original and the most versatile intellect that the Americas have so far produced? The answer "Charles S. Peirce" is uncontested, because any second would be so far behind as not to be worth nominating. Mathematician, astronomer, chemist, geodesist, surveyor, cartographer, metrologist, spectroscopist, engineer, inventor; psychologist, philologist, lexicographer, historian of science, mathematical economist, lifelong student of medicine; book reviewer, dramatist, actor, short story writer; phenomenologist, semiotician, logician, rhetorician [and] metaphysician[.[
> He was, for a few examples, the first modern experimental psychologist in the Americas, the first metrologist to use a wave-length of light as a unit of measure, the inventor of the quincuncial projection of the sphere, the first known conceiver of the design and theory of an electric switching-circuit computer, and the founder of "the economy of research." He is the only system-building philosopher in the Americas who has been both competent

and productive in logic, in mathematics, and in a wide range of sciences. If he has had any equals in that respect in the entire history of philosophy, they do not number more than two.[3]

Fisch then went on to list some of Peirce's many achievements, including his graduation from Harvard University's Lawrence Scientific School summa cum laude in 1863; his thirty-year career as a research scientist in the Coast and Geodetic Survey, which ended in 1891 and during which he became the first American delegate to any international scientific association; his influential lectureship in logic at the Johns Hopkins University from 1879 to 1884; his courses of lectures at Harvard in 1865, 1869–70, 1903, and 1907, and at private homes in Cambridge in 1898 and in other years; his reviewing for the *Nation* from 1869 to 1908; his many and major contributions to the *Century Dictionary* and to James Mark Baldwin's *Dictionary of Philosophy and Psychology*; and his membership in learned societies such as the American Academy of Arts and Sciences, the National Academy of Sciences, and the London Mathematical Society. Fisch identified Peirce's major focus in the great range of his inquiries as logic,

conceived at first as a branch of a branch of semiotics [the study of signs and their function and interpretation, what Peirce called "the science of representation"], but eventually as nearly coextensive with it, though with a distribution of emphasis different from those of semioticians who are not logicians. The purpose was to distinguish the possible kinds of semioses or sign-functions, and, among them, to make the most thorough study he could of arguments in particular, and above all of their functions in mathematics and in the sciences. His major single discovery was that what he at first called *hypothesis* and later *abduction* or *retroduction* [now often called the logic of discovery] is a distinct kind of argument, different both from deduction and from induction, and indispensable both in mathematics and in the sciences. This discovery came at least as early as 1866. . . .

Whatever the technical name and definition of this third kind of argument should be, and the exact working out of its relations with the other two, an essential element of it is something for which the colloquial name is *guessing*.[4]

Fisch accurately places Peirce's work at the source and center of all inquiry, be it scientific, biographical, literary, or whatever. However, he does not respond to the extraordinarily daring, grand, and powerful vision which Peirce expressed in his intention "to outline a theory so comprehensive that . . . the entire work of human reason . . . shall appear as the filling up of its details." Nor does he recognize the hubris manifest in Peirce's intention to make "the entire work of human reason" a string of footnotes to his own philosophical system.

Peirce was a close student of the history of science, philosophy, and mathematics. He well knew, from personal experience as a man of both science and religion as well as from his knowledge of the past, what a tremendous and culture-wracking revolution in basic beliefs the invention of modern science required. The threat and the dislocation still haunt us. Like Darwin, Peirce was unwilling to accept any metaphysical or religious doctrine which did not face up to the chilling implications of scientific knowledge for the traditional views of the nature of reality embedded for millennia in every facet of human culture. Unlike Darwin, he believed that Aristotelian and medieval realism provided the basis for a reconstruction of the nature of knowledge, not only consistent with but embodied in the practice of science itself. Peirce fervently believed that he had discovered a model of thinking which exemplified this belief and which was, at the same time, the key to understanding the way the universe is made. In this model, the universe could be known by means of the logical elaboration of an architectonic containing only three categories, first, second, and third. In 1887–88, in his dazzling cosmological speculation "A Guess at the Riddle," he said, " . . . three elements are active in the world, first, chance; second, law; and third, habit-taking . . . . Such is our guess of the secret of the sphynx [sic]."[5] Fifteen years later, he called his full-fledged theory of logic broadly *semeiotic*, one of whose applications was the formal logic of science, which itself contained a doctrine for the clarification of meaning called pragmatism. It was this conviction which led Peirce to make his extraordinary claim.

Of course, like claims have been put forth by philosophers, theologians, scientists, and cranks of all kinds. What is there about Peirce's ideas that could conceivably justify considering his grand hypothesis seriously and testing it by the methods of science, as he himself required be done? The answer lies in two levels of response to Peirce's work, especially in the last thirty years or so. In the first place, disconnected inquiries into various aspects of his work by specialists in such varied fields as the logic of relations, semeiotic, psychology, sociology, mathematics, phenomenology, metaphysics, and literary criticism have resulted in remarkable agreement on the originality and usefulness of Peirce's proposals. In the second, the realization that all of these various proposals were generated by the same method of thinking has led to serious consideration of the validity of his architectonic system taken as a whole. Among the few who have recently worked through Peirce's lifelong investigations into the logic of science (which for Peirce was how we know anything) is Karl-Otto Apel, one of the leading contemporary German philosophers and one of the half-dozen philosophers in any time and place to have examined Peirce's writings systematically and in depth:

> If we look back at Peirce's Pragmaticism [the name Peirce took to distinguish his position from those of other pragmatists such as James and Dewey] from the perspective of the present, then we see in it primarily the outline and program of a "logic of science" for the future. It goes without saying that the logic of science that has been developed in the meantime by analytic philosophy, with the aid of mathematical logic, has come much farther than Peirce in technicalities. But it seems just as certain to me that the basic, two dimensional (syntactic-semantic) approach which modern work in the logic of science took over from logical Positivism's anti-metaphysical program is fundamentally inferior to Peirce's three-dimensional semiotic approach. The two-dimensional approach forces philosophers of science to reduce the metaphysical problems of the so-called pragmatic dimension, that is, problems regarding the subject who interprets and engages in science, by making them problems of an empirical science. Moreover, unless all contemporary developments mislead me, we are now already witnessing a restructuring and dissolution of the two-dimensional logic of science. This view . . . has begun now to give way to a three-dimensional, cybernetically oriented, "systems theory" of science which conceives it as a human, social undertaking. . . .
>
> . . . If we take to its logical conclusions the idea, which Peirce had already implicitly founded in his logical Socialism [the ideal of a practicing community of inquirers], that the world cannot be known or explained merely by its previously fixed, lawful structure, but must rather continue to be developed as a historical, social world of institutions and habits for which we must assume responsibility, then it becomes evident that man confronts mankind with other tasks besides that of objectifying and explaining the world through science or of converting science into efficient behavior, that is, technology in the broadest sense. As members of the community of interpreters, human beings must remain for mankind the subject engaged in science and nonetheless be capable of being made the topic of rational knowledge and praxis.[6]

Apel's judgment that Peirce's pragmaticism should be taken as "the outline and program of a 'logic of science' of the future" (and he is by no means alone in this view) and the reasons he gives for so thinking, especially the reintroduction of the value judgments of the scientist as a normal element of the scientific method, begin to give a glimpse of the credibility of Peirce's claim for the comprehensiveness of his hypothesis. Whether or not Weiss, Mumford, Fisch, and Apel, and others of far greater prominence, prove correct in their judgments is not so much an open question as it is a question of the degree of Peirce's greatness. In 1877, the great British mathematician and logician William Kingdon Clifford placed Peirce as a logician on a par with Aristotle and George Boole. In 1936, the process philosopher Alfred North Whitehead named William James and Peirce as the founders of the renascence in American philosophy, which was itself becoming a center of importance for the discipline. He said, "Of these men, W. J. is the analogue to Plato, and C. P. to Aristotle. . . . "[7] Karl Popper, likely the most influential modern philosopher of science, said in 1965:

> Among the few dissenters [to physical determinism—the doctrine that clouds are clocks] was Charles Sanders Peirce, the great American mathematician and physicist and, I believe, one of the greatest philosophers of all time. . . . So far as I know Peirce was the first post-Newtonian physicist and philosopher who thus dared to adopt the view that to some degree *all clocks are clouds*; or in other words, that *only clouds exist*, though clouds of very different degrees of cloudiness. . . . I further believe that Peirce was right in holding that this view was compatible with the classical physics of Newton. I believe that this view is even more clearly compatible with Einstein's (special) relativity theory, and it is still more clearly compatible with the new quantum theory.[8]

Noam Chomsky, the inventor of generative and transformational grammar, was asked in 1976 which philosopher was his kindred in ideas. He answered, "In relation to the questions we have been discussing [concerning the philosophy of language], the philosopher to whom I feel closest and whom I'm almost paraphrasing is Charles Sanders Peirce."[9] From the other side of the spectrum of inquiry, the novelist Walker Percy said in his 1989 Jefferson lecture that modern science is utterly incoherent in its view of "man *qua* man, man when he is peculiarly human," and that Peirce's theory of signs laid the groundwork for a coherent science of man.[10] In 1989, an international congress was held at Harvard University to honor the 150th anniversary of Peirce's birth; it was attended by over 400 scholars representing the United States, Canada, Brazil, Colombia, almost every country in Western Europe, Finland, the Soviet Union, Poland, Austria, Hungary, Greece, Algeria, Israel, India, Australia, Japan, the Republic of Korea, and the People's Republic of China. The disciplines addressed included logic, the philosophy of science, semeiotic, metaphysics, epistemology, aesthetics, ethics, psychology, linguistics, geology, and religion. Among those attending were such major international scholars as Willard Van Orman Quine, Klaus Oehler, Jürgen Habermas, Gérard Deledalle, Umberto Eco, Thomas Sebeok, Takashi Fujimoto, Christopher Hookway, Robert Tobin, and Carolyn Eisele.[11] The conference clearly underlines the broad international importance of Peirce's ideas.

The great mystery is why, almost eighty years after Peirce's death, such an extraordinary man and his ideas could still be so little known. The only studies of Peirce's life to appear since his death in 1914 have been (with the exception of the 1960 dissertation of which this biography is an expansion) short and incomplete, based for the most part upon cursory examinations of the vast manuscript sources available. The first was the philosopher Morris Raphael Cohen's introduction to the first collection of Peirce's work, *Chance, Love and Logic*, which he edited in 1923. It remains the best brief account of Peirce's life and, more particularly, of his thought. This was followed by Weiss's insightful article in the *Dictionary of American Biography* in 1934. Although Fisch wrote a sketch in 1939, his best biographical work, which unfortunately does not contain his thorough account of the Cambridge Metaphysical Club in which pragmatism made its first appearance, is included in a collection of his essays, *Peirce, Semeiotic, and Pragmatism*, published in 1986. It contains a number of pioneering studies of both his life and thought and their interrelationships and is certainly, despite its piecemeal nature, the most useful single source of biographical information in the form of journal articles. The mathematician Carolyn Eisele has written numerous essays on Peirce in her fields of interest. These were collected in 1979 in *Studies in the Scientific and Mathematical Philosophy of Charles S. Peirce*, which contains a brief scientific biography and her enlightening introductions to her collection of Peirce's mathematical writings. In 1985, Eisele edited a large collection called *A History of Science: Historical Perspectives on Peirce's Logic of Science* in two volumes. This, too, has a most useful biographical introduction. The introductions to the first four volumes of *Writings of Charles S. Peirce: A Chronological Edition*, which began appearing in 1982 and so far cover Peirce's life to 1884, are useful, especially that of Nathan Houser in volume four, which covers the Johns Hopkins period. There are a number of accounts of alternative ways in which Peirce's philosophical evolution can be explained, but only one, *The Development of Peirce's Philosophy* by Murray G. Murphey, shows an intimate knowledge of the biographical sources. Murphey's book is particularly penetrating in its analysis of the relationship between Peirce and his father.[12]

Why has it taken so long for a full-length American biography to be written and published about this major figure in the intellectual history of the United States and, indeed, of the larger world as well? (There is irony in the fact that two brief European biographies have recently been published, though neither is based on extensive manuscript research.)[13] It is not because of any lack of documentation. There is, if anything, too much. For some periods of Peirce's life it is possible to give, on the basis of varied and extensive primary sources at Harvard University and elsewhere, an almost daily account of much of what he did and thought. His philosophical manuscripts and letters at Harvard's Houghton Library number in the tens of thousands of pages, his published works in the thousands.

The spectacle of great individuals spurned in their own times and rehabilitated in the next is one of the clichés of history. Each case exhibits an open or suppressed threat to the dominant ideologies of its world, but each one is different in spirit and detail. What were the reasons for Peirce's obscurity and rediscovery? With regard to his rediscovery as a philosopher, the reason is clear: there have always been a small company of those who respected Peirce's genius and were inspired by it, at first friends and later scholars, and they have done their best to preserve and publish his work, especially under the enthusiastic auspices of the Charles S. Peirce Society and its *Transactions*. It was only a matter of time until their labors raised Peirce's philosophical reputation to prominence again. The rediscovery of his life is another matter. The problem of Peirce's obscurity is complicated and twofold. First there is that kind of obscurity which depended on the fortunes of his writings after his death, and second that kind which he found forced upon him during his life.

After Peirce's death in 1914, the philosopher Josiah Royce, who was deeply indebted to Peirce for some of the most important ideas in his late works, saw to it that Peirce's papers and his large working library of about 12,000 books, with its many interleaved and annotated volumes, were transferred as soon as possible to the department of philosophy at Harvard University. It was at first difficult to find an editor for the manuscripts. In the late twenties, largely through the efforts of the philosopher Morris Raphael Cohen, a student of Royce's, sufficient funds were raised to make it possible for Charles Hartshorne and Paul Weiss to edit and publish portions of the philosophical manuscripts with the Harvard University Press. Between 1931 and 1935, six volumes of the *Collected Papers of Charles Sanders Peirce* appeared under their editorship, and twenty-three years later, two more under the editorship of Arthur W. Burks. Thus, forty-four years after his death, a large selection—unfortunately misleading in chronology and organization—of Peirce's philosophical writings (and of some biographical material) had been published. In those years an unknown number of manuscripts disappeared, and the papers themselves were mishandled.[14] After another break of almost twenty years, Carolyn Eisele published an exhaustive collection of Peirce's mathematical writings in 1976, and ten years later a collection of his writings on the history of science.[15] Between 1975 and 1979, Kenneth L. Ketner and James E. Cook published three volumes of Peirce's contributions to the *Nation*. In 1982, the Peirce Edition Project at Indiana University at Indianapolis, under the initial editorship of Max H. Fisch, began publication with Indiana

University Press of a selected edition taken from the approximately 80,000 pages of manuscript and 12,000 pages of published papers, entitled *Writings of Charles S. Peirce: A Chronological Edition*. To date, four volumes of a projected thirty have appeared, covering the period 1859–1884. In 1992, the press will issue *The Essential Peirce: Selected Philosophical Writings*, under the editorship of Nathan Houser and Christian Kloesel, a chronological selection of Peirce's most important philosophical works, an expansion of *Chance, Love and Logic*, published almost seventy years before.

On the other hand, the manuscripts at Harvard University relating to Peirce's personal life were (with a small number of formal and informal exceptions) restricted from use until 1956, forty-two years after his death, when all but four boxes of biographical documents were opened for research. However, these four boxes contained some of the most important biographical information in the Harvard collection. The largest collection of Peirce manuscripts and correspondence is in the Houghton Library at Harvard, for which annotated catalogues were prepared in 1967 and 1971 by Richard S. Robin. Most of these are available on microfilm, and all are now open to scholars.

While the delay in publishing Peirce's philosophical manuscripts can be attributed almost entirely to skepticism or disinterest, on the one hand, and a lack of funds, on the other, the delay in producing a biography was directly caused by the inaccessibility of the biographical portion of the Harvard Peirce collection. This suppression was justified by its owners, the Harvard department of philosophy, on the grounds that there was information in the letters that would seriously damage Peirce's reputation and that must, therefore, be withheld in order to protect his reputation and the sensibilities of his family (and perhaps those of Harvard University). Lewis Mumford wrote in 1931 that the legend of Peirce's immorality had been allowed to grow "like a fungus," for lack of a little directness in revealing it:

> Charles Peirce [was] an unconventional soul, who followed his own track, and whose reflections on life and the moralities were not merely out of harmony with those of his own generation but are equally remote, apparently, from the notions held by some of the present possessors of his letters. Even the publication of Peirce's collected papers has lagged for lack of a few thousand dollars to guarantee the initial expenses of publication.[16]

The restrictive policy led to rumors about homosexuality, sexual promiscuity, chronic drunkenness, violence, and drug addiction, and since there was no published evidence to either support or disprove such accusations, Peirce's reputation has varied according to rumors about the contents of his letters and the tastes of the persons concerned with it. In fact, many of the rumors were true, but because of the decision to deny access, the research which would have put his life into its true light, that of the dignity of deep tragedy, was discouraged or forbidden. An attempt to correct this mistaken policy was made in 1959 by the designation by the Harvard department of philosophy of Max H. Fisch as Peirce's "official biographer." Thirty years later, during which time other biographers were actively discouraged, Fisch retired, having produced a series of intriguing and sometimes brilliant articles, but without completing even the first volume of his long-awaited full-length study. Even with the appointment of Fisch in 1959, it was far too late to interview those who had known Peirce well—former students, friends, philosopher-correspondents, wives (Peirce was married twice), business associates, and others. The last of those still living with a personal knowledge of Peirce, E. L. Burlingame, the editor of Scribner's and a member, like Peirce, of the Century Club, died the year before Fisch's appointment. Such knowledge was permanently lost. Fisch did leave a valuable legacy, however. His biographical research (including the author's contribution at Fisch's request), housed at the Peirce Edition Project, constitutes a massive collection of great importance for the study of Peirce's life and, generally, for the study of nineteenth-century American thought.

Neither the National Academy of Sciences nor the American Academy of Arts and Sciences, in both of which he was a prominent member, has ever published a memorial biography of Peirce. The person whom the American Academy of Arts and Sciences originally entrusted with the job was Josiah Royce, but he was unable to accomplish it before he died, and none of those assigned since has been able to carry it out. The National Academy of Sciences first designated Lawrence Joseph Henderson, a Harvard professor in biological chemistry, to do a memorial; he, too, died leaving it undone. The task was then given to Edwin Bidwell Wilson, a chemist and occasional lecturer in economics at Harvard, but he gave it up, in 1958, as too difficult, and no one else has since attempted the job. These facts help to explain the depth of the obscurity which has surrounded Peirce since his death.

Yet, only ten years before he died, Peirce was a very well-known figure in intellectual circles. His public prominence in his lifetime was clearly demonstrated when, in 1902, he applied for a grant from the Carnegie Institution which would have allowed him to complete and publish his studies in logic; President Theodore Roosevelt himself recommended that Peirce be given the money. Secretary of War Elihu Root delayed the vote on the grant until he could be present to vote in its favor as a member of the executive committee of the institution. When Peirce failed to receive the grant a year later, Andrew Carnegie expressed his disappointment to Peirce's younger brother. In the same year, Peirce was prominently mentioned in the *National Cyclo-*

pedia of American Biography, where he received the accolade of a picture and a column of text. Peirce was also the subject of a complimentary account in the *Biographical Dictionary of America* published in 1906. In the same year, and more appropriate to his work as a scientist and philosopher, was the brief but respectful account of his major achievements in *American Men of Science,* edited by the psychologist J. McKeen Cattell.

His failure to receive the Carnegie grant in spite of such strong support reflects another and more puzzling aspect of Peirce's life, which was hinted at by Mumford when he called him "an unconventional soul." Even though he was described by many eminent academic figures, including Josiah Royce and William James, as the most brilliant and original mind of his place and time, Peirce was dismissed from every important professional position he held and died a poverty-stricken outcast. In his own day he was personally notorious and considered by many influential academics and prominent men in other professions as something of a charlatan in his philosophical and religious pretensions, while at the same time he was highly respected as a scientist and logician.

Like any writing about history, this study attempts to elucidate the enigma of fact. The facts are those of Peirce's life, the course and signifi-cance of which have been obscured by the intricate entanglements of his personal relationships, his rejection in his own times, the suppression of documents necessary to understand him, the great range and depth of his interests, and the jealousy of academicians. Facts do not speak for them-selves. They are the puzzling and recalcitrant debris of human life. As Peirce pointed out well over a century ago in his model of explanation, facts speak only in the fallible voices of the guesses, conjectures, and hypotheses that imply them, deductively, and which are then verified inductively. No history, no matter how trivial or significant, has meaning unless we can create, some-how, the hypotheses that indicate the explanations we search for. Much that the historian does is described by the logic, centered on the nature of hy-pothesis, that Peirce spent his life obsessively trying to work out.

In 1936, in the course of a conversation, Norman Fay, a brother of Peirce's first wife, Harriet Melusina Fay, and a man known to dislike the Peirce family, commented that "very few men are as great as their works, and it is better not to try to dig up their lives, but let them stand on their own merits." This comment, uttered in reference to Peirce himself, was made in protest against any thorough examination of his life. Fay, then in his late eighties, expanded further by adding, "Peirce was a very selfish man, com-pletely absorbed in his work, and not one whose private life would add anything to the understanding of his philosophy."[17] But what did Peirce philosophize about, if not his experience of living? As Peirce might have put it, his life and thought were two intimately related aspects of the same sign, Peirce himself. In his later studies of great men, Peirce included as many of the intimate details of their lives as the evidence provided, convinced that understanding these was necessary in order to understand what made them great.[18] This study follows his lead.

The position that there is no instructive connection between a person's life and work is not new by any means. Typically, the historian of philosophy looks only for connected strands of ideas and deals with, say, "the influence of Kant on Peirce," meaning not the men themselves but their works. But historians of ideas (often called intellectual historians, as if the study of history in any of its aspects were not intellectual), if they are to be differentiated usefully from historians of philosophy, must be distinguished by their belief in the necessary connection between the person and the work—by a concern with the embodiment of ideas in the actions of people in the context of their history. This point of view about the relation between ideas and actions is a hypothesis in the sense meant by Peirce, and its concern with their consequences makes historians of ideas pragmatists, since they adhere to the doctrine that one can tell an idea by what it may lead to. As Peirce put it with more precision in his "pragmatic maxim" in 1878, "Consider what effects, which might conceivably have practical bearings, we might conceive the object of our conception to have. Then, our conception of these effects is the whole of our conception of the object."[19] In short, meaning is the result of what physicists call a thought experiment; it is the consequence of the testing of a hypothesis by way of its conceivable results. Meaning is virtual, not actual. In 1905, almost thirty years later, after he had decided that logic depended on ethics (and ethics on aesthetics), Peirce wrote that the value of an idea "lies exclusively in its conceivable bearing upon the conduct of life. . . . For it is to conceptions of deliberate conduct that Pragmaticism would trace the intellectual purport of symbols; and deliberate conduct is self-controlled conduct."[20] I take this to mean that Peirce may be held accountable for his actions not only to the extent that they will help to make his ideas clear, but also to the extent that ideas did govern his conduct and justify it not only implicitly, but concretely as embodied in his actions.

Much of Peirce's life has an obvious bearing on the development of his thought: for example, his rearing in the Brahmin world of Cambridge and Boston; his introduction as a boy to experimental chemistry; the intellectual dominance of his father in his mathematical, scientific, and philosophical education; his early fascination with logic; his passionate study of Schiller and Kant with his college friend Horatio Paine; his relationships as a young man with Chauncey Wright, William James, Francis Ellingwood Abbot, and other original philosophic minds of his own generation; his career in gravimetrics; and his five years of teaching and research at the Johns Hopkins University.

Much of it does not have so obvious a bearing. His way of thinking, which he called *pedestrianism* as a young man, was in part a consequence of his being left-handed and of the strict mental discipline forced on him by that fact and by the time he lost to the effects of neurological maladies. He spent much time alone, ill, and depressed. "Illustrations of the Logic of Science," which appeard in 1877–78, were thought through during the period 1875–76, while Peirce was alone in Europe under great stress and suffering from periods of severe nervous collapse. He wrote his brilliant and pioneering 1880 work "On the Algebra of Logic" while he was under treatment for possible insanity and suffering from a number of additional afflications. He made a profound return to metaphysics after his father died in 1880 and his academic career collapsed in the mid-1880s. During the desperate period after his dismissal from the Coast Survey, he wrote his extraordinary 1892 piece "The Architecture of Theories" (and four other articles for *The Monist*), which much modified his earlier thinking; the model and inspiration for this work were the remodeling and expanding to his own design of the 1854 farmhouse in Milford, Pennsylvania, that became Arisbe, his beloved home. His experience of great suffering and extreme poverty during the three years between 1895 and 1898, while he was living as a fugitive from Pennsylvania law in New York City, changed fundamentally his view of the importance of his philosophic direction and brought him to announce the doctrine that logic depended on ethics and ethics on aesthetics, which he introduced, along with advances in his system of logic, in Cambridge in 1898. After his return to Milford in that year, so poor that Arisbe became a virtual prison, he was dependent on the vagaries of his editors for the books which kept him in touch with his world, and the charity of family and friends. In general, though with some important exceptions, the worse for him the times were, the more remarkable was his work.

Charles Sanders Peirce was a stocky, dark, and extremely handsome man of about five feet seven inches in height. Although less Byronic, he closely resembled his father, Benjamin, the brilliant and honored Harvard mathematician and astronomer. The most noticeable feature of Peirce's face were his eyes, which were ardent, dark, and brilliant. His voice was high and piercing. From about the age of thirty he wore, like his father, a dark and straggling full beard that slowly silvered and grew steadily longer. In temperament Peirce was impulsive, quick-tempered, and often perverse and arrogant. His nephew described him as "a highly emotional, easily duped, rather snobbish youngster going his own way indifferent of consequences," and added that "his father had neglected to teach him self control with the consequence that later he 'suffered unspeakably.' "[21] He loved luxury and taking risks. Indeed, his view of inquiry required the risk of inventing hypotheses at every critical point. When speaking he sometimes dropped his g's, thereby adding to the general air of dandified gentility which he affected. He had a pervasive and prickly sense of personal honor and a general suspicion of the motives of others, which, together, brought almost every personal and professional controversy in which he was involved to a disagreeable end. At the same time, he often showed a sweetness of temper and a warm consideration for others which endeared him to those close to him.

He was, when he chose, a thoroughly charming companion and a delightful and brilliant conversationalist. When he did not feel threatened, he seemed shy and vulnerable, but his mien often changed without warning to one of suspicion and hostility. For the listener who seemed taken in by his manner, he often showed contempt. On the other hand, he was generous to a fault in giving credit to others for their ideas. He was very clever and indulged a corrosive and scurrilous sense of humor upon slight provocation, often directed accurately at himself. Peirce's sensitivity to insult, his arrogance and impulsiveness made him a suspect acquaintance and a difficult friend, but these same traits, together with his underlying vulnerability and glossy appearance, made him a ladies' man of considerable notoriety. To the pain of both his wives, he was unfaithful. Peirce lived a profoundly lonely life, despite its manic and often desperate bustle, and had very few close friends, perhaps only two.

All his life Peirce endured the effects of two physiological disorders: trigeminal neuralgia—then medically termed *facial neuralgia*—an excruciatingly painful neurological disease, and left-handedness, which he strongly believed affected the way he thought and wrote. Together, these conditions help to explain aspects of his more extreme behavior. He and his father both suffered frequently from attacks of trigeminal neuralgia and used ether and tinctures of opium to manage its pain (Charles later also used morphine and probably cocaine), which likely led to their becoming addicted. It is to the extreme pain of this disease—described as unbearable by its sufferers—and his use of drugs as palliatives that much of Peirce's erratic behavior can be attributed. The disease worsens with age, and by the time he was fifty, more than one friend—and sometimes Peirce himself—believed that he was no longer sane. One conspicuous effect of the pain was that Peirce (and his father) fell into cold, sometimes uncontrollably violent rages, often for no apparent reason.

In large part as a consequence of the disease, Peirce was plagued all his life by dangerous psychological instability. Because of his affliction, his father and mother spoiled him, indulged his excesses, and protected him as best they could from the world of affairs well into his thirties—and even his forties. Peirce was, as a result of these troubles and arrangements, neurotic in the extreme, or perhaps manic-depressive. The malady took the form of what he called, contemptuously, his "emotional slush." Despite these frightening personal ills, Peirce, with the aid of his father, developed such a high degree of self-discipline that he could work on the most intricate philosophical problems with concentrated intensity for several days at a time. Because of the unexpected and sudden onset of neuralgia and his fear that his periods of lucidity were threatened by it, from the age of about twenty he spent every spare moment abstractedly scribbling away at his work. He spent the greater part of his life philosophizing in this piecemeal way. It is amazing that he accomplished so much of value in a life filled with such harsh obstacles.

Peirce attributed a number of his problems to his left-handedness, referring to himself on occasion as "sinister," punning on the Latin meaning of the word. Peirce here lends his own authority to the idea that he was wrongheaded, or as he himself described it, that he thought in a way "that to a normal mind seems almost inconceivably awkward."[22] He also blamed his left-handedness for his "incapacity for linguistic expression," the extreme difficulty he had in putting his thoughts into words. Recent research supports Peirce's opinion that left-handers are different, and that they are marked at birth by a deviation from normal neural patterns that is pathological, and it also points out that they appear in unusually high numbers among children who are, as Peirce was, extremely precocious in mathematical abilities.[23] The logician Beverley E. Kent has placed this trait in the context of recent studies of brain hemisphere dominance and points to the great similarity between Albert Einstein and Peirce in their visual and diagrammatic way of thinking, which she suggests was the result of the ability of both to use the imaging hemisphere to create the visual language of "thought experiments." She also suggests that in neither man was either brain hemisphere dominant, so that Peirce was able to shock his students with the uncanny ability to use both hemispheres at once.[24] The fact, as reported by his nephew, that Peirce was able to write on the blackboard, ambidextrously and simultaneously, a logical problem and its answer, was a remarkable example of his mental discipline.[25] One of Peirce's students at

Johns Hopkins, William Pepperell Montague, may himself have witnessed such a performance and wrote of a Faustian being:

> For Pierce himself, I had a kind of worship. While his intellect was cold and clear, his metaphysical imagination was capricious, scintillating, and unbridled, and his whole personality was so rich and mysterious that he seemed a being apart, a superman. I would rather have been like him than like anyone else I ever met.[26]

Throughout his thinking life, Peirce's greatest passion was the study of logic, which he understood to be the only useful approach to the riddle of things. For him, logic was nothing like the mechanical truth tables and theorem proving found in a modern college course (though Peirce's influence extended to both); it was the only way to approach reality. Surprisingly, Peirce claimed that his mind was completely lacking in imagination, and that his philosophical achievements were the results of pedestrian "Peirce-everence" (along with "Peirce-istence" one of his favorite puns). This self-evaluation is intriguing, and the principal clue to it, and to many of the twists of his character, probably lies in his relationship with his father. When Charles was still a boy, his father draped on his shoulders the crushing mantle of genius and engaged him from that age well into his manhood in an intense and extremely demanding training in the rigorous efforts needed to make fine distinctions. It was this laborious and exacting but delicate distinction-making that Peirce called pedestrianism and which became in time the basis for the power of his philosophical system. The effects of this training were to aggravate his neuralgia, to nourish his arrogance, and to set his ambition afire.

Not surprisingly, the idea of genius fascinated him all his life. He was a practiced actor, belonging for many years to amateur performing groups. Peirce assumed the role of the genius with a sort of desperate diligence, always unaware of what was happening on the other side of the footlights and constantly uneasy with his father's insistence on his genius. Peirce was deeply puzzled by himself, and he was never truly satisfied that he knew what his genius was. He didn't know quite what to do with it, though he tried out many different ways, none of which were, finally, successful. His ambivalent feelings about himself were expressed characteristically when on the one hand he wrote that he possessed no imaginative faculties, while on the other he confidently proclaimed that his philosophical system would form the foundation of a philosophical tradition as great and long-lasting as Aristotle's. In sum, Peirce was, as the close friend of his maturity William James remarked sympathetically, "that strange and unruly being."

Around 1887, when he was approaching fifty, perhaps as a prefatory note to his projected book "A Guess at the Riddle," Peirce described the essentials of his intellectual life and his philosophical views:

> The reader has a right to know how the author's opinions were formed. Not, of course, that he is expected to accept any conclusions which are not borne out by argument. But in discussions of extreme difficulty, like these, when good judgment is a factor, and pure ratiocination is not everything, it is prudent to take every element into consideration. From the moment when I could think at all until now, about forty years, I have been diligently and incessantly occupied with the study of methods [of] inquiry, both those which have been and are pursued and those which ought to be pursued. For ten years before this study began, I had been in training in the chemical laboratory. I was thoroughly grounded not only in all that was then known of physics and chemistry, but also in the way in which those who were successfully advancing knowledge proceeded. I have paid the most attention to the methods of the most exact sciences, have intimately communed with some of the greatest minds of our times in physical science, and have myself made positive contributions—none of them of any very great importance, perhaps—in mathematics, gravitation, optics, chemistry, astronomy, etc. I am saturated, through and through, with the spirit of the physical sciences. I have been a great student of logic, having read everything of any importance on the subject, devoting a great deal of time to medieval thought, without neglecting the works of the Greeks, the English, the Germans, the French, etc., and have produced systems of my own both in deductive and in inductive logic. In metaphysics, my training has been less systematic; yet I have read and deeply pondered upon all the main systems, never being satisfied until I was able to think about them as their own advocates thought. . . .
>
> Thus, in brief, my philosophy may be described as the attempt of a physicist to make such conjecture as to the constitution of the universe as the methods of science may permit, with the aid of all that has been done by previous philosophers. . . . Demonstrative proof is not to be thought of. The demonstrations of the metaphysicians are all moonshine. The best that can be done is to supply a hypothesis, not devoid of all likelihood, in the general line of growth of scientific ideas, and capable of being verified or refuted by future observers. . . .
>
> I am a man of whom critics have never found anything good to say. When they could see no opportunity to injure me, they have held their peace. The little laudation I have had has come from such sources, that the only satisfaction I have derived from it, has been from such slices of bread and butter as it might waft my way. Only once, as far as I remember, in all my lifetime have I experienced the pleasure of praise—not for what it might bring but in itself. That pleasure was beatific; and the praise that conferred it was meant for blame. It was that a critic said of me that I did not seem to be *absolutely sure of my own conclusions*. Never, if I can help it, shall that

critic's eye ever rest on what I am now writing; for I owe a great pleasure to him; and, such was his evident animus, that should he find out, I fear the fires of hell would be fed with new fuel in his breast. . . .

The development of my ideas has been the industry of thirty years. . . .

For years in the course of this ripening process, I used for myself to collect my ideas under the designation *fallibilism*; and indeed the first step toward *finding out* is to acknowledge you do not satisfactorily know already; so that no blight can so surely arrest all intellectual growth as the blight of cocksureness; and ninety-nine out of every hundred good heads are reduced to impotence by that malady—of whose inroads they are most strangely unaware!

Indeed, out of a contrite fallibilism, combined with a high faith in the reality of knowledge, and an intense desire to find things out, all my philosophy has always seemed to me to grow. . . . [27]

Peirce had strong, though unorthodox, religious convictions. Although he was a communicant in the Episcopal church for most of his life, he expressed contempt for the theologies, metaphysics, and practices of established religions. At the same time that he thought of himself as a first-rate, tough-minded, antimetaphysical experimental scientist, he perceived the logic of science as leading to a realist metaphysics. Peirce often thought of his life as the joining of these two strands of his thinking in a search for the right guess (or hypothesis) to explain the constitution of the universe. Into this attempt to unify what most of his scientific peers thought to be at the opposite poles of inquiry, Peirce poured many of his talents and, above all, his enormous capacity for work. Because his views on religion were unorthodox and his personal life was so thoroughly unconventional, he had a reputation for hypocrisy among powerful members of the elite of the religious and scientific orthodoxy.

Especially after his father's death in 1880, Peirce did his best to show the underlying unity of religion and science. In later life, he tried to achieve knowledge of God through the application of the logic of science, in particular through the use of the method of hypothesis, which he then called "the play of musement." There is an unexpected similarity here between Peirce and the empirical mystics, and also between his metaphysics and the mystical *philosophia perennis*. This similarity exists because both Peirce and the empirical mystics held that one could find God only in experience. The difference lies in the fact that Peirce made the statement from the viewpoint of the scientist and depended for verification on the community of inquirers, whereas the mystic would insist on the community of mind and nature, as Peirce himself was to do in time. Peirce may have achieved a mystical knowledge rather than an empirical verification of religious experience; his later letters and philosophical writings exhibit a strong tendency in that direction, as this eloquent passage shows:

> If, walking in a garden on a dark night, you were suddenly to hear the voice of your sister crying to you to rescue her from a villain, would you stop to reason out the metaphysical question of whether it were possible for one mind to cause material waves of sound and for another mind to perceive them? If you did, the problem might probably occupy the remainder of your days. In the same way, if a man undergoes any religious experience and hears the call of his Saviour, for him to halt till he has adjusted a philosophical difficulty would seem to be an analogous sort of thing, whether you call it stupid or whether you call it disgusting. If on the other hand, a man has had no religious experience, then any religion not an affectation is as yet impossible for him; and the only worthy course is to wait quietly till such experience comes. No amount of speculation can take the place of experience.[28]

Peirce's writings contain no description of such an experience other than his musing about the reality of God. He surely would have reported it had it happened. Peirce's case was that of the person in between, drawn powerfully by intimations of the supernatural, yet without direct experience of it. Whatever the actual case of his religious experience, he denied that any barrier should exist between religion and science in their nature as inquiries after truth.

Peirce's father, Benjamin, the eminent mathematician and astronomer, was a Unitarian and undoubtedly influenced his son in religious matters, though Charles became a trinitarian as a member of the Episcopal church. In a published reminiscence, one of the father's students described how he stopped in the midst of a lecture on celestial mechanics and then turned to the class and said,

> Gentlemen, as we study the universe we see everywhere the most tremendous manifestations of force. In our own experience we know of but one source of force, namely will. How then can we help regarding the forces we see in nature as due to the will of some omnipresent, omnipotent being? Gentlemen, there must be a GOD![29]

This anecdote pointedly illustrates the influence of the father on the son, for it is an example of an argument which Charles Peirce elaborated in a 1908 article he called "A Neglected Argument for the Reality of God": in brief, the more we muse about the hypothesis that God is, the more certain of the reality of that idea we must become.[30] But, curiously enough, there remains missing from most of Peirce's life the core of strongly ethical conduct that would be expected in a person so concerned with religious issues.

Although Peirce's intellectual prowess was widely acknowledged and his achievements were numerous and important, his contempt for convention, his difficult character, his reckless involvement in get-rich-quick schemes, and recurring questions about his morals caused him to fail at every turn of his career. When he was a young man known for his brilliance in philosophy, the Harvard Corporation, and later President Charles W. Eliot, pointedly refused to consider him for membership on the faculty at a time when his father held a prestigious chair and was a powerful and respected national leader in science, because, according to William James, he was not a "safe" man. So strong was the Corporation's antipathy to Peirce that, after 1870, when he was thirty-one, they refused even to allow him to lecture on the Harvard campus, despite James's periodic requests, until he was in his sixties. He was abruptly dismissed from his lectureship at the Johns Hopkins University on unspecified moral grounds after five years, despite the fact that President Gilman had intended from the first to offer him a tenured professorship. Peirce spent over thirty years as the scientist in charge of gravimetric experiments at the United States Coast Survey. His career there was ended by forced retirement on grounds of dereliction. The Carnegie Institution denied his request for a grant because of questions about his morals and his mental state. Along the way, Peirce became involved in a number of foolhardy ventures, all based on his inventions. He expected each one to make him a millionaire. Even after the depression of 1893 destroyed whatever chances he might have had for a financial windfall and placed him so heavily in debt that his brother felt obliged to save him from bankruptcy and the loss of his Milford home, he never quit believing that sudden wealth would save him. He continued to live extravagantly even after he had lost his position and salary at the Coast Survey and was reduced to the little income he could make from writing articles. At one point, impending lawsuits against him for assault and nonpayment of debts forced him to become a fugitive from the law. His situation became so desperate that he several times threatened suicide. At the end, a sick and malnourished old man, he was sustained only through the largess of his family and friends, living off the contributions to a fund organized by his close friend William James.

This shadowed side of Peirce's character was explored in a letter to Weiss in connection with his Peirce article in the *Dictionary of American Biography* by Edwin Bidwell Wilson, then (in 1946) beginning research for a memorial biography on Peirce, never completed, for the National Academy of Sciences:

There is probably something you would not say in your biography that is true of Peirce though proof might be impossible to obtain. L. J. Henderson referred him to me once as probably an "essentially wrong-headed individual." I take it he was not referring to Peirce's contributions to logic or science, and perhaps not to philosophy, but to matters of personal behaviour or attitude. I have been told by others that when Peirce was very poor some of his friends took the position that he should be encouraged to come to Cambridge to pick up some private tutoring, but that there was great opposition on the part of members of the Faculty one would not designate so particularly squeamish to having the Harvard student exposed to contact with him, whether this was a suggestion of homosexuality or something else, I never made out, but there seems to be no doubt that several worthy scientific gentlemen thought his influence on the youth would be bad morally. Finally, ⌊Peirce's student at Johns Hopkins, the logician⌋ Mrs. ⌊Christine⌋ Ladd-Franklin who was patently a great admirer of his work and of him told me that once when he dropped in on them in New York with no place to stay (and very poor) they asked him to stay over night with them (as he was always welcome to do) on an occasion when President Gilman of Johns Hopkins University was to be there; and that when Gilman came and found that Peirce was there he took his leave, saying that he would not remain under the same roof with so immoral a man. Clearly Mrs. Ladd-Franklin considered this attitude extreme and unnecessary and well nigh inexplicable, but she also seemed to feel that Gilman did have some background for his attitude. I have often wondered whether you did not too readily excuse in your biography the low standing of Peirce in college. Bright sons of professors went to college early in those days. ⌊The physicist⌋ J. Willard Gibbs was graduated at 19, I believe ⌊as was Peirce⌋—2nd in his class. That Peirce may have had an irregular preparation is probable but with his native ability I fail to see how lack of appreciation on the part of his instructors of a brilliant son of Harvard's leading professor could have resulted in a ranking of Peirce in the lowest fifth of his class unless Peirce himself had been decidedly negligent, about his work and exceptionally antagonistic in his attitude, or something that properly could be described as "essentially wrong-headed."

I saw Peirce only on one occasion, that of the meeting of the Nat⌊ional⌋ Acad⌊emy of⌋ Sci⌊ences⌋ in New Haven about 1905. His paper was quite unintelligible to every member of the audience; . . . and moreover when Peirce terminated the paper he did so in a manner considered by the audience to be rude by remarking curtly that was all he would say upon that occasion on that subject to that audience. In the evening I spent a lot of time with him and a few others at the north end of the lounge in the Graduates Club. His conversation might justly be described as brilliant flashes against cimmerian darkness ⌊a reference to William James's characterization⌋ but the flashes were few and not very clearly directed and the darkness was heavy. In my young way I made up my mind that he had lost much of his—that he must have been wonderful 20 years earlier at Johns Hopkins, but that cerebral arteriosclerosis or something (possibly morphine?) had dulled him and rendered him incoherent.

It was therefore interesting to me several years later to hear Mrs. Ladd-Franklin tell me that she thought he was losing his mind as early as the first half of the nineties. She thought his essay "Man's Glassy Essence" showed it very definitely. And I must say that it has always seemed to me that his writings after 1890 gave much evidence of this compared to those before 1885. However, he never had been particularly clear to me.[31]

In this tension between intellectual strength and moral weakness, there is much that reminds me of the great French poet Charles Baudelaire. Both men were obsessed with their different, but equally demanding, callings, poetry and logic, both of which are self-consciously embedded in the universe of signs. Both had a precocious taste for women. Both lived extravagantly beyond their means and were constantly in debt. Both used drugs and had special knowledge of their effects. Both were fascinated by Edgar Allan Poe. In midlife, after becoming increasingly disgusted with himself, each searched passionately for spiritual enlightenment and proclaimed the need for a transcendental realist metaphysics. Baudelaire, the poet, wrote philosophically of his realism in a passage closely similar to many of Peirce's:

> Every idea is endowed of itself with immortal life, like a human being. All created form, even that which is created by man, is immortal. For form is independent of matter: molecules do not constitute form.[32]

Peirce, the scientist, put the same idea poetically in a different vein, also from the standpoint of the creator:

> Suppose, for example, that I have an idea that interests me. It is my creation. It is my creature; . . . it is a little person. I love it; and I will sink myself in perfecting it. It is not by dealing out cold justice to the circle of my ideas that I can make them grow, but by cherishing and tending them as I would the flowers in my garden.[33]

Both men were social outcasts whose lives and works engendered disgust and dismay in the respectable bourgeoisie of their respective countries. Both men were bohemians and were in their turn disgusted and dismayed by the bourgeois culture that surrounded them. Peirce would have given his laughing and sardonic agreement to Baudelaire's characterization of that culture in his journal:

> All these imbecile bourgeois who ceaselessly utter the words: immoral, immorality, morality and art, and other idiotic phrases, make me think of

Louise Villedieu, the five-franc whore, who, having accompanied me one day to the Louvre, where she had never been before, began blushing and covering her face with her hands. And as we stood before the immortal statues and pictures she kept plucking me by the sleeve and asking how they could exhibit such indecencies in public.[34]

Both men were forced by their ostracisms to make their livings by their wits and from writing articles for journals, and both lived their last years on the charity of others. Both men had deserved reputations for brilliance and depth and breadth of knowledge and achievement, spiced with a sharp originality and insulting arrogance.

Peirce, like Baudelaire, recognized the great cost of his obsession in "dangerous cerebral activity & excitement."[35] He might well have written, as Baudelaire did, "I have cultivated my hysteria with delight and terror. Now I suffer continually from vertigo, and today, 23rd of January, 1862, I have received a singular warning, I have felt the wind of the wing of madness pass over me."[36] Peirce did say more prosaically, in 1902, that his study of logic had derived from " . . . uncontrollable impulse. . . . it has been necessary for me at all times to exercise all my control over myself, for fear that my mind might be affected. . . . "[37]

Both men thought of themselves as modern heroes and are, in their unique ways, progenitors of modern thought. The culture they were born into changed as they grew up in it from the closed society of tradition and inheritance into an open—a public—society of competition and choice. It was no longer possible for gifted men to move safely into already established places of influence and power. Instead, they were forced to make deliberate choices in which they were both actors and critics. Faced with this nineteenth-century Western predicament, Baudelaire created the ideal of the Dandy, who is the modern heroic individual, and named his enemies, the Bourgeois, the Woman, and the vulgar Mass. Baudelaire's concept of the Dandy, which helps to understand the Peirce who was not the logician and scientist, was not the insultingly arrogant fop of eighteenth-century European nobility as he was later copied in an unconscious satire by the wealthy bourgeoisie of the nineteenth century. For Baudelaire, whose *Les Fleurs du Mal* was still notorious at the time of Peirce's first extended visit to Paris in 1875, the ambition of the Dandy was "to be a great man and a saint *by one's own standards*, that is all that matters."[38] As W. H. Auden points out in his introduction to the intimate journals, Baudelaire gave the idea philosophical garb:

> The Dandy . . . is like the hero of poetry, in that he requires certain gifts of fortune, such as money and leisure, and like the hero of philosophy,

in that he must be endowed with the will to make himself into a dandy out of the corrupt nature into which he, like everyone else, is born. On the other hand, the Dandy is neither a man of action nor a seeker after wisdom; his ambition is neither to be admired by men, nor to know God, but simply to become subjectively conscious of being uniquely himself, and unlike anyone else. He is, in fact, the religious hero turned upside down—that is, Lucifer, the rebel, the defiant one who asserts his freedom by disobeying *all* commands, whether given by God, society, or his own nature. The truly dandyish act is the *acte gratuite*, because only an act which is quite unnecessary, unmotivated by any given requiredness, can be an absolutely freely self-chosen individual act.[39]

The Dandy lives and sleeps in front of a mirror, is rich, and is consumed by his work, which he yet does in a disinterested manner. He is solitary and unhappy. If, like both men, the Dandy cannot endure the loneliness which this heroic ideal brings, he can at least choose to debauch himself and yield deliberately to what he despises in order to make himself as despicable as possible. Baudelaire said, "When I have inspired universal horror and disgust, I shall have conquered solitude."[40]

The concept of the Dandy was deliberately carried to this self-loathing conclusion by Baudelaire, but Peirce did not much consider the consequences of his actions apart from his work, and in this it could be said that he was typically American in his relentless optimism, especially in the folly of his schemes for quick wealth. When his world of fantasy collapsed in the late 1890s, Peirce began to examine the moral world of the individual as if for the first time, and, unlike Baudelaire, who knowingly chose to debauch himself, he learned that he had arrived in his own degraded state by going his own way, most unpragmatically, indifferent of the consequences. Only then did he stop to consider his life seriously—distinct from his labors in philosophy and science—in a moral context.

Peirce's first wife, Zina Fay, was apparently thoroughly convinced of Peirce's Dandyism. In her feminist novel, *New York: A Symphonic Study in Three Parts*, there appears a description of a man so like her husband in physical appearance and mannerisms that I believe he was the model. Of her marriage to Peirce, which she ended by leaving him in 1876 after fourteen years, Zina said, "The human heart is a complicated, and in marriage a perfectly inscrutable thing." Her reasons for thinking so can be understood from the description of her husband as

> . . . the handsome demi-mondaine . . . a fashionably dressed young man, very dark, of un-American aspect, and with an expression of complete self-will. . . . [He] had large ability. A certain foundation of grandeur and no-bleness was his. It is conceivable that *some* women walking with him as the

best women best love to walk with men—on the plane of the Mind, of the Soul—might have engaged and uplifted his energies to good. . . . [But] he came out still more material, cynical, brutal—still better fitted to wage merciless war on helpless animals and almost equally helpless women and thus deeper to betray the interests confided to him as a free and potent American—than before. For him humanity had now no sacredness, and God was blotted out.[41]

Clearly, these opinions were very close to those expressed by Presidents Eliot and Gilman and the members of the Harvard faculty reported a generation apart by William James and E. B. Wilson.

Peirce developed a Dandyish attitude toward life at least as early as sixteen, when he wrote that he would not "turn obedient lad" or "go by any rules that other people give me" but would go his own way because on such conduct was his theory of life built.[42] He always dressed, as long as he could possibly afford it, very well, with a rakish elegance. Henry James expressed his opinion of Peirce's personal style with a neat economy of phrase when he wrote his brother William from Paris, in 1875, that he had met "Mr. Chas. Peirce, who wears beautiful clothes, &c." A decade later, Peirce described the manner in which he intended to achieve his unique greatness and become a modern hero in his extraordinary intention "to outline a theory so comprehensive that . . . the entire work of human reason . . . shall appear as the filling up of its details."

It is the second aspect of Peirce's character, the Dandy, which has been suppressed for so long. This study will attempt to portray both the Philosopher and the Dandy as two intimately related aspects of the same sign, Peirce himself.

1

Father, Son, and Melusina

1 8 3 9 – 1 8 7 1   My life is built upon a theory: and if this theory
turns out false, my life will turn out a failure. And
just in proportion as my theory is false my life is a
failure. Well, my theory is this. But first, I am not
to be an old fogy or go by any rules other people
give me—if I should turn old fogy or obedient lad
my life would in troth and indeed be a failure. For
on not doing it is my whole theory built.

CSP, 1854

Charles Sanders Peirce was born on Tuesday, September 10, 1839, into the
thoroughly gentle and Protestant world of well-bred Cambridge and Boston.
This privileged world was entering a time of transformation. Cambridge was
a small, quiet college town of about 8,000 population, more rural than
urban. Boston was a small city of some 85,000, whose overseas trade was in
rapid decline in a losing competition with New York City, while its banking
and manufacturing enterprises were on an equally rapid rise, not to be outdistanced by New York until after the Civil War. No longer was Boston's
harbor a forest of square-rigged masts, although its fleets of fishing and
coasting schooners still presented a busy nautical prospect. On the other
hand, to the pleasure of the sober Brahmins, State Street, still a generation
away from any threat from Wall Street, had grown to be a solidly imposing
bastion of wealth that seemed likely to protect and increase Boston's fortunes for the foreseeable future. Even more imposing was the rapid growth of
manufacturing of many kinds, but especially cotton, railroads, and machin-
ery. The Irish were still a small percentage of the population and though
generally despised were not yet felt to be an immediate danger. Within
fifteen years, they came to number half of Boston's population and a third
that of Cambridge and constituted most of the labor force there. In such

mill towns as Lawrence and Fall River, they would be considered by those of English descent a serious threat to their culture and even their persons. Within twenty years, the Irish controlled many city police forces and much of the state's urban politics.

Cambridge, the scholastic suburb, had the air of a village, and Harvard College's several buildings, which housed about three hundred students, were bounded by a low wooden fence. A horse-trough stood in the Square next to a hand water-pump near the huge "Cambridge Elm," an ailing symbol of the Revolution, and cows were pastured in still-vacant lots on the far side of the Common. Charles Peirce, William James, and Chauncey Wright, three young men who, along with Boston's Oliver Wendell Holmes, Jr., in the late sixties and early seventies were to form the nucleus of a revolution in philosophy, lived in comfortable federal houses within no more than a five-minute walk of each other along neat tree-shaded streets bordered by ample, well-kept gardens.

Harvard College was a family matter and more to the patrician families

The last home of Benjamin and Sarah Mills Peirce, his sister Charlotte Elizabeth Peirce, and James Mills Peirce. The home is located at 4 Kirkland Place, Cambridge, Massachusetts.

of Boston and Cambridge. Not only did they send their sons to the college as a matter of course, they also considered it their duty to support it by endowment for the sake of the poor, and to watch closely over its standards and oversee its smallest details through the Harvard Corporation. Learning was not so important for them as the formation of character. They could describe clearly the traits they had in mind:

> A clear, distinct mentality, a strong distaste for nonsense, steady composure, a calm and gentle demeanour, stability, good principles, intelligence, a habit of under-statement, a slow and cautious way of reasoning, contempt for extravagance, vanity and affectation, kindness of heart, purity, decorum, profound affections, filial and paternal.[1]

The curriculum was intended to perpetuate, in the Boston manner, the merchant, the lawyer, and the man of God. The center of the curriculum was logic (the subject of Peirce's lifelong obsession), the prerequisite for Locke, theology, and the law. Students were required to memorize Professor Frederick Hedge's and later Archbishop Richard Whately's text in logic.

Beneath this cold Ciceronian surface, memorialized in Boston's many marble busts, existed a world in cultural and intellectual ferment that Van Wyck Brooks called "the flowering of New England." The year before Peirce's birth, Ralph Waldo Emerson had read his mildly unsettling "Divinity School Address," an elaboration of the mystical meaning of transcendentalism, to the assembled men and women of the local gentry and intelligentsia. Transcendentalism was one of three powerfully attractive ideologies that occupied much of their attention. A second and far more controversial one, abolitionism, a naive and often racist political expression of Protestant morality intended to purify the American air of the moral taint of slavery and to prepare the nation for greatness, had begun in earnest eight years before, when William Lloyd Garrison published his first issue of the *Liberator*, proclaiming that he would be "as harsh as truth and as uncompromising as justice." The third was the appearance, eight years after, of modern, experimental science in the guise of Harvard's Lawrence Scientific School, named for and endowed by the Boston industrialist Abbot Lawrence, who headed the Essex Company and the Atlantic Cotton Mills Company and founded the Boston and Albany Railroad. Lawrence intended the school to generate technologies and engineers, but its effect was far broader and deeper by the time it was effectively broken up in 1908.

A variety of less well known but equally subversive causes also arose. Cambridge and Boston were becoming self-consciously literary on the Oxford model. Henry Wadsworth Longfellow, James Russell Lowell, and Dr.

Oliver Wendell Holmes, the Autocrat of the Breakfast Table, led a growing group of disciples into the fascinations of writing and reading poetry. Charles Eliot Norton began his lifelong study of Dante and became friends with John Ruskin. Others were editing Homer, Spenser, and Sallust. Emerson, Thoreau, and Hawthorne, each in his different way, brought metaphysical light to the dark pessimisms of Calvinism. The *North American Review* under George Bancroft, Bronson Alcott's *Dial*, and the *Atlantic Monthly*, begun by Dr. Holmes, all commented on the world with a kind of self-satisfied smartness that touted Boston, or Concord, as the modern Athens, or Delphi. Margaret Fuller and her women cohorts began the long struggle to weaken male privilege. By the time Charles was eight, Harvard's curriculum and faculty had begun their transformations, unrecognized in their uncentered force by the merchant-bankers and churchmen of the Corporation, into a new and unruly means to knowledge. Among other upsetting changes in the perspectives of learning, Cornelius Conway Felton and Francis J. Child introduced and refined the modern world-historical view in their approaches to ancient and modern literature. Asa Gray, the original theoretical botanist, Louis Agassiz, the great Swiss paleontologist, and Benjamin Peirce, the inspiring mathematician and astronomer, brought the sharp, transforming instruments of science into the complacent midst of the Brahmin world.[2] It was an extraordinary time and place to be born, especially as the favored son of a patrician father and mother.

Not only was the Peirce family among the most prominent socially and politically, but it was one of the most eminent intellectually as well. Peirce's mother, Sarah Hunt Mills, was the daughter of Senator Elijah Hunt Mills, whose seat was taken on his retirement by Daniel Webster, a family friend. Peirce's father was a much-admired teacher whose students included two Harvard presidents and the eminent astronomer Simon Newcomb. (Newcomb, one of Benjamin's favorite students, would later play a decisive role in undermining the career of his mentor's son Charles.) Charles was the second son and in many ways the favorite. The other children were James Mills (1834–1906), professor of mathematics and dean of the graduate faculty at Harvard; Benjamin Mills (1844–1870), who studied engineering, showed great promise, but died young; Helen Huntington (1845–1923), through whom came most of the family correspondence relating to her brother Charles; and Herbert Henry Davis (1849–1916), who entered the Foreign Service, where he had a distinguished career and represented the United States as host at the Portsmouth Conference.

The Peirce ancestry is typical of New England in its course.[3] The family descended from John Pers (pronounced "purse"), a weaver from Norwich, England, who emigrated to Watertown, Massachusetts, in 1637 in the first wave of the Puritan exodus. For the next four generations, the family were farmers, craftsmen, or shopkeepers. Then Jeramiel, in the Peirces' spelling (1747–1831), married up, moved to Salem, entered the China Trade, and made a fortune. Charles's grandfather Benjamin (1779–1831), after failing in the China Trade, became librarian at Harvard during the last five years of his life, leaving the first catalogue of the contents of the Harvard Library and a manuscript history of the college which was published posthumously. It was this grandfather who thus established the scholarly precedent for his son Benjamin (1809–1880), Charles's father, who held the chair of mathematics and astronomy at Harvard College and who was easily the most brilliant and outstanding mathematician to appear in America before the Civil War. He had a fine reputation in Europe, as well. Benjamin had a brother, Charles Henry, a physician and later professor of chemistry in the Lawrence Scientific School, and a sister, Charlotte Elizabeth, who never married, kept school, read French and German novels and other literature, and commented volubly on the Peirce family in her letters, many of which survive.

Charles was in the eighth generation and was interested in the more unusual aspects of his ancestry. In 1911, at age seventy-two, still searching for the means to understand his own failed life, he reexamined this ancestry in the light of the theory of biologically determined traits, in which he believed. This theory, often set forth in racial terms, had been developed by his contemporaries Sir Francis Galton, the anthropologist, and Cesare Lombroso, the criminologist and physiologist. Peirce was deeply troubled by his own behavior:

> In my case, it is undeniable that *three mental twists* [italics mine] are strongly marked in the families that have given me being, and seem to be so in myself. Of course, the name Peirce, being merely another form of Peter, was given to numberless humble individuals no more related to one another than they were to the Stones. But in the line of Peirce's from which I come, back considerably further than my great-great-grandfather, had been marked by an unusual proportion of mathematicians and persons given to exactitude. This trait, unless it is sedulously broadened, is, I think, distinctly opposed to sound sense in such a matter as religion. . . .
>
> Two of my direct ancestors, Lawrence and Cassandra Southwick, were sentenced to death by the Massachusetts General Court; nor was this considered sufficient punishment for their abominable deed. In addition, all their children were ordered to be sold as slaves. But they contrived somehow to escape to Shelter Island [a Quaker refuge]. That is highly characteristic, and my father was regarded in much the same way by the majority of his Massachusetts fellow-citizens,—i.e. of those who knew his crime [of supporting Negro slavery], though it differed from that of the Southwicks

in consisting in a political, not a religious belief. I myself fully share my father's abomination. For I do not regard such slavery as an owner is likely to exercize as half as horrible as that to which many,—not to insist on saying the great majority of us,—subject ourselves. Freedom of thought is, to my thinking, so much more valuable than any other kind. . . . It is curious that my great-grandfather [Jeramiel], was, on account of his shocking opinions, "read out" of that same Quaker Society, for belonging to which the Southwicks were so signally disgraced. That same great grandfather amassed a considerable fortune, founded at first I think upon some process for making morocco, but later in the adventurous China trade.[4]

The third trait, after aptitude for mathematics and a strong tendency toward contentiousness, regardless of the outcome, he believed to be exaggerated sensibility, which he found expressed in both ancestries. In his father's he found greatness of heart, and in his mother's " . . . the warmest, if not the hottest family I ever came near enough to judge of."[5] This romantic sentimentality, especially in matters of the heart, of the sort made influential by Goethe in *The Sorrows of Young Werther*, Peirce later saw expressed in himself as a failure of moral self-control: "For long years I suffered unspeakably, being an excessively emotional fellow, from ignorance of how to go to work to acquire a sovereignty over myself."[6]

In surveying his life, Peirce was looking for biologically determined mental kinks that he was unable to resist as the explanation of his moral failure. In his analysis, he made the same self-serving argument that Augustine did in his *Confessions* about sex, that its pleasures and attractions were irresistible, not that he lost control of himself. Peirce's search was not for the theological sources of evil, however, but for hereditary traits having the same origin in biology as the physical and psychological stigmata which Lombroso had thought he found in his studies of criminals, such as prominent superciliary arches and insensibility to pain, which signaled the personality irresistibly drawn to criminal acts.[7] Clearly, Peirce felt himself to be the victim of an overwhelming and uncontrollable passion. He found the same three traits in his formidable father that he found in himself: great mathematical ability, contentiousness bordering on the pathological, and exaggerated sensibility.

Benjamin Peirce was an extraordinary man. He was successful as both an academic and a public figure, and he was at the center of the movement to improve American education, especially higher education in the sciences. As a member of the Lazzaroni (the Beggars), an informal group of leading American scientists, he lobbied Washington for funds for science and also supported the movement for a national university. He was instrumental in convincing Abbot Lawrence to endow the Lawrence Scientific School at

Harvard in 1847. In 1853 and 1854, he was elected president of the American Association for the Advancement of Science, and in 1863, with Louis Agassiz and others, he helped found the National Academy of Sciences. From 1867 until his resignation in 1874 (while still holding his Harvard professorship), he was superintendent of the United States Coast Survey, and thereafter until his death in 1880 served as its "consulting geometer." He published two major works (along with many lesser ones), both influential, *Analytic Mechanics* and *Linear Associative Algebra*.

Charles's father was also by all accounts a most unusual and unconventional man. Students remembered him with great respect and affection and thought of him as a genius who, as often as not, they were unable to understand. This description of a typical class was written by one of his students:

> I have hinted that his lectures were not easy to follow. They were never carefully prepared. The work with which he rapidly covered the blackboard was very illegible, marred with frequent erasures, and not infrequent mistakes (he worked too fast for accuracy). He was always ready to digress from the straight path and explore some sidetrack that had suddenly attracted his attention, but which was likely to have led nowhere when the college bell announced the close of the hour and we filed out, leaving him abstractedly staring at his work, still with chalk and eraser in his hands, entirely oblivious of his departing class.[8]

Benjamin's eccentricities added to the appeal and eminence of his popular and professional image:

> The appearance of Professor Benjamin Peirce, whose long gray hair, straggling grizzled beard and unusually bright eyes sparkling under a soft felt hat, as he walked briskly but rather ungracefully across the college yard, fitted very well with the opinion current among us that we were looking upon a real live genius, who had a touch of the prophet in his make-up.[9]

When public lectures were instituted at Harvard in the early 1860s, Benjamin became a popular lecturer known throughout Massachusetts. When he heard of Benjamin's appointment as superintendent of the Coast Survey, President Charles W. Eliot of Harvard later recalled how amazed he was:

> When Professor Bache retired from the superintendency of the Coast Survey, he procured the appointment of his intimate friend Benjamin Peirce as his successor in the superintendency. Those of us who had long known Professor Peirce heard of this action with amazement. We had never supposed that he had any business faculty whatever, or any liking for ad-

Engraving of Benjamin Peirce by H. Wright Smith. The National Academy of Sciences used it as the frontispiece to vol. II of *The Mathematical Monthly*, 1860.

ministrative work. A very important part of the Superintendent's function was to procure from the Committees of Congress appropriations adequate to support the various activities of the Survey on sea and land. Within a few months it appeared that Benjamin Peirce persuaded Congressmen and Congressional Committees to vote much more money to the Coast Survey than they had ever voted before. This was a legitimate effect of Benjamin Peirce's personality, of his aspect, his speech, his obvious disinterestedness, and his conviction that the true greatness of nations grew out of their fostering of education, science and art.[10]

Benjamin Peirce taught mathematics as a kind of Pythagorean prayer. He proclaimed the mystical doctrine that, however the supernatural might be, it existed in the natural world and was experienced there. In 1889, in the *Century Dictionary*, Charles, under the heading of "ideal-realism," described his father's position (essentially his own in time as well) as " . . . the opinion that nature and the mind have such a community as to impart to guesses a tendency toward the truth, while at the same time they require the confirmation of empirical science." Among many other examples of a similar nature is this statement of Benjamin's, the closing of a formal paper read before a learned society upon the subject "mathematical investigation of the fractions which occur in phyllotaxis [the formal arrangement of leaves on a plant stem]":

> May I close with the remark, that the object of geometry in all its measuring and computing, is to ascertain with exactness the plan of the great Geometer, to penetrate the veil of material forms, and disclose the thoughts which lie beneath them? When our researches are successful, and when a generous and heaven-eyed inspiration has elevated us above humanity, and raised us triumphantly into the very presence, as it were, of the divine intellect, how instantly and entirely are human pride and vanity repressed, and, by a single glance at the glories of the infinite mind, are we humbled to the dust.[11]

Although a professed Unitarian, the dominant Boston sect, Benjamin was thoroughly unorthodox in many of his opinions and was considered a disgrace by many of his coreligionists for his opinions on Negro slavery, which he supported. He agreed with Louis Agassiz's belief in a separate creation of the races and believed in the superiority of the Anglo-Saxon race as a justification for the continued enslavement of what he believed to be the mentally inferior Negro. Benjamin had friends among Souther planters, and he wrote to his son Charles, in 1860, as if he were Thomas Jefferson himself:

> No pure blooded African had ever yet become a mathematician. This could not be from want of opportunity for they had been in the most intimate relations with the Egyptians, Carthaginians and Romans in ancient times, with the Arabs in the middle ages, and in modern times in our own and other countries. Hence it follows that races differ. To decide what is suited to each race must be left to the wise lovers of mankind who have the opportunity to observe. . . . [12]

Benjamin also viewed the Irish and other recent immigrants as dangerous inferiors. These deeply held biologically determinist views of a racist and nativist kind, not at all unusual for the time, and especially sophisticated among university-educated men both North and South, influenced Charles's views about human nature all his life.

Benjamin was influenced by the unorthodox religious views of the Swedish scientist and mystic Emmanuel Swedenborg, to whose writings both he and Charles were introduced by Benjamin's friend Henry James, Sr. That Charles shared this interest is demonstrated by his 1870 review of James's study of Swedenborg's mystical theology.[13] This review was the first public expression of his interest in mysticism. It also provided him with an explana-

The founders of the National Academy of Sciences with Abraham Lincoln in 1863. *From left to right*: Benjamin Peirce, Alexander Dallas Bache, Joseph Henry, Louis Agassiz, President Lincoln, Senator Henry Wilson, Admiral Charles H. Davis, and Benjamin Apthorp Gould. The original, painted by Albert Herter, hangs in the Board Room of the National Academy of Sciences Building.

Benjamin Peirce and his graduating mathematics students at Harvard, 1869.

tion for his suffering from neuralgia in Swedenborg's idea that evil is a good because it challenges us to become spiritually whole, that we must love it as a degenerate form of the good. His father's deeply religious attitude had a profound effect upon Charles, which manifested itself increasingly as he became older. Murphey wrote that the "religious spirit was always present in [Charles] Peirce's work, whether overtly expressed or not, and was an important factor in determining the nature of his philosophy."[14] In general, Charles's father influenced his philosophy in three ways: in giving it a religious foundation of a mystical flavor, in providing it with the exacting methods of experimental science and mathematics, and in developing in him a rigorously critical and skeptical attitude and approach to both philosophers and philosophical issues.[15] The latter probably had much to do with his rebellion against the Brahmin hierarchs of his youth and young manhood.

With the exception of Herbert Henry Davis, who became a successful diplomat and administrator in the Department of State, married only once, and raised a family, all within the accepted rules of his time and class, the Peirce men were self-consciously unconventional and unique. Benjamin saw to the education of each personally. Individualism was encouraged in the Peirce home by a lack of all discipline, except that which fostered the intellect. The family was unusually indulgent of its male members, who behaved much as they wished. Sarah was particularly indulgent of her husband and Charles. At the same time, Benjamin towered over the family, an awe-inspiring figure to his children made even more so by his massive rages, of which a relative said discreetly:

> Like many men devoted deeply to wife, children and family; and who in fact seemed to greatly enjoy the company of all his young relatives, and their companions; Prof. Benjamin Peirce was subject at times to violent outbreaks of impatience, and temper. This may have been manifest to his colleagues and associates.[16]

In announcing Charles's birth, Benjamin wrote delightedly and eloquently in a prophetic vein, already ambitious for him:

> The boy weighs $8\frac{3}{4}$ pounds, and is as hearty as possible. He offered to go out and throw the bar with me today; a certain sign that he will either make an eminent lawyer or a thief. As soon as he publishes his Celestial Mechanics I will send you a copy, and I have no doubt he would be glad to correspond with you about your last mathematical researches. He has two splendid optical instruments—each of a single achromatic lens—which is capable of adjustment!—and so wonderful is the contrivance for adjustment that, by a mere act of the will, he is able to adapt it to any distance at pleasure. But one fault has been found with these instruments and that is,

the images are inverted; our new born philosopher, however, our male Minerva, contends that this is a great advantage in the present topsy-turvy state of the world. . . . The first proof of his genius which he exhibited to the world consisted in sounding most lustily, a wonderful acoustical instrument whose tones, in noise and discordancy, were not unlike those of a . . . fish-horn. Is not this a singular coincidence? A sure omen of his coming, almost come, celebrity?[17]

Little record remains of Charles's first ten years. What exists portrays a happy and imaginative boy. In an obituary, his younger brother Herbert remembered him

forever digging into encyclopedias and other books in search of knowledge upon abstruse subjects, while discussions with his learned father upon profound questions of science, especially higher mathematics and philosophy, were common matters of astonishment, not only to his brothers and sister, but to his parents as well.

Charles however was no prig or pedant. His mirthful, contagious laugh, his keen sense of humor and ready wit made him a bright and forever welcome companion in all gatherings. He was always capable of holding his own with unconscious ease whether among his elders or with simple unpretentiousness joining in the sports of the youngest and smallest. His own choice was for intellectual games, especially chess, of which he early became a master.[18]

Another side of young Charles, recalled after his death by his friend and cousin Mary Huntington, was his dangerous temper:

Our games of chess were of daily occurrence, because he demanded it. I had no aptitude for the game, though I liked to play with him to please him, but would often have liked to escape; though I dared to refuse but once. Then, he showed such displeasure, that I was glad at the end of a few days to play as often as he wished. This was the only occasion when he showed toward me his violent temper, but I knew it was there and instinctively avoided any danger of rousing it.[19]

Peirce himself provided a gnomic outline in "My Life Written for the Class Book" as a senior in 1859, which he extended to 1861:

1839 September 10. Tuesday. Born.
1840 Christened.
1841 Made a visit to Salem which I distinctly remember.
1842 July 31. Went to church for the first time.
1843 Attended a marriage.

1844 Fell violently in love with Miss W. and commenced my education.

1845 Moved into new house on Quincy St.

1846 Stopped going to Ma'am Sessions and began to go to Miss Wares—a very pleasant school where I learnt much and fell violently in love with another Miss W. whom for distinction's sake I will designate Miss W'.

1847 Began to be most seriously and hopelessly in love. Sought to drown my care by taking up the subject of Chemistry—an antidote which long experience enables me to recommend as sovereign.

1848 Went to dwell in town with my uncle C. H. Mills and went to school to the Rev. T. R. Sullivan, where I received my first lessons in elocution.

1849 In consequence of playing truant and laving in the frog-pond, was taken ill. On my recovery, I was recalled to Cambridge and admitted a member of the **Cambridge High School.**

1850 Wrote a "History of Chemistry." [never found]

1851 Established a printing-press.

1852 Joined a debating society.

1853 Set up for a fast man and became a bad schoolboy.

1854 Left the High School with honor after having been turned out several times. Worked at Mathematics [with his father] for about six months and then joined Mr. Dixwell's school in town.

1855 Graduated at Dixwell's and entered College. Read Schiller's *Aesthetic Letters* [with his great friend Horatio Paine] and began the study of Kant.

1856 SOPHOMORE. Gave up the idea of being a fast man and undertook the pursuit of pleasure.

1857 JUNIOR. Gave up the pursuit of pleasure and undertook to enjoy life.

1858 SENIOR. Gave up enjoying life and exclaimed "Vanity of vanities! All is vanity!"

1859 Wondered what I would do in life.

[added in 1861]

Appointed Aid on the Coast Survey [1859]. Went to Maine and then to Louisiana.

1860 Came back from Louisiana and took a Proctorship in Harvard. Studied Natural History and Natural Philosophy [with Louis Agassiz].

1861 No longer wondered what I would do in life but defined my object.[20]

Three major recurrent themes in Peirce's life are sketched in this brief and intriguing list: the cross-fertilization of science and philosophy (e.g., chemistry, mathematics, and Kant), a strong inclination to Dandyish dissipations and romantic involvements (e.g., falling in love, fast man, bad schoolboy, pursuit of pleasure, enjoying life, and Schiller's *Aesthetic Letters*), and confusion about his purpose in life, which, despite its unspecified resolution in 1860 by his decision to devote his life to the study of logic, continually reappeared.

Charles also mentioned in passing a fourth such recurrent theme: sickness. The apparently isolated event of getting sick when he was ten from "laving in the frog pond" was, in fact, one of a constant stream of illnesses from which he suffered in his lifetime. Often the complaint was of nervous disorders. The Peirce family correspondence mentions his high-strung behavior and frequent bouts of various kinds of the usual sicknesses throughout his childhood, including severe colds, headaches, and fevers, but beginning in the late 1850s the most serious complaint was neuralgia, a disorder from which his father also suffered. Particularly in 1859, Charles's senior year in college, which was particularly bad for sickness, recurrent neuralgia accompanied by excruciating and debilitating pain was reported in his father's and other family correspondence.[21] Aunt Lizzie wrote at about that time, underlining its seriousness, that "Charley Peirce has the neuralgia too—& at times suffers from it dreadfully. Alas for the sufferings of the world! But we must have faith has St. Paul had. Perhaps St. Paul's 'thorn in the flesh' was neuralgia."[22]

Among many other such reports is this one, in 1864, to Benjamin Peirce's close friend Alexander Dallas Bache, then superintendent of the Coast Survey: "I reached the house yesterday morning and last night came as close as possible to one of my attacks. But I escaped with a few hours of intense suffering & without being compelled to resort to opium or ether."[23]

A year earlier, Charles's wife Zina (they were married in 1861) had written to his brother Ben:

> Poor Charley [then 23] is at this moment slumbering on that lounge he is so proud of, under the influence of *ether*, having been suffering all day from neuralgia. I am almost discouraged about his neuralgia, it hangs on so long & keeps him weak and languid even when it does not pain him, so that he gets through but little work, and even if he does get better, a breath of [winter] air will give it to him again as badly as ever.[24]

Peirce reported recurrent episodes of the affliction for the rest of his life. In one example while he was lecturer there, forty years old at the time, he wrote to President Daniel Coit Gilman of the Johns Hopkins University:

> I have had an unfortunate week in New York. Whether I had already taken cold in working on some coefficients of expansion or whether it was on the sleeping-car, certain it is that when I arrived I was so ill with rheumatism I had to go directly to bed & shortly after came a violent neuralgia in my face

& also an obstinate & severe diarrhea. From these two last I have suffered all the week & have past most of my time in bed, so that to my intense regret I shall miss another week's lectures. . . .

I have been deeply disappointed at being ill so much this year.[25]

Peirce and his father were extremely well-versed in medical literature, and his use of the medical term *facial neuralgia* (or *neuralgia of the face*, thus distinguishing it from migraine, intercostal neuralgia, or sciatica) suggests that he suffered from what is now called trigeminal neuralgia, a neurological disease for which only in the past decade has a cause and treatment been found. Until this discovery, the specificity of the pain and the lack of a cure for the disease were its defining characteristics. It is always marked by the kind of acute, intense, and sometimes unbearable facial pain described by both father and son. The term *facial neuralgia* was used medically in the nineteenth century to refer to the same neurological disorder as the modern term *trigeminal neuralgia*: acute pain affecting one or more of the three branches of the fifth cranial nerve on either side of the face, usually thought to be the result of pressure on the nerve sheath from a then-unknown source. "There are few ailments which give rise to greater suffering."[26] An attack may be triggered by a draft, a touch somewhere on the face, or stress, or sometimes for no apparent reason. Sometimes the pain occurs every few minutes for several days or even weeks. Sometimes it does not recur for months. Peirce often associated the incidence of neuralgia with other disorders and conditions, such as prolonged fever, rheumatism, bronchitis, excessive stress, high emotion, bad weather, depression, overwork, and even madness of a kind. To abate the terrible pain, both father and son regularly took ether and decoctions of opium. Charles probably also later used morphine regularly, since it does not leave behind the kind of long-lasting lassitude produced by the other two drugs.[27] Charles, at least, appears to have been addicted, and to have later used cocaine as well. Support for the likelihood of his early addiction comes from a letter written to him when he was twenty-one by Carrie Badger, apparently asking him to give up opium: "regarding the request I made of you the other evening about the opium— would you do for me when my husband what you would not do as a lover?"[28]

Trigeminal neuralgia causes the kind of two-sided behavior which many of Peirce's friends and colleagues reported. They very seldom were made aware of its cause, about which Peirce was close-mouthed, except with his family and a very few others such as Gilman. When free of pain he was often pleasant, considerate, cheerful, loving, charming, and good company, but when the pain was on him he was, at first, almost stupefied and then aloof, cold, depressed, extremely suspicious, impatient of the slightest crossing, and subject to violent outbursts of temper. The attacks often left him in a confused state, sometimes lasting for days. These swings of temperament were reported in passing to Gilman by one of Peirce's Johns Hopkins colleagues, who said that Peirce "has been kind to me in his way, and if he were always as he can be sometimes, he would be a charming companion."[29] There are many such bemused accounts of Peirce's ambivalent behavior made by his colleagues and by those who, though not close to him, were concerned for him. His family and close friends, knowing of his affliction, did their best to protect him from the time he was a young man. Their indulgence helped to create the "highly emotional, easily duped and rather snobbish" young Dandy he became. Much of Peirce's pursuit of luxury and pleasure flowed from his intense and constant desire to escape terrifying pain.

That the family of his boyhood was close and loving is obvious from the remaining correspondence. This benediction closing a letter from husband to wife will suffice to establish the point:

> Kiss darling little Bertie, dear sweet gentle Nellie, warmhearted, imaginative Benjie, and bright eyed, bright souled, fervently loving Charlie, and when Jem gets home . . . tell him that he is every day dearer to me, and that I am every day prouder of such a son. Goodbye my own true loving wife—dearer to me than ever. How dearly I love you.[30]

The children led a close and active life, entertaining themselves with considerable imagination, especially with games, and spending their summers usually either in Northampton or at the family home in Salem. There are two examples of storytelling among the children told by young Charles, aged about ten. These stories also indicate the quality of the intellectual life in the Peirce household and the standards of competence which were required of the male children, not unusual for the time and class:

Charles one day write [sic] a couple of stories, asked his mother to read them, and said they was handsome little stories, and a little while afterwards his father came in, and Charles asked him to read them. Father read them, said they were pretty simple stories. Charles says they are not are they? You ought not to say they are simple.

CHARLES AND BEN

Charles & Ben were two brothers. Ben was four years older [sic] than Charles and when he was a little boy—he thought he would try to climb the hill of knowledge. Now this is a very high hill & full of stones and briars—& rough places—but at the top there is a beautiful palace where there are many good & sensible people assembled. Ben was very successful & in a few years had reached the palace, & had begun to make quite a

Helen Mills Peirce, age ca. 15 years.

figure among its learned inhabitants; when Charles undertook the same journey. He is now on his way there & though he has not pursued exactly the same path yet he goes on so slow & sure that there can be no doubt of succeeding as well I hope as his brother.

THE LIBRARY

Charles was one day sitting in his room when suddenly he heard a rustling noise & looking up he saw all the books moving from their places & coming towards him. The Latin grammar was first & opened of itself & said—"Look not frightened my dear Charles; for you are so well acquainted with me that I can say nothing to trouble you." In this way he was addressed by Viva Romae—Greek Grammar & several other books—Colburn's Arithmetic to be sure sputtered a little but Charles did not care for he could not understand him. At last came Virgil—& said—Charles my friends the Latin grammar & Caesar have told me how well they like you & I have a strong wish to be acquainted with you—let us never have one quarrel & then you may be sure that I shall speak so favourably of you to

Mr. Horace—& Mr. Quintillian [sic] that you will be delighted with their affable & sociable manners—& if we are not friends I fear that you will not be able to be acquainted with these illustrious men.[31]

The image of himself going "slow & sure" to success is one which Peirce always considered the true one. As a young man he developed the idea he called "pedestrianism," and a few years before he died he stated that what he had accomplished in philosophy had been done by plodding. Faced with his brilliant and impatient father, Charles was to adopt the strategy of the tortoise in his race with the hare. Logic, with its step-by-small-step progress, gave him, in the long run, the advantage over his facile, brilliant, impatient, and error-prone father. But there was another, more fundamental, because also physiological, reason for Peirce's inchmeal approach to thinking. As he described it to the mathematician Cassius J. Keyser when he was approaching seventy:

> But I am left-handed; and I often think that means that I do not use my brain in the way that the mass of men do, and that peculiarity betrays itself also in my ways of thinking. Hence, I have always labored under the misfortune of being thought "original." Upon a set subject, I am likely to write worse than any man of equal practice. . . .
>
> I am not naturally a writer, but as far from being so as any man. If I have ever written anything well, it was because the ideas were exerting a tremendous tension,—almost to the bursting point. Moreover, I write much better when I have a definite proposition to prove. It should also not be intricate; for otherwise my mental left-handedness makes me express myself in a way that to a normal mind seems almost inconceivably awkward.[32]

Peirce also complained of difficulty in using language. He thought English no less foreign than Greek or German, and at about the same time as the letter to Keyser, he wrote, "One of the most extreme and lamentable of my incapacities is my incapacity for linguistic expression." He explained himself further:

> I will remark, by the way, that I am led to surmise that this awkwardness is connected with the fact that I am left-handed. For that my left handedness is not a mere accidental habit, but has some organic cause seems to be evidenced by the fact that when I left the last school where it had attracted attention, I wrote with facility with my right hand, but could not write legibly with my left; and yet when I ceased to make the effort to continue this habit of three years standing, I soon fell back to using my left hand, though I have always used knife, fork, and spoon, *at table,* just as others do. [(crossed out) Now supposing that my cerebral organ of speech is on the

left side as in other people . . . [Now, since my heart is placed as usual, it would seem that the connections between different parts of my brain must be different from the usual and presumably best arrangement; and if so, it would necessarily follow that my thinking should be *gauche*.[33]

Peirce clearly knew about the discovery of Broca's Area in the left hemisphere and the control of speech located there in the great majority of people. He also speculated accurately on the pathology associated with left-handedness and on the possible alternatives of brain hemisphere asymmetry which modern research has uncovered in left-handed people. In a discussion of the effects of left-handedness, Kent, in her study of Peirce's diagrammatic thinking, suggests three related possibilities to account for Peirce's "awkwardness":

> When such persons are obliged to use their right hands to write, shift gear levers, and so on, their imaging hemispheres must adapt to these atypical functions. Confusion, distress, and lack of co-ordination may occur in some. Others may acquire a visual/creative content in the extended linguistic use; that is, left-handed persons whose language dominant hemisphere is atypical and who have successfully converted to right-handedness may be able to make more facile connections between analytic and imaginative/creative activity than those who have not been so constrained. In some persons, it has been suggested, neither hemisphere is dominant and, without a definite left-to-right orientation, they may experience difficulty in learning to read and write.[34]

On the basis of this general hypothesis, Kent compares Einstein and Peirce and makes a number of unusual and, I believe, accurate suggestions about the origins of Peirce's thinking. Apparently, in neither man was either brain hemisphere dominant. Both did poorly in school work. Both thought in diagrammatic terms, and both thought their differences from the normal to be of physiological and not cultural origin:

> Einstein began using his thought experiments (Gedankenexperimente) at sixteen, and Peirce began training himself to think in diagrams when a young man, finding it a great advance over algebraic thinking. There is, indeed, a remarkable similarity in their analyses of this thought process: both men emphasized the elements of reiteration and association in imagery; both maintained that inquiry advances in reaction to experiences that conflict with established thought patterns and, in doing so, create surprise or wonder. The result in Peirce's terms is the "eradication of doubt," the "production of belief," the "settlement of opinion." Einstein referred to it as a "continuous flight from wonder." Both men traced their own creative initiatives to systematized diagrammatic thought. . . .

Beginning with a suggestion from Berkeley's work on vision, Peirce conceived the possibility of forming habits from imaginary practice. . . . He claimed that by exercising the imagination, we can visualize the occurrence of a stimulus and mentally rehearse the results of different responses. That which appears most satisfactory will influence actual behaviour as effectively as a habit produced by reiteration in the outside world. From this Peirce was led to pragmatism, conceived as a philosophy in which thinking involves manipulating diagrams in order to examine questions; that is to say, problems would be expressed in diagrams and analysis would proceed by executing transformations upon those diagrams. . . .

Peirce's objective was to have the operation of thinking literally laid open to view—a moving picture of thought.[35]

To put his ideas into words was laborious and stressful in the extreme. The picture of himself as a plodder is singularly consistent and was his explanation of the way in which he gained the rank of a philosopher on the same level with Leibniz. It is also consistent with the evidence of thousands of pages of repetitious manuscripts, each one of which, nevertheless, shows the growth of the idea on which he was working. This view of himself was quite the reverse of the contemporary commentary of others about Peirce, who found brilliance, obscurity, arrogance, impulsiveness, and other similarly contrasting characteristics more suitable to describe him.

The family itself was not the only intellectual resource, however. The academic culture of Harvard College and Boston and many illustrious guests played an important role in the development of the children's attitudes and minds. Frequent visitors at the Mason Street house in Cambridge where Peirce lived until he was six were J. J. Sylvester of mathematical eminence and later Charles's colleague at Johns Hopkins University; the poet Henry Wadsworth Longfellow; the poet and essayist James Russell Lowell; the historian Francis Parkman; the abolitionist theologian Theodore Parker; the Autocrat of the Breakfast Table, Oliver Wendell Holmes, and his brother Dr. John Holmes; Ralph Waldo Emerson, the Seer; the abolitionist feminist Margaret Fuller; the jurist Rufus Choate; the paleontologist Louis Agassiz; Senator Daniel Webster; Superintendent Alexander Dallas Bache of the Coast Survey; and Secretary Joseph Henry of the Smithsonian Institution, among others. Of Emerson, Peirce said, tongue in cheek, that his "address in the early forties greatly impressed me; for it was not necessary to understand Emerson or to have more than the slightest contact with him to be greatly impressed."[36] Despite his often expressed opposition to transcendentalism, Peirce, with heavy irony, did proclaim, when he was fifty-two, its profound influence on him:

I was born and reared in the neighborhood of Concord. . . . at the time when Emerson, [Frederick H.] Hedge, and their friends were disseminating the ideas they had caught from [Friedrich von] Schelling [with whom Peirce identified his own metaphysical position in the *Monist* papers of 1891–93], and Schelling from Plotinus, from Boehm[e], or from God knows what minds stricken with the monstrous mysticism of the East. But the atmosphere of Cambridge held many an antiseptic against Concord transcendentalism; and I am not conscious of having contracted any of that virus. Nevertheless, it is probable that some cultured bacilli, some benignant form of the disease was implanted in my soul, unawares, and that now, after long incubation, it comes to the surface, modified by mathematical conceptions and by training in physical investigations.[37]

To illustrate his unorthodox cast of mind, Peirce, in a fragment written when he was in his early seventies, recounted how, when a boy, he had decided in opposition to his teacher that animals and birds possessed reasoning powers similar to those in people. He had come to this opinion

Sarah Mills Peirce, Benjamin's widow, in the living room of their last home, on Kirkland Place in Cambridge, Massachusetts.

through observing a dog and a parrot that were family pets. When his brother Jem (James Mills) was a day student at Harvard, he kept a fine spitz which stayed in his rooms until he came home in the afternoons and called him with the words "spitz, spitz, spitz." The dog then ran down the stairs past the old parrot, whose perch was in the hall and who watched this daily ritual with interest. Peirce was both instructed and pleased by the game the parrot invented, in which it would take advantage of the dog by calling out "spitz" in imitation of its master's voice and then would jeer at it when it came running in, wagging its tail in welcome.[38]

Charles's interest in science was awakened early and was assiduously strengthened by his father, who seldom missed a chance to bring home a scientific curiosity from his many trips and expeditions and taught him at length when at home. This scientific romance, written in 1851, when Charles was twelve, is typical:

> Tell Charlie that last night we ground through a shower of rain, in which there were twin drops, falling within a few feet of each other, of which one was destined to pass into Lake Erie, over the falls of Niagara, through Lake Ontario and the St. Lawrence to the Atlantic; while the other running into the Mississippi, through the Gulf of Mexico, up the Gulf Stream and meeting the other upon the banks of New Foundland cry out "Have you a strawberry on your left shoulder" and when the other said, "I have not" would again burst out with . . . "It is my long lost brother" and rushing into each other's arms they would expire in a briny tear, rise again to the skies, and after making once and again the circuit of the earth; again face and separate upon the dividing ridge of the crater, of the great lakes and the great river of the west.[39]

Four years earlier, when he was eight, Charles had been introduced to chemistry by his father. This study took place in the context of the development, beginning in 1847, of the Lawrence Scientific School, among whose sponsors were Benjamin Peirce and Louis Agassiz. In keeping with the pattern of the times, its origins were in German graduate schools, in this case Giessen, where Eben Norton Horsfeld had studied under the innovative experimental chemist Baron Justus Von Liebig. Von Liebig's importance lay in creating a radically experimental method for chemistry, which Horsfeld then introduced at the Lawrence Scientific School when he was made professor there. Charles's uncle Charles Henry Peirce, a practicing physician, was made his assistant. He and his sister, Charlotte Elizabeth (Charles's maiden Aunt Lizzie, the family commentator and fluent in French and German), helped the eight-year-old boy to set up his own laboratory at home and to work his way through Liebig's program of quantitative analysis. These experiments, structured in such a way as to encourage the student's own explanations of the effects produced, introduced Charles to the idea of scientific hypothesis. When his uncle died in 1854, he left Charles a study he had written while he was inspector of drugs for the port of Boston. Titled *Examination of Drugs, Medicines, Chemicals, &c, as to their Purity and Adulterations*, it was useful to Charles, among other things, for determining the appropriate drugs and their dosages for managing the pain of neuralgia, and contained an annotation in his hand on the uses of opium.[40]

In his late sixties, Peirce remembered that he also began the study of logic in 1851, when his brother Jem was a sophomore at Harvard.

> I remember picking up Whately's [*Elements of*] *Logic*, in my elder brother's room, and asking him what logic was. I next see myself stretched on his carpet, devouring the book; and this must have been repeated on following days, since subsequent tests proved that I had then fairly mastered that excellent and charming treatise. From that day to this, logic has been my passion.[41]

It was also from Archbishop Richard Whately that the younger Peirce learned his early fascination with the reductionist power of nominalism. Whately had a chapter criticizing realism, whose arguments about the nature of language Peirce used in the more nominalist passages of his "Illustrations of the Logic of Science," published in 1877–78. It was Whately, as well, whose views characterized the Harvard group, including his father, which professed what was known as the "Cambridge Metaphysics." It is an irony that it was from Ockham, Hobbes, Leibniz, Berkeley, and Whately, nominalists all, that Peirce derived his realist doctrine that all thoughts are signs.[42]

Charles was his father's favorite, and Benjamin spent long hours with him teaching him the art of concentration. In his short biography, written in 1934 when details of Peirce's life were still available directly from members of his family, Paul Weiss described the relationship of father and son:

> From time to time they would play rapid games of double dummy together, from ten in the evening until sunrise, the father sharply criticizing every error. In later years this training perhaps helped Charles, though ill and in pain, to write with undiminished power far into the night. His father also encouraged him to develop his power of sensuous discrimination, and later, having put himself under the tutelage of a *sommelier* at his own expense, Charles became a connoisseur of wines. The father's main efforts, however, were directed towards Charles's mathematical education. Rarely was any general principle or theorem disclosed to the son. Instead, the father would present him with problems, tables, or examples, and encouraged him to work out the principles for himself. . . . At college he again had the benefit

of his father's instruction. . . . Pacing up and down the room, they would deal with problems in mathematics beyond even the purview of the elder brother, himself destined to become a mathematician.[43]

In the relationship between father and son, there is much that is reminiscent of the extraordinarily intensive education of John Stuart Mill by his father, James, and much similarity in its psychological effects upon the boys. Most important, perhaps, was the constant strain—the continual stress and nervous tension—that such training imposed upon them both. Both assumed wrongly that rational judgment ruled the world of affairs, and both misjudged the importance of motive in human action. Neither son ever felt constrained by the rules of conventional conduct, as their relationships with women showed. Both were very lonely men, dependent on women. In Peirce's case, this dependence may have been a direct result of his neuralgia, which made him a patient in search of the solace of a nurse, mother, lover, confidante, and scapegoat. When he was seventy, trying to discover what went wrong with his life, Peirce wrote feelingly of the kind of upbringing he deeply regretted he had not been given:

> If I had a son, I should instill into him this view of morality, (that is, that Ethics is the science of the method of bringing Self-Control to bear to gain satisfaction) and force him to see that there is but one thing that raises one individual animal above another,—Self-Mastery; and should teach him that the Will is Free only in the sense that, by employing the proper appliances, he can make himself behave in the way he really desires to behave. As to what one ought to desire, it is, I should show him, what he will desire if he sufficiently considers it, and that will be to make his life beautiful, admirable. Now the science of the Admirable is *true* Esthetics. Thus, the Freedom of the Will, such as it is, is a one sided affair. . . . There is no freedom to be or to do anything else. Nor is there any freedom to do right if one has neglected the proper discipline. By these teachings, by showing him that a poor dog is more to be respected than an improvident man, who has not prepared himself beforehand to withstand the day of temptation, I should expect to render him eager to submit to a pretty severe discipline.[44]

Charles's performance in school seldom showed a disciplined mind or reflected his brightness and originality. He disliked school work intensely, and his failure to do well is entirely consistent with the difficulty in writing out his ideas that he described as directly a result of his left-handedness. The Peirce family saved a few exercises, including compositions, from his years at Cambridge High School. One, entitled "Caesar and Hannibal. Decision of Character 2 Kinds. For Exhibition. Not Spoken," showed considerable grasp, but like other examples from this period was disorganized and messily and carelessly done. Significantly, after he was graduated from high school after being suspended several times, his father saw fit to send him to Dixwell's School for one semester's intensive preparation before entering Harvard. Epes Dixwell did not think highly of Charles's intelligence, or, if the work which remains is an accurate example, of his ability to produce finished work. One of the English compositions written for Dixwell, entitled "The Parthenon," was badly done, poorly executed, and confused in understanding. It is inconsistent with the picture of a youthful genius which others attributed to him at this age. This essay and several other compositions exist only in draft form, probably for oral presentation, so that it is impossible to judge their finished quality. Of the Latin exercises which remain, many are unfinished. One of the compositions is of interest, however, in that it foreshadows many of Peirce's later ideas and interests. Written in 1854, when he was fifteen, it was called "Every Man the Maker of His Own Fortune" and expresses in its youthful form his Dandyism, his interest in the traits of genius, and an embryonic pragmatism which derived from Scotch common-sensism:

> . . . For the practical man grace is important indeed; but it is impossible to be acquired without perfect confidence. Lord Kames says, I believe [sic], that grace is a union of energy, boldness, magnificence, simplicity, ease, and neatness; and what one of these can be acquired without confidence.
> . . .
> . . . the successfull man must posses [sic] the faculty of seeing & understanding affairs. The Genius for making plans. A talent for executing them. But it is the wondrous combination of all these with life which make a man the master of his own fortune. Napoleon called himself the child of destiny //and/but// he well knew that the way to be beloved by . . . fate was to perceive and to turn to his use whatever she spun him.
> There are four things necessary, for successfully prosecuting any undertaking
> First a knoledge [sic] of the Facts of the
> Circumstances of the case
> Second. An ability to form the best plans
> Third, A Talent for executing plans
> Fourth. Presence of mind[45]

That the thoughts Peirce dashingly expressed in this exercise were not merely the fancy of the moment is established in a piece which his first wife considered significant enough to keep all her life. The manuscript, not in Peirce's handwriting (although his comment "true" appears on it in his unique hand), consists of the notes made of his exposition, most likely taken down by his then-future wife Zina, and is entitled "Theories, of C. S. Peirce 1854." The irony is clear enough:

> My life is built upon a theory: and if this theory turns out false, my life will turn out a failure. And just in proportion as my theory is false my life is a failure. Well, my theory is this. But first, I am not to be an old fogy or go by any rules that other people give me—If I should turn old fogy or obedient lad my life would in troth and indeed be a failure. For on not doing it is my whole theory built.
> "Theory I" "Every one's mind has a certain basis, which can't be decreased or enlarged. This can be filled, covered with *mind* or with *memory*, And everyone can take their choice and cover their Foundation with MIND or MEMORY; or PASSION or GENIUS"
> "II" "Genius is the result of thinking 'till—'till—'till—Genius 'till you turn a corner and find yourself in another world. Genius is above reasoning"
> "III" Love is the foundation of everything desirable or good"
> "IV" Impudence—Grace—[Knowledge] These three are requisites for every thing"
> "V" "Witty people have the least sympathy"
> "VI" "Every truth may be infinitely extended, but when all truths are expanded to universal principles they make a parallelogram of forces which can't be calculated. Hence the need of particular rules"
> "VII" Grace consists of Energetically bold magnificence & easy neat simplicity, variously combined" Put beauty instead of grace, perhaps . . .
> "XI" "Will will. . . . " Fill up the blank with what you will.[46]

Both these examples of Peirce's youthful philosophizing foreshadow later formulations and attitudes of mind. "Impudence—Grace—[Knowledge]" is an epigram of the concept of the Dandy. Peirce's nephew characterized his uncle at college as emotional, gullible, snobbish, and indifferent of the consequences of his actions, but it should be understood that in this attitude he was following the example of his Brahmin family, which set itself apart from the crowd as patricians on the heights of American culture and looked down on other groups in the society, especially Irish Catholics, whom his Aunt Charlotte characterized as " . . . born and bred *cheats—as a rule.*"[47] Thus, Peirce's arrogant Dandyism should be understood as emerging in the form provided by his family, class, and education. Well illustrated are the beginnings of Peirce's description of the pedestrian—and pragmatic— origins of genius in such statements as "Genius is the result of thinking 'till—'till—'till—Genius 'till you turn a corner and find yourself in another world." He seems to have anticipated, with his father's eager encouragement, his own genius.

The general origins of pragmatism in the popular common-sensism of

Henry Home, Lord Kames, seem clear, since Peirce did not begin the study of Kant until the following year. Pragmatic statements such as "every truth may be infinitely extended . . . " derived from such a source. Kames was an eighteenth-century Edinburgh judge whose writings were still much in vogue at that time, and whose various essays were used by Dixwell in his school, and by Harvard. Justus Buchler suggested that Peirce later identified the Scottish philosopher Thomas Reid (and perhaps also Reid's follower Dugald Stewart) as a principal source of the category of Secondness. Reid proposed that, while the existence of external objects is mediated in the mind, sensation, as the raw data of experience, is given directly and undeniably by physical objects. Buchler pointed out that it was from this sense of duality in perception, "the sensation of *reaction*," that Peirce drew his concept of what he later called the "outward clash."[48] Much of Peirce's concentration on the experience of the irresistible otherness of sensation probably came from his thoughts about the undeniability of his knowledge of pain. Peirce also identified Reid as the origin of his "critical common-sensism." Because of close similarities between some aspects of Reid's philosophy and that of the philosopher Immanuel Kant, it was perhaps also Reid who provided an introduction for Peirce's study of Kant, and for his denial of Humean skepticism and Cartesian doubt as well.

While Charles was still at Dixwell's School, his father wrote his mother, "Charlie appears very well, and I have great hopes that his is coming bright, Dixwell to the contrary notwithstanding." Even halfway through Charles's freshman year, his family still seems to have thought that he was doing well, but at the end of the year he stood only seventy-third out of eighty-nine and had already begun to cut classes and generally to misbehave in a way that placed him for his undergraduate career among the select group of half-a-dozen or so considered to be the recalcitrants of his class.

He followed his own course, and one of the enterprises in which he was engaged during his freshman and later college years was a more formal development of the idea which he called "pedestrianism," an early form of his lifelong passion for logic. The term was sufficiently well known in his family that his father could write in 1856, "How has Charlie got along with his pedestrianism . . . ?"[49] By this time, pedestrianism was becoming a more formed idea as he became more familiar with logic and mathematics and the philosophies of Aristotle and Kant. There was an element of the utopian in Peirce's pedestrianism which came from his own experience. He became convinced, I think because of his experience with left-handedness, that if ordinary people were taught logic, they would thereafter behave more in tune with reality. He acted on this belief in his late forties when he attempted a correspondence school with a singular lack of success.

Charles's sophomore year was only slightly better; he placed in about the lower third of the class. Peirce's father began to show some concern for his lack of scholarship during this year and remarked to him that he ought to master chemistry at least. And although he placed in the upper half of the class in that course, it is indicative of their future relations that Peirce was fined one dollar for cutting up a bench in the classroom in the charge of the instructor in chemistry and mathematics, Charles W. Eliot, who became president of Harvard twelve years later and opposed Peirce's joining the faculty thereafter. Peirce was in serious trouble during his sophomore year for drinking and was considered an unhealthy influence by at least one indignant uncle, with whose nephew Peirce was discovered "coming out of Boston in a state of intoxication." The nephew, Horatio Paine, was the dearest friend of Peirce's young manhood and the one with whom he studied Schiller's *Aesthetic Letters*. The letter the uncle wrote President Walker of Harvard concerning his nephew's relations with Charles illuminates the character of both.

> I learned, also, that he continued his intimacy with Mr. Peirce, again, and while I have admonished him for the best interests of both, I must therefore appeal to your goodness, and to your confidence to remonstrate with him. . . . I think, too, that Professor Peirce will feel obligated by having the intimacy between his son and my nephew broken up; as they only administer temptations to each other. . . . I think that Mr. Peirce has a great ascendancy over him, and that Horatio's social habits and love to pleasure are injurious to Mr. Peirce.[50]

The intimacy between Peirce and Paine involved much more than giving in to the temptation to do mischief. It was a romance of searching minds inspired by Schiller's idea of *Spieltrieb,* what Peirce later called "the play of Musement," a phrase which became for him a synonym, after 1900, for hypothesis in the sense of a description of its activity. Play as a free kind of doing also anticipated his later development of the idea of chance, what he then called *tychism*. Almost fifty years later, Peirce recalled poring over the work with Paine, spending "every afternoon for long months upon it, picking the matter to pieces," and realizing how that study led him at last to conclude that though "esthetics and logic seem, at first blush, to belong to different universes . . . that seeming is illusory, and that, on the contrary, logic needs the help of esthetics," and "When our logic shall have paid its *devoirs* to Esthetics and the Ethics, it will be time for it to settle down to its regular business."[51] Schiller developed an aesthetics which, in form, strongly anticipated Peirce's categories. As Thomas A. Sebeok summarized Schiller's triadic system, it

> presented an analysis of human nature as comprising three "impulses": *Stofftrieb,* the drive for diversity, forever striving for change, contrasted with *Formtrieb,* the demand for "form" in the abstract, alien to time, hence

oppugnant to change (this pair corresponding to Kant's well-known dualism), plus a third component he himself dubbed *Spieltrieb,* or play *(ein ernstes Spiel)*—the aesthetic tendency, mediating and harmoniously reconciling the twofold way of sense and reason on the level of the individual's faculties (microcosmos, the particular) as well of those of society (macrocosmos, the lofty).[52]

This impassioned study of Schiller's aesthetics was formalized in his senior year in the short piece "I, It, Thou," the romantic forerunner of his triadic categories. The two friends then moved on to the study of Kant.

In this, his sophomore year, Charles placed only sixty-first out of a class of ninety, and in his junior year forty-seventh of ninety-three, the best showing in his undergraduate career. Obviously, he was not much impressed by the requirements of class work, which he placed in priority well below his father's informal but rigorous teaching. During the summer of 1858, between his junior and senior years, Charles presented for the Boylston Prize an essay entitled "Judge Choate's Eulogy of Daniel Webster," which, despite his well-known ability in declamation, did not win or place; the previous summer he had entered an essay on Lord Byron and the Isles of Greece, which did no better.

The summer of 1858 also saw the beginning of Peirce's connection with the United States Coast Survey, when he joined a surveying party in Machias, Maine. The joining of summer survey parties was a fairly common practice among young and well-connected, scientifically inclined college students of the period, although none continued their connection with the Coast Survey for more than thirty years as did Charles Peirce. This summer also marked the beginning of ten years' association with his father's friend Alexander Dallas Bache, the Survey superintendent, who, with Joseph Henry and his father, was one of the three most important men of American science. These three men, along with Louis Agassiz, often determined the futures of the new generation of scientists through their personal influence.

Charles's senior year, the year his debilitating bouts with neuralgia began, was the worst of his undergraduate years, his standing being only seventy-ninth of ninety. After graduation, Charles remained at Harvard as a resident graduate for a year, a classification signifying that he was not aiming for any degree. During this period, he also did occasional tutoring. The records show that in 1862, he received a Master of Arts degree, the subject of which is not recorded. In 1863, he received the first Bachelor of Science, summa cum laude, in chemistry from the Lawrence Scientific School, at the time the most important of the new experimentally oriented scientific schools being established in American colleges. Unfortunately, the records

Charles S. Peirce, from the Harvard Class Album of 1859. Photograph courtesy of Houghton Library, Harvard University.

of the school are spotty where they have been kept, and aside from the fact that Peirce received such a degree, nothing can be discovered. From 1863 until 1867, Peirce was again carried on the Harvard rolls as a resident graduate.[53]

Two things stand out in Peirce's college career, with the single exception of the highest honors in chemistry: his indifference to the academic requirements of the college and his consistent resistance to any authority but that of his father. A sophomore assignment will serve to illustrate the spirit in which he approached assigned work, most of which he seems to have considered beneath his abilities and tastes. The assigned topic of the forensic was, "What is your favorite virtue? Do you select it, because you delight to practice it, or because you think you need it, or because you have seen it beautifully exemplified in a Friend?"

> Here the simple question is put to me. No prevarication, no equivocation will do. I am not asked to state what my favorite virtue ought to be, nor

upon what one I can write the best theme, but, with my hand upon my heart, to tell what it is.

I have no favorite virtue. A regular oration, with its Exordium, Proposition, Explication, Arguments, Pathetic Parts, and Conclusion, would hardly add to the strength of this assertion. I shall take the liberty, therefore, since a theme must be written, of attempting to show that no one ought to have a favorite virtue, and that *favoritism* is as bad in morals as anywhere else.

In the first place, then, there are different ways of understanding the words, "your favorite." If they signify that which is liked best, disregarding its moral claims (of course, the *only* claims of virtue, as such), the question is answered, at once; for we ought not to disregard the moral claims of virtues in deciding which we like best. But if the words mean "which virtue is it your opinion, has the most claim to be liked?", a doubt arises as to the meaning of the word, virtue.

For there are two kinds of virtues—moral *states*, and moral acts of the soul. Of the virtues of the first kind, it is not a matter of opinion, which has the most moral claim, (as I shall show below) and therefore it is not a matter for favoritism;—we might as well have a favorite between the dollar and the dime.

If, then, the other kind is intended, I wish to inquire, in what the moral claim of an act upon our admiration consists. Does it lie in the origin of the act, in *the act itself* of the soul, or in its effect?

The effects of acts have only an *intellectual* claim, for morality does not deal in effects; and acts, in themselves considered, have only an *aesthetical* claim, for the same act may be moral and immoral, instructive & deceptive, politic & impolitic, in different circumstances. It is only the origin of acts, then, which have a moral claim. And what is the origin of acts but states of the soul? And as to these, there abide, Faith, Hope, Charity—these three—and the greatest of these is charity.[54]

Having thus accurately—and arrogantly—called his teacher stupid for asking a silly question and then concluding with a sophistical twist of phrase that he deserved charity for doing so, Peirce expressed his contempt for the majority of his college education. Despite the low standing, Peirce, like most of his peers, mastered Latin and particularly Greek, which became the source of his own inventive philosophical language, and he learned passable French and German. He also mastered Shakespeare, much of which he memorized and often declaimed. In 1864 he wrote a study of Shakespearean pronunciation.[55] Shakespeare's use of language supplied the model for the concept of the sign in much of his own work. Peirce often quoted as a poetic version of his own theory of signs this passage from *A Midsummer Night's Dream*:

And, as imagination bodies forth
The forms of things unknown, the poet's pen
Turns them into shapes, and gives to airy nothing
A local habitation and a name.[56]

Peirce's attitude toward Harvard's curriculum was likely derived from his father, who did not consider Charles's academic performance of great importance and laid considerably greater stress upon his own education of his son. Peirce recalled in his old age that

> . . . even in my teens, when I was reading Kant, Spinoza, and Hegel my father, who was the celebrated mathematician Benjamin Peirce, not a powerful analyst of thought, so that his demonstrations were sometimes faulty, but a mind who never once failed, as well as I can remember, to draw the correct conclusion from given premises, unless by a mere slip, my father, I say would induce me to tell him about the proofs offered by the philosophers, and in a very few words would almost invariably rip them up and show them empty. He had even less mercy for such philosophers as Hobbes, Hume and James Mill. In that way, the bad habits of thinking which would have been impressed upon me by those mighty powers were in great measure, though I confess not entirely, overcome.[57]

One effect of this training for genius was to engender in the young man an arrogance toward and impatience with others who exhibited superficial understanding or lack of clarity in their thinking. It must be corrosive of character to be placed, at the age of sixteen, in the unlikely position of believing that your own philosophical abilities are demonstrably superior to those of some of the most respected and revered philosophers of the past, such as Kant, Spinoza, Hume, and Hobbes. I imagine Charles in 1857, at age eighteen, brilliantly discoursing in class "that the PERFECT is the Great Subject of Metaphysics," elegantly dressed, in negligent posture, completely self-assured and cool, the picture of the arrogant Dandy. William James commented on this aspect of Peirce's character in 1861, writing, "There is a son of Prof. Peirce, whom I suspect to be a very 'smart' fellow with a great deal of character, pretty independent and violent though."[58]

Peirce lived his social and intellectual life almost entirely apart from the regular activities of the college. His attitude toward society drew, in part, on the way his family had for some time been involved in theater and opera, even to the unusual extent of inviting performers into their homes. While still a boy, Charles had a reputation for oratorical talent both from membership in the debating society at Cambridge High School and in reading dramatic pieces, such as Poe's "The Raven." He continued this interest in college in his junior year as a member of the W. T. K. (Wen Tchang Koun, meaning hall of literary exercise in Chinese), which presented debates, orations, mock trials, and readings in various literary styles. In his senior year, he was a founding member of the O. K. Society, an elite group dedicated to the performance of literary works. He carried these interests over into adult life; he was in some demand among friends and family as an amateur performer and at one time considered going on the lecture circuit.[59]

A list of some of the topics which Peirce concerned himself with and wrote about at this time shows the extent to which he was studiously unconcerned with issues considered important by his Harvard instructors, and also the extent to which he continued independently a course of studies deeply influenced by his father:

> Oct. 13, 1857 Scientific Book of Synonyms in the English Language. Classified according to their meanings on a definite and stated philosophy.
> May 21, 1859 That the PERFECT is the Great Subject of Metaphysics
> May 21, 1859 That There is No Need of Transcendentalism
> May 22, 1859 Of the Stages of the Category of Modality or Chance
> July 25, 1859 Comparison of our Knowledge of God & of other Substances
> July 25, 1859 Of Realism: It is not that Realism is false; but only that the Realists did not advance in the spirit of the scientific age. Certainly *our ideas are as real as our sensations.* We talk of an unrealized idea. That idea has an existence as noumenon in our minds as certainly as its realization as such an existence out of our mind. They are in the same case. *An idea I define* to be the neumenon [sic] of a conception.
> [On the other side of the sheet on which this note appears, Peirce had written, with nominalism conspicuously absent,]
> List of Horrid Things I am: Realist, Materialist, Transcendentalist, Idealist.
> Oct. 25, 1859 That Infinity is an Unconscious Idea.
> Oct. 25, 1859 Of Objects: 1. The thing 2. Influx 3. the Unconscious idea 4. the Act of thinking 5. the Soul
> July 3, 1860 The Infinite, the Type of the Perfect
> [Spring, 1861] I, It, Thou
> Aug. 21, 1861 [From notebook] "Metaphysical and Private" [on the definition of metaphysics:] . . . Why is Metaphysics so hard to read? Because it cannot be put into books. You may put suggestions towards it into books but each mind must evolve it for himself—& every man must be his own metaphysician.
> [From notebook] "On the Fundamental Distinction of Metaphysics" The Real Worth of Metaphysics must lie, of course, in its practical application. . . . To learn how to analyze ideas, therefore, and to analyze them—in short to study metaphysics—will be *par excellence* education.[60]

In this list, Peirce begins to show the characteristic patterns and concerns of his thought, and that already at twenty he was no novice philosophizer but an experienced critic of arguments. First is his lifelong passion for a critical metaphysics and his belief in its primary importance for philosophy and education. Second, the original version of his categories, derived from his study of Schiller, appears expressed as the pronouns I, It, and Thou. Third, the subversive purpose of the pragmatic maxim is suggested, seventeen years before the publication of "How to Make Our Ideas Clear," in the formulation that "the real worth of metaphysics must lie, of course, in its practical application."

The pieces that these titles introduce are among the first clear fruits of Peirce's pedestrianism, which were in time to lead to his architectonic system. He kept them, as he kept almost everything he wrote, and returned to them time and again, finding useful elements even in his earliest work. Sometimes he used these early starts verbatim as introductions to his much later attempts to clarify his views. As he described his pedestrianism on December 13, 1865: "It is necessary to reduce all our actions to logical processes so that to do anything is but to take another step in the chain of inference. Thus only can we effect that complete reciprocity between Thought & its Object which it was Kant's Copernican step to announce."[61]

Murphey accurately described the spirit and process of Peirce's long life of "pedestrian" philosophizing:

> Because he believed in the architectonic theory [developed by Kant as embedded in formal logic], Peirce was always a system builder, and in each stage of his career he had in mind a definite concept of an over-all philosophic system. In general, his method was first to formulate his position as systematically and completely as possible, and then, having found certain difficulties in it, to solve these difficulties piecemeal. During the time he was occupied with these specific problems, he paid little attention to the remainder of the system, returning to it only when the specific difficulties had been eliminated. He would then revise the whole system to incorporate his new results. Thus the fact that Peirce worked on different problems at different times does not mean that he had made a radical shift in position: it rather indicates that the chief problems confronting the system were different at different times.
>
> But it also follows from this interpretation that since logic is the basis of the architectonic order, the creative and dynamic agent in the development of Peirce's philosophy should have been his logic. And it further follows that each major discovery in logic should have led to a major reformulation of his philosophy. This is in fact the case. . . . [62]

In the fall of 1859, in large part to get away from another northern winter after his year of intermittent suffering from neuralgia and other illnesses, Charles joined a Coast Survey party in Biloxi, Mississippi, with which he stayed until the late spring of 1860, when he returned to Cambridge to study fossil classification under Louis Agassiz. In the meantime Darwin's *Origin of Species* had appeared, so that Peirce's brief apprenticeship to Agassiz put him at the center of the arguments about evolution. After Clausius's and Kelvin's proposal of the second law of thermodynamics, which challenged Newton's time-reversible dynamics with the irreversibility of the expenditure of energy and of time, made it conceivable, Peirce believed that it was Darwin's theory of irreversible biological evolution which inaugurated "the greatest mental awakening since Newton and Leibniz."[63] While Peirce was deeply influenced by the evolutionism of Darwin's hypothesis and fully agreed with his idea of fortuitous variation which he later called "tychastic evolution," he never accepted the doctrine of natural selection as sufficient to account for the evolution of mind, which he later proposed to be dependent on the gentle purposive action of love and named "agapastic evolution." He thought that Darwin's most interesting innovation lay in his interdisciplinary application of Malthusian statistical economic concepts to biology, but he passionately opposed the use of natural selection as a justification for dominance in human society. He wrote in 1892, after losing disastrously in an inventing venture, "As Darwin puts it on his title page, it is the struggle for existence; and he should have added for his motto: Every individual for himself and the Devil take the hindmost!"[64]

In the fall of 1860, he was appointed a proctor at Harvard during the absence of the regular incumbent; he apparently did not carry out his duties to the liking of the Harvard Corporation because he was never again asked to do that job, principally a matter of keeping dormitory.

On January 19, 1861, in keeping with customary obligation, Charles Peirce "called on Miss Harriet Melusina Fay for the first time" for the purpose of becoming engaged to her.[65] Zina, as she was called, was descended from the Fays, a seventeenth-century Huguenot family who had settled in Massachusetts. On her mother's side, the Hopkinses were a well-to-do Dublin family who had emigrated in the late eighteenth century. The first settler, her grandfather John Henry Hopkins, Episcopal bishop of Vermont, was infamous among abolitionists for a tract entitled "Slavery Vindicated." Zina's father, Charles S. Fay, was Benjamin's Harvard classmate and friend.

Zina and Charles were already well known to each other, as Zina's notes on Charles's 1854 "theories" show. Some doggerel he wrote for her and some undated letters are not the work of a young man of twenty. One of these, entitled "Apology to Miss *Fay* Alias *Junks* for not writing some Promised Verses," is the best of the lot:

> The temple of my heart flows oer
> With ardent sentiment

Which does so crowd about the door
Of Speech that none finds vent
To reach the audience hall of thine.
That door a charm must ope
The potent queen of *fays* my lips
Inspire. Then would I hope
To sing a lay which should eclipse
Een Codman's song divine.
While sweet Titania? Junks my ditty should approve,
Who by the by is requested to reply to the above.

There are a number of other examples of this schoolboy doggerel, the beginning of one of which contains a chemical metaphor:

Nor wintry sky, nor chilly air,
Nor frost, nor sleet nor snow,
Congeals my truest love for thee—
I laugh at 5° below.[66]

Charles was appointed to his first official position in the Coast Survey
seven months later, in July 1861, as an assistant computer at thirty-five
dollars per month.[67] A year later, this appointment stood him in good stead
when he came face to face with the possibility of being drafted into the
Union Army. He then wrote anxiously to Bache, the superintendent:

Does my appointment in the C. S. service exempt me from draft or
not? . . . This town has just raised a full company, tho' considerably above
its quota. But I perfectly dread going. I should feel that I was ended &
thrown away for nothing.
Yours, with much respect and love . . . [68]

He was exempted, and this letter represents the only mention of the Civil
War written by Peirce, with the exception that in later life he said that he did
not feel the case for or against slavery very strongly, and that he sympathized
with the strong pro-slavery views which made his father so distasteful among
abolitionists. Charles's maiden aunt, Charlotte Elizabeth, expressed political
opinions regarding the Civil War, race, and ethnicity which were typical in
the Peirce family and most others of British descent:

I have no objection to the blacks, provided I am not obligated to see them
or be very near them, which proximity to me cannot, I suppose, be of any
material advantage to them. [She continued in a similar vein concerning
the Boston Irish:] To whisper the truth I have a similar objection to the

Irish—and in fact to all the lower classes who, in general, seem to ignore the existence of soap and water. . . . [69]

In a family whose opinions were so opposed to the abolitionist orthodoxy of the time, it is not surprising that Peirce considered the Civil War no more than a personal inconvenience to be avoided if possible.

Within four months of his letter to Bache, on October 16, Charles Peirce, at his urgent insistence driven by fear for his soul, married Harriet Melusina Fay in a ceremony conducted by her father in the Episcopal church at St. Alban's, Vermont. As a condition of marriage, four months before at Zina's insistence, he had been baptized into that sect with Bishop Hopkins present. He was twenty-three, she twenty-six. The engagement, which had occurred in the spring of 1862, was approved by both families, but the marriage was looked upon as hasty. As Benjamin put it,

> Charlie . . . understands, distinctly, that although we do not object, nei-
> ther do we approve and that the responsibility of the affair must rest wholly
> upon him and Zina. With my present income, I can help him along, until
> he gets something to do[,] more than he has at present[,] and which shall
> be a permanent means of living.[70]

The newlyweds took up residence in the Peirce family house until they could move into modest quarters of their own at 2 Arrow Street in 1864, but owing to the meagerness of Charles's income they took their meals in the elder Peirce's house until 1870.[71] Before the marriage, Benjamin had written approvingly of Zina to his closest friend, Alexander Dallas Bache:

> What do you say to Charley Peirce's having fallen in love with a young lady
> of Vermont, daughter of my old friend and chum in College, Rev. Charles
> S. Fay of your church, and grand-daughter of Bishop Hopkins. Of course
> she is poor as the crows and ravens who fed the prophet in the wilderness.
> But then she is very full of knowledge and really a person of great mind—
> and although far from a beauty, Charles is quite in love with her. She has
> begun by converting him to episcopacy and his mother thinks that her
> influence upon him has been in all respects of the best possible character,
> and that he is a greatly improved person. . . . I thank God that he feels the
> need of religion. He can only be on that account the dearer to me, and Zina
> is all the more acceptable that she has been the instrument of bringing him
> to a serious state of mind.[72]

Zina, to whom the Peirce parents were so grateful for the reformation of their wayward son, was a romantic, strong-minded, and puritan feminist intellectual, one of a growing group in and around Cambridge and Boston founded in the previous generation by Margaret Fuller. In her dissertation on Zina's life and thought, Norma Pereira Atkinson has provided a lively and perceptive picture of both Zina and Charles and their marriage.[73] The main source of Zina's feminism was the life of misery forced upon her mother, Emily, the daughter—one of thirteen children—of a dour clergyman who recognized Emily's remarkable gifts, but drew her out of school at fourteen, because "she knew enough for a woman," and insisted she marry a clergyman. Emily obeyed him, had seven children of her own who lived and a half-dozen more who did not, and was constantly ill and constantly overworked.[74] In the summer of 1859, Zina, then twenty-three, experienced a religious conversion in which the conviction came to her that the "'Holy Ghost the Comforter,' is the Infinite Eternal Feminine of the Infinite Eternal Trinity." She believed that in this true trinity of Father, Mother, and Only Son, the feminine principle was referred to cryptically throughout the Scriptures as The Spirit, Wisdom, The Holy Ghost, The Comforter, and The Woman clothed with the sun and crowned with the stars and with the moon under her feet.[75] This belief was central to her feminism and to her life.

Zina was also a rabid nativist, especially toward the Irish, who she, like her father-in-law, feared would destroy New England life and culture through their barbarism, Catholicism, and resentment. Although she sup-

Harriet Melusina Fay Peirce, ca. 1870.

ported the anti-slavery movement, she believed that blacks were an inferior race, at least mentally. Like Charles, she suffered from physical problems, principally gynecological, and nervous disorders, especially extreme depression. She was repelled by the sensual in love and saw marriage as a Platonic ideal. She never had a child or became pregnant, and the evidence is silent on whether this childlessness was because of physical disability or by choice. Obviously, there was much in the characters and illnesses of both Zina and Charles that made their marriage difficult from its beginning.

Among Zina's friends as a young woman were such literary figures as Ralph Waldo Emerson, James Russell Lowell, and George Eliot. To Eliot, she ended a letter:

> Don't answer this dearest. I don't require you to think of me anything more than the evening breeze that sometimes kisses your cheek. I *love* to love you, you are so loveworthy. And once in a long time I love to say so to you. But I would not have it burden you with the weight of a rose leaf.[76]

With Emerson, she carried on a brief but intense correspondence, filled with Episcopal—almost Calvinist—exhortations against his Unitarianism, which she called

> one of that terrible sect which is the ancient Pharisee under another name and in different circumstances, and with all the angles rubbed off. I love you too much, however, for some things in that book of yours, not to hope that your spiritual pride and confidence is not like theirs, though alas! I can see no *Christianity* in your book from one end of it to the other. . . . If I have said anything impertinent or self-conceited, I beg your pardon most humbly, since next after Religion I bow to Intellect.[77]

Zina had finished her formal education, on Emerson's recommendation, at the Agassiz School for Young Ladies in Cambridge, where she studied science, philosophy, literature, history, and other subjects usually well outside the educational limits for young women, even of her class. She was so fine a student that, on graduation in the summer of 1861, she delivered the class oration. With her intelligence and force of character, Zina played an important part in both Charles's intellectual and moral life. Charles gave her to read his early explorations into metaphysics and dedicated a number of his early essays to "Z. F." I believe that their discussions of the Trinity and community influenced his thinking about categories of being and the nature of validity in science. For example, in the last Lowell Institute Lecture in the fall of 1866, in which Peirce proposed "adopting our logic as our metaphysics," he said, toward the end:

Here, therefore, we have a divine trinity of the object, interpretant, and ground. . . . In many respects, this trinity agrees with the Christian trinity; indeed I am not aware that there are any points of disagreement. The interpretant is evidently the Divine *Logos* or word; and if our former guess that a Reference to an interpretant is Paternity be right, this would be also the *Son of God*. The *ground,* being that partaking of which is requisite to any communication with the Symbol, corresponds in its function to the Holy Spirit.[78]

Zina's feminism, which meant to her a complete dedication to the improvement of the condition of women, combined with her intensely religious reforming urge, led her to take up various projects soon after the marriage. Her activities were concentrated in three fields: education, particularly higher education, for women; the creation of institutions to give women a public voice without directly competing with men; and the transformation of housework in order to free married women from its drudgery for higher things. In education, she was one of the organizers of the Women's Education Association, where she worked toward the founding of Radcliffe College. Politically, she was a strong supporter of the formation of a Woman's Parliament and was elected president of its first convention when it met in New York in 1869.

Her great project in these early years (second only to her husband in importance) was the establishment of the Cooperative Housekeeping Society in Cambridge. The actual experiment was preceded by a series of five well-received articles on the subject in the *Atlantic Monthly* in 1868 and 1869 (the same years in which Peirce published a series on logic in the *Journal of Speculative Philosophy*). The enterprise soon achieved respectable proportions with the blessings of figures such as Horace Mann, Benjamin Peirce, William Dean Howells, and Professors Francis J. Childs and Nathaniel S. Shaler. At first the society planned to buy the Cambridge Armory, but when this was found to be impossible, it rented a house instead. The Society was incorporated in May 1869, with a capital of $3,400, and planned for a laundry, storeroom, and bakery. Zina was established as the secretary at a salary of $100 a month. But before a year was out, the society began to disintegrate; it was permanently dissolved in the spring of 1871, largely, I believe, because Zina left Cambridge to join her husband in observing a solar eclipse in Sicily in the fall of 1870, leaving the cooperative without her driving force. She did not return until March of 1871.[79]

Zina and Charles's married life was devoted at first. His Aunt Lizzie reported to his father in February 1867:

I was at Charley's not long ago & admired his new book cases & his nice comfortable study—then the little back parlor looked very pretty & pleasant. Rosa [Zina's sister] was seated in an armchair studying—Zina came in dressed for walking—short skirts and no crinoline. Charley was giving a lesson to one of his students & looking bright & spirituelle as you can well imagine. Zina turned to me & whispered "Is he not lovely?" looking perfectly delighted.

To Charles's brother Jem, she wrote in June:

> I went yesterday to Charley's—He was seated in his comfortable & handsome study—himself the handsomest object in the room. They say that every person resembles some animal—& I guess that Charley is like a squirrel & never will grow old if he lives to be a hundred. He called out—"Zina! Zina! Here is Aunt Lizzie"—so Zina came in & we three had a very pleasant half hour.[80]

In the same year, Aunt Lizzie also explained Zina's character to her nephew Benjamin Mills in a very different way, a view which eventually dominated the family, Charles perhaps excepted: "she is busy teaching some of the Episcopal children their catechism & also to become good & useful citizens of the *church* and of society. You see Zina is the same old sixpence—full of plans for reforming the world." She elaborated fifteen years later, in retrospect after Zina and Charles were divorced:

> . . . Zina is no saint & never was and never will be in this world. I wonder how she will contrive to get along in the next world with Moses & Aaron & Solomon & Queen Elizabeth & whether she will open a cooperative store with their aid & counsels? She never will be happy unless she has something & somebody to manage—and no doubt she will find her niche there & become a very useful and happy member of the heavenly society.[81]

Their difficult characters and divergent careers and interests put too great a stress on the marriage, and it slowly disintegrated. Charles became abusive and increasingly unresponsive to Zina's attempts to reform his character, and she spent less and less time with him. Despite their continuing affection for each other, the marriage broke up in 1876 when she left him, and it ended in 1883 when he divorced her.

The period beginning with Charles's marriage in 1862 and ending in his trip to Europe in the spring of 1870 was a time of intensive philosophical study under his father's critical eye, dealing in the earlier years principally with Kant and his Categories and in the later years with the study of logic—principally the British logicians, such as Hamilton, J. S. Mill, De Morgan, and especially George Boole, but also the scholastic philosophies of Ockham and Duns Scotus. Much of Peirce's early study of Kant is outlined in his correspondence with Francis Ellingwood Abbot during the 1860s, in which he discussed Kant's ideas of logic, hypothesis, categories, infinity, his own rejection of the idea of an unknowable "Thing in Itself," and other Kantian proposals.[82] Much of the study in logic was inspired and aided by a close friendship with Chauncey Wright, with whom Peirce had also been arguing and studying since 1857, particularly about Mill and Darwin. Peirce called Wright, nine years his senior, his boxing master and made him a model both in person and in method of thinking.

Chauncey Wright, unlike Peirce, was from a poor family in Northampton. He was famous for his Socratic sessions with the elder Henry James and with the young men who became the members of the Metaphysical Club. He was "a local sage and character" who lectured, tutored, and wrote for the *North American Review*, but he made his living from computing for the *Nautical Almanac* and the *American Ephemeris*:

> He devised new ways of computing, for he was a mathematical genius, and he forced the work of a year into two strained months. No one saw him then, and he saw neither sunlight nor moonlight; but he emerged from his cave with time to burn. He walked and talked for weeks at Mount Desert;

Chauncey Wright, leader of the group which became the Metaphysical Club. Harvard Class Album, 1852. Photograph courtesy of the Harvard University Archives.

he philosophized all over the Franconia mountains. Once he went abroad for a visit to Darwin, who had brought out one of his essays as a pamphlet in England; and he remarked that 'Paris was as good as Cambridge,'—perhaps to annoy Henry James. A big man, with mild blue eyes, somewhat sluggish and inert, he was remote, slow, melancholy, but not unfriended; he was shy, but he was serene; he was simple and frugal, and his freedom from all cares and wants, material and mental, reminded the Cambridge circle of the antique sages. Like them, and like Emerson, he slighted books and reading; indeed, as he never read, the wonder grew,—he seemed to know much more than if he had. This lonely soliloquizer, with his corncob pipe, excelled by the sheer, bleak power of unaided thought. But he was a lover of children, and, like Thoreau, he delighted in entertaining them with magic and juggling. He was a master at sleight-of-hand, and he used his mathematical genius to invent and exhibit all manner of puzzles and games. There were no Christmas parties like those of the Norton's at "Shady Hill," where Chauncey Wright was busy with his marvels and Child and his three little girls performed old ballads, which they turned into Robin Hood plays with their gestures and costumes.[83]

Wright had studied extensively in mathematics, physics, and botany, and this knowledge, together with the study of Darwin, John Stuart Mill, and Alexander Bain, led to his interest in the nature of scientific method. From this study he made a distinction between science as myth and science as a fruitful means of uncovering the laws that extend our knowledge of the physical universe. His model scientist was Newton, who formulated the mathematical laws from which one could not only deduce the positions of the planets as they were known, but also predict the existence of the unknown planet, Neptune, from perturbations of planetary movement. His conclusion was that scientific laws do much more than summarize existing knowledge, they lead to new knowledge. This idea that the scientific method is a means for arriving at new experimental results was a starting point of Peirce's pragmatism. Peirce was also indebted to Wright for the origins of his ideas about chance in Wright's notion of "cosmical weather," which held, against the mechanists, that there is genuine novelty in nature which no knowledge of its laws can predict or even foresee.[84] Peirce had derived a like view from his study of Schiller and his idea of *Spieltrieb*. Wright, too, despite his acknowledged brilliance, was ostracized from the regular Harvard teaching staff and lectured at Harvard only on psychology in 1870–71 and in mathematical physics in 1875, the year he died, at age forty-five.

Peirce's studies with Wright and his father bore fruit in lectures and articles. The first series of lectures, eleven in all, were to have been given in March 1865, at the request of the Harvard Corporation, but these fell through, according to Peirce, " . . . for want of an audience. Rather mortifying, but I was not sorry. I study for my own satisfaction and am bored with my own thought if I have to explain it & don't wonder others are."[85]

However, in February 1866 they were given in revised form as Lowell Lectures, a high honor for a twenty-five-year-old. His father was greatly impressed, which no doubt meant more to Charles than the official honor: "My son Charles has been delivering a course of Lowell lectures upon the Logic of Science, in which he has quite astonished me by the breadth, and depth and thought of his arguments, and his powers of research."[86]

In January 1867, Peirce was elected a resident fellow of the American Academy of Arts and Sciences, of which his father was a founding member. In the same year he presented five papers to the academy on the subject of logic, the third of which he considered the most important writing of his life, and of which he wrote in 1905,

> It was in the desperate endeavor to make a beginning of penetrating into that riddle [of human existence, conduct, and thinking, and their relation to God and Nature] that on May 14, 1867, after three years of almost insanely concentrated thought, hardly interrupted even by sleep, I produced my one contribution to philosophy in the "New List of Categories" in the *Proceedings of the American Academy of Arts and Sciences*, Vol. VII, pp. 287–98.[87]

Peirce considered that this essay represented his "first self-controlled work and set forth the substance of my central achievement."[88] The central achievement to which he referred was not the pragmatism expressed ten years later in "How to Make Our Ideas Clear," which he described as an application of " . . . Bain's definition of belief, as 'that upon which a man is prepared to act.' From this definition, pragmatism is scarce more than a corollary." The substance of what Peirce considered his central achievement was far removed from Bain's psychological theory of belief, and, though Peirce tried to bridge the gulf by the introduction of "pragmaticism" after 1900, the effort seems to have been strained and unconvincing, more the result of the sudden publicity given to the doctrine of pragmatism after 1898 than of any deep unity of ideas beyond that of synechism, the connectedness of things. In the twenty years between 1870 and 1890, Peirce exhibited a curious reticence about openly setting forth his adherence to the doctrine of realism, partly, perhaps, because he was confused himself, but also because he was unwilling, as an ambitious scientist and logician, to risk the contemptuous rejection by his peers, Francis Ellingwood Abbot and perhaps William James excepted, of the realist concept that the suprasensible is embedded in the very body of natural science, the very thing they were intent to throw out.

In Peirce's maturity, he said it was his discovery "of the theory of the categories which is (if anything is) the gift I make to the world. That is my child. In it I shall live when oblivion has me—my body."[89] The new list was the triad of categories: quality, relation, and representation or sign. The first category is monadic, the second dyadic, and the third triadic, the relations which, in his metaphysics, became Firstness or feeling, Secondness or reaction, and Thirdness or mediation. Joseph L. Esposito has written that this metaphysical theory of logical categories had its origin in Peirce's discovery that "our concepts . . . literally 'participate' in the reality of what is conceived. . . . It is of the nature of an idea to be a *representation* of something beyond our direct awareness of it. . . . "[90]

For Peirce, the fact of representation is the link—the sign—embedded in the otherness of the finite thing and is the bond between the inescapable duality of our inner world and the world without. As he put it, "perception represents two objects reacting upon one another," and "it is downright nonsense to dispute the fact that in perception two objects really do so react upon one another."[91] In a passage that reflected his weight-lifting regimen, he also insisted that in the act, perception is experienced as a unified whole:

> that perception is a two-sided consciousness in which the percept appears as forcibly acting upon us, so that in perception the consciousness of an active object and of a subject acted on are as indivisible as, in making a muscular effort, the sense of exertion is one with and inseparable from the sense of resistance.[92]

This brief formulation may clarify the manner in which Peirce approached this still-unexplained phenomenon of perception:

> In the constitution of the object, which in the act we perceive as a seamless whole, there is that which is perceived by sense and that which is not so perceived.

To take the case of vision, the eye perceives color, but not, say, space, time, number, change, or form, or any of their myriad aspects, such as, respectively, here, now, three, cause, and the historical Charles Peirce, all of which, in any guise, are really represented by sensible signs. These concepts do not exist; they have being independent of sense and can be neither created nor destroyed, but only represented. For this commonplace mystery of perception, we have found no explanation, or even the hope of one. (The mystery can be made more interesting. For example, in camouflage, form can be represented and not perceived; in mimicry it can be misperceived.) It is this mystery that interests the empirical mystic, who finds in it transparent evidence of the representation of the supernatural in the natural world, or, less controversially, of the suprasensible in the sensible world. Put in a slightly variant form, mystical doctrine speaks paradoxically of the supernatural as both immanent and transcendent, and this doctrine is almost invariably expressed in trinities, sometimes, as with Plotinus, Boehme, or "the monstrous mysticism of the East," worked out in as intriguing detail as by Peirce himself.[93]

Peirce criticized Aristotle and Berkeley, among others, for not looking behind the ordinary appearance of things. He claimed that he had examined the phenomenon and found it to be complex, but not in the Kantian sense, since he rejected the possibility of an unknowable "Thing-in-Itself." In 1871, in his review of Fraser's edition of Berkeley's works, Peirce attacked Berkeley's nominalism for its inadequate representation of reality:

> the coherence of an idea with experience in general does not depend at all upon its being actually present to the mind all the time. But it is clear that when Berkeley says that reality consists in the connection of experience, he is simply using the word *reality* in a sense of his own. That *an object's independence of our thought about it* is constituted by its connection with experience in general, he has never conceived.[94]

Almost thirty years after the publication of this review, Peirce remarked, "1st, that all the intelligible philosophers, even Hegel, have been more or less nominalistic; 2nd, that nominalism is false in all its shades and degrees; and 3rd, that it has had a baleful influence upon civilization."[95] He went on to note that F. E. Abbot had made "a tolerable defence of realism," but that he could do better, and that in the review quoted above, he himself had treated it "without committing myself nor making the subject very clear."

The fact of the hybrid nature of our perceptions, so much a part of the philosophical vision of the British empiricists whom Peirce studied so closely, influenced him deeply, but his way to bridge the chasm was not theirs, nor was it the way of the empirical mystic, although his realist doctrine was closely similar to mysticism, a similarity he later examined. Peirce's way was that of the scientist and logician.

In 1867, in "A New List of Categories," Peirce had found in every act of perception (or cognition) an irreducible trinity of elements: quality, relation, and representation, each one of which, when logically analyzed, is itself made up of three more such elements—trinities begetting trinities. Briefly, and without reproducing his arguments, all representation is by means of signs, of which there are three kinds: likeness (later icon), index, and symbol. Symbols are of three kinds: terms, propositions, and arguments. Arguments are in their turn of three kinds, which exhibit three relations between premises and conclusions: hypothesis, induction, and deduction. Each of these triads expresses the characteristics of the original triad, so that an icon is the sign of a quality, an index is the sign of a relation, and a symbol is the sign of a representation. Similarly, a hypothesis is iconic, an induction is indexical, and a deduction is symbolic. Thus, Peirce's architectonic system is not only triadic but strictly hierarchical as well. In his late working out of his triadic system of signs, Peirce at one time tentatively named sixty-six classes of them.

Peirce called the activity of perceiving such aspects of the real as space, time, number, and form a hypothetical inference (later a perceptual judgment). Through this strategy he avoided the issues of perception by bypassing phenomenology and starting his system with the logical world of cognition, which placed hypothesis, or guessing, at the center of knowing. As he put it in his sixties in a graceful account of having hypotheses, or as he then named them, abductions:

> Looking out of my window this lovely spring morning I see an azalea in full bloom. No, no! I do not see that; though that is the only way I can describe what I see. *That* is a proposition, a sentence, a fact; but what I perceive is not proposition, sentence, fact, but only an image, which I make intelligible in part by means of a statement of fact. This statement is abstract; but what I see is concrete. I perform an abduction when I ⎿do so much⏌ as express in a sentence anything I see. The truth is that the whole fabric of our knowledge is one matted felt of pure hypothesis confirmed and refined by induction. Not the smallest advance can be made in knowledge beyond the stage of vacant staring, without making an abduction at every step.[96]

Such, briefly, was "the substance of his central achievement" on which he worked, with increasing passion and desperation, for the rest of his life.

Beginning in January of 1868, Peirce began a correspondence with the St. Louis Hegelian William Torrey Harris, who had just founded his quarterly *Journal of Speculative Philosophy*, the first philosophical journal in the United States. This correspondence began as a challenge by Harris to Peirce to defend the nominalism of the "Cambridge Metaphysics," and more particularly to show how on nominalist grounds the laws of logic could be anything other than inexplicable. In the process of responding to Harris in two letters and three articles, the last and most important of which was called "Grounds of Validity of the Laws of Logic: Further Consequences of Four Incapacities," Peirce found himself forced by his examination of the matter to recognize that generals, such as the laws of science, are real and to examine the meaning of his doctrine of signs.[97] The interest which Harris's

Journal had for Peirce was probably its Hegelian character and its concern with "first principles." Although Peirce objected to what he termed the illogical aspects of Hegel's philosophy, he was sympathetic with his attempts to create a triadic dialectic and was curious about philosophers of a Hegelian tinge. What Peirce ended up doing in these papers was to develop the grounds for his semeiotic theory. Fisch wrote:

> The central positive doctrine of the whole series is that "all thought is in signs" ([CP[5.253). Every thought continues another and is continued by still another. There are no uninferred premises and no inference-terminating conclusions. Inferring is the sole act of the cognitive mind. . . . Cognition is a minimally three-termed or triadic relation. . . . ([CP[5.283)
>
> The sign-theory of cognition leads into a semeiotic theory of the human self, "the man-sign" ([CP[5.313), and thence into a social theory of logic. . . . "The real, then, is that which, sooner or later, information and reasoning would finally result in, and which is therefore independent of the vagaries of me and you. Thus, the very origin of the conception of reality shows that this conception essentially involves the notion of a COMMU-NITY, without definite limits, and capable of an indefinite increase of knowledge" ([CP[5.311). "So the social principle is rooted intrinsically in logic" ([CP[5.534).[98]

William James spoke to Henry Bowditch soon after the appearance of these articles:

> I have just been quit by Charles S. Peirce, with whom I have been talking about a couple of articles in the St. Louis *Journal of Speculative Philosophy* by him which I have just read. They are exceedingly bold, subtle and incomprehensible and I can't say that his vocal elucidations help me a great deal to their understanding, but they nevertheless interest me strangely.[99]

Thus, Peirce, "the man-sign," began his lifelong inquiry into the nature of the Logos, his semeiotic journey to solve the riddle of being and of being represented, and to find the reality represented by his "glassy essence."

That Peirce did not make so favorable an impression on A. Bronson Alcott, the dean of the St. Louis Hegelians, is evident from a letter to Harris in which Alcott commented upon an article of Peirce's critical of his position. "I take [him] to be the son of the Cambridge Mathematical Professor, and perhaps defending as he best can the Professor's metaphysics, if not of the College."[100]

While Alcott could not influence Peirce's career for the worse, this matter of Peirce's "credit" first became a real problem for him in 1868, when it became clear that he would have great difficulty in finding the kind of academic position he desired. As James put it:

> The poor cuss sees no chance of getting a professorship anywhere and is likely to go into the ⌊Harvard⌋ observatory for good. It seems a great pity that as original a man as he is, who is willing and able to devote the powers of his life to logic and metaphysics, should be starved out of a career, when there are lots of professorships of the sort to be given in the country, to "safe" orthodox men. He has had good reason, I know to feel a little discouraged about the prospect, but I think he ought to hang on, as a german wd. do till he grows gray.[101]

The problem of Peirce's reputation dogged him for the rest of his life, despite the efforts of his influential father, friends such as James himself, and his politically powerful first cousin, Henry Cabot Lodge. Peirce's stubborn hanging on in Cambridge was a practice dictated by his desire to gain a permanent appointment at Harvard. The various employments which he held during this period—odd tutoring, minor assignments for the Coast Survey and for the Harvard Observatory, along with occasional invitations to lecture—were all considered temporary until he should be accepted into the charmed circle of permanent Harvard professors. But by 1870 it had become clear that unless a stroke of fortune intervened in his favor, Peirce would get no academic employment in philosophy at Harvard, or likely, in consequence, at any other college or university which interested him. In 1868, in response to a hint from Peirce, W. T. Harris had gone so far as to offer him an instructorship at Washington University in St. Louis, but Peirce refused it summarily on the grounds that a professorship was more appropriate. Peirce never gave up his hope of a permanent academic position during his active life, and this hope brought about an ambivalence of loyalties which detracted from both his scientific and his philosophical work. Peirce's father had become the third superintendent of the Coast Survey in 1867, and increasingly it seemed that in that organization lay the only certain and permanent employment, though even this connection was to fail in time. Gradually, Peirce found himself tied to the Survey more and more strongly against his true desires, and also against his father's strong belief that his son would do best to pursue a career in chemistry, his strongest field outside of logic.

In the winter of 1869–70, again at the request of the Harvard Corporation, Peirce gave a series of lectures on the British logicians which included Ockham, Scotus, Roger and Francis Bacon, Hobbes, Locke, Berkeley, Hamilton, Whewell, J. S. Mill, De Morgan, and Boole. These were the men of the British tradition in philosophy, ranging from the thirteenth to the late nineteenth centuries, whose work (and lives), along with that of Aristotle, Leibniz, and Kant, Peirce studied intensively for their contributions to the development of logic. Among those present was William James, to become in time his only great friend:

> I heard Chas. Peirce lecture yesterday—one of his 9 on "British Logicians." It was delivered without notes, and was admirable in matter, manner, and clearness of statement. He has recently been made assistant astronomer with 2500 a year [at the Harvard Observatory]. But I wish he could get a professorship of philosophy somewhere. That is his forte, and therein he is certainly *tre's-fort*. I never saw a man go into things so intensely & thoroughly.[102]

Two possibilities existed in 1869 for Peirce to remain at Harvard. The first and most desirable was that the occasional lecture courses might be transformed into a permanent appointment in philosophy; the second, desirable principally because it would keep him in Cambridge, as well as provide a small additional income, was that a position might be available in the Harvard Observatory, of which Joseph G. Winlock, a close and obligated friend of his father's, was director and for whom Charles had been making observations since 1867. Peirce was appointed assistant to Winlock in October 1869, in the same academic year that Charles William Eliot became president of Harvard College. Within a year Peirce and Eliot were in conflict with each other over this appointment and other matters. That Peirce was interested in the science of astronomy there can be no doubt, but he always considered both his Observatory and Survey work (geodesy was considered at the time a branch of astronomy) as secondary to his passionate interest in logic.

Since these positions were by no means full-time responsibilities, Peirce had the leisure to pursue his own studies as he desired. Moreover, he looked upon his scientific work as a kind of testing ground for his logic of science and, as well, as a competitive sport. In a draft fragment of 1911, he wrote, "in my own feeling, whatever I did in any other science than logic was only an exercise in methodeutic and as soon as I had the *method* of investigation thoroughly shown, my interest dropped off."[103] The kind of passing interest any particular scientific inquiry had for him, as well as his insistence on his own priority in discovery and invention, is illustrated in a reminiscence about his forays as a young man upon the fields of science:

> It was . . . my fortune to be one of the first of mortals to look upon the spectrum of Argon. My impression is, that I was the first to measure the wave-length of its most characteristic line. I was assistant to Professor

Winlock in the Harvard College Observatory. He had arranged an apparatus,—very ill-calculated for the purpose,—to observe the spectrum of zodiacal light. He was called away for a week or two; and I was left to conduct the observations . . . but it so happened that there was, one evening, a fine auroral display. I think we had heard that someone in Europe had seen an unexplained line, or band, in the spectrum of the aurora. I had the good luck to pin it down,—not that line only, but several others,—and to measure their wavelengths, after a fashion. I telegraphed the figures to Prof. Winlock; and he announced them to the Academy of Sciences, whose session he was attending. My measure is given in the article Astronomy in the Encyclopedia Britannica.[104]

On April 22, 1870, Charles's younger brother, the mining engineer Benjamin Mills, died unexpectedly at Ishpeming, Michigan, at the age of twenty-six. Benjie was, if possible, a more unusual fellow than Charles himself. The Peirce papers are remarkably silent about him, with the exception of disapproving hints that he was at one time engaged to Zina's lovely musician sister, Amy, and had a serious affair with her. Fortunately, Peirce's first cousin, Henry Cabot Lodge, wrote an autobiography which contains a

Benjamin Mills Peirce, ca. 23 years old.

reminiscence of his good friend Ben. There is no mention of Charles at all, despite Lodge's long connection with him, but the character presented is extraordinarily suggestive of him, nevertheless, in spite of its radical politics:

> Ben. Peirce, the son of Professor Peirce, the eminent mathematician, who had graduated from Harvard the year before [1864], was completing his education at the École Polytechnique and lived in two small rooms in the Latin Quarter. . . . [He] was a man of really brilliant talent, but was wearing himself out by a reckless disregard of health and of all the necessary limitations of human existence. He understood almost everything except self-control. He worked very hard and distinguished himself in his studies; he also played very hard, and in short burned the candle not only at both ends, but at every other point on its surface. Not content with all the amusements affected by the students of Paris, he flung himself violently into French politics. He was one of the drollest human beings I ever knew, as well as one of the most hard-working, and he had a wild humor which would carry him into all sorts of excesses, and very dangerous when applied to French politics, which at that particular time were none of the safest. Haunting the cafés frequented by students, and speaking French with the utmost fluency, although with a strange accent, he became a violent republican and an ardent foe of the empire.
>
> He was wont to discourse about the infamy of established government, half seriously and half humorously, but with a violence and an eloquence which used to startle my youthful mind. Unfortunately he would not always stop there. One night, returning from dinner with his cousins, he insisted upon climbing up onto the high fence of the Tuileries, and from that point of vantage shouting: "Vive la République!" "A bas l'Empereur!" . . . The natural result was the appearance of the sergeant de ville and his immediate arrest. He was rescued with difficulty by his cousins, who explained that he was an American, and that he was only joking. . . . To me Ben. Peirce seemed then, as he does now in memory, one of the most fascinating beings I had ever seen. His fun and humor were unbounded, but he was equally interested in serious matters, and if he did not always think soundly, he rarely failed in originality. He graduated at the Polytechnique with distinction, came home and entered at once upon a career which was full of promise. But the candle had been burned too freely and in too many places. He died young, leaving a sense of loss which still endures among all those who knew him.[105]

The Peirce family produced an unusual and, as it turned out for three of them, a tragic group of sons. Of the four only one, Herbert Henry Davis, lived a regular life, going respectably and conventionally through the expected steps leading to a distinguished foreign service career, ending as assistant secretary of state. He was the only son to have children. Benjamin

Mills, the brilliant youngest son, lived a wild life far from his family and died young in circumstances and from causes hidden under what Murphey called "that queer blanket of obscurity" which the Peirces threw not only over the life of Charles, but over the lives of all three of their unusual sons.[106] James Mills was a discreet but deeply convinced homosexual who, after considering a career in the ministry, then law, mathematics, and finally education, became dean of the graduate school at Harvard University through an astute use of camouflage. About 1890, he wrote of his passionately held views on sex and love under the pseudonym of Professor X in a letter quoted as Appendix D of Havelock Ellis's *Sexual Inversion:*

> I have considered & enquired into this question for many years; and it has long been my settled conviction that no breach of morality is involved in homosexual love; that, like every other passion, it tends, when duly understood and controlled by spiritual feeling, to the physical and moral health of the individual & the race. . . .
>
> Passion is in itself a blind thing. It is a furious pushing out, not with calculation or comprehension of its object, but to anything which strikes the imagination as fitted to its needs. . . . Sexual passion is drawn by certain qualities which appeal to it. It may see them, or think it sees them, in a man or a woman. . . . The two directions are equally natural to unperverted man, and the *abnormal* form of love is that which has lost the power of excitability in either the one or the other of these directions. It is *unisexual* love (a love for one sexuality) which is a perversion. The normal men love both.[107]

Charles, blessed with extraordinary intelligence and tenacity, went to the brink of brilliant success before falling, not into death, as Benjie did, but into disgrace. Charles burned his candle, too, "at both ends and at every point on its surface." So single-minded was he in continuing his study of the logic of things that even the example of the shocking death of his shooting-star of a younger brother could not budge him from his own unique obsession. He wrote many years later:

> When my father and I went out to Marquette together and brought back my brother Ben's body, my father talked to me very earnestly, representing that I was sacrificing all hopes of success in life by devoting myself in logic, and that people would never think I amounted to much if I did so. I told him that I fully realized the truth of that, but that my bent of mind was so strong in that direction that it would be a very hard struggle to give up logic. That I intended, however, to try to do so and to take a good long time to come to any conclusion. . . . [108]

At about the same time, the United States Coast Survey, in conjunction with a number of other American and European astronomical and geodetical institutions, proposed an expedition to observe the solar eclipse of that year. It was determined that the optimum conditions for observation would be in the western Mediterranean, and Charles and his brother James Mills were given the assignment of scouting various locations in that area in order to establish the most feasible sites for occupation later in the year by observation parties. The brothers went ahead, combining in the easy and unbureaucratic atmosphere of the nineteenth century the pleasure of a Grand Tour of Europe with a program of scientific investigation. On the eve of his departure, Peirce was informed by President Eliot that his Observatory salary would be suspended during his absence. This event marked the beginning of a widening rift between the two men, since Peirce took the suspension personally. Although the policy of suspending salaries under similar conditions had been in effect for a year, Peirce had been delegated to perform Observatory as well as Survey work in connection with the eclipse, so when he learned of Eliot's action, he felt reasonably assured that Harvard intended to be rid of him.[109] His opinion was strengthened when, at the same time, the course of lectures he was scheduled to give at the college the next year was canceled, presumably by Eliot.

On June 18, Charles and his brother sailed for Europe, where they began an extensive tour. Their itinerary included London, Berlin, Dresden, Prague, Vienna, Munich, Venice, Florence, Rome, Naples, Sicily, southern Spain, Greece, and Thessaly.[110] In the autumn, Benjamin Peirce, taking Zina with him in the official capacity of an assistant in the Coast Survey, went to make final preparations and then to join Charles and James Mills at the villa of the Marquis de San Giuliano in Sicily to observe there the December eclipse.

In June, in London, Charles had visited the logician Augustus De Morgan, with an introduction from his father, giving him copies of his paper "Description of a Notation for the Logic of Relatives, Resulting from an Amplification of the Conceptions of Boole's Calculus of Logic (DNLR)," one of the most important works in the history of modern logic, "for it is the first attempt to expand Boole's algebra of logic to include the logic of relations."[111] The paper may well have arisen out of the argument between Charles and his father over which discipline held primacy—logic, as Charles held, or geometry, as Benjamin held. While Charles was working on the DNLR, his father was working on his "Linear Associative Algebra." Peirce also gave a copy to the logician W. Stanley Jevons, and the paper subsequently became a part of the discussion of Boole's *Laws of Thought* at the Liverpool meeting of the British Association for the Advancement of Science in September, where the logician Robert Harley remarked that "the most remarkable amplification of Boole's conceptions which the author has hitherto met with is contained in a recent paper by Mr. C. S. Peirce, on the 'Logic of Relatives.' "[112] De Morgan and Jevons are major figures in the development of exact logic.

The scientific expedition was also a success, for it largely validated the American observations made the year before at the solar eclipse in Kentucky, which had convinced them that the newly observed effects of the sun's corona and protuberances required new explanatory theories. (Charles had also been present there as assistant in both the Coast Survey and the Harvard Observatory.) The amateur, Zina, had a particularly pleasing success as well in witnessing and reporting an unusual effect in the corona of the sun.[113] This expedition was Charles's first experience of large-scale international scientific cooperation, and it illustrated for him the importance of the community of science in reevaluating and validating its hypotheses.

Observers of the Solar Eclipse of December 22, 1870, near Catania, Sicily. Standing fourth from the left is Charles S. Peirce; fourth from the right is his father, Benjamin, and second from the right is Zina Peirce. Sitting in front of them is Herbert H. D. Peirce, Charles's younger brother. C. A. Schott is standing on the far left, and Norman Lockyer is standing on the far right. Photograph courtesy of Mrs. Peirce Prince, Herbert's granddaughter.

While in Europe, Peirce had come to a final decision about his future at Harvard and wrote to Winlock, director of the Observatory, "I do not mean to go back to the observatory at all, because I wish to devote myself to Logic as much as I can."[114] Charles and his father had concluded that he would be able to spend more time on his researches into the logic of science, as well as earn a comfortable living, if he became a permanent member of the staff of the Coast Survey. Although neither looked upon the position only as a sinecure and, to the contrary, both fully expected that the responsibilities pertaining to such work would be competently carried out, it is likely that the decision was dictated by a desire not so much to benefit the Survey as to solve Charles's financial and professional problems. The decision also provided the father with the means to protect his son from himself. Already, as of September 21, 1868, Peirce's salary had been increased from $1,200 to $1,500 (it had earlier been increased from $720). Until 1871, he had performed mainly mathematical computations and astronomical observations. From December 1, 1872, when he was promoted from aide to assistant (the rank just beneath superintendent), until December 31, 1891, Charles was employed full-time only by the Coast Survey.

Peirce believed himself to be in a very fortunate position as he considered his future when he returned, aged thirty-one, from Europe in March 1871. He had made a strong impression on Britain's finest logicians and philosophers. He had published, if not extensively, influentially in his chosen field of logic and in a number of other fields as well. He was asked regularly to review books for the *Nation*, the *North American Review*, and other journals. His scientific reputation was increasing in stature. His father was one of the most influential and respected men of science in the United States. He was married to an intelligent, strong-minded, and loving wife from a good New England family, whose beliefs and politics, though considered eccentric, did not detract from her respect in the Brahmin world. Although with a characteristic edge of desperation and doubt, Peirce anticipated as his due a brilliant life and career.

2

"Our Hour of Triumph Is What Brings the Void"

1 8 7 1 – 1 8 8 2

The genius of a man's logical method should be loved and reverenced as his bride, whom he has chosen from all the world. He need not contemn the others; on the contrary, he may honor them deeply, and in doing so he only honors her more. But she is the one that he has chosen, and he knows that he was right in making that choice. And having made it, he will work and fight for her, and will not complain that there are blows to take, hoping that there may be as many and as hard to give, and will strive to be the worthy knight and champion of her from the blaze of whose splendors he draws his inspiration and courage.

CSP, "The Fixation of Belief," 1877

When Charles and Melusina returned from their European adventure in March 1871, they moved into their second house, at 6 Arrow Street in Cambridge. Peirce's salary from his two assistantships approached $2,500, a good income for the times. At thirty-one, he was full of himself and of the glimpses he had had of the glittering intellectual life, especially in philosophy and the sciences at Oxford and Cambridge, and he wished to prove to himself and to that world that he and Harvard could equal it. In this intention, he had been preceded by William James, who had already written three years earlier from Germany to Oliver Wendell Holmes, Jr., urging the formation of a " . . . philosophical society to have regular meetings and discuss none but the very tallest and broadest questions—to be composed of none but the very topmost cream of Boston manhood."[1] That the group was organized and that it met is evidenced by a letter written on November 24,

1872, by Henry James to his friend the Dante scholar and translator Charles Eliot Norton:

> Wendell Holmes is about to discourse out here on Jurisprudence. [He] some day, I think, will *percer*, as the French say, & become eminent—in a specialty, but to a high degree. He, my brother, & various other long-headed youths have combined to form a Metaphysical Club, where they wrangle grimly & stick to the question.[2]

During the years 1871–74, and especially in the winter of 1871–72, Peirce spent a significant portion of whatever time remained to him from Coast Survey and other scientific work in the small company of "long-headed youths" who made up what has since become famous among students of Peirce as the Metaphysical Club. Peirce's version of this club has been the subject of considerable controversy because so little mention of it was made by the members themselves, with the exception of Peirce, who claimed it to be the birthplace of pragmatism. Peirce's exhumation of the club was driven by his desire to establish his priority as the progenitor of pragmatism. John Dewey described Peirce's problem clearly:

> The term pragmatism was introduced into literature in the opening sentences of Professor James's California Union Address in 1898. The sentences run as follows: "the principal of pragmatism, as we may call it, may be expressed in a variety of ways, all of them very simple. In the *Popular Science Monthly* for January, 1878, Mr. Charles S. Peirce introduces it as follows": etc. The readers who have turned to the volume referred to have not, however, found the word there.[3]

This embarrassing absence was what Peirce sought to explain.

The members of the club, as he recalled them, were Peirce himself; Chauncey Wright; William James; Nicholas St. John Green and Joseph Bangs Warner, both Cambridge lawyers; Oliver Wendell Holmes, Jr., later Supreme Court justice; and more or less occasionally John Fiske, the historian and philosopher; Francis Ellingwood Abbot, author of *Scientific Theism*; Professor Henry Bowen of the Harvard philosophy department; and C. C. Everett of the Divinity School.[4]

There are two mentions of members of the club by James. In 1905 he wrote to T. S. Perry, who had asked about John Fiske's part in the club, reminiscing about " . . . how, when Chauncey Wright, Chas. P[eirce], [Nicholas] St. John Green, [Joseph B.] Warner & I appointed an evening to discuss the Cosmic Phil[osophy], just out, J[ohn] F[iske] went to sleep under our noses."[5] Among the papers of Francis Ellingwood Abbot is an invitation from James to " . . . join a Club for reading and discussing philosophical authors, which meets once a week at present and is composed of C. C. Everett, N. St. J[ohn] Green, O. W. Holmes jr., John Fiske, Thos. Davidson, J. B. Warner, Prof. Bowen, and one or two others . . . " which was then reading Hume.[6] Although written in January 1876, the letter gives a membership which, with the exceptions of Chauncey Wright, who had died the year before, Peirce, who had left for Europe almost a year earlier on Survey business, and Thomas Davidson, who was Peirce's friend and former pupil, is the same as that listed by Peirce. Peirce himself claimed that he began the club both in the late sixties and shortly after his return from Europe in the spring of 1871. It is more likely that, on his return, he rejoined the group, which had been meeting informally with Chauncey Wright as its focus since the middle sixties. Wright, James, Green, and Holmes had continued to meet during Peirce's absence; on his return, at his suggestion they called themselves the Metaphysical Club after the Metaphysical Society of London, founded in 1869.

An explanation for the evanescent nature of the club was offered by Peirce in an unpublished draft in 1909. He stated that it was thoroughly informal and kept no minutes of attendance, and that its name had been chosen to alienate those whom it might.

> its constitution was equally effective, for it simply consisted in a single clause forbidding any action ever being taken by the Club as a collective body, thus preventing it from wasting the only intrinsically precious element in the world, as so many other societies waste it, in the idle frivolity they call "business," while moreover since without action there could be no officers and in particular no secretary and so no acknowledged record of debate, to gentlemen desirous of distinguishing themselves or of taking out patents as it were upon such ingenious combinations of ideas as they might contrive, an adequate motive was presented to hold their peace and abandon the arena of debate to those who only sought to draw as near the truth as they could.[7]

In a 1904 characterization of the club's members and the parts they played in its doings, Peirce wrote:

> In the sixties I started a little club called the Metaphysical Club. It seldom if ever had more than half a dozen [members] present. Wright was the strongest member and probably I was next. Nicholas St. John Green was a marvelously strong intelligence. Then there were Frank Abbot, William James, and others.[8]

In 1906, Peirce wrote a somewhat contradictory account in a fragment called "Pragmatism Made Easy":

> I went abroad [in June 1870] and in England, Germany, Italy, Spain, learned from their own mouths what certain students at once of science and of philosophy were turning in their minds. After my return [in March 1871], a knot of us, Chauncey Wright, Nicholas St. John Green, William James and others, including occasionally Francis Ellingwood Abbot and John Fiske, used frequently to meet to discuss fundamental questions. Green was especially impressed with the doctrines of [Alexander] Bain, and impressed the rest of us with them; and finally the writer of this brought forward what we called the principle of pragmatism. Several years later, this was set forth [but not named] in two articles printed in the Popular Science Monthly (Nov 1877 and Jan. 1878) ["The Fixation of Belief" and "How to Make Our Ideas Clear"] and subsequently in the Revue Philosophique.
>
> The particular point that had been made by Bain and that had most struck Green, and through him, the rest of us, was the insistence that what a man really believes is what he would be ready to act upon, and risk much upon.[9]

William James wrote his brother Henry on November 24, 1872, that "He [Peirce] read us an admirable introductory chapter to his book on logic the other day," almost certainly the paper referred to by Peirce.[10] On the following day, Thomas Sargeant Perry, an editor of the *North American Review* and a friend of both James and Peirce, wrote to the latter begging for a copy of the piece read before the club; he did so again in December, after Charles and Zina had moved to Washington. Peirce did not send the piece, and because of his work with the Survey was able to work on his logic only sporadically, which probably explains why it did not appear until five years later. In none of this, nor in any of the other evidence bearing on the club—nor, indeed, in the essays published in the *Popular Science Monthly* in 1877–78 referred to by Peirce and James, or even in the *Monist* series of 1891–93—does the word *pragmatism* appear. The first edition of the *Century Dictionary*, published in 1889, contains no entry for *pragmatism* as a philosophical term, even though Peirce was responsible for, including other categories, philosophical terms, among which he provided definitions for *realism, nominalism, idealism,* his father's *ideal-realism,* and many others. There is an entry for *pragmatism,* however: "Pragmatical character or conduct; officiousness; busy impertinence," and for *pragmatist:* "One who is impertinently busy or meddling," an irony which Peirce surely appreciated. This absence of the term *pragmatism* from published writings and correspondence more than ten years after its presumed coinage seems extraordinarily puzzling, especially in the light of Peirce's usually aggressive insistence on receiving the credit for his inventions.

Much of the puzzle is resolved by an exchange of letters between James and Peirce in November 1900. James Mark Baldwin, the psychologist and editor of the *Dictionary of Philosophy and Psychology*, was in need of assistance in developing definitions for a large range of terms. He turned to Peirce, no doubt knowing of his work on the *Century*. Peirce wrote to James:

> Now, however, I have a particular occasion to write. Baldwin, arrived at J in his dictionary, suddenly calls on me to do the rest of the logic, in the utmost haste, and various questions of terminology came up.
> Who originated the term *pragmatism*, I or you? Where did it first appear in print? What do you understand by it?[11]

James responded in a postcard, "You invented 'pragmatism' for which I gave you full credit in a lecture entitled 'Philosophical Conceptions and practical results' of which I sent you 2 (unacknowledged) copies a couple of years ago [the California Union Address of 1898]."[12] This was the first time in the long and often voluminous correspondence between the two men that Peirce used the term *pragmatism*. Almost all the accounts of the club and of the origins of pragmatism are, therefore, retrospective creations of the two men. By 1900, James had entertained his students and colleagues with numerous tales of the club and of Peirce, its most mysterious member, so that they had become Harvard lore. Among these is an account by one of James's students, reported by Fisch, which sets just the right tone:

> In conversation James told of a philosophical club of which Chauncey Wright, John Fiske and others were members, at which Peirce was to read a paper, They assembled; Peirce did not come; they waited and waited; finally a two-horse carriage came along and Peirce got out with a dark cloak over him; he came in and began to read his paper. What was it about? He set forth, James said, how the different moments of time got into the habit of coming one after another [for Peirce all regularity is the result of taking habits].[13]

Peirce, on the other hand, had no reason to become involved with his recollections of the club until Baldwin forced its importance on him with his request for help in defining terms for his forthcoming dictionary. It was only then that Peirce reconstructed the club in various versions and wrote definitions of *pragmatism*, *pragmatist*, *pragmatic*, and *pragmaticism* for Baldwin's dictionary and, five years later, the *Century Dictionary* (which were probably edited by Dewey), which appeared in the revised 1909 edition *Supplement*, five years before his death. Peirce's interleaved copy of the *Century* at Harvard is probably the most enlightening source of these and many other later definitions.

Facts such as these led Ralph Barton Perry in his 1935 study of William James to state categorically that "though the origin of pragmatism be obscure, it is clear that the idea that pragmatism originated with Peirce was originated by James." Professor Perry concluded that "the modern movement known as pragmatism is largely the result of James's misunderstanding of Peirce."[14]

In his book *Evolution and the Founders of Pragmatism*, published in 1949, Philip P. Wiener also raised serious doubts, writing that the club may have been "primarily a symbol in Peirce's metaphysical imagination," and that it may have been in imagination that he "conferred membership in his Metaphysical Club" on Chauncey Wright and the rest. He concluded:

> But, after all, what's in a name? The most significant fact for the historian of thought is that Peirce brought together in his account of the genesis of pragmatism a historically important group of persons who really lived in the same place and time, moved in the same intellectual atmosphere, and influenced each other in ways that shaped the growth of certain pervasive ideas current in our thinking today.[15]

In his 1954 article "Was There a Metaphysical Club in Cambridge?" Fisch showed that there must have been one, thereby removing one of Wiener's doubts; but he did not at the same time refute Perry's claim that Peirce's priority in the matter of the origination of pragmatism was entirely James's idea. Nor did he give reason to believe that the club was not "primarily a symbol of Peirce's metaphysical imagination" as Wiener suggested.[16]

The only published reference to the club and its role in the origins of pragmatism provided by Peirce in his lifetime appeared in passing in his 1908 article "A Neglected Argument for the Reality of God." It consisted in a single sentence with much-reduced claims: "In 1871, in a Metaphysical Club in Cambridge, Massachusetts, I used to preach this principle as a sort of logical gospel, representing the unformulated method followed by Berkeley, and in conversation about it I called it 'Pragmatism.' "[17] Peirce had a number of opportunities to publish a more complete version of the club, but he chose not to do so. He was probably frustrated by the embarrassing fact that the term *pragmatism* was nowhere to be found in the papers which set forth its doctrine. Also, as proposed in those papers it was too nominalistic to sit well with the logical realism he openly professed by 1900; nor did it fit in with his later insistence that the basis of logic was not at all a matter of psychology. And, too, there was his realization that his sometimes contradictory re-creations of the club contained the pungent scent of nostalgia, and that his own principle of scientific ethics therefore brought some of his recollections into question.

From his beginnings as a philosopher, Peirce made a strong and consistent effort to give credit to the originators of any idea he was aware of using. For Peirce, the pursuit of knowledge, especially in science, was not an individual concern. It was, in fact, the opposite: it was social praxis, the creation of a community of inquirers. Peirce's idea that the continuity or persistence (a pun Peirce enjoyed) of an idea had much to do with the degree to which it approximated truth meant that any individual contribution was simply added to the innumerable ones of five thousand years of searching for it. He felt, therefore, that every effort ought to be made to clarify the origins and continuity of any important idea, and he established this as a principle of philosophical and scientific ethics.

Since pragmatism was to him one of the most important ideas, it would have been inconsistent of him and against his most deeply held principle to falsify its origins. The club probably existed much as Peirce described it in his recollections. Where Peirce romanticized it was in assigning it such a general historical importance. For the other members, except James, the club was important as a gathering place for the purpose of pursuing philosophical issues of joint interest as intensely as they knew how. For Peirce it was the place in which he had originated pragmatism, his "beloved creature," the "living idea" *he* had "cherished and tended like the flowers in his garden," and so the club was for him hallowed ground. Peirce gave his personally unsatisfactory, but truthful, account of his claim to priority as the founder of pragmatism in the revised *Century Dictionary Supplement*, where it appeared after the entry for James's definition of the term:

> (b) A theory concerning the proper method of determining the meaning of conceptions. . . . This theory was first propounded by Mr. Peirce in an article on "How to Make Our Ideas Clear" in the "Popular Science Monthly" in 1878. The term "pragmatism" does not, however, appear there. In an article in the "Monist" for 1905, Mr. Peirce says that he "has used it continually in philosophic conversation since, perhaps, the mid-seventies." The term was publicly introduced in print by Professor William James in 1898 in an address upon "Philosophic Conceptions and Practical Realities," in which the authorship of the term and of the method is credited to Mr. Peirce. The latter has recently used the term 'pragmaticism' to express this meaning.

The thirty-three-year-old Peirce, anticipating as he then did a brilliant career in philosophy and science, could not have imagined such a convoluted and humiliating ending for his great expectations. The idea that Ralph Barton Perry, the biographer of Peirce's great friend William James, would, twenty years after Peirce's death, hint maliciously that the value of his life's work was no more than the pitying invention of his friend James would have seemed to him not only inconceivable and wrong, but a misreading of James's personal honesty and a violation of the very essence of philosophical inquiry.

The remaining months of 1871 Peirce spent partly in Washington and partly in Cambridge, preparing to take up what he and his father had decided would be the central focus of his career, one of the most important aspects of Coast Survey work, a branch of geodesy called gravimetrics, the measurement of gravity. He was also engaged in photometric researches as assistant to Winlock in the Harvard Observatory and in other bits and pieces of astronomical research. He and Zina were often separated, because of both his time in Washington and her pursuit of her own feminist career. He wrote her just before Christmas 1871:

My dearest Zie,

I do so wish we could be together this evening, darling. It is so long since I have heard your voice or have seen you, my littel [sic] Zero [A Political Zero was the pseudonym Zina used as author of *The Democratic Party: A Political Study*, published four years later]. Could writing letters only bring us any nearer, I should write twice a day. But, alas, they do not seem to have much effect of that sort. You have no idea—though I suppose you can imagine—how delightful a Sunday in this office would be together. My sweetest wife.

Simon Newcomb came to see me today [they discussed political economy]. He asked after you. At the [Washington] Philosophical Society last evening I made a little communication on Enke's [comet] which was well received & occasioned some discussion. There was a baloonist [sic] there who was questioned a good deal. He told how he went up once & had a young man with him & the baloon [sic] began to swing violently when they were about two miles high. The young man said he didn't know about this.

I have been quite interested in political economy which I generally spend my evenings in studying. I will try my hand at explaining my views to you. 1. Political Economy I conceive treats of the relations of these three qualities, the *price* of a thing, the yearly sales of it which I term the *demand*, and the *cost* to the . . . [letter is incomplete].[18]

On April 8, 1872, Benjamin Peirce appointed his son, over the heads of the more experienced assistants, to the position of acting assistant in charge of the Coast Survey office in Washington for the period that Julius Hilgard, the assistant in charge, was in Europe on Survey business. Charles remained in that position until December 1, when his father appointed him assistant in charge of gravimetric experiments at a salary of $2,500.[19] Charles insisted that he have complete freedom of operations in carrying out his responsibilities. Benjamin's letter of instruction was unusually broad and generous:

> You are hereby directed to take charge of the Pendulum Experiments of the Coast Survey, and to direct and inspect all parties engaged in such experiments. . . . In combination with the pendulum experiments you will investigate the law of the deviations of the plumb line and of the azimuths from the spheroidal theory of the earth's figure. . . . [Charles added and received his father's agreement to even greater authority and scope:] When you are not in the field you will direct the mathematical investigations of the force of gravity in the office, and will also oversee the publication of results of the Coast Survey under the assistant in charge and will assist him in the superintendence of the chemical operations going on there and in such business of the office as he may desire; and you are hereby authorized to recommend to me a person to be appointed clerk not exceeding $1200 a year, to report to the assistant in charge of the office and assist you in the performance of the duties imposed upon you by these instructions. . . .
>
> You will make an annual report to the superintendent of the state of your department of investigations, and make such suggestions and investigations as may be required.[20]

In the structure of the Survey, the rank of assistant was immediately below and responsible only to the superintendent; thus, these instructions meant that as long as his father retained his authority over the Survey, Charles would be protected from the consequences of any ill-considered actions, and from the jealousies and resentments of his colleagues. As Murray Murphey wrote of this policy, "No one ever questioned Charles Peirce's brilliance—he earned his recognition by his own ability: but because he was his father's son he was not held to account as others were. The indulgence was to bear bitter fruit."[21] At the time of his appointment, Peirce knew very little about geodesy and gravimetric research. The Survey had to provide the considerable funds and time for his education in the field.

For the entire time the elder Peirce was superintendent, he stayed for the most part in Cambridge, where he continued as professor of mathematics. He needed a person in Washington who could act as his extension and who could also assess the lay of the land. This function was normally carried out by Julius Hilgard, his assistant in charge of the Washington office, who expected to succeed to the superintendency, so the temporary appointment of his son to that position gave Benjamin, if only briefly, a completely loyal and perceptive spy in that office. An obvious advantage for Charles was that his appointment gave him detailed knowledge of the administrative workings and internal politics of the Survey, which ought naturally to have facilitated his advancement to assistant in charge of gravimetrics. But there was an ominous side to the appointments. They were both obvious instances of nepotism, and Charles's appointment to the charge of pendulum experiments removed the scientist then concerned with them, Charles A. Schott, thereby creating jealousy and resentment on his part which were later to damage Peirce's position in the Survey. That Peirce realized this danger is shown in a note to his father: "I shall avoid any hard feeling on Schott's part if I can by talking & consulting with him[,] but at any rate I want to do it as I think it important for my own reputation & for the interests of astronomy."[22]

Peirce's acceptance of the appointment made it necessary for him to resign his assistantship in the Harvard Observatory (though he was to remain on its rolls until the end of 1875), but as his photometric researches were at least one year from completion, he made a formal arrangement with the director, Joseph G. Winlock, whereby he would continue the work until it was finished and published.[23] After Winlock's sudden death in June 1875, Peirce proceeded, without informing Eliot, as if the arrangement were still in effect, an action that was to bring him and Eliot into serious conflict.[24]

Concurrently with his appointment in charge of gravimetrics, Peirce moved to Washington with Zina. William James commented in a letter to his brother that Peirce was " . . . appreciated there, & only tolerated here [in Cambridge] and wd. be a fool not to go there."[25] The Washington they moved to was not Cambridge. Its buildings were mostly ramshackle and wooden, with randomly located government offices in various stages of completion. The town was filled with saloons, brothels, rooming houses, and the other sordid accompaniments to politics. As described a few years earlier by an Ohio congressman, Washington was

> as unattractive, straggling, sodden a town, wandering up and down the left bank of the yellow Potomac, as the fancy can sketch. Pennsylvania Avenue . . . stretched drearily over the mile between the unfinished Capitol and the unfinished Treasury building on Fifteenth Street . . . where it turned north for a square and took its melancholy way to Georgetown. . . . It was the only paved street in the town. . . . As may be supposed the Capital of the Republic had more malodors than the poet Coleridge ascribed to ancient Cologne. There was then the open canal, a branch of the Chesapeake and Ohio, from Rock Creek to Anacosta, breeding malaria, tadpoles, and mosquitoes. . . . Politically, the city—the fixed population—was intensely Southern, as much so as Richmond or Baltimore.[26]

Zina thoroughly disapproved of the place and wrote a piece published in the *Atlantic Monthly*, "The Externals of Washington," which took the government to task for the squalid ugliness of the city.[27] Soon, she spent as little time there as she decently could, leaving her husband to his own devices while she pursued her own interests. At first, things went well between them, as Sarah wrote her son Jem:

> This is Charley's new papers of which he is very proud . . . [official embossed Coast Survey stationery]. He has been showing me his Sanctum & reading me what he has written of his logic which it seems to my "untutored mind" he has begun well. Have you read or has he sent it to you? . . . Charley I think I never saw looking better or apparently happier, & they both continue to be much pleased with their life here. . . . No rural sabbath could be more quiet than today is here. No sounds but the wind . . . & the hymns from the chapel which it bears on its wings are to be heard, for the birds are too far off—too far below this lofty abode [the Survey offices in the elegant Richards building] for their pipings to reach us.[28]

Until August 1873, Peirce was occupied principally with preliminary research into theoretical and practical problems in geodesy and gravimetrics. Even when he and Zina were together, he spent his odd hours absorbed in work. Where he could fit them in, he worked on his double star observations, his photometric researches, and his logic book. Measurements of gravity are of great practical importance for the accurate measurement of land masses, since variations in gravity are related to the distance of the land surface from the center of the earth's spheroid and are capable of giving the distance from a given point on the surface of the earth to its center with great precision. When integrated, numerous such measurements produce an accurate model of the shape of the earth and thereby increase the accuracy of land surveys. The method which was used to make these measurements (and is still one of the methods used today) was the swinging of pendulums. The principle involved is that the length of time a given pendulum at a given location and altitude takes to complete one arc, when compared to the same information for the same pendulum placed at a different location and altitude, results in a mathematical difference which can be used with a gravitational constant to determine the distance of the pendulum from the center of the earth. Since this mathematical difference is very small in any case, and variables such as barometric pressure, temperature, tolerances in the mechanical linkages of the pendulum, and flexure of the pendulum support can result in a percentage of error greater than the gravitational difference itself, the procedures used in measuring gravity obviously require unusually refined techniques.[29]

What Peirce seemed not to understand at the beginning of his research into gravimetrics, a minor though critical aspect of geodesy, was that there was little more to it than the refinement of techniques of measurement, a line of investigation which quickly became a dead end for him. Since he found his interest in any science concentrated primarily on its logic and method and only minimally on its techniques, his commitment to gravimetrics was bound to lessen drastically in a few years. He quickly expanded his researches to include the theory of errors of observation, the logic and mathematics of measurement as such, and other, more interesting problems associated with gravimetrics, but the Survey proved increasingly resistant to these lines of original research and pressured him constantly for "results." Even more threatening was the drudgery involved in reducing the thousands of results from pendulum swings to a single value. This was done by human, not mechanical (or electronic), computers during Peirce's thirty years with the Survey. While Peirce had the assistance of computers, a great many of the reductions and all the checking of results had to be done by him. For a man whose interests really lay in the freer air of the logic of all the sciences, this aspect of gravimetrics was stifling.

In August 1873, Peirce began his gravity experiments on Mt. Hoosac and in the shafts of the Hoosac railway tunnel near North Adams, Massachusetts. There were innumerable delays caused by periods of blasting in the tunnel and by inexperience, not only on his part but also on the part of American instrument makers, whose techniques were insufficiently refined to meet the demands of gravimetrics. These delays made it necessary to reoccupy the Hoosac site in the spring of 1874 in order to complete the first group of experiments. In addition to problems caused by lack of scientific knowledge and experience, Peirce suffered from his inexperience and failure of tact in handling his subordinates, many of whom quit on him; Henry Farquhar, his regular computer for many years thereafter, was later to testify against him before Congress in 1885. Zina deplored the rough camping life necessitated by the location of the tunnel, and in the second year they occupied lodgings in the nearby village of Florida. During the progress of swinging pendulums, which continued twenty-four hours a day, there always had to be someone performing the dull but difficult and exacting task of timing the swings. Since there were often only three and never more than four persons involved in the experiments, the shifts were usually eight and often twelve hours in length. One of the two men assisting Peirce consistently shirked, forcing Peirce to dismiss him. Thus, Peirce was shorthanded and required to stand two shifts himself, which led to his becoming seriously overworked and a prey to bouts of illness.[30]

In the spring of 1874, the elder Peirce gave up his double life and retired from the superintendency of the Coast Survey to become its "consulting geometer." He was thus able to maintain his influence within it without being burdened with the administrative responsibilities of office. All major decisions within the Survey, including those affecting Charles, continued to be made by him. The new superintendent was Carlile P. Patterson, a naval captain with many years' service in the Survey, who made it a practice not to act without consulting Benjamin, whom he called "My dear Chief" and "My darling Chief."[31] Benjamin supported the appointment of Patterson in place of Julius Hilgard, who had been expecting to occupy the position. Hilgard's resentment was, in time, to undermine Charles both in the Survey and at the Johns Hopkins University. As Sarah described the situation at the time of her husband's resignation:

> The officers are all lamenting the change, excepting Captain Patterson who is jubilant & assumes the chair with great confidence altho' all the men almost without exception dislike him. As for poor Hilgard he is bitterly disappointed as he has always looked forward to being Superintendent himself when Ben retired.[32]

By the end of 1874, the elder Peirce and Patterson had decided that Charles should spend at least one year in Europe in order to bring the

Carlile P. Patterson, superintendent of the United States Coast Survey, 1874–1881. Photograph courtesy of the National Oceanic and Atmospheric Administration.

science of geodesy in the United States up to European standards.[33] But before the Peirces left for Europe in April 1875, where Charles was to study European techniques of gravimetric research, Zina brought up with him and his parents her suspicions that he was having affairs during her absences. One woman in particular, the attractive wife of a Captain Bradford of the Survey, was the object of her jealousy. Charles's mother wrote to her sister-in-law about her reluctant and ambivalent meeting with Mrs. Bradford:

> Mrs. Bradford appeared remarkably well in her own house. I think the intimacy between her & Charlie is as innocent & merely friendly as possible. I have looked anxiously at their intercourse since I have been here because I know how Zina feels & *am sure* it is all right—perfectly so—she is very free in her manners—but in an innocent kind of way. She kisses Ben & takes his hand & all that & altho' she takes no *such liberties* with Charlie she treats him too very familiarly & seems to depend on him a good deal— for numerous friendly offices which seem right eno' as her husband is away & Charlie very intimate with him—Charlie certainly does not go there now very much & he told me he had asked Mrs. Throckmorton who is a perfect lady if she considered him too intimate with Mrs. B. and she assured him that she saw nothing at all wrong in it. I wish Zina could feel differently about it for as Mrs. B. is among the very few neighbors Charlie has it is a pity he should [not] have the relation he gets from hearing her prattle. She is a great deal such a woman as Mrs. [Joseph] Le Conte with less talent. Thoroughly southern.[34]

Zina spent much of the winter of 1873–74 in Cambridge with her parents. She shared her feelings about her marriage with her sister Amy, including her belief that Charles no longer loved her and the possibility of leaving him. Atkinson believes that the marriage must have been in serious trouble already if Zina was considering separation, because she was absolutely opposed to divorce. Atkinson quotes her extreme views on adultery and divorce:

> That Creative Deity having entrusted to monogamic marriage *the transmission of the human soul*, adultery is not only the violation of the most intimate and solemn contract of the universe, but is also the betrayal and corruption of the *source of life itself*—consequently is treason to the unborn, to the future offspring of the unborn, to society, and to the race. Therefore its proper penalty is not divorce, but death or prisoning for life.[35]

Despite her profound reservations, Zina accompanied her husband and his aide, Farquhar, to Europe in 1875. Charles may have met William H. Appleton, publisher of the *Popular Science Monthly*, on this trip:

> The leisurely voyages of those days gave one time to make acquaintances, even friendships. Mr. Appleton and I used to pace the deck together, and I

would talk to him about my studies of the nature of scientific reasoning . . .
he offered me a good round price for some articles for the *Popular Science
Monthly.*[36]

Charles and Zina landed in Liverpool in mid-April and spent the next
week sightseeing and living so well that it put a strain on his finances, a
pattern of extravagance which soon became an overwhelming problem.
Peirce discussed geodesy with a number of British scientists, including the
renowned physicist James Clerk Maxwell at Cambridge, who agreed with his
views on the characteristics of the resistance affecting pendulums. He also
questioned instrument makers and, after a delay occasioned by English re-
serve, swung the Coast Survey pendulum at Kew Observatory for purposes of
comparison with his swings made in the United States. His father, in a letter
from Superintendent Patterson, heard that there had been " . . . a most
interesting and 'informing' letter from Charlie—a good representative of
young America to match Clerk Maxwell and others of that ilk."[37] He also
spoke with—and impressed—the great mathematician William Kingdon
Clifford about the logic of relatives and his proposed book on the subject.

In June, he heard of the death of his father's friend and his patron,
Joseph Winlock, the director of the Harvard Observatory; he wrote later to
his mother, "I didn't write either for the day I heard of it I was taken ill,
partly caused by that, for I am weak and emotions effect [sic] me physically,
& I had to go to bed for several days."[38] Five days after Winlock's death,
Benjamin telegraphed Patterson that he supported Hilgard for the position.
On the same day, he wrote to him privately:

> I want you to write President Eliot, and commend Charles S. Peirce, as a fit
> person for the directorship of the observatory. I wish you would especially
> [write] of the efficiency with which He [sic] administered the office during
> the absence of Hilgard . . . if you can truthfully do so.[39]

Patterson responded immediately:

> Yes, most gladly would I do all in my power to help Charlie to a position in
> which he could show to the world the dazzling brightness of the metal that
> is in him. Enclosed I send letter to Presdt Eliot. If not in proper shape, "lick
> it in" as the dear old bear told the young one, & I will rewrite it. Should
> Charlie be appt'd however, what shall we do for the gravity? . . . Newcomb
> is, I presume, a candidate and very formidable. . . .

He continued ten days later:

> I trust that Prof. [Joseph] Henry's [secretary of the Smithsonian] view as to
> the succession at the Naval Obsy may induce Newcomb to hold on there,

and so allow C. S. P. to be appointed to Harvard. Of the two I think the latter has more originality and creative power, has fully at [his] command as great mathematical resources as the first, and is the best observer. Such a place is not the best possible one for Charley's special powers, but it is the next best, and his present place is the third best.[40]

As it happened, Eliot and the Harvard Corporation gave little consideration to either Hilgard or Charles as a replacement for Winlock. (In 1877 they would choose instead Edward C. Pickering, who had been an assistant in the Observatory for some time. Newcomb would choose to stay with the Nautical Almanac.) From Paris in November, Peirce commented to James with deep ambivalence about these machinations:

> You are very kind in wishing me back in Cambridge. I don't know whether I shall ever live there or not. I like the place but there is something about it too which I find very antagonistic to me. I had ambition once to be a professor there, which I have outgrown. Why put myself in such a position of obloquy almost if I could—why be Charley Eliot's man when I have already a position where I am engaged in original research & where even that is my duty & is counted positively for me—instead of being something to be excused as it is in College. As for the observatory, it is of all situations I know of the one which has the most of thankless, and utterly mechanical drudgery, together with vexatious interference from two different sources, certain members of the committee & the president. I speak of *Directorship* of it, for my own connection with it was most delightful. Winlock was charming. I am not quite through with it because my book of photometric researches isn't out & they began at once after Winlock's death to try to nag at me, but fortunately I am too far off.
>
> But don['[t let me speak as if I did not feel the warmest gratitude to you and my friends who wanted to get me into the observatory. I don['[t know that I would have declined it even although it does not seem to me altogether desirable. But I always speak too strongly when I think of Eliot.[41]

From England, Zina, Charles, and Farquhar went first to Hamburg to pick up the Bessel reversible pendulum ordered two years before from A. G. Repsold and Sons, and then on to Berlin, where Zina visited with her sister Amy, who was studying music there. Charles had several interviews with Lieutenant General Johann Jakob Baeyer, the founder and president of the Royal Prussian Geodetic Institute, who questioned the stability of the Repsold support. In October Peirce went on to Geneva, where he arranged with Professor Emile Plantamour, director of the Geneva Institute, to swing his new pendulum there and, in addition to his usual routine, found and measured the flexure of the support suspected by Baeyer. In September, he established a fairly permanent base of operations in Paris. There, within days of his arrival, he attended a meeting of the Permanent Commission of the International Geodetic Association and reported the discoveries he had made in Geneva to its Special Committee on the Pendulum, thereby becoming one of the few Americans of his time to participate directly in the deliberations of an international scientific association.[42]

Although six months had already passed, Peirce had as yet made no accounting to Washington of his expenses, and he began to be anxious that he might find himself seriously in debt. In his constant traveling about, he had allowed his accounts to become inextricably tangled, making it impossible for him to document them according to regulations. Peirce had permitted this condition to become so serious because he did not know whether to base his accounts on the exchange rate of gold or currency; the use of one or the other could change the amount of money available to him by as much as one-quarter. Further complicating his situation, he had opened accounts with two bankers, both of whom were authorized to draw from the Coast Survey. And finally, on leaving the United States, Peirce had neglected to leave a forwarding address with the Survey office (and later provided one where he stayed only a short time), which made it impossible for that office to reach him. Over the months his letters to Superintendent Patterson became more and more frantic, while Patterson on his part tried without success to reach Peirce. And then, as the unvouchered accounts with his two bankers arose, the bankers wrote his father, who in turn became increasingly distressed.[43]

Zina did not accompany Charles to Geneva as they had planned. In the same month that he arrived in Paris, giving both illness and her reservations about continuing the marriage as the reasons, she left for Cambridge with her sister. The Paris in which Peirce found himself deserted and alone in the fall of 1875 was in the midst of one of its grandest, most extravagant and creative periods, the *fin de siècle*. In that year, undaunted by the German defeat of 1870 at Sedan and their occupation of Paris for one day, or by the violence of the ensuing civil war in which revolutionaries of the "Commune" barricaded the streets, assassinated the archbishop, and burned the Tuileries, or by the French army's immediate and brutal repression, which either killed the radicals or shipped them off to colonial exile, the city opened the opulent Paris Opéra with the premiere of Georges Bizet's *Carmen*, which Peirce, with his love of opera, luxury, and spectacle, may well have seen. Society glittered through the streets and in the salons and the more than 30,000 cabarets and cafés. Literature flourished, well primed by the scandals and ideological and conceptual excitement surrounding the appearance of Charles Baudelaire's volume of poems *Les Fleurs du Mal* and

Gustave Flaubert's novel *Madame Bovary*, both in 1857. By 1875, Emile Zola was already writing his host of gritty naturalistic novels, Guy de Maupassant was polishing his literary jewels, and Paul Verlaine, following Baudelaire, was inventing symbolist poetry. In 1863, Edouard Manet had shown *Olympe*, his portrait of a naked harlot, at the Salon des Refusés, thereby not only shocking the respectable bourgeoisie but announcing a new aesthetic. Baudelaire gave his critical support to the nonconformists and also to the impressionist painters, such as Claude Monet, Camille Pisarro, and Gustave Caillebot, who gave their first show in 1874 (the year before Peirce visited Paris), presenting their novel and revolutionary experiments with light, color, form, and subject matter. Paris influenced him deeply. It was this great bohemian world that gave Peirce his love for French novels and his mature style as a Dandy. He learned there to appreciate French wines and otherwise follow his father's encouragement to refine his palate. He hired an expensive *sommelier* and spent two months acquiring a fine knowledge of Médoc wines. His experiences in Paris may also have inclined him toward Juliette, a woman who reflected the glamour of that world. He began a scandalous affair with her less than two years later in New York, and they married in 1883. In Paris, too, alone with his obsession, he started to bring into final form the ideas that began to appear two years later as "Illustration of the Logic of Science."

In December, from New York, Zina wrote a long and remarkable letter to Superintendent Patterson, explaining her reasons for deserting her husband and asking his help:

Dear Captain Patterson:

I have long been wanting to write and ask you whether those pictures of ours are still hanging up in the Coast Survey parlours where I left them, for I think they would do something toward making this room we are boarding—my sister and myself—more home-like. I had a very blue letter from Mr. Peirce the other day. He says he has never yet understood from you whether his appropriation is on a gold or a currency basis and so he is all at sea with his accounts. I cannot but think there is some misconception on his part about it and write not to interfere or suggest, dear friend, in what is none of my affair, but merely to say that if you can write a few cheering words to poor Charley, I think they will do him good. In your official capacity toward my darling husband, as well as from your sincere and long friendship for *him* (I doubt not) as well as for his father—you have now, dear Sir, in your power to do him a great deal of good. I do not know how far you may have noticed it, but I have known for a long time that he has been going on in a way that could not but end in wretchedness if not in humiliation. His parents and brother [Jem] are utterly incapable of seeing that anything is amiss in one of their children and so he has never had a word of advice or warning from any one but me, and to them wives, husbands, as you know—are proverbially dear. I at last took the extreme course of leaving him to himself in Europe and returning home without him, giving him to understand that unless he changed I could not any longer live with him. This I think has at last brought him to his senses, and I think he feels now that to make duty one's *first* instead of one's last object is not only the only safe—it is the only *happy* . . . principle of action. Charley has one trait which unfortunately has never been taken advantage of by any one in authority over him—and that is docility to what he recognizes as *law*. It has been peculiarly unfortunate for his temperament that his father's position on the Survey has always been so influential that he has not (at least so I have judged from my imperfect observation) been held as strictly to account as other officers in similar positions are. All his life from babyhood it seems as though everything had conspired to spoil him with indulgence—Now while I do not suggest or counsel a sudden tightening of reins that have perhaps been held too loosely I *would* hope that a grave and kindly and earnest letter from yourself enlarging upon his responsibilities to the Survey, to family, to his own talents, to his Maker and strengthening him by expressions of confidence in his genius if *only* he will act prudently, cautioning and carefully in everything—instead of rushing things through with recklessness and extravagance—would do him a great deal of good. He ought to see to things personally himself—not go off to the next station and leave subordinates who do not understand packing scientific instruments as well as he does—the task of sending them after him, etc. etc. Of course they arrive broken and then ensure trouble and expense and delay in getting them replaced.

Charley is now at a great crisis of his life and if the good in him is encouraged, disciplined and called to the front, he will rise as a man to the level of his wonderful intellectual gifts and be a shining ornament in the practice to his country. I hope and trust, dear sir, that you will act a noble, wise and paternal part to this brilliant but erratic genius who is now, as it were, in your charge. To no one but my sister have I said as much as I have here *in strict confidence* to yourself. I shall confide in you that not even the wife of your bosom, dearly as I love her, knows anything about my writing to you. Be good to my Charley, dear Captain Patterson, and be above all judicious with him. Let us save him *together* . . . if we can. Please *burn* this *immediately* and believe me ever truly respectfully and for all previous kindness to him I am gratefully yours.

Zina Fay Peirce[44]

Despite her discretion, Zina's letter seems a remarkably accurate analysis of the weaknesses of her husband's character. Patterson thought so as well, placing the letter on file for reference despite Zina's plea for him to burn it and Benjamin Peirce's eloquently patriarchal protest: "Should Zina's letter come in your way, do not hesitate to declare that it is her own independent firework, let off in one of her fits of explosion, for the amusement of her sex. It is as harmless as the firefly, and will not burn the most combustible gauze."[45]

Although he continued with his work of swinging pendulums and learning about European geodesy, Zina's desertion left Peirce in a profound depression. His Survey party's accounts seemed insoluble, parts of his instruments had been broken in transit, and, to cap it all, the Académie Française persisted in treating him as an American of no account by putting him off and refusing him the use of the laboratory facilities necessary for continuing his pendulum research. By October 1875, both his personal funds and his credit were exhausted, and he was forced to consider returning home with his work unfinished. He wrote to Superintendent Patterson:

> Before this reaches you, I fear that I shall have been obliged to lay my case before our minister here and apply to him for relief from his private means.
>
> I have been working faithfully. For the last two months I have certainly not taken so many days recreation as there have been Sundays. I have completed an exclusive series of experiments in Geneva, and the International Geodetical Conference have expressed by a unanimous resolution their approval of my work in Europe & their desire that it should be completed. My reports it is true are behind hand; but on the 1st of September I was in the midst of work which could not be interrupted & have not been able yet to complete the rather long report of my operations. I do feel that I have done my duty here fully & have not been seduced by a tourist's impulses.
>
> I think it would be very wrong to allow me to go home with my work all in its present condition. But as for me I cannot pay for the work any longer. I cannot be reimbursed for what I have spent without knowing how to make out my vouchers. And therefore I must make this last appeal to you to answer my inquiry. I dont know why you haven't before answered it, but I rest entirely confident in your friendship.[46]

Patterson had tried to answer, but with no current forwarding address had been unable to do so. Simultaneously with the letter of October 1, Peirce sent a telegram which read, "Will party expense be paid gold? /s/ Peirce." Patterson replied, "Expenses gold, salaries currency—wrote you July 26 in Berlin." A few days later the telegraph company in Paris notified Patterson that it was unable to find Peirce in Paris. This state of affairs had begun the previous April when Peirce first sailed for England and continued until February 1876, altogether a period of eleven months.[47] That Patterson should have been unable to reach him for such a length of time seems beyond possibility, yet that is what happened. Had Zina remained with her husband, she easily would have managed the problem for him as she had done in many similar circumstances. Peirce seems not to have realized that Patterson must have been responding to his frantic communications, and he never thought to check his original arrangement or to send Patterson a new address. A final settlement of Peirce's expenses was not made until over a year later, in February 1877. This was accomplished by giving Peirce $2,000 in return for the extra expenses which he had incurred and paid from his own pocket, a significant portion reflecting his high style of living and the breakage of instruments. If Superintendent Patterson can be believed, the settlement was not achieved without financial sleight of hand.[48] The whole affair seems no more than an extreme instance of Peirce's odd inability to handle ordinary practical matters.

Fortunately for Peirce's spirits at this time, a letter from his friend William James mentioned that James's brother Henry was in Paris, and Peirce wrote that his "presence here is a great thing for me as I am lonely & excessively depressed."[49] Henry reported to his brother that he had seen

Chas. Peirce, who wears beautiful clothes &c. He is busy swinging pendulums at the Observatory, and thinks himself indifferently treated by

Henry James and William James, 1904–1905. Photograph courtesy of the Harvard University Archives.

the Paris scientists. We meet every two or three days to dine together; but though we get on very well, our sympathy is economical rather than intellectual.[50]

The correspondence between the brothers continued with some advice from William on the handling of his difficult friend:

> I am amused that you should have fallen into the arms of C. S. Peirce, whom I imagine you find a rather uncomfortable bedfellow, thorny & spinous, but the way to treat him is after the fabled "nettle" receipt: grasp firmly, contradict, push hard, make fun of him, and he is as pleasant as anyone; but be overawed by his sententious manner and his paradoxical & obscure statements, wait upon them as it were, for light to dawn, and you will never get a feeling of ease with him any more than I did for years, until I changed my course & treated him more or less chaffingly. I confess I like him very much in spite of all his peculiarities, for he is a man of genius and there's always something in that to compel anyone's sympathy.[51]

The acquaintance between Peirce and Henry James continued intermittently into the next year, Henry writing his brother that he saw

> a little of a few people, but form no intimacies. . . . Apropos of "intimacies" Charles Peirce departed a week since for Berlin—my intimacy with him my mother says "greatly" amuses you. It was no intimacy for during the last two months of his stay I saw almost nothing of him. He is a very good fellow & one must appreciate his mental ability, but he has too little social talent[,] too little art of making himself agreeable. He had however a very lonely and dreary existence here & I should think would detest Paris. I did what I could to give him society.[52]

In the letter which describes their last meeting, in July 1876, Henry commented, having apparently followed his brother's advice, that he had seen Peirce several times

> and enjoyed, by way of a change, his profound first-class intellect reflected in his ardent eyes. It will amuse you to hear that he is an *extreme* admirer of *Roderick Hudson*: a conquest which flatters me. He wrote me a few days since from Kew Observatory, Richmond, where he seems to be dwelling,—a charming berth.[53]

For his part, Peirce wrote William equally appreciatively:

> I see your brother very frequently. He is a splendid fellow. I admire him greatly and have only discovered two faults in him. One is that his digestion isn't quite that of an ostrich & the other is that he isn't as fond of turning

over questions as I am but likes to settle them and have done with them. A manly trait too, but not a philosophic one. He is looking better than when he first came & Paris is the place for him; Paris & he are adapted to one another.[54]

Into this already confused state of things came a letter to Charles from his father reporting that William James had recommended him in November to President Daniel Coit Gilman of Johns Hopkins University, founded in that year, as the best mind in the country after Chauncey Wright—who was, after all, dead.[55] Peirce was already recommended to succeed Winlock at the Harvard Observatory. Peirce immediately wrote his friend James, explaining how torn he was by this chance which could open the way for him to do that philosophic work which was all that really interested him:

> I hear from my father that you have written a beautiful letter to the President of the Baltimore University proposing me for the chair of logic and I am asked if I would accept.
> It is a question impossible to answer in my present state of information. I dont know what the conditions are.
> My place in the Coast Survey is agreeable to me. I have with great trouble learned to swing pendulums & Uncle Sam has spent a good deal of money upon teaching me. It is a very difficult business. I do not know that I could honorably disconnect myself from the Survey now. Just at present, I don't *think* I could.
> On the other hand, I feel that in a chair of Logic, I should be using my best powers, which I never shall use elsewhere. Elsewhere, in an observatory or anywhere, I shall always be a mediocrity, which doesn't disturb me in the least. In a chair of Logic, I should reach some eminence and leave some ideas which would ultimately be found very useful, I dont doubt. It is not very clear to me what I ought to do. But if I dont change my profession very soon, I never shall. On the whole, I think I will leave the question to my wife to decide as she is on the ground.[56]

Despite this diffidence, his desire to go into the academic life almost got the better of him even then. Had he not been so acutely aware of his wife's accusations of irresponsibility in his Survey work, and had his hope of repairing their marriage been weaker, if asked he would have joined Johns Hopkins in 1876 rather than three years later.

In January 1876, Superintendent Patterson wrote the letter that Zina had urgently requested from him, and its effect was to rejuvenate Peirce's sense of obligation to the Survey. He wrote Patterson that, although he had been recommended to Johns Hopkins, he would not so much as consider the position; he went on to propose grandiosely that he edit a monumental

Treatise of the Determination of the Force of Gravity in five books, which was never completed.[57] His plan for the project was pleasing both to Patterson and to his father, and it was approved before Peirce left Paris for Berlin.

In May 1876, Peirce suffered a serious nervous collapse, the principal symptom of which was temporary but complete paralysis. This collapse, taken together with his irresponsible performance, his exaggerated sensibility, and his tendency to break down under strain, indicates that Peirce had suffered an attack of conversion hysteria (also called dissociative reaction), of which a major symptom is complete paralysis.[58] The illness is not organic but psychosomatic. The victim, unable to cope, retreats into complete physical impotence. Benjamin wrote Patterson in July that Charles had been "attacked very strangely and suddenly—so as to be utterly incapable of motion. [Since that time] his health seems to be better although he has had another of his *immovable* attacks."[59] Charles described these attacks as involving "excessive sensibility & muscular contractions," also symptomatic of the condition.[60] This type of attack occurred twice in 1876, once in 1877, and once in 1879. In 1880, he put himself under treatment for possible insanity, and in later years he also suffered from fugues (blackouts), three cases of which he reported to James in 1904.[61] At the same time, he was afflicted periodically by the exquisite pain of facial neuralgia.

Peirce probably would have been susceptible to conversion hysteria, given his highly emotional and impulsive nature. His situation was drastic. He was in a strange country alone, under great pressure to live up to his brilliant reputation with his father and Patterson by convincing the leading European geodesists of his ability, an extremely difficult if not quixotic enterprise. In addition to Survey work, he was engaged in the considerable research necessary to expand crucial parts of his *Photometric Researches*. He had made a mess of his party's accounts and allowed himself to get heavily in debt with two banks, in part through extravagance and carelessness about his instruments. He was a candidate for two positions, the directorship of the Harvard Observatory and a professorship in logic at Johns Hopkins that attracted him intensely and, despite his protests to the contrary, eroded his loyalty to the Survey. As the final blow, his wife, on whom he was emotionally dependent in the extreme, left him.

Benjamin Peirce's reaction to his son's illness was to blame Zina for having deserted him in Europe and to order her to England to his side. By the middle of July, Peirce had recovered sufficiently to continue work and prepare for his return to the United States. Although the physician who attended him during his first attack blamed it on overwork, in long letters to Patterson and his father, Peirce stated that what he called his "affection of the nerves" was the result not so much of overwork as of the breakup of his marriage.[62] In giving emotional stress as the reason for his mental collapse, Peirce underlined his own awareness of his lifelong mental instability. His family, on second thought, blamed excessive drinking for his breakdown, an accusation which Peirce himself denied categorically.

At his father's insistence, Charles and Zina departed for Boston on August 8, 1876, to allow him to rest and regain his health. He left behind some unfinished research, but on the whole he was satisfied and confident of the success of his expedition. Patterson and his father were pleased and, in fact, enthusiastic. He had proved himself, and therefore the Survey, to be knowledgeable in the science of gravimetrics. He had swung the Repsold pendulum in the main European stations and thereby generated data which tied Survey pendulum experiments into the international practice in geodesy and, as well, established the basis for setting up the first American stations. Most remarkable, by demonstrating that the flexure of the pendulum stand was a source of serious error in measurement, he had attracted the interest and respect of leading European figures in the field. Patterson decided to overlook Peirce's extravagance; he concluded that his European trip had been a distinct success for the reputation of the Coast Survey, and the evidence clearly supported him.

The new year brought little relief for Peirce, whose difficulties then began in earnest with President Eliot of Harvard over the publication of the book *Photometric Researches*. In it he proposed an original use of the relative brightness of stars as a means of determining an approximate shape for the solar galaxy and the mode of distribution of stars within it, based both on the observations he had made as an assistant in the Observatory and on existing star catalogues, such as those by Ptolemy and Tycho Brahe. Peirce placed considerable importance on the publication of this, his first major entry into the front ranks of scientific research, an effort which had already been noticed favorably in England by William Kingdon Clifford.[63]

The problem of Peirce's connection with the Observatory had become complicated before the death of Director Winlock the previous year, because of the conflict between Eliot and Winlock. When Eliot first became president of Harvard, as part of his campaign to bring the various parts of the university under his control, he wanted to put the Observatory under his immediate direction and get it out of the sway of the Survey, then headed by Benjamin Peirce. Winlock successfully rebuffed this effort, wishing to remain as independent as possible from the Harvard administration. Eliot next tried to force Charles Peirce to resign by suspending his salary while he was in Europe for the balance of the year as a Coast Survey (and Observatory) representative in 1870–71.[64] This action convinced Peirce of Eliot's enmity toward him.

When Peirce accepted a position as assistant with the Coast Survey in 1872, he resigned as assistant in the Observatory, but he and Winlock agreed that he would complete his photometric researches for the sum of $1,200.[65] (Peirce was not removed from the Observatory's roster as assistant until Winlock's death in 1875.) At the time of his departure for Europe in 1875, it had become clear that the original sum would be insufficient, and an agreement was made between Peirce and Winlock which committed the Observatory to pay Peirce $500 and furnish him with an aide to assist him in undertaking several revisions and seeing the text through the press in Europe. They also discussed the likelihood of increasing the figure to $1,200. Winlock died without telling Eliot about the agreement, and Peirce did not take the trouble to clear up the matter for him. Peirce explained his inertia in a letter to Patterson, saying that he did not think Eliot would "consent to any proposition about it [the *Photometric Researches*]."[66] The ensuing six-year conflict between the two men undermined Peirce's professional life, because as James remarked, "he dished himself at Harvard by inspiring dislike in Eliot."[67] The quarrel also throws light on the characters of the two men, the life of the mind each espoused, and the dominant educational ideology of the times.

From 1870 until he died, Winlock consistently supported Peirce against Eliot, not only because of his high regard for the elder Peirce and his admiration for Charles's astronomical researches, but because he wished to retain his autonomous position within the administrative structure of the university. While this may have protected Peirce at first, it made him a controversial figure for Eliot, and with the death of Winlock while Peirce was in Europe, there ensued a two-year period during which there was no one in charge of the Observatory and, therefore, no one but Eliot with whom Peirce could deal. Instead of informing Eliot of the arrangement made between himself and Winlock, whereby he was to receive Observatory assistance in putting his *Photometric Researches* through the presses in Europe, Peirce procrastinated and made the mistake of proceeding as if the arrangement, of which Eliot knew nothing, were still in force. In doing so, he gave Eliot the opportunity he needed to refuse him further assistance. A month after Winlock's death, Peirce wrote Arthur Searle, the Observatory secretary:

> I consider the immediate publication of the photometric researches important. They are intended not merely to commemorate facts to the astronomical world, but also to inculcate ideas. If there happens to elapse a sufficient time for their due digestion before the photometric stomach receives anything else of importance, I am in hopes they may acquire a certain influence on the current research in this direction. . . .
>
> In accordance with my understanding with Professor Winlock, which your letter encourages me still to act upon, I came yesterday to Leipzig and

applied to Engelmann, the greatest publisher of such things in the world, to furnish an estimate of the cost of printing the photometric researches. His son, who is not only a professional astronomer but also has practical acquaintance with photometric work would read the proof *con amore.* I enclose an estimate. . . .

Please bring the question before the government of the observatory and telegraph me care of McCulloch London, simply "yes" which means just what I propose is agreed to or else add a few words such as "stereo" etc. to indicate how my plan is to be modified. Mr. Eliot, you say, wishes to print at once. The thing will be much better & cheaper done here and much more quickly.[68]

The relationship between Eliot and Peirce was further complicated by the fact that he had been so strongly recommended to succeed Winlock as director of the Observatory. To be sure, Peirce was ambivalent about taking the position, but when he learned that he had been summarily rejected, he became certain that it was Eliot alone who was hostile to him; he did not realize the depth of opposition to him on the part of some members of the Harvard Corporation, partly because of his reputation as an atheist and partly because of Zina's family's strongly expressed disapproval of him. What Peirce thought was enmity on the part of Eliot was more likely the effect of the suspicions he had formed of Peirce's "unsafe" character over the years since Peirce was his student at the Lawrence Scientific School. These suspicions were transformed to positive dislike and distrust during the course of the quarrels over publication of the *Photometric Researches.*

Peirce, for his part, had marked contempt for Eliot, much of it reflecting the uncomplimentary views his father had of Eliot's intellectual qualities. Others close to Peirce, such as William James, remarked that Eliot had been named president despite "his great personal defects, tactlessness, meddlesomeness, and disposition to cherish petty grudges. . . . "[69] As James had commented in 1864, the criterion for choosing a new member of the Harvard faculty was above all that the nominee be "safe," that he be orthodox in his views. Although Charles Eliot was the first noncleric president of Harvard, his views were unorthodox only to the extent of accepting an orthodox social Darwinism. A Socratic mind such as Peirce's, which delighted in putting every idea to the test and in following an argument irrespective of where it led, was bound to raise Eliot's suspicions. In his eulogy of Benjamin Peirce, Eliot remembered the precise moment when he had closed his mind to the play of original thought:

One day in my senior year, when Professor Peirce had already acquired the habit of giving me the highest possible marks on all my notes of his lectures and on every other exercise for which marks could be given, to the great concern of my competitor for the first place in the class . . . —I graduated second—I ventured to say that what he had just been saying to us about functions and infinitesimal variables seemed to me to be theories or imaginations rather than facts or realities. Professor Peirce looked at me gravely, and remarked gently, "Eliot, your trouble is that your mind has a skeptical turn. Be on your guard against that tendency or it will hurt your career." That was new light to me; for I had never thought at all about my own turns of mind. The diagnosis was correct.[70]

That Charles's father should have been the one unwittingly—and quite contrary to his sarcastic intention—to convince Eliot that skepticism was a moral weakness is a surpassing irony. In a period when a Protestant apologist such as James McCosh was president of Princeton University, and close copies of him and of Eliot presided at almost all American colleges; when the study of religion, logic, ethics, history, science, and philosophy was carefully limited to "safe" courses and instructors, the "spinous" Peirce would indeed have made an impossible colleague for the likes of Eliot. In this he was the victim of his times, as were Chauncey Wright, John Fiske, Francis Abbot, and others. Only William James's remarkable personality can explain his presence as a professor at Harvard, and surely even that delightful character must have been aided substantially by his medical studies in Germany. In sum, in addition to his defects of character, which President Eliot considered grave indeed, it was Peirce's unsentimental and unyielding quest for truth, regardless of conventional sanctities, which so disturbed him.

The squabble over the publication of the *Photometric Researches* undoubtedly changed Eliot's suspicions of Peirce to outraged dislike. In January 1877, Edward C. Pickering, already an assistant in the Observatory and a man with whom Peirce had been friendly for at least ten years, was appointed director of the Observatory. Peirce immediately called to see him, hoping to settle the difficulties over pay and publication. Reporting the meeting to Eliot, Pickering spoke very highly of Peirce's work. He stated that had Winlock lived, he probably would have accepted Peirce's offer to finish the work for an additional $1,200, but Pickering himself did not see how it could be done in view of the meager financial resources of the Observatory.[71] Pickering then wrote to Peirce offering some money from the Observatory funds and suggesting that he would try to obtain further money from the Rumford Committee. In reply, Peirce made it offensively clear that he felt he was being defrauded of what was his due. Presumably, Peirce's misplaced suspicions derived not so much from the sense of a loss of money as from his conclusion that his professional honor was under an attack instigated by Eliot. Pickering then suggested that the *Researches* be taken off Peirce's hands. Peirce appealed to Eliot, saying, "The printing of my Photometric Researches has been for a long time stopped in consequences of my being unable to induce Prof. Pickering to make any equitable arrangement for their continuance," an accusation which does not fit the facts.[72] Eliot replied curtly that under the circumstances "it seems quite clear that you should give us no more time and labor of any description."[73]

Meanwhile, at Eliot's request, Pickering had made an exhaustive examination of the letter-books of the Observatory to determine whether Peirce had in fact any claim upon Harvard. From the search it was obvious that the relations between Peirce and Winlock had often been informal, but that Peirce did have reason to expect at least $500 and an aide to help complete the book.[74]

Peirce's reply to Eliot's letter was a masterpiece of injured dignity, in which he said that Pickering had humiliated him, something which he could never forgive. He added grandly:

> There is a quality of labour in every trade, which cannot be hired, which is never adequately paid, which often goes wholly unpaid, because the workman will not chaffer about it; and my photometrical work is of this sort. Of course a man is a sort of fool to do such work; but then universities encourage it.[75]

Eliot responded shrewdly that if such qualities were beyond hire, he saw no reason for Harvard to extend itself simply to increase Peirce's reputation. In the midst of this bickering, Pickering wrote to Peirce requesting his permission, as a representative of the Coast Survey, to take down and store a small observatory on the college grounds which had been erected some years before by the Survey but never used. Peirce immediately assumed that the letter represented a further slight and told Pickering that he was writing Eliot "to know the intention of the College more clearly than I learn it from your note."[76] Eliot replied with exaggerated courtesy that Pickering had no hidden motives in his request and concluded by chastising Peirce for his groundless irritation with Pickering.[77] This petty, crucial controversy dragged on until the summer of 1878, when the *Photometric Researches* were finally printed, by Engelmann in the form demanded by Peirce (but without further payment to him), as Volume IX of the *Annals* of the Harvard Observatory. The final set-to concerned the preface that Peirce had written for the volume, to which Eliot objected because it gave no credit whatever to Winlock, who had supported the work for so long, or to Harvard, which had paid for it, but gave effusive praise to the Coast Survey, which had little to do with the work. He wrote to Eliot,

I send you a preface to my Photometric Researches. In this, I can consent to no essential change.

I never was an assistant in the Observatory. My name was erroneously inserted as such in one catalogue, but I called your attention to the error and it was not repeated. [In fact, he was assistant from 1869 to 1873 and was carried on the roster in error only from that time until December 1875.]

The whole of this research is mine, its idea, plan, execution, everything. No credit is due Prof. Winlock in the matter except as director of the observatory for which it was executed. It is true, I was under personal obligation to him, but I will express my sense of these in my own manner in my own time [which Peirce never did].[78]

It would have been too much to expect President Eliot to have any attitude other than dislike and distrust for Peirce after such a performance. By 1878, he also knew about Zina's separation from him and the reasons for it as expressed by the Fay family, which placed Peirce in a bad light. Peirce obviously gave little weight to the fact that Eliot was one of the most powerful men in American higher education. Thereafter, any request to Eliot for information about Peirce in connection with university employment was bound to kindle Eliot's moral outrage.

In October 1876, Peirce had moved to New York to make preparations for the initial United States pendulum station, to be set up at the Stevens Institute in Hoboken, New Jersey. Stevens had excellent laboratory facilities and a faculty in physics of high caliber, including Lewis M. Rutherfurd, who had developed diffraction gratings for the measurement of light, which Peirce hoped to use in his own experiments. Zina did not accompany her husband, and they were never together again, though Charles continued for some time to hope for a reconciliation. He wrote her from New York the following spring:

My darling little girl! [She was forty years old and more feminist than ever.] If you were to decide to come on here, no doubt Berts [the youngest brother, Herbert] would pack up my things & I dare say you would enjoy coming. We would have a bed hired from a furniture place or have that one from Washington. As you didn't answer my telegram I wanted to return tonight; but they persuaded me not to do so. I have been doing a lot of good work; have written one long article ["The Fixation of Belief"] for the *Popular Science Monthly* and begun another ["How to Make Our Ideas Clear"]. That is the reason I allowed myself to be persuaded to stay, though I am downright homesick for the sight of my own heart's darling, my sweet and precious little wife . . . let me know how you are doing and whether you will come here or want me to return.[79]

Considered in the light of the times, Zina's decision to separate permanently from her husband was unusually modern in its feminism and quite out of keeping with her rigidly churchy New England background. No doubt she was aware of the price her drastic action would demand, and no doubt her fierce morality would require that she pay it. She was forty years old and had been married to Charles for fifteen years. The fact that she left her husband could be construed legally only as desertion, so that, with no money of her own, she faced a life of poverty and exile from her own world and, since principle forbade her from divorcing him, was unable to remarry. More than her suspicions of her husband's infidelity and her own experience of his abuse, irresponsibility, and extravagance, the main reason for Zina's action was probably her refusal to be complicit any longer in what she saw as his reckless descent into personal disaster. Knowing intimately as she did the terrible cost to him of the pain of neuralgia and his dangerous dependence on drugs to abate it, such a fateful step must have appeared to be her only choice. At the same time, Zina was well aware of the depth of his dependence on her, and, as she explained to Patterson, she must have hoped her leaving him in Europe the year before would be enough to shock him into behaving as she thought he must to save himself. He did not, and she separated from him permanently.

Sarah wrote Charles's brother Jem about her confusion and misery over this part of her son's life:

> It is very sad to me to think of those two wrecked lives & all the fault & sorrow there must be somewhere. Charley seemed so loving to me & was so pleasant & thoughtful. I could not feel that all the wrong was with him. Ah well. . . . Life is full of sorrow & if we could not have the solace of loving hearts how could we sustain its burden.[80]

As for Zina, she turned even more passionately to the emancipation of American womanhood and wrote in the preface of her book *New York: A Symphonic Study* that her motive in writing was to

> . . . rescue my own sex from profanation and ruin. . . .
>
> For the cause of Inviolate Womanhood is the cause of the Republican Institutions. Profaned and ruined womanhood presupposes profaning and sensual manhood, and profaning and sensual manhood in every age and clime of the world has meant autocratic government—the many, in some form, by some means, ruled by the few.[81]

Zina stayed on at the Arrow Street house in Cambridge for some months, then moved to New York and started the first of a series of boarding houses there and in Chicago, from which she gained most of her income. Charles's sister Helen and his brother Herbert visited her on occasion in New York. Magazine articles continued to bring her some money for a time. She edited her sister Amy's letters from Germany under the title *Music Study in Germany*, which went through several editions.[82] More and more, her life became lonely and poor. Although she suffered from heart trouble and re-current attacks of severe depression, she continued to involve herself in women's issues and worked obsessively on her novel, *New York*, reworking it again and again until, forty years later, in 1918, it was finally published. She died five years later.

In 1878, Charles published what appeared to be a poignant, public, but cryptic elegy for the marriage in "How to Make Our Ideas Clear":

> Many a man has cherished for years as his hobby some vague shadow of an idea, too meaningless to be positively false; he has, nevertheless, passionately loved it, has made it his companion by day and by night, and has given to it his strength and his life, leaving all other occupations for its sake, and in short has lived with it and for it, until it has become, as it were, flesh of his flesh and bone of his bone; and then he has waked up some bright morning to find it gone, clean vanished away like the beautiful Me-lusina of the fable, and the essence of his life gone with it. I myself have known such a man; and who can tell how many histories of circle-squarers, metaphysicians, astrologers, and what not, may not be told in the old German [French] story?[83]

The late medieval tale, which encourages symbolic and psychoanalytic interpretations, tells how Melusina, resident spirit of the noble house of Lusignan, near Poitiers, and eldest daughter of the fairy Pressine, imprisoned her father in a mountain in Northumberland for wrongs he had done to her mother. In punishment she was condemned to change every Saturday into a woman-serpent, a snake from the hips down. She could save herself from this punishment and gain a soul only if she could find a husband who would vow never to see her on Saturdays. She found her love in Raymond, nephew of the count of Poitiers, whom she made famous and wealthy by her machi-nations, building the castle of Lusignan and other family fortresses. The pair had six sons, all of them monsters and each one hideously different. Of course, Raymond was unable to resist his curiosity and, peeking through the keyhole, he saw her sinuously taking her Saturday bath of purification, whereupon she became a frightful dragon and flew away around the battle-ments, making a terrible noise.[84] Whatever secret of Zina's Charles found out, it seems certain that he intended the angry metaphor, and that Zina well knew the tale.

On the other hand, Peirce's gravimetric work for the Survey seemed to be progressing successfully and to the great satisfaction of Patterson and his father. By February 1877 his accounts had been settled, and the next month he began pendulum experiments at the Stevens Institute, though not without an angry controversy with some of its faculty.[85] There, in addition to his gravimetric experiments, Peirce began to develop what he termed a "spectrum metre" (a spectrometer), using a diffraction grating developed by the physicist Lewis M. Rutherfurd of the Stevens Institute, with which he intended to determine, more exactly than was possible with existing instruments, an exact standard for the meter by using the wavelength of sodium light.[86] In spite of his apparent satisfaction with his Coast Survey position, Peirce threatened in June 1877 to quit it. This threat drove Patterson to write Peirce's father a hurt and angry letter:

> That boy Charley of yours "worritted" me much and I want you to—well—scold him [Peirce was then 37]. Enclosed is a note received from him two days since which you notice is marked "*confidential.*" With 3 or 4 years of preparatory work on the Pendulum and its system not yet perfected, what *shall* I do if he quits! He is getting well through the "experimental age" with much greater than ordinary success and all will be lost if he leaves. At his suggestion, under the impression he was perseverant, I have arranged with Rutherford [*sic*] to conduct the necessary experiments to build up a "spectral metre" for a wave length, expecting Charley to be the chief of that party and adjunct in the work.
>
>   I cannot reconcile myself to the thought of his going for I lean on him greatly and yet I can fully appreciate and commend the feeling & sense of duty to himself to endeavor to better his position pecuniarily—If he abandons science just as he has opened the door of its temple! I wish the C. S. were rich enough to outbid the "adversary." What does he mean? Possibly he has not written you & may not wish a discussion until he tells more. I have written him earnestly but, of course, think first it my duty to further his interests in whatever direction he may think they lie at whatever loss or inconvenience it may be to me. I trust sincerely he is not chasing a temporary & false light.[87]

Peirce was considering the likelihood of an offer by Johns Hopkins to become a member of its faculty, the position for which his friend James had recommended him six months before. But he was easily persuaded by a letter from Patterson, to whom he wrote on June 25, "I had quite determined in my mind that if I received such a letter from you as you have written that I would think nothing like abandoning the Survey to which I am equally bound by honorable obligation and my own best interests."[88]

Nevertheless, his treatment by the Survey continued to rankle him.

Even greater than his conviction that his salary was less than his value as a scientist deserved was his disgust at the haphazard manner in which he and his salary were treated. A month after he had agreed to stay on with the Survey, he wrote Patterson:

> I myself am far from well and since the cause still subsists and must continue until Monday at least, I fear that I shall be seriously ill. The cause is that I haven't the money to buy myself a meal, so that I have had to subsist for several days off casual crackers and cheese which I have picked up at the Century [Club]. . . .
> I desire to hold to the Survey, but I can't starve.[89]

A letter written to William James about two months earlier gives a very different picture of his style of life:

> I am in process of moving & was forced to come here [to the Brevoort House] for the night. Imagine my disgust at seeing in the Herald this morning that Prof. C. S. Peirce of Harvard College is sojourning at the Brevoort. Particularly as I am rather ashamed of my partiality for the Brevoort. But I have always come here for many years; I am known to every waiter etc. & find myself at home. It is frequented by a class of people very comme il faut but not in my line. I insensibly put on a sort of swagger here which I hope I have nowhere else, & which is designed to say "You are a very good fellow in your way; who you are I don't know & I don't care, but I[,] you know[,] am Mr. Peirce distinguished for my varied scientific acquirements but above all for my extreme modesty in which respect I challenge the world." I noticd that if one goes into the niceties, scarcely any one is totally without swagger & in those few the dryness is disagreeable. Required an essay on good taste [in] swaggering.[90]

The juxtaposition of these two letters illustrates something about Peirce which was true: he was extravagant and vain, and he could not afford extravagance on his salary, with the result expressed in the first of the two letters.

In September, Peirce wrote to Patterson that he should go to a meeting of the International Geodetic Association at Stuttgart to read some scientific papers, particularly the one containing his controversial claim that the flexure of the pendulum stand substantially decreased the accuracy of pendulum measurements. There was a nice point of protocol involved, since the association was then debating whether or not to invite him. Peirce maintained that he should go in any case and thereby sidestep the problem with a *fait accompli*. Patterson decided to send him, and he left for Europe in September 1877.[91]

It was on this trip that Peirce finished the second in the series of

The elegant Hotel Brevoort, on the northeast corner of Fifth Avenue and Eighth Street, New York City, in 1904. Along with the Century Club, it was one of Peirce's favorite haunts. Photograph by Byron, courtesy of the Museum of the City of New York.

articles published the next year in the *Popular Science Monthly* ("How to Make Our Ideas Clear") and completed the translation into French of the first ("The Fixation of Belief"). Peirce described the trip in these words:

> There were only four first-cabin passengers beside myself, two ladies travelling separately alone and two gentlemen travelling separately, equally unprotected. They found themselves very congenial and paired off. This left me the smoking room entirely to myself; and I occupied myself by writing an article in which I enunciated a logical maxim.[92]

He also amused himself by writing a long mock official letter to Patterson in which he invented bizarre abuses of foghorn procedures by the French naval authorities.[93]

The two essays finished on this trip and the four others ("The Doctrine of Chances," "The Probability of Induction," "The Order of Nature," and "Deduction, Induction, and Hypothesis"), all of which were published in

Official Coast Survey photograph of Charles S. Peirce, ca. 1875.

1877 and 1878 under the general rubric "Illustrations of the Logic of Science" in the *Popular Science Monthly*, were expressions of Peirce's intimate experience of doing exact experimental science over the past decade. He had begun the project of explaining how science proceeds with his "Logic of 1873." The "Illustrations" were the first formal expression of the scientific method as the logic of science. Not only that, they constituted the first thoroughgoing and convincing attack on the deductive foundationalism of Cartesian doubt, and on traditional metaphysics generally—"The demonstrations of the metaphysicians are all moonshine." At the same time, Peirce offered the alternative and self-consciously fallible starting point of accepting the world as we experience it and going on from there step-by-testing-step. This is not to say that other philosophers and scientists had not thought and written about the method of science, because they had, beginning with the Greeks. But Peirce put that method in its modern form with such an elegant fit that the "Illustrations," though revolutionary, appear to us now merely the common-sense of it. To read Popper or Carl Hempel on the logic of science after reading the "Illustrations" shows how little has been added to the model first proposed by Peirce over a century ago, and may also show that some elements, particularly the essentiality of hypothetical inference, have been removed with damaging effect to our understanding of science.

The physicist Victor F. Lenzen, who had been a student of Josiah Royce, summarized a typical early example of the interaction between Peirce's scientific method and logic in his 1870 paper "On the Theory of Errors of Observation," itself a pioneering topic:[94]

> all our knowledge is derived from induction, and its analogue, hypothesis. Peirce states that the general nature of induction is everywhere the same and is completely typified in the following example. From a bag of black and white beans I take out a handful, and I assume that the black and white are nearly in the same ratio throughout the bag. If the experimenter is in error in this conclusion, it is an error which a repetition of the same process must tend to rectify. It is, therefore, a valid inference. But it clearly teaches nothing in reference to the color of any particular bean. Only the approximate general ratio can be inferred and this is represented by the probability for black or white beans. Given a large number of bags in each of which we know the relative number of black beans, then if the black beans have a value and the white beans none, the man who knew the relative number of black beans in every bag would act as though the bean he would draw from the bag which contained the larger proportion of black ones were known to be black, and as though the bean he would draw from the other would be certainly white. For knowledge derives its practical importance from its influence on our conduct.[95]

The last sentence is a summary of the pragmatic maxim which Peirce enunciated at much greater length eight years later in "How to Make Our Ideas Clear." The example illustrates clearly that, in formulations before 1900, the practical importance of the influence of knowledge on conduct has no larger ethical dimension. The scientist, as portrayed by the maxim, has no interest in any effects other than those within the limited universe of experiments dealing with the physical world. As it is with modern science, ethical consequences beyond that limited field are considered outside the use of the maxim. Peirce, at this point of his philosophical development, saw no reason to import ethics into inquiry beyond what was needed to give validity to methodological issues. Ethics was limited to implications drawn from the ideal of truth as embodied in the community of inquirers, and the individual partook in knowledge only as a member of it. Outside the sacred circle, since worthless there, the individual was not bound by ethical considerations. As he had already explained the position in 1868 in "Some Consequences of Four Incapacities":

> The individual man, since his separate existence is manifested only by ignorance and error, so far as he is anything apart from his fellows, and from what he and they are to be, is only a negation. This is man,

> proud man,
> Most ignorant of what he's most assured,
> His glassy essence.[96]

This moral blindness cost Peirce dearly. It was twenty years before he proposed the doctrine that logic, and therefore pragmatism, depended on ethics in the larger sense. "Illustrations of the Logic of Science, Second Paper—How to Make Our Ideas Clear" appeared in January 1878. The year before, just before the appearance of "The Fixation of Belief" in November, Edward Livingstone Youmans, editor of the *Popular Science Monthly*, had written his sister from London: "Charles Peirce isn't read much on this side. [W. K.] Clifford, however, says he is the greatest living logician, and the second man since Aristotle who has added to the subject something material, the other man being George Boole, author of the Laws of Thought."[97]

Surprisingly, not only did none of the papers contain his coinage *pragmatism*, but none of them referred to his "new list of categories," that is, to the three original elements of his architectonic from which the rest of his system was drawn, distinction by distinction, or to semeiotic, the theory of signs. The reason may have been that Peirce was exhilarated at the time by the hard power of science and by the idea that he had embodied that force in this conception of its logic as expressed in his pragmatic test for meaning, in his analysis of probability, and in the logical categories of hypothesis, deduction, and induction. His positivist and apparently anti-metaphysical identification of himself with the irresistible juggernaut of scientific inquiry, together with the praise he had received from European scientists and logicians, increased his arrogance. Important for his later influence in philosophy, the papers also lack, probably for the same reason, the expression of what was already his distinctively realist perspective on science. Since the "Illustrations" were his best-known writings, they were taken quite plausibly by the members of the "Vienna Circle" and their logical positivist and neopositivist kindred as an important predecessor of their own anti-metaphysical and nominalistic doctrines and their operationalist view of meaning.

The meeting in Berlin in 1877 of the International Geodetic Association was the personal triumph of Peirce's scientific career, and he staged an entry into the affair which gratified him hugely. He wrote to Patterson:

> I waited over one day [at Ostend] to repose & look about and took the train at 11 PM and came right through here [Brussels] getting here [to Stuttgart] this afternoon in time to be late for dinner. Going down, I saw a number of my old friends at one table which was full. I sat down quietly to another, not wishing to interrupt dinner with explanations. However, [The-

odor von] Oppolzer soon spied me out & came over & spoke to me & then the others came & were much surprised at my sudden appearance.[98]

Two days later the crowning event of Peirce's geodesic career occurred when, as he wrote to Patterson:

after the preliminary business the president read your letter[.] The entire company rose and the president welcomed me to the association, to which I responded thanking him in my own name & that of the Coast Survey. After the usual reports from different countries had been read, . . . the pendulum business was at once taken up though out of turn. Professor Plantamour as chairman of the special Committee on that subject opened & described the experiments [concerning the flexure of the pendulum stand] which he had been led to make in consequence of my researches. . . . Everyone speaks of my work as most important and as making an epoch in pendulum work.[99]

Patterson and his father were, of course, immensely pleased, and he was heartily recommended for an increase in salary. Peirce returned home in November, and a month later suffered another breakdown brought on by overwork, the third in two years, though he seemed recovered by January 1878.[100]

Late in 1877, Benjamin Peirce had written to President Gilman of the newly founded Johns Hopkins University to recommend Charles as head of the department of physics, not long after Henry Augustus Rowland's appointment to the same department. Charles and Julius Hilgard, among others, were invited to meet Gilman and Rowland in early January 1878. Charles wrote Gilman a long letter on January 13, in which he began by commenting patronizingly on Rowland's standing as a physicist and then went on to praise, quite confusingly and grandiosely, his own qualifications as a potential master of any science:

In regard to my own *personlichen Wenigkeit,* I understand that my father has suggested my name for the place of general professor of physics. But supposing it were determined to call me to the University, (a call which would be very agreeable to me) I think it would be more advantageous to make use of me, first, to fill the precise want of the physical department and, second, to utilize my logical studies. . . . [Peirce then described the needs of the department and his proposed methods of instruction.]

But as for me[,] I am a logician. The data for the generalizations of logic are the special methods of the different sciences. To penetrate these methods the logician has to study various sciences rather profoundly. In that way, I have learned nearly the whole trade of the physicist though there are a good many instruments relating to electricity particularly with which I am not practically familiar. However, being a delicate manipulator in other branches of physics and in chemistry, I should not fear taking hold of anything, especially as I have seen most of the instruments, the quadrant electrometer[,] etc[.,] worked & know the points to be attended to. Thus though I am a logician, I consider it necessary to have a laboratory.

In logic, I am the exponent of a particular tendency, that of physical science. I make the pretension to being the most thoroughgoing and fundamental representative of that element who has yet appeared. I believe that my system of logic (which is a philosophical method to which mathematical algebra only affords aid in a particular part of it) must stand, or else the whole spirit of the physical sciences must be revolutionized. If this is to happen, it cannot be brought about in any way so quickly as by the philosophical formularization of it and the carrying of it to its furthest logical consequences. If on the other hand it is to abide, its general statement will be of consequence for mankind. I have measured my powers against those of other men; I know what they are. It is my part to announce with modest confidence what I can do. My system has been sketched out but not so that its bearings can be appreciated. If the world thinks it worth developing, they have only to give me the means of doing it. But if not, I shall follow another path, with perfect contentment.

It would be a great pleasure to me to enter your society of scholars in Baltimore, the idea of which I approve from the bottom of my heart. You are the only real university in America.

But there are two things I ought to say by way of premonition. The first is that I could not give up the direction of the pendulum operations of the Coast Survey, which require my guidance though they will not in the future occupy much of my time. The second is a very painful personal matter upon which I dislike to speak at all, & and of which I will say the least possible. It is that I have been for a number of years in disagreement with my wife, not having lived with her for a long time, & not having seen her for over a year; and the reasons for this on the one side and on the other will, I hope, never be made known. It is however certain that we shall never live together again. This is a fact to which you will naturally give a weight, should you seriously consider inviting me to Baltimore.[101]

On March 12, after receiving a definite offer of a lectureship from Gilman, Peirce replied with obvious disappointment that it was not a professorship. "On the whole, I feel bound to accept your suggestion that I should retain my place in the Coast Survey, and to give the University what might be reckoned as half-service as Professor of Logic, and I beg that you will bring the matter before the authorities."[102]

Two days after sending off this letter, Peirce received one from George Bruce Halsted, a graduate student at Hopkins with whom he was acquainted, which described Peirce's apparent reputation there. Halsted had proposed to spend some time on Peirce's work in a course he was to give,

> But the opinion was expressed here to me that I had better not do it and that you had exhibited in your writings a tendency to undervalue everybody and everything you mentioned. Besides this I was particularly discouraged by Prof. [James Joseph] Sylvester's adding that your articles in the Popular Science Monthly were pretentious without being at all profound and that anybody could have written them. For my part[,] I had enjoyed your articles exceedingly and could find no fault with them except, as I have already mentioned, obscurity in places.[103]

Peirce wrote immediately to Sylvester, his father's old mathematical colleague and a regular visitor to the home of his youth:

> I was surprized to learn from the enclosed letter that you are acting against my being invited to the Johns Hopkins University. I thought you had given me to understand that you would be friendly to me in this matter.
> In regard to your opinion, in itself, I have nothing to say. I am satisfied with the reception which my writings met with in the logical world, and the opinion of outsiders does not greatly concern me. I cannot say that young Mr. Halsted appears to me remarkably distinguished for *savoir-vivre*. He is in no way entitled to address personal comments to me. Unless you indicated to him your willingness to have your observations repeated to me, his action would seem to have been somewhat indiscreet.[104]

These letters marked the beginning of a turbulent relationship between Peirce and Sylvester during their stay at Hopkins. Peirce resented Sylvester's criticisms deeply and personally, and three years later this resentment came out into the open in a nasty dispute.

A week after his letter to Sylvester, in the wake of Sylvester's attack and in response to a letter from Gilman that effectively retracted the offer of a part-time lectureship, Peirce wrote Gilman, "I have no desire to have my name pressed upon your trustees at a moment when they have resolved that it is inexpedient to make further appointments."[105]

During the winter months of 1877 and the spring of 1878, Peirce continued in Hoboken his pendulum experiments and his experiments with the spectrometer of his design, by which he proposed to use a wavelength of light to greatly increase the accuracy of measuring the length of the meter. By June, he was preparing plans to occupy stations in the Rocky Mountains, but a shortage of Survey funds forced him to abandon this idea. During the summer he went to Cambridge, whence he hoped to initiate experiments in the White Mountains of New Hampshire and nearby Mt. Washington. But his mother wrote:

> Charley lingers here still—having been disappointed in his White Mountain plan he seems at a loss where to pitch his tent for work, & indeed seems to have abandoned the Pendulum operations for the present. Meantime Madame P[ourtalai[is at Intervale [in the White Mountains]— & sends him occasional missives of which he speaks with perfect freedom. . . . [106]

Peirce's indecision reflected the conflict between his strong desire to leave the Survey for a position with Johns Hopkins and his feelings of obligation to the Survey, but his lingering in Cambridge had mostly to do with Juliette, the mysterious Madame Pourtalai, who, after a public love affair of five years, became his wife. To the great misfortune of them both, the fact that Charles was still married to Zina until two days before his marriage to Juliette was never forgotten in academic or society circles. Peirce returned to New York in August, where the pressures for leaving the Survey became more evident. Patterson objected to the many books Peirce was buying at Survey expense, many of which had no connection with Survey matters. Peirce commented sarcastically: "I had perhaps supposed myself higher in your esteem than I really was, exaggerating doubtless the slight importance of my scientific work. . . . I owe you my thanks for the condescending manner in which you have shown the error of my interpretation."[107]

Peirce was increasingly dissatisfied with his salary and with the failure of the Survey to provide him and his party with what he considered necessary funds for the support of his field operations. The September before he had made a list of the eight Survey assistants and their salaries. He was at the bottom, and none of the others had produced anything approaching the kind of results or scientific reputation that he had achieved. But Peirce adjusted his plans for pendulum work for the coming year to an occupation of the region of the Alleghenies within easy reach of Washington—and of Johns Hopkins. He also made a request for another trip to Europe, which was put off till the following year. Patterson wrote Benjamin Peirce asking him to go to New York to "confer" with his son and attempt to improve his behavior and spirits.[108] In December, Peirce went to Allegheny City to examine the area for sites, but before he could accomplish his mission, he came down with pneumonia, frightening both Patterson and his father, and was sent home to spend Christmas in Cambridge with his family.[109]

In January 1879, Benjamin Peirce, dismayed that his brilliant son Charles, almost forty years old, still received a salary of but $2,870, wrote a long letter to Superintendent Patterson insisting that his son's scientific achievements deserved a higher reward. Patterson replied that he had already attempted to have Charles's salary raised, but to no avail because of the political situation in the Treasury Department.[110] Not satisfied with this answer, Charles Peirce himself put in a request for an increase in salary, supported by four of the more eminent astronomers and physicists of the time.[111] The enclosures from Alfred M. Mayer, professor of physics at Stevens Institute of Technology; Wolcott Gibbs, Rumford Professor at Harvard University; Ogden Rood, professor of physics at Columbia College; and Benjamin Peirce show their high opinion of Peirce's work. Gibbs wrote:

> In fact I do not hesitate to say that both the spectroscope and spectrometer are the most perfect instruments of the kind in existence and I have been both delighted and *instructed* by a critical examination of the experiments introduced in their construction.[112]

Rood wrote:

> It would be very difficult to find another scientist having similar qualifications with Mr[.] Peirce either in the special education required, or in natural ability—I certainly know of no one in this country who would be at all qualified to take the position which he now holds on your survey.[113]

And Benjamin Peirce wrote, commending his son even more highly:

> It is a most remarkable achievement to have thus determined the length of the meter from the wavelength of light, which is the shortest length which has ever been measured; and the only sure determination of the meter, by which it could be recovered if it were lost to science. It will certainly secure for the Survey the applause of all scientific men.
>
> When combined with Mr. Peirce's admirable measures of the pendulum, which have justly been regarded by the savans of Europe as adding a new era to this most difficult branch of observation. It places him among the great masters of astronomical and geodetic research—and it would be most unfortunate if such grand strides in science were not suitably acknowledged.[114]

In June, Peirce received yet a third offer from Johns Hopkins, to become lecturer in logic during the academic year 1879–80. He wrote to Patterson:

> I have received a proposition from the Johns Hopkins people to deliver some lectures there and superintend the introduction in logic. As they expressly say that they do not desire to interfere with my duties to the Coast Survey, I think I shall accept, as I believe you have already told me you had no objection to such an arrangement. They won't pay much [$1,500] but it will be something.[115]

In his acceptance to Gilman on June 6, Peirce said:

> My views respecting my giving instruction in Logic in the Johns Hopkins University remain substantially as last year. I should require in the first place to have sole charge of that branch, and in the second that there should be an intention of ultimately making a full professorship for it. . . .
>
> I think you would do better not to press me to come to a definite agreement as to the amount of time I should give to the matter. You know my devotion to Logic. . . . But if I were to make a contract about it, I should consider much more what it was fitting that I should promise for so small a sum as $1500, than how much I was willing to do.
>
> In one respect I am in a different position from last year & that is that I now have such engagements as will require me to be in Europe during the early autumn of this year so that I could not be in Baltimore at the beginning of the term. I should like to take occasion of my being abroad to purchase some books upon logic for Library.
>
> Should you desire to see me, I shall be in New York next week, where the Brevoort and the Century Club are my headquarters. . . . [116]

The Hotel Brevoort was an expensive, continental-style hotel on Fifth Avenue at Washington Square which catered to the wealthy, titled, and socially important. Peirce was well known to the hotel staff, and he probably met Juliette Pourtalai there at a great ball in 1876.[117] Their indiscreet affair may very well have begun at the Brevoort. The Century Club was the gathering place for the most interesting and important men of the time. Its membership included bankers, scientists, writers, publishers, explorers, entrepreneurs, promoters, politicians, poets, inventors, eccentrics, and mountebanks. Peirce met there a number of men with whom he later became involved in speculative schemes for quick wealth. The most influential with Peirce was the maverick stock speculator and poet Edmund Clarence Stedman. Later, in the 1890s, when these ventures and national economic collapse bankrupted Peirce and left him sunk in poverty, the Century Club became a major source of the food he cadged on which to live. Because his brilliant and amusing company was prized by his fellow members, he remained welcome there until his expulsion in about 1898.

On second thought, when he considered the depth of his desire to make a good impression on President Gilman, Peirce decided to change plans and go immediately to the Alleghenies, then to Europe the following summer, so that he would not be absent from his first term at Johns Hopkins. He did not give this reason for his change in plans to Patterson.[118]

In July, Superintendent Patterson tried again to raise Peirce's salary. He sent a letter of recommendation, in which he included the letters of support from scientists earlier sent him by Peirce, to Secretary of the Treasury John Sherman. In it he said, no doubt in close consultation with his chief, Benjamin:

> Mr. Peirce is forty years of age, has been employed on the Survey for eighteen years, and on account of his exceptional ability for special investigations, was during eleven years service rapidly advanced to his present pay in 1873. Since that date Mr. Peirce has made extraordinary advances in Pendulum observations of a very original character, exciting the deepest interest in this important scientific subject on the part of all physicists, both in this country and abroad, and leading to a complete revision of all past observations at the main initial points for Pendulum observations in Europe. In fact Mr. Peirce is the first person in this country who has with any success attacked this problem, the subject having remained in abeyance for many years, awaiting a truly scientific observer. Mr. Peirce has also succeeded in comparing the accepted standard unit of length (the meter) with a permanent (so far as now known) length in nature, a wave length of light, a task hitherto never attempted on account of the inherent difficulties of the case, over which after many discouragements and failures he has at last triumphed. These results of Mr. Peirce's work have greatly advanced the science of Geodesy, the scientific reputation of the Survey, and therefore that of the country.
>
> The enclosed extracts from letters of eminent American Scientists offer the best evidence of the value of Mr. Peirce's work.[119]

A month later, Patterson wrote Peirce that his salary would not be raised by the secretary of the treasury and that he assumed Peirce would continue to carry out his duties to the best of his ability as he had in the past. But he added:

> If, however, at any time you deem that your interests can be advanced by any other engagements or employment, I should certainly do anything in my power to advance them, although the loss to the Survey might not be supplied in reference to the problems you now, or might hereafter have in hand.[120]

Peirce answered noncommittally, "I desire to thank you very warmly for the manner in which you laid my case before the Secretary. I shall endeavor to do my duty as long as I remain on the Survey."[121]

The way was now open for Peirce to leave the Survey, and if, as he had been assured, President Gilman of Johns Hopkins intended to turn the lectureship into a permanent professorship, his great hope would be realized. In September, Peirce moved to Baltimore; for the sake of convenience, he moved the pendulum station from Ebensburgh in the Alleghenies to York, Pennsylvania, less than an hour by train from Baltimore.

The city of Baltimore was, by 1880, a polyglot mixture of European immigrants and African-Americans numbering about 400,000. Originally populated by English, Scots, Irish, German, and French and predominantly Catholic, after the Civil War it was inundated with African-Americans, Italians, Poles, Lithuanians, Russians, and other ethnic groups. It was a major seaport and the eastern terminus of the Baltimore and Ohio Railroad, with a large manufacturing capacity employing a largely immigrant workforce. During the Civil War, the city was occupied by Union troops, and its older population were still fiercely unreconstructed Southerners. The society ladies wore dull black, and many never wore colors as long as they lived. During the occupation they had been the "Monument Street Girls" who secretly distributed copies of the Maryland anthem, "Maryland, My Maryland," with its opening line, "The despots' heel is on thy shore, Maryland." After the war, the city produced a small group of wealthy men of deeply Southern loyalties and of narrow and largely Methodist and Presbyterian convictions, and it was they who raised the money for a university that would bring honor to them and to Baltimore.

The Johns Hopkins University, which opened in 1876 as an elite institution, was intended to match European, especially German, standards of scholarship in graduate and professional education. Gilman, appointed president the previous year, recruited his faculty accordingly. In only four years, its published research matched the entire production of all American universities by the previous generation of scholars. Its first class had an enrollment of 89 students, its fourth, 159, many of whom were graduates of other universities seeking advanced degrees. Hopkins attracted brilliant students, and among the 50 or so taught by Peirce were John Dewey, Fabian Franklin, Benjamin Ives Gilman, Allan Marquand, Oscar Howard Mitchell, Thorstein Veblen, and the two who were to remain closest to him, the psychologist Joseph Jastrow and the logician Christine Ladd. With such small enrollments and about forty instructors, the university was an intimate institution with both the virtues and the faults of the type. Peirce's unconventionality stood out sharply in this respectable assembly of scholars. When Sylvester, who had questioned Peirce's intelligence, asked a student about his teaching, he was told that his lectures "were always substantial, often very subtle, never trite, often not easy to follow, frequently so lacking in clearness that the hearers were quite unable to understand," and he added, "there can be no question that Mr. Peirce is a man of genius." "Well," Sylvester replied, "if he is a genius, isn't that enough? Isn't it men of genius that we want here?"[122]

Peirce spent five years at Hopkins. During that time he taught courses in elementary and advanced logic, the logic of relatives, philosophical terminology, medieval philosophy, probabilities, and one of his lifelong interests, the psychology of great men. He founded a new Metaphysical Club, which was a genuine success as a crucible for philosophical ideas. He participated in many university academic functions, such as meetings of the Scientific Association and Mathematical Seminary, to both of which he presented a number of original and important papers. Peirce assumed an active and influential role in the intellectual life of the university. He did not, however, take part in its political life, from which he was effectively excluded by his part-time status, much to his anger and frustration. In this connection, two Hopkins colleagues were important for Peirce's career: G. Stanley Hall, the psychologist, because, as a "safe" man, he was chosen above Peirce (and James) for the philosophy professorship that Gilman had promised him; and Simon Newcomb, the eminent astronomer, for his successful destruction of it.

For Peirce, the great achievement of his Hopkins career was the publication, in 1883, of *Studies in Logic by Members of the Johns Hopkins University*. As its title suggested, it was the work of Peirce and his students, and it covered with considerable originality much of the field of symbolic logic. Even though he had a hand as teacher in the book's preparation during its two years of gestation and he edited it, his name does not appear on the title page. He took no credit for his students' work, which was, indeed, at the leading edge of research in the field. John Venn, who reviewed the book for *Mind*, praised it highly, especially the paper by Peirce entitled "A Theory of Probable Inference."[123] For Peirce, the book was the embodiment of his ideal and ethic of a community of inquirers after truth. For his students it was the brilliant start of their careers, though because she was a woman, Christine Ladd-Franklin, who had completed all the requirements for it, was not granted her doctorate by John Hopkins for fifteen years.

In 1916, Ladd-Franklin recalled her experience of Hopkins and of Peirce:

> Probably there has never been in this country a center of learning where the conditions were more ideal for producing in its best form the joy of the intellectual life—nor a group of students better fitted to profit by their novel opportunities.
> Peirce . . . sat when he addressed his handful of students (who turned out afterwards, however, to be a not unimportant handful) and he had all the air, as has been noted by Professor Jastrow, of the typical philosopher who is engaged, at the moment, in bringing fresh truth by divination out of some inexhaustible well. He got his effect not by anything that could be called an inspiring personality, in the usual sense of the term, but rather by

Charles S. Peirce, early 1880s.

creating the impression that we had before us a profound, original, dispassionate and impassioned seeker of truth. No effort was made to create a connected and not inconsistent whole out of the matter of each lecture. In fact, so devious and unpredictable was his course that he once, to the delight of his students, proposed at the end of his lecture, that we should form (for greater freedom of discussion) a Metaphysical Club, though he had begun the lecture by defining metaphysics to be the "science of unclear thinking."

Several of Professor Sylvester's students—understanding that the New Logic which Professor Peirce professed had connections with existing mathematics and that, even if it had not, it was something which, unlike the mechanical logical exercises of the schools, was expected to have a vivifying and clarifying effect upon one's actual reasoning processes—joined his class in logic, composed otherwise, of course, of students of philosophy. This mixed character of the audience, as is too often the case in lectures on modern logic, made it impossible for the lecturer to adapt his subject-matter with exactness to the needs of either part. Peirce's lectures did not go very extensively into the details of his mathematical logic. . . . His lectures on philosophical logic we should doubtless have followed to much greater advantage if he had recommended to us to read his masterly series of articles on the subject which had already appeared in the *Popular Science Monthly* in 1878 under the title "Some Illustrations of the Logic of Science."[124]

After Peirce's death, Joseph Jastrow, with whom Peirce had carried out original research into the measurement of small variations in sense experience, reminisced that Peirce's courses in logic "gave me my first real experience of intellectual muscle," and that his greatest gift was his "fertile suggestiveness." He went on to describe him as a teacher:

> Mr. Peirce's personality was affected by a superficial reticence often associated with the scientific temperament. He readily gave the impression of being unsocial, possibly cold, more truly retiring. At bottom the trait was in the nature of a refined shyness, an embarrassment in the presence of the small talk and introductory salutations intruded by convention to start one's mind. His nature was generously hospitable; he was an intellectual host. In that respect he was eminently fitted to become the leader of a select band of disciples. Under more fortunate circumstances, his academic usefulness might have been vastly extended. For he had the pedagogic gift to an unusual degree. . . .
>
> The young men in my group who were admitted to his circle found him a most agreeable companion. The terms of equality upon which he met us were not in the way of flattery, for they were too spontaneous and sincere. We were members of his "scientific" fraternity; greetings were brief, and we proceeded to the business that brought us together, in which he and we found more pleasure than in anything else.[125]

Both Fisch in "Peirce at the Johns Hopkins University" and, more recently, Nathan Houser in his introduction to volume 4 of the *Writings of Charles S. Peirce* have provided excellent and detailed accounts of Peirce's academic connection with the university.[126]

Peirce carried the extraordinarily demanding double load of logic courses requiring intensive preparation and overseeing ongoing pendulum experiments until December, when he had another nervous collapse brought on by overwork. Peirce wrote Gilman a letter on Christmas Day explaining the nature of his affliction:

> I have an odd thing to say to you which is to be perfectly confidential unless something unexpected should occur. In consequence of certain

symptoms, I yesterday went to see my physician in New York, & he after calling in an eminent practitioner in consultation, informed me that he considered the state of my brain rather alarming. Not that he particularly feared regular insanity, but he did fear *something* of that sort; and he must insist on my being some little time in New York and he could not promise that I should go back on January 5th. For my own part, I do not think the matter so serious as he thinks. The intense interest I have had in the University and in my lectures, combined with my solitary life there, & with the state of my physical health, has undoubtedly thrown me into a state of dangerous cerebral activity & excitement. But I feel convinced that I shall surprise the doctors with the rapidity with which I regain my balance. I don't think the matter of any particular importance. However, I think it best to say to you as much as I do say; both that you may understand why I may possibly not be on hand Jan[.] 5, and also because the matter might turn out worse than I anticipate, and I might do some absurd thing.

I have said nothing to anybody else than you; & I beg you will not let me see that it is in your mind when I go back; for I shall not go back until it is quite over.[127]

Following this breakdown, facial neuralgia, bronchitis, and various other ills kept Peirce in bed until mid-January 1880, at which time he was sufficiently recovered to return to Baltimore and take up his lectures again.[128] His father heard him there and was delighted with him; after talking with President Gilman, he was convinced that his son's connection with the university would shortly become permanent.[129]

Benjamin Peirce had come to Baltimore in part to give a series of lectures at the Peabody Institute, which had been given the year before as Lowell Lectures. Later printed as *Ideality in the Physical Science*, these lectures presented an evolutionary theory of the universe which anticipated the essentials, with the exception of a theory of probability, of what Charles was to write in "Design and Chance" (1884), "A Guess at the Riddle" (1887), and his *Monist* papers (1891–93). Benjamin proposed that the evolution of the universe is structured mathematically by means of a "law of continuity" in such a manner that the process of science is recursively arranged through the transition from "unconscious induction" to the conscious activity of hypothesis, both of which exist within a preexisting harmony. Benjamin summarized:

The universe . . . commences with an all-pervading substance, in which there is no apparent structure nor division into parts, but the same monotonous uniformity throughout. Passing through innumerable transformations, it terminates in a system, whence disorganization has been wholly eliminated, and where vast multitudes of individuals, each a perfect organism in itself, are combined in indestructible harmony. In the beginning, it has the unity of monotony; in the end, it has the unity of complete organization.[130]

Peirce continued to lead his exacting and wearing double life, and the pressures of it resulted in late February in another siege of sickness. In April 1880, before the end of the spring term, he had recovered and left for Europe to attend conferences on geodetic matters for the Coast Survey, but in late May, while in England, he came down with bronchitis. In July, he was suddenly called home by the grave illness of his father. He arrived in Cambridge in early August, where he stayed until his father's death in September. Benjamin's death affected Charles profoundly, both personally and professionally. His father had raised him as an extension of his own genius and had said as much to a meeting of the Boston Radical Club a year before his death, when he "observed that his son Charles was now engaged in carrying on his investigations in the same line to which he had specially applied himself; and it was a great gratification to him to know that his son would prosecute the work to which he had devoted the latter part of his own life."[131]

With his father's death, Charles lost his sense of direction and purpose. This loss was particularly dangerous to him because he no longer had his father's powerful influence to protect him and advance his professional career, or Zina's strong presence to help him keep his emotional balance. He soon began to behave very erratically and against his own best interests.

Although in August Peirce had felt confident that his position at Johns Hopkins would shortly be made permanent, on December 18, coincident with a particularly severe attack of neuralgia, he decided to quit his lectureship there. In giving his reasons, he said:

> Although there is no life which I could enjoy more than one which should attach me to the Johns Hopkins university, yet I fear that in the spring my connection with Baltimore must cease. I could not arrange to be here another season without modifying my connection with the Coast Survey, which I do not certainly care to do for the sake of the subordinate position which I hold here. . . .
>
> Upon leaving the University I shall bid adieu to the study of Logic and Philosophy. . . . [132]

He offered to sell his logic and philosophy library to Hopkins for $550. Gilman accepted within a week, and at commencement exercises on February 22, 1881, he praised Peirce and thanked him for his excellent collection. But Peirce was vacillating; in early February, he had written to Gilman:

Not long ago[,] you were kind enough to express the wish that my lectures might be continued another year. As you know, I am unwilling to remain on the same terms. But it would be gratifying to me to receive a distinct proposal in writing, in order that I might carry away with me this evidence that the University considers that I have earned my pay. I do not hesitate to ask this, because I think, myself, that I have been of use to my pupils and that I am entitled to an expression of satisfaction.[133]

Although the trustees did not present him with the written offer he asked them for, they did give him a vote of thanks. In light of the sentiments which Peirce expressed to Gilman, the fact that Peirce accepted, in June, a third appointment as lecturer in logic, the same position he had refused in February, seems strange, yet the problem is easily solved. Peirce had remarked a week after his letter reporting his resignation that he was " . . . quitting the University upon a pure question of price for my services . . . ," and, by the end of March, Sylvester convinced Gilman to keep him (although the trustees had already accepted his resignation), and his salary was raised from $1,500 to $2,500.[134] His combined salaries from both the Survey and Hopkins came to almost $5,500, a large income for the times (the superintendent was given $6,000), but not enough to support his extravagant lifestyle. Sylvester wrote to Gilman to thank him for keeping Peirce:

Allow me to express the great satisfaction I feel in the interest of the University at the measures adopted by the Trustees to secure the continuance of Craig and Peirce. We now form a corps of no less than eight working mathematicians—actual producers and investigators—real working men: Story, Craig, Sylvester, Franklin, Mitchell, Ladd, Rowland, Peirce; which I think all the world must admit to being a pretty strong team.[135]

The letter points out the extent to which Sylvester considered Peirce and his students Franklin, Ladd, and Mitchell primarily as mathematicians. Ladd-Franklin herself commented on the fact that the majority of Peirce's students were mathematicians. Peirce did much of his work at Hopkins as part of this group of working mathematicians, and his thinking reflected their influence. Two major works he completed there, the most difficult written during his severe nervous illness in 1880, were concerned with the algebra of logic and the relations of mathematics to logic. The other major publication, included in his joint publication with his students, the *Studies in Logic*, was on the logic of probability, also mathematical in nature.

His lectureship settled, Peirce spent the summer in Nahant and Cambridge and returned to Baltimore in time to begin his fall semester classes at Johns Hopkins. During the summer, Superintendent Patterson had died; he was replaced by Julius E. Hilgard, who had been in the Survey all his professional life and whom Benjamin Peirce had passed over for the superintendency in favor of Patterson. The death of Patterson removed Peirce's only defender in the Survey. Unfortunately for Peirce, Hilgard resented the extravagant genius who was now his employee. Furthermore, Hilgard was a lax administrator whose public drunkenness was welcomed to feed the charges of bureaucratic corruption in the Survey made by the Allison Commission in 1885, in which Peirce was to find himself a major target.

During the spring of 1882, Peirce continued his course of lectures and submitted a plan of operation to the Coast Survey which included summer in Mt. Desert Island, the Isles of Shoals, Mt. Washington, and Nantucket, while during the winter, in close proximity to Baltimore, he intended to occupy Frederick and Hagerstown, Maryland, and one or two points in the Alleghenies.[136] These pleasant plans were changed owing to the pressures for results in pendulum research, emanating originally from Congress and amplified by the secretary of the treasury, who as a good Cleveland Democrat was drastically cutting the budgets under his control, especially the funds for the Coast Survey. Hilgard probably did not wish to, nor in all likelihood

Julius Erasmus Hilgard, superintendent of the United States Coast Survey, 1881–1885. Photograph courtesy of the Library of Congress.

could he place effective pressure on Peirce for results. Therefore, he and his assistant in charge, General Richard Cutts, passed on to Peirce the pressures from Congress and the secretary by pointing out to him that future appropriations depended on his providing his long-overdue reports as soon as possible. Peirce played the difficult game of satisfying both his increasingly demanding employers, but the situation finally forced him to give up his course of lectures for the fall semester of 1882, and instead of spending a pleasant summer in New England, he worked in the heat of New York to produce publishable monographs for the Survey *Annual Report*, which included in some cases results from as far back as 1876. From May through September, he occupied stations at Washington, Hoboken, Albany, and Montreal. Peirce had traveled to Montreal and Albany openly with Juliette in a fashion which attracted Hilgard's interest. In December, he set up a station in St. Augustine and at Savannah in connection with a French field party. At year's end, Peirce was back in Washington awaiting the turn of events which would make him professor of logic at Johns Hopkins.

The new year was full of promise for Peirce. He was certain of his professorship, since it had been promised by President Gilman. Patterson's failure to get his promotion in the Coast Survey meant that he could leave it honorably and without regrets, especially since Hilgard seemed bent on humiliating him. He eagerly looked forward to spending the remainder of his life in the intense and fruitful study of the logic of science, as he had so deeply wished to do for so long. Yet, a course of events had already begun which was to lead in a decade to poverty and ruin.

3

Expulsion from the Academy and the Search for a New Eden

1 8 8 3 – 1 8 9 1

I want to be appointed Professor of scientific Logic in the University of St. Helena. Could not some people be found who would subscribe something handsome to induce me to go there and never come back? . . .

I have something very vast now. I shall write it for Mind. They will say it is too vast for them. It is, or within it has as a part of it, an attempt to explain the laws of nature, to show their general characteristics and to trace them to their origin & predict new laws by the law of the laws of nature. The new philosophers will say, "How crude!"

CSP to William James, 1885

In the sixteen years following the appearance in 1867 of "On a New List of Categories," Peirce had amassed an extraordinary record of accomplishment in logic, science, and the logic of science as he broadly conceived it. In the United States, Peirce had received little recognition for what he had done, with one major exception—his appointment by Gilman as lecturer in logic in 1879 with the promise of tenure. By 1883, however, in Britain and the Continent, his reputation was well established in at least three fields: astronomy, geodesy, and logic, especially algebraic logic and the logic of science. His recognition in Europe and his lack of it in the United States were an expression of the comparatively low level of American philosophy and science at the time. Since the professionals of the American academy, with a few exceptions such as William James and Josiah Royce, were unable to appreciate Peirce's originality of mind and his real achievements until well after the turn of the century, the American academy rejected him the more easily because of his eccentricities and suspect character. In the United States and even in Europe, his major ideas were almost a century ahead of their time.

In astronomy, beginning with his work as a computer for his father in Cambridge in 1861 when he became involved in the computations of theoretical astronomy, until his removal from the roster of assistants in the Harvard Observatory in 1875 (he had resigned in 1872), he produced a steady stream of minor publications involving such procedures as the reduction of stellar observations, the observations of solar phenomena in two eclipses in 1869 and 1870, and, of more importance, an inquiry into the theory of errors of observations. The Harvard Observatory obtained its first spectroscope in 1867, and Peirce's experience with it enabled him, in the late 1870s, to apply spectroscopy to determine the length of the meter in terms of a wavelength of light, a major improvement in the techniques of metrology.

Peirce's major contribution to astronomy was his monograph *Photometric Researches*, published in 1878. The purpose of stellar photometry is to establish the relative brightness, or magnitude, of stars. Peirce's major interest in doing so, apart from establishing standards for magnitude using his own and other astronomers' observations, including Ptolemy and Brahe, was to determine, admittedly on the basis of scant evidence, the form of the Milky Way galactic cluster, for which he proposed the form of a disc, among the first to do so. The book received recognition by the Royal Astronomical Society (1883), in *Publicationen des astrophysikalischen Observatoriums zu Potsdam* (1883), in Gustav Müller's *Die Photometry der Gestirne* (1897), by the Carnegie Institution (1915), and in the comprehensive *Handbuch der Astrophysik* (1929–1936), which states, "The first photometric star catalogue, which contains calculated magnitudes, appears to be the one of C. S. Peirce which appeared in 1878."[1]

Peirce became involved with geodesy, then a field of astronomy, in 1872. His demonstration in 1875 that the flexure of the pendulum stands used in gravity experiments was a factor large enough to bring the results of earlier measurements into question added significantly to the accuracy of gravimetrics. This finding was presented to a special committee in 1875, and then, in 1877, to the general conference of the International Geodetic Association at Stuttgart, where his results were confirmed and praised very highly, and new experiments were outlined to increase the accuracy of measurements of gravity. This was the first triumph for an American scientist at a gathering of so eminent a group of European scientists. At the same meeting he proposed, on the basis of his earlier experiments, which were later built upon by Michelson and Morley, to use the wavelength of sodium light to measure the length of pendulums more accurately. At the association meeting in 1880 he reported his progress on this procedure. At the meeting in 1883 held in Rome, which he attended, Peirce was again mentioned prominently in connection with the means to increase the accuracy of measurements of gravity. His "Measurements of Gravity at Initial Stations in America and Europe" is regarded as one of the early classics of geodesy and as the first significant American contribution to the field.[2] It is listed as a basic monograph in the *Encyklopedie der mathematischen Wissenschaften* (1904).

Peirce produced a number of presentations to and publications by the American Academy of Arts and Sciences and the National Academy of Sciences, but he enjoyed his highest academic and professional reputation in Europe. His early publications in logic—the series including "A New List of Categories," published in the *Proceedings of the American Academy of Arts and Sciences* in 1867; the series arising out of his controversy over nominalism with W. T. Harris, published in the *Journal of Speculative Philosophy* in 1868 and 1869; but especially the "Description of a Notation for the Logic of Relatives . . . ," published in 1870 and distributed by him in England and the Continent in 1870–71—were known and appreciated by British logicians shortly after their appearance. The *Popular Science Monthly* series of 1877 and 1878 titled "Illustrations of the Logic of Science" included such influential pieces as "The Fixation of Belief" and "How to Make Our Ideas Clear," which William James later called the "birth certificates" of pragmatism. These two essays were also published at the same time in French in the *Revue Philosophique de la France et l'Étranger*.

W. Stanley Jevons, a major figure in the study of logic in Britain, remarked in *Nature* in 1881 that "the most elaborate recent contributions to mathematico-logical science, at least in the English language, are the memoirs of Prof. C. S. Peirce, the distinguished mathematician, now of the Johns Hopkins University, Baltimore."[3] In 1883, three years after Peirce's appointment as lecturer at Hopkins, the influential and original British logician John Venn wrote in the British publication *Mind* that

> Mr. C. S. Peirce's name is so well known to those who take an interest in the development of the Boolian or symbolic treatment of Logic that the knowledge that he was engaged in lecturing upon the subject to advanced classes at the Johns Hopkins University will have been an assurance that some interesting contributions to the subject might soon be looked for. . . . Such assurance is justified in the volume under notice [the 1883 Johns Hopkins *Studies in Logic* edited by Peirce], which seems to me to contain [a] greater quantity of novel and suggestive matter than any other recent work on the same or allied subjects which has happened to come under my notice.[4]

Pierce was forty-four years old in 1883. He had produced at least twenty-six important publications, including a few which changed the course of philosophy. Any modern major American (or foreign) university would be delighted with such a record, despite the eccentricities of its author. The one American acknowledgment of his accomplishments by 1883 which reflected the high level of his work, other than his appointment as lecturer in logic at Johns Hopkins, came from Benjamin Eli Smith, a staff member of the *Century Dictionary*, soon to become its managing editor, who recruited Peirce in 1883 as a contributor and editor. Smith gave him primary responsibility for terms in logic, philosophy, mathematics, mechanics, astronomy, and weights and measures, and all words relating to universities, a list of subjects which showed clearly the remarkable breadth of his knowledge and interests and yet which fell well short of the actuality. Peirce also influenced the dictionary's underlying rationale through his development of a systematic approach to terminology. Within three years, his employment by this great and pioneering dictionary was the only tangible American recognition of his internationally recognized distinction as a philosopher, logician, mathematician, and scientist. The one exception was the psychologist G. Stanley Hall's judgment published four years before in his 1879 article for *Mind* (a British journal), "Philosophy in the United States," in which he said, "The author [of "Illustrations of the Logic of Science"] is a distinguished mathematician, and this discussion, in which he long ago interested himself, promises to be one of the most important of American contributions to philosophy."[5]

The years 1883–91 marked the destruction of Peirce's career and the beginning of his descent into ruin and poverty, a descent in which he sometimes seemed actively to conspire. Before the deaths of his father in 1880 and of Superintendent Patterson of the Coast Survey in the summer of 1881, Peirce had been protected by their powerful influence. From 1879 to 1883, all the signs had seemed to point to a brilliant academic career for him under the wing of Daniel Coit Gilman, president of what was then the finest graduate school in the United States. However, his world changed drastically when, within a span of seven years, he was suddenly and unexpectedly dismissed from Hopkins; accused by a congressional investigative commission of dereliction of his Survey responsibilities; then forced to resign from the Survey for failing to complete the important geodesic researches for which he was solely responsible. Thereafter, only William James, who was well aware of Peirce's personal faults, and a few others, including his brother Jem, his cousin Henry Cabot Lodge, and Josiah Royce, were willing to champion his cause in the academic world. Unprepared as he was by both his sheltered upbringing and his professional life to face the harsh realities of making a living, he made disastrous, often childishly innocent blunders, and his brittle arrogance pushed many who would have helped him into neutrality, if not enmity. Between the two dismissals, the focus of his interests changed drastically both philosophically and professionally. He moved away from the accepted tracks of inquiry and livelihood to explore risky new territory in both.

One of the reasons which may have led to Peirce's dismissal from Hopkins was his characteristic attraction to controversy. In early February 1883, after his return from the Deep South on Survey business, Peirce had almost become involved in a dispute with J. J. Sylvester, the British mathematician at Hopkins who had impugned his reputation three years earlier. It began in a letter to Gilman:

> I am obliged to go to Philadelphia today to meet [the British geodesist] Major Herschel.
>
> I have printed a brochure on the Algebra of Relatives but it is not yet issued. It occurs to me that it is possible that (although I am unable myself to see it at all) there may be some just cause of offence in my references on the last page to Professors Sylvester & Cayley. Of course, you will see none at first glance; but will you see them & find out 1st whether they think they see anything out of the way and 2nd whether if so it is merely the systematic arrogance of these Britishers or whether it is just. I will keep back the issue until I hear from you.
>
> You understand that I do not *expect* them to find anything but what is flattering in the allusions; but then I want to avoid the possibility of doing wrong in the matter.[6]

Peirce had discovered that Arthur Cayley's work had anticipated his own, but he claimed that his own was more inclusive. Why he did not deal directly with Sylvester and Cayley and instead asked for Gilman's intercession is not clear, but it may well be that he placed Gilman in his father's place as protector. Peirce withheld the brochure. A year later, a more serious conflict came out into the open, this time because Peirce placed a sentence of his own, "These forms can be derived from an algebra given by Mr. Charles S. Peirce (*Logic of Relatives*, 1870)," in an abstract of a paper (on nonions) written by Sylvester and issued in the university *Circular* of August 1882. Sylvester had entrusted Peirce with checking the proofsheet, and he was incensed. He issued an "Erratum" which corrected the line to read, "Mr. Charles Peirce informs me that . . . " Peirce was in his turn angered because Sylvester had been reported in a *Circular* as saying in April 1882 that "Mr. Charles S. Peirce, it should be stated, had to the certain knowledge of Mr. Sylvester, arrived at the same result in connection with his theory of the *logic of relatives*." This earlier recognition did not change the fact that Peirce had put the disputed sentence in Sylvester's mouth without asking his permission. There ensued a nasty battle of letters which thoroughly embarrassed Gilman and the Hopkins trustees. On March 27, Peirce wrote that he considered Gilman's showing his statement to Sylvester

> not quite fair, because his was not shown to me. Still, if it were possible to avoid further dispute, I should heartily consent. I do not think, however, that it is possible; because he is blinded by arrogance & I shall not go without having the imputations that have been made upon my conduct, completely refuted.[7]

A week later Sylvester wrote angrily that Peirce's "virulent and disingenuous statements" ought not to be allowed to appear in the circular "without giving me an opportunity of replying."[8] On April 17, after two months of trying to resolve the matter, George William Hand, chairman of the executive committee of the trustees, wrote to Gilman, "After thinking over this annoying matter, it appears to me that nothing is to be done but to publish the articles as they stand. This should however be the last of it and would it not be well to say so to both in advance."[9] Despite the controversy, Sylvester continued to be impressed with Peirce's work and supported its publication in the *Journal of Mathematics*, of which he was editor. Several years later, Sylvester, who had left just before Peirce's dismissal and did not hear of it immediately, wrote to Gilman: "What was the cause of C. Peirce's leaving? I am truly sorry on his account. I regret the differences which sprang up between him and me for which I was primarily to blame. I fear that he may not have acted with entire prudence in some personal matters."[10]

In April 1883, Peirce's contract with Johns Hopkins was renewed for the coming year. In the same month he decided to marry the woman who called herself "Mme. Pourtalai." In September 1881, in preparation for the marriage, Peirce had begun divorce proceedings for desertion against Zina, who had left him in 1876; he received the final decree on April 24, 1883.[11]

Juliette Annette, whose true surname remains unknown, called herself both Pourtalai and Froissy. The marriage certificate in the bureau of records in New York City, dated April 26, 1883, gave her maiden name as Juliette Annette Froissy, daughter of August Froissy and Rose [E]yem or [S]yem; the first letter of her mother's claimed maiden name is blotched. Despite thirty years of searching, to date no one has found a French family related to Juliette by the name of either Froissy or [E]yem. Elisabeth Walther, in her 1989 biography of Peirce, presents a number of conjectures as to Juliette's identity, but points out that at every crucial point, there are contradictions in the evidence.[12] Since the names were undoubtedly chosen to deceive, this failure is hardly surprising. Juliette listed her marriage to Peirce as her second and herself as a widow, giving her first husband's name as Pourtalai, a name which was also made up. No record exists of the first marriage. As Walther points out, there is a French family with a Swiss branch called de Pourtalès. One of the Swiss members, a former student of Louis Agassiz named Louis François de Pourtalès, served for a time in the 1870s as assistant with the Coast Survey, but there is only the most speculative connection with Juliette. Peirce identified himself as a chemist despite his ten-year career in the Coast Survey as a physicist. Even Juliette's age is uncertain. The wedding certificate lists her age as twenty-six, but her death certificate and obituary notice gave her age at death as sixty-nine, which would have made her sixteen at the time of her marriage, twenty-seven years younger than her husband.[13]

Juliette made sure that her identity would not become known. In the Gifford Pinchot collection in the manuscript division of the Library of Congress, there is correspondence and information about her in the papers of

Juliette Peirce, 1889.

her close friend Mary Eno Pinchot, Gifford's mother. All references to Juliette's identity, which was known to Mrs. Pinchot, were cut out.

According to Cornelia Bryce Pinchot, Gifford's widow, Juliette claimed to be a Hapsburg princess and to have played on intimate terms with the boy who later became Kaiser Wilhelm II. She told how young Wilhelm had taken her dolls away and thrown them violently against the ceiling, breaking them to bits and pretending they were blasted by cannon fire. She said that, because of an innocent involvement in the Mayerling Affair in which she played the dupe of an evil brother, she was forced to leave her home, was smuggled into Belgium, and was spirited away, incognito, to the United States, where an income was settled on her on condition that she never return. To cover her identity, she took upon arrival the name of Pourtalai. Mrs. Pinchot pointed out that Juliette was inventing this, because the suicide of Archduke Rudolph of Hapsburg that ended his doomed love affair with Maria Waleska had occurred in 1889, thirteen years after Juliette's arrival in America. Juliette boasted that, by her own efforts, she could have prevented the First World War. As she told them, Mrs. Pinchot discounted these stories as figments of a madwoman's mind. She also speculated that Juliette may have been one of a small group of "*fille de joie*, but cultured, you know the French!" among those forced into exile by the Third Republic for political reasons, and that this best explained her origins. But after telling Juliette's tales, she reconsidered, remarking on the authenticity of Juliette's jewelry and her mysterious income, and on her mother-in-law Mary Pinchot's knowledge of Juliette's aristocratic family connections and her devotion to her. Walther reports similar tales given to William James's son Henry, Jr. Joseph Jastrow's account of Juliette, published in 1934, which portrayed a frail, impoverished, and pathetic widow with her mind intact, tends to support Mrs. Pinchot's second thoughts.[14]

In the early spring of 1883, Juliette told Charles that she would not marry him unless they went to Europe and had the ceremony repeated there. Peirce immediately wrote a long letter to Superintendent Hilgard, outlining his professional reasons for wanting to make a trip to Europe: to swing pendulums of his own design at Berlin, Kew, and Geneva, to consult with the French on the progress of gravimetrics there, to attend the seventh international meeting on geodesy in Rome, and to order a better pendulum from Gautier, the renowned instrument makers. The letter also points to the beginnings of a policy of excluding Peirce from decisions about his own field of gravimetrics as a consequence of his impending break with the Survey:

> I have been consulted by those men before & have discussed with them their plans. . . . I very carefully went over with Villarceau & St. Clair

Deville their work upon the geo-gravimeter. . . . I learn accidentally that experiments on this subject have been conducted by [Assistant] Mr. Schott under [Assistant in Charge] Gen'l. [Richard D.] Cutts. I do not think that it is either friendly to me or advantageous to the survey to keep what they are doing a secret from me.[15]

Peirce's proposed itinerary would take them to France, then London, and then they "would stop on my way up the Rhine and by that route to Geneva. We might diverge to go the seashore. Thence, to Rome . . . ," and then to Paris and home in the fall. Peirce continued:

> I will now privately state to you my personal reasons for wishing to go abroad.
>
> I wish to marry a French lady, Madame Pourtalai, who has been in this country for a good while being detained here by the bad state of her health. Her condition of health has now become almost desperate, her financial affairs are going wrong and demand her presence. She will not consent to being married here unless I will go to France to have the ceremony repeated, and for all these imperative reasons she *must* go and I must go with her. I propose and you will dispose I ask a great favor. But the occasion is exceptional and unique. The excuses [are] remarkably good and solid. I hope you will [be] able to act favorably.[16]

A few days later, Peirce wrote President Gilman deceptively that "something having gone wrong at the Coast Survey, I am obliged to go on to Washington . . . and I think I had better bring my course to a close."[17] Peirce married Juliette April 26, and a week later they sailed for Le Havre. In Europe, as he had proposed to Hilgard, he combined his Survey business, which included placing the order for new pendulums on the Defforges model with Colonel Gautier, with a three-month honeymoon in Paris and London, up the Rhine to Geneva, to the Riviera, to Rome to attend a meeting of the geodetic association, and back to Paris. For reasons that remain unclear, Peirce did not stay in Paris the short time needed for the completion of the Gautier pendulums, which included some minor redesign, so that he did not return with them. This decision was to leave him without the refined instruments his pendulum research required and, therefore, to bring the research results and his scientific reputation into question.

On their return to New York on September 19, Charles and Juliette went first to Baltimore, where, on the assurance from President Gilman that Peirce's appointment at Hopkins would soon become permanent, they immediately rented a large brick house at 272 North Calvert Street, then in the most fashionable part of the city, five blocks from the harbor and a half-hour ride by trolley or hansom from the university. Peirce resumed the nerve-racking burden of both teaching his courses, effectively full-time, at the university and carrying out his researches, full-time, for the Coast Survey. Hoping to reduce his constant traveling, Peirce recommended that pendulum experiments be carried out at Hopkins, but Superintendent Hilgard, now apparently convinced that Peirce was too obviously using the Survey for his own convenience, refused. Peirce responded by saying, "as for the J. H. University, I must admit on reflection that in recommending it ⎰as a station for pendulum work⎱ my judgment was rather warped by considerations of convenience."[18]

In November Charles and Juliette went to Cambridge to visit the Peirce family. There they found the family—and society in Cambridge and Boston—arrayed against them. The first warning had already been sounded by Peirce's mother, Sarah, in a letter to her daughter, Helen, on September 19, 1883:

> I have this moment received a telegram from Charlie announcing ⎰his⎱ arrival at N. Y. I can do nothing of course about them—with Jem away, but Bert and Helen ⎰his brother Herbert and his sister⎱ I know will be kind and take *some* notice of them in N. Y. I dread the troubles which are sure to be in store for them & thro' them for me in the family and in society. Poor Charlie is like a child about conventionalities & has no idea that anything stands in the way of her being received everywhere!!![19]

Juliette arrived in Cambridge ill. She spent much of her time in bed, adding to the already painfully difficult burden she and Charles had placed on the family. Sarah spent time with her and came to change her initial disapproval:

> She seems to me a very feeble person & looks delicate. Of course I am with her a part of the time & she talks while I am there as fast as her tongue can go. . . . My impressions of her life & character are a good deal *modified* for the better by what I have seen of her. She is certainly intelligent & *amiable* I believe—seems quite devoted to C. & he to her. Yet he is as usual quite absorbed in his work & tossing up his hands drawing into himself ⎰in the⎱ old way a great deal of the time,—then with his pen & paper making profound calculations & entirely abstracted for a long time—just the old Charlie—& just as affectionate as ever. . . . I do not know precisely when they mean to leave.[20]

Charlotte Elizabeth (Aunt Lizzie) never forgave either of them for marrying, though she came to pity Juliette and continued to indulge Charles. Her moral outrage, which was reflected by the Cambridge matrons, was profound. At the same time she remained fascinated by the scarlet woman she believed Juliette to be. She wrote Helen:

> I do not hear anything of Charles' going—I hope and trust they will go this week and never return. They could not have a worse place for them than Cambridge—where all the White Mountain scandal [where Charles and Juliette had indiscreetly conducted their affair three years before] & others of a similar nature is known. However it is not worthwhile to worry. No doubt of her badness & I fear of his also—I have sufficient that is personal against them to prevent my having *any* intercourse with them.[21]

They stayed six days, four of which Juliette spent in bed, and after they left, Sarah described Juliette sympathetically:

> She told me a great deal about herself [but not about her identity] & about her intercourse with Charlie—& I am very sure there has been less impropriety than has been supposed between them. Her manners are very pleasing & sometimes when she is animated her eyes are beautiful. Her teeth & hair too are very handsome, & she has a pretty figure & hands— but her cheeks are hollow & she is deathly pale. They have taken a house in Baltimore & are fitting it up. I think it will be a tax upon her strength & do not see how she is to get through with it. . . . Aunt L. was quite attentive to her all the time & as J's manner to her was flattering & deferential she seemed quite taken with her & accepted her flatteries as thoroughly earnest expressions of opinion. She [Lizzie] began however, as soon as her [Juliette's] back was turned to take a different tone. . . .
> Darling—Excuse this hurried scrawl & burn it.[22]

Nine years later, when Peirce came to Cambridge, bringing Juliette with him, to talk in Royce's house on synechism, Francis Abbot described her as a "timid, gentle little woman."[23]

In the aftermath of this short visit, Aunt Lizzie, then an energetic eighty years old, engaged in a spate of gossip with Helen, describing Juliette's views on fashion—"she says that this year strawberries are *the* most to be sought after in all figured stuffs"—and her own views of Juliette, Charles, and the marriage. These letters show, among other things, that Juliette, unlike Zina, had no knowledge of and no interest in Charles's passionate involvement in the world of ideas. She was the extension of Peirce the Dandy:

> [December 18] I will say this of her that she was always lady-like, gentle & thoughtful of others. I could not help being interested in her—yet I was not in the least fascinated. I do wish Charley would come out openly & tell her true history—yet I am afraid if he did I should not like her any better than I do—now—though I do hate mystery. It seems to me that she is a spoilt

child—& I should be wretched if I had to pass any length of time with her; it wd be so impossible to satisfy her or make her happy. Your mother says she pities Charley—so of course we all do to a certain point. But he married Juliette with his eyes open—& he is no mere child & when he swallowed the pill—he could easily foresee all the consequences. Well—as we brew so must we bake—& it is easier to jump into a ditch than over it. What in the world did Charley want to marry her for? is the question always uppermost on my mind.[24]

[March 18, 1884] Jem had a letter from Charley saying that Juliette was very sick. Well I do pity Charley, still it was his own choice to marry J. contrary to the advice or wishes of all his friends. I never could imagine what he could discover fascinating in or about her. It was not her beauty— since she *had none*—& never could have had much if any of that article. The fact is she bewitched him, I suppose. If she had lived in Salem during witch time she wd certainly have been tried as a witch & been sentenced accordingly. . . . At any rate she is just the reverse of Zina—in some respects—& Zina is no saint & never was & never will be in this world.[25]

In April 1884, just after Charles had lost his Hopkins lectureship, an event which so shamed and angered him that at first he could not bring himself to tell his mother about it, he and Juliette visited again. This time Juliette stayed there for some days without her husband and talked at length with Aunt Lizzie about the misery of her life with her husband.

> Yesterday afternoon I was alone with her in the parlor & she began to tell me what a horrid winter she has had & all owing to Charles' treatment of her. . . . She said she had not been much sick—only she has a slight falling of the womb which requires her to be careful—but she has been able to be about & working most of the time. When she was sick it was entirely owing to Charles' treatment of her. It is strange that Zina & now Juliette should have the same sort of experiences. She (Juliette) told me that when Charles gets into his passions it is "perfectly awful." . . . She said she was on the point of leaving the house, never to return. She told Charles she would & he said "Why don't you try it for six months?" & then she said to him "Why, I did not marry you *on trial*—if I go away it will be forever." One of her complaints was that he interfered with the housekeeping & the girls . . . & the servants would not stay. She told me that within a few weeks he *lent* Bradford nearly a hundred dollars, that he had often lent him money but *never* got it back, & that it was in reality *Mrs.* Bradford to whom he lent the money. . . . I suppose you remember Zina's old long jealousy of Mrs. Bradford. . . . I said to Juliette, "This then . . . was the cause of your coming on now?" "Yes," said she, it was, he thought that if I came here I might "give in" to him—"but I shall not." . . . I cannot understand such women. What a sad, terribly sad fate! Pity she cannot go in to a convent. Perhaps she *can*. . . . [26]

Well Juliette and Charley still here. Yesterday I went to Boston simply to get a change of thoughts. . . . When I came home, Juliette, whom I had left sick in bed, was sitting with your mother & apparently quite restored. She told me afterwards that her sickness was caused by something unkind, that Charley had said to her. She says that all her sicknesses have been caused by that. In the afternoon I was sitting in the dining room & she came & sat beside me. We talked German & then French together. Her pronunciation of her native language is really beautiful—so clear, easy & distinct—& so fluent and expressive. She tells great stories of her father & her bringing up. She is a real mystery to me. She seems so artless & simple. It is most strange that a woman brought up as she says she was could have gone round with Charles & been so intimate with him as she has been for many years. . . . If I had a husband & he did not treat me well I *would* go away from him—for I know I should hate him. I should rather "dig clams" than live in the same house with a man who was unkind to me and if he treated me *brutally* I should be afraid to live with him.[27]

Juliette and Charles left yesterday [April 16] after lunch. . . . She laid down on the sofa while I washed the things & then I sat down & we talked together in French & in German. & I got some of the French novels Charley had given me—to ask her about them. I shall not have them bound on her recommendation. . . . I asked her if she had money of her own—independently of Charles. She said she had—but that *she did not let him know she had any, because he would get it & spend it right & left—she did not know how—only he was so extravagant.* I *had* heard that she was in Boston at the time of your father's sickness that long sad summer—you remember Charles came from Europe. I said to Juliette "Were you in Boston the summer, when my brother was sick?" "I was sick in New York" she said. But there was a woman whom Charles had brought with him from Europe & she was in Boston at that time! . . . She told me also that there was another woman, to whom Charles gave a great deal of money & whom he sent for to come here & she came. She was a handsome "Dutch" girl! How strange Juliette could have married if she knew these things to be true! She said, she did not want to marry him, but he [forced] her—& he came to her with a pistol in his hand & said he would shoot her if she did not consent to marry him & then your mother wrote to her [urging her to marry him]. . . . Charles told your mother that he shall probably have to give up his connexion with the Johns Hopkins University. . . . Well altogether they are in a bad fix—& I am *very, very,* sorry; but the only thing for Charles to do is stand on his own foundation—to turn over a new leaf. . . . [28]

One thing is certain—that Zina's & Juliette's accounts of Charley agree in the main.[29]

Zina, to a lesser extent, and Juliette were abused wives. That Peirce was psychologically abusive to his wives is supported by the evidence. That he was physically abusive as well is not clearly stated, though the letters certainly suggest it. Like his father, (and probably the fathers of his two wives), Charles was a domestic tyrant. Juliette lived in the shadow of her husband, as much his daughter as his wife—a pale, sickly, and childless exile who did her best to be the elegantly mannered woman her Charles desired. He called her "my little girl," and she called him "Papa." The marriage was perverse but loving. They depended completely on each other and were inseparable. Charles said later that if Juliette were to die, he would be unable to continue with his life and work. He protected her against her shadowy enemies, and she shielded him from the moral censure of his peers. They cared for each other with close attention during their almost constant illnesses and comforted each other in their different but equally painful exiles. Juliette may even have shared her husband's dependence on drugs.

A new factor seems to have played a large part in the development of this aspect of Peirce's character, beginning with his decision, in 1879, to carry out simultaneously both his exacting Survey work and his even more demanding courses of lectures and research in logic at Johns Hopkins. This factor was the use of cocaine—in addition to the morphine he took to abate his pain—to help him try to manage the impossible undertaking he had set himself. He longed so intensely to return to the academic life he had grown up in that he drastically overestimated his capacities. Opiates, especially laudanum and morphine, and cocaine were legally dispensed, commonly used, and easily available at the time. Opiate addiction was a common tragedy in middle-class life, especially among women. Cocaine had become of considerable medical interest by the 1880s, when it was (as it still is) often used as an anesthetic. Freud recommended its therapeutic use in psychoanalysis in 1884. Among those known to use the drug were a number of Peirce's prominent contemporaries, such as Thomas A. Edison, Ulysses S. Grant, Henrik Ibsen, Emile Zola, Jules Verne, Pope Leo XIII, and Edward, Prince of Wales. With his long-time interest in drugs, Peirce was no doubt aware of its psychoactive properties. Although there is no direct evidence that Peirce used cocaine, it seems the most plausible explanation for the oddly random inconsistency of content and feeling, and the depth of his swings of mood as expressed, for example, in his letters to Gilman and later to other correspondents. Cocaine is known to cause abnormally aggressive behavior, such as that characteristically exhibited by Peirce, and for the way in which it disastrously undermines judgment. The drug also causes paranoid suspicions of persecution of the kind that Peirce increasingly used to account for his failures after his dismissal from Hopkins.[30]

On their return to Baltimore in early November 1883, Peirce continued with his self-destructive double life while Juliette, still in poor health, put the finishing touches on their house. Neither had the slightest doubt that Peirce would be given a permanent position at Hopkins. In connection with his work on scientific and philosophical definitions for the *Century Dictionary*, Peirce had begun that semester a new course on philosophical terminology which required the borrowing of a dozen books at a time from the Peabody Library, most of them in the collection he had sold to Hopkins in 1881. When this privilege was not accorded him, he offered to buy back $100 worth of his collection. Gilman was offended, and Peirce responded:

> I deeply regret having said anything which seems to offend you, since I am bound to you by every bond of official respect, personal esteem, gratitude, and if you will permit me to say so even of affection.
>
> You have certainly always treated me with the most generous justice; but when you ask me so indignantly when you ever refused a similar application, you give me particular pleasure in thus showing that you are not conscious of having done so.
>
> Then, let me say with candour, my dear Mr. President, that although I believe I have never complained of it to anybody, I have not thought that any heed at all had been given to any of the suggestions which I have made in regard to wants in the library, although I considered them important. . . . I think, without of course comparing you to the jailer [W. Hand Browne, the librarian] of the Peabody library, that Cambridge is a trifle ahead of Baltimore in its appreciation of the wants of its students in the way of books. You have always permitted me to express myself with great freedom to you, and I always think a misunderstanding should be seized as an occasion to have a mutual understanding. Therefore, I beg you will not find offence in what I am saying. I have lately been offending people everywhere by my speeches. Pray excuse me if I unconsciously go too far; I only wish to express my strictly personal and very humble opinion, which you will take for what it is worth. . . .
>
> On reflection, I don't think my proposition to buy certain books of the University in good taste or temper, and I withdraw it. . . .
>
> I will buy the various books I need, as I can pick them up, & let the work wait until I get them.[31]

During the month of December, Peirce heard a rumor that he would not be continuing at Hopkins, but he thought nothing of it, secure in Gilman's promise of tenure. The first sign in the official record that a change in Peirce's position at Hopkins was about to happen was a letter from Simon Newcomb to President Gilman written three days before Christmas:

> I felt and probably expressed some uneasiness in the course of our conversation the other evening lest I might have been the occasion of doing

injustice to persons [Charles and Juliette] whose only wrong had been lack of prudence. I have therefore taken occasion to inquire diligently of my informant [and early mentor and long-time friend Superintendent Hilgard], and am by him assured that every thing I said was fully justified. Furthermore, he deemed it part of the obligation of friendship to make known to you the exact state of the case, and would avail himself of the first opportunity to do so.[32]

Neither Newcomb's nor Hilgard's revelations ever became part of the official record, and the only reference to them was made obliquely by Gilman to the executive committee almost a year later:

It is true that [at] the beginning of the academic year 1883–4, I knew of no disposition to disturb Mr. Peirce in his relation to this university. It was not until several weeks later that one of the Trustees made known to the Executive Committee & to me certain facts which had been brought to his knowledge quite derogatory to the standing of Mr. Peirce as a member of an academic staff. These facts & their bearing upon the philosophical instruction in this university were considered by the Executive Committee, at their meeting, January 26, 1884.[33]

Newcomb himself clarified the reason behind Gilman's drastic shift of feeling in a letter to his wife written a week after his letter to Gilman:

I have been somewhat exercised at being the unintended means of making known some of the points of C. Peirce's marital history at Baltimore. When last going to N. Y. I went from Balt. to Phil. in the same seat with Dr. Thomas, a J. H. U. Trustee, and supposing they all knew more or less of the affair got talking of it, and let several cats out of the bag. What I gave as reports, Dr. Th[omas]., I suspect, told Gilman as facts, and troubled the latter greatly, as it seems Mrs. P(2) had begun to cultivate Mrs. G's acquaintance. The supposition is, that the marriage last summer made no change in the relations of the parties. Mr. Hilgard assures me that it is all true, they having occupied the same apartments in N. Y. some years ago. It is sad to think of the weaknesses which may accompany genius.[34]

For a sanctimonious man of affairs of the period such as Newcomb, for Peirce to have a mistress was both understandable and acceptable if the affair were carried on discreetly, but to marry her after such a public liaison was outrageous because to do so attacked the sanctity of marriage. Obviously, by the time of Newcomb's letter, Peirce's love life had become a staple in the gossip of the academy and the Survey. Peirce was never again offered a regular academic job, and his reputation and his dismissal from Hopkins were a large part of the reason. When his friend William James, in his continuing efforts to find him a place, recommended him for a position in philosophy at the University of Chicago when it opened in 1892, its president, William Rainey Harper, who soon hired Thorstein Veblen, a man whose sexual exploits and vile reputation far exceeded those of Peirce, relied for his rejection of Peirce on the advice of Harvard University's George H. Palmer, who wrote:

> I am astonished at James's recommendation of Peirce. Of course my impressions may be erroneous, and I have no personal acquaintance with Peirce. I know, too, very well his eminence as a logician. But from so many sources I have heard of his broken and dissolute character that I should advise you to make most careful inquiries before engaging him. I am sure it is suspicions of this sort which have prevented his appointment here, and I suppose the same causes procured his dismissal from the Johns Hopkins.[35]

The actions in which Newcomb engaged which damaged Peirce did not end with the information he gave to Gilman. When he succeeded Sylvester as editor of the *American Journal of Mathematics*, he refused the second part of Peirce's "Algebra of Logic," the first part of which Sylvester had already accepted and which appeared in 1880, on the grounds that its subject was not mathematics. In 1890, Newcomb's denial of the value of Peirce's Survey work led quickly to his dismissal there. In 1899, he refused to support (and probably acted against) Peirce's application to the Survey to head the newly established Department of Weights and Measures. In 1902, when Peirce applied to the Carnegie Institution for a grant to complete his great work on logic, it was again Newcomb's denial of the value of Peirce's work which prevented his receiving the grant. And these acts were not the whole story of Newcomb's carefully disguised ill-treatment of his presumed friend. In an odd failure of insight, Peirce never understood the extent of Newcomb's malign influence on his professional life and invented complicated and unlikely conspiracies to explain his constant failures.

Unlike Peirce, who was born into the wealthy and privileged world of Harvard University and the upper crust of Cambridge and Boston society, Newcomb, who was four years older, was born in deep poverty to an exiled New England family in the remote town of Wallace on the rocky and hostile island of Nova Scotia. His father was an itinerant teacher who eked out a subsistence living and was forced to hire his son out at thirteen as a manual laborer. At sixteen, Newcomb was apprenticed to a doctor who turned out to be a quack. He fled and, after three years of wandering, ended up as an underpaid and overburdened teacher in a Maryland country school. In 1856, at the age of twenty, his prospects improved when he became tutor to a Maryland plantation family who lived close enough to Washington to allow him to indulge his passion for learning at the Smithsonian Institution, where Joseph Henry and Julius Hilgard became his patrons. At twenty-two, because of their sponsorship, he became a computer for the *Nautical Almanac* and was admitted to the Lawrence Scientific School at Harvard, where he studied mathematics under Benjamin Peirce, earning a B.S. in that discipline the next year, in 1858.

Although the elder Peirce and Newcomb became friends and political allies, Charles and Simon did not. Newcomb never joined the small, pioneering, and exclusive group, led by Chauncey Wright—who was five years Newcomb's senior and worked with him at the *Nautical Almanac*—that became the Metaphysical Club. He was probably not asked, because his interests were entirely conventional. In 1875, he refused an offer from President Eliot to become director of the Harvard Observatory and instead, two years later, became head of the Nautical Almanac Office, and soon after of the Naval Observatory, both in Washington, where he had found the political and scientific world in which he felt most comfortable. In 1881, when Patterson died, Newcomb refused the superintendency of the Coast Survey. This refusal was likely a consequence of his marriage to Mary Hassler, granddaughter of Ferdinand Hassler, first superintendent of the Survey. She was well aware of the problems there and took a special interest in finding out the worst about Peirce.[36]

Newcomb was a self-made man who resented Peirce's privileged arrogance and his great talent, despised his morals, and was able to move effectively against him because he was a politically astute scientist whose influence was powerful and pervasive. He was elected Foreign Associate to the French Academy of Sciences in 1895, an extraordinary honor, and to the presidency of the American Mathematical Society in 1897 and 1898. He also had a well-established reputation as a popularizer of science and wrote numerous books on various scientific topics in a facile style.[37]

In the thirty-seven-year correspondence between the two men, the attitude of each toward the other was expressed between the lines. For Peirce, it was an inappropriate, almost fawning deference, intended to gain Newcomb's patronage. For Newcomb, it was an irritated resentment of Peirce's constant begging for help in finding employment in the same breath that he flaunted his superior mathematical invention. Although Newcomb made significant contributions in astronomy—Einstein wrote to his daughter that "your father's life-work [in the field of calculating planetary perturbations] is of monumental importance to astronomy"—his knowledge of mathematics and logic was superficial.[38] At a time when the discoveries of Cantor, Riemann, and others were revolutionizing mathematics, Newcomb wrote Peirce on the subject of mathematical infinity:

Simon Newcomb, ca. 1905, in full regalia as director of the Naval Observatory, wearing the gold Huygens and Copley medals awarded him for his achievements in astronomy. Photograph courtesy of the Library of Congress.

Your last letter seems decisive in favor of a proposition which I have often been inclined to maintain, to wit, that all philosophical and logical discussion is useless. . . . I have always held that infinity, considered in itself, could not be treated as a mathematical quantity, and that it is pure nonsense to talk about one infinity being greater or less than another. . . . The very meaning of the word infinity is something without bounds. But we can compare two magnitudes only by comparing their bounds. Therefore I say the reasoning in question is baseless. What more can I say?[39]

This opinion that infinity could not be treated as a mathematical quantity revealed a mind virtually closed to mathematical inquiry and invention. When Newcomb judged Peirce's work to be of little scientific or mathematical value, his eminent reputation in both fields effectively camouflaged his ignorance of their theoretical dimensions. This led other men, often powerful and eminent themselves, who were otherwise sympathetic to Peirce to undervalue his profound originality and accomplishments and to weigh his personal faults more heavily against him.

Newcomb's revelations about Peirce resulted in the passage by the executive committee of the trustees, on January 26, 1884, of a resolution which went to extreme lengths to make it appear that there was no desire on their part to be rid of Peirce. First a directive was issued which affected all the members of the department of philosophy and psychology who held the position of lecturer and who were not members of the regular faculty. This directive stated that because of a lack of funds, none of these lectureships would be renewed the following year. Then, very shortly, all but Peirce's lectureship were renewed. Although the committee intended this indirection as a way to protect Peirce's feelings and reputation, he responded as if the trustees had attacked him personally and without just cause. Later he was to argue that he should have been allowed to resign. He wrote Gilman:

> You will doubtless be surprized at my condescending to write such a letter as the enclosed [to the executive committee]. Only one thing moves me to do it,—the knowledge that to communicate to my wife the resolutions of the committee would be her certain death. . . .
>
> I would offer the following observations which I will thank you to lay before the committee.
>
> On returning to Baltimore last September, I was unable to obtain a suitable house for one year. Therefore, as soon as the President returned I went to him and explained my difficulty and asked whether in his judgment it would be prudent for me to take a house for two years. To this important inquiry he replied that he knew of no disposition to disturb me in my place. The Treasurer suggested my purchasing a house. In view of these encouragements, I did take a house for two years. I have never heard the smallest whisper of dissatisfaction or suggestion of a possible change until I yesterday receive your resolutions. My lectures have been much better than hitherto. There has been more cooperation between the different branches of philosophical instruction. There has, in short, been no reason for a change which did not exist before. I, therefore, appeal to your sense of fairness, gentlemen, with great confidence; for to cut short my lectureship at the end of this year, though it be perfectly within the letter of the contract, is not one of the things which it is open to you under the circumstances to do. I have no doubt that President Gilman spoke truly and sincerely in encouraging me to take my house. He now tells me he has for a long time seen this crisis coming; this long time must however have been altogether subsequent to last October. And though he was not formally authorized to speak for you, you cannot disregard such encouragements given by the President of the University,—you cannot, I mean, consistently with your characters and consciences as fair men.
>
> All of this has the more force, inasmuch as the engagements of Professors [George S.] Morris and [G. Stanley] Hall have another year to run; so that you cannot make at the end of this year any change except to get rid of me.
>
> But I desire to be heard in person before your honorable board upon the condition of logical and philosophical instruction in the University.

I will undertake to show you that the defects of the present arrangements are not due to my fault or to that of Professors Morris and Hall. I will show you [by] demonstration what the difficulty is.

I also desire to address you briefly upon the present state of philosophy, and to show you that the difficulty of finding a *modus vivendi* between different schools of thought, between philosophy, science, and religion, is now much less than it has been for a very long period; so that you have only to make the philosophical department really true to the actual condition of thought, and you will bring it into a state of warm sympathy and friendship with science on the one hand and Christianity on the other.[40]

Peirce guessed accurately that his unorthodox religious views were a factor in the trustees' decision. Within a week he told Juliette, and she collapsed from both the shock and disgrace of the dismissal and his abusive behavior toward her. He himself was thoroughly demoralized. He wrote to Gilman:

My wife's condition is alarming and I am advised to throw up everything and take her abroad. I have not decided to do so, but would like to ask you a question. It was understood at the beginning of this year that I was to give 40 lectures. I have given about that number, but I am extremely loath to relinquish my courses which are just now as I think profitable to my students. Should I however decide to bring my lectures to a close,—say in three weeks,—would you think that I had fulfilled my engagement amply and was perfectly entitled to the balance of my salary although I should leave the country?[41]

The executive committee had already decided to reimburse Peirce for any loss in renting his house, but to stick to their purpose in letting him go. George W. Brown, chairman of the committee, wrote to Gilman:

Peirce's case is the most difficult to deal with. The last letter furnishes the new proof of the desirableness of making a change. I feel strongly tempted to advise payment of his year's salary and let him go, but what is to become of him and his wife in Europe unless they have money and friends? The plan seems to be too wild even for him to attempt to put it in execution. If we could part on friendly terms by paying him the rest of his year's salary and seeing him transferred elsewhere I should be glad.[42]

Gilman informed Peirce that he would be paid in full and released from further service, but Peirce had already decided not to abandon his lectures and to stay on until his contract ran out in September. By this time he was nearly prostrate with shame, exhaustion, stress, and the effects of neuralgia. Peirce intended by his decision to prove to Gilman and the executive com-

Daniel Coit Gilman, President of the Johns Hopkins University, ca. 1900. Photograph courtesy of the Library of Congress.

mittee that the reasons given for his being let go were unjust and that his teaching and research were of high caliber. He had no idea of the true cause of their action and continued to defend and justify himself on professional grounds. As he wrote with scarcely controlled outrage to Gilman on March 7, to argue that he be given an additional year's contract, since he was then convinced that his performance would justify a permanent appointment:

> I maintain that if I have fulfilled my present engagement as well as I did fulfill previous annual engagements, there would be a distinct breach of understanding in not renewing the engagement for one year more.
>
> Now in point of fact I have this year devoted about 2½ times as much time and energy to my university duties as I ever did in any previous year. My regular [logic] course, showed the fruit of a special study. . . . I have also greatly improved the inductive part of the course by introducing a practical exercise, which has greatly interested the students . . . and which (without consulting their own impressions) will, I will take it upon me to say, give them ideas of logic which will influence them [Dewey, B. I. Gilman, Ladd-Franklin, Marquand, O. H. Mitchell, and Veblen, among others] through life. Many of the lectures of this course have been master-

pieces, relatively, at least, to anything I have previously done in the university. I began and should have been glad to continue a course upon philosophical terminology, of which I have made a special study; but the students did not come, for reasons which I shall presently consider. I am giving a successful course upon the logical and mathematical doctrine of probabilities, which attracts some of the best men in the university. . . . I have guided and aided Mr. Jastrow, one of my pupils, in an experimental enquiry of a logico-psychological nature [published jointly as "On Small Differences of Sensation" in the same year[, which has certainly been advantageous to him and which will be an addition to science of some consequence. . . . [Pierce had also aided in improving the Metaphysical Club,] to which I have presented two considerable papers ["Design and Chance," which President Gilman, Dewey, Jastrow, and Professors Ira Remsen and Morris, among others, attended, and "Logic of Religion" to justify his unorthodox views on religion[and for which I have prepared several others.

Thus, I have worked far harder and better than in any previous engagement with the university, I have been regular in my attendance, I have done all that could possibly be expected of me, and all that in me lay to render my instruction useful. Still, the students have not frequented my lectures much, and in so far I have not been successful. But the reason of that is not that far to seek. It lies in the jealousy (I speak of the effect not the motive) with which I have been excluded from all participation in or even knowledge of the conduct of instruction in general. . . . I am of the opinion that to make my higher instruction thoroughly good, I ought to enter into the lower life of the university by giving some elementary instruction. . . . I would even now, for the remainder of the year, be only too glad, quite irrespective of the future, to devote as much as ten hours a week to such work. . . .

In view of these things, I say that the university is itself to blame that my work here has not been more successful; and if the executive committee are either to act with fairness or to regard the interests of the university, they will offer me another annual appointment.

My former letter contained the expression of a desire to address the executive committee (in case my connection with the university were brought to a close) upon the present condition of philosophical thought in its relation to university instruction. As the committee ignores this wish, I will no longer urge it, inferring from your silence that the committee is indifferent to the subject.[43]

Five days later on March 12, Gilman gave his final word in the matter, saying that he had read Peirce's letter to George W. Brown and Dr. Thomas, but that he did not

discover in them any disposition to change the position they have already taken, that it is better for the university that your engagement should be terminated. As to any pecuniary loss which may come to you from having hired a house for two years, I am confident the Trustees will meet you in a spirit of equity.

It gives me great pain to say this so plainly because I appreciate your high intellectual powers, & your lofty conception of the Science & Art of Logic,—but I am forced to believe that you are ⌊more⌋ adapted to the work of an investigator than ⌊crossed out: you are to the guidance & instruction of young men in their university studies⌋ to that of a university professor.[44]

The final (edited) sentence of this letter was the closest that Gilman, or any of the Hopkins trustees, ever came to explaining to Peirce their reason for dismissing him. Even the hint of moral censure which might have given him the clue was denied him. Some six months later, he may have learned directly from Hilgard the immediate reason for his great personal and professional tragedy. Peirce stayed on in Baltimore and commuted to Washington, in spite of his public disgrace, until the end of the year, four months after his contract ended in September. As a practical matter, his remaining so long was necessary because he could not sublet his house, but the main reason was that he rightly feared that his academic career was ended, and he wanted to continue, as long as he could, the intense and fruitful comradeship in learning that he had created with his students and with those of the faculty for whom he had respect in the heartening intellectual environment provided by Gilman and the trustees.

Peirce did not mention in his letter to Gilman the course on the psychology of great men which he had begun in the fall of 1883 and continued through the summer and fall of 1884. Peirce had a personal interest in the course because, as he had written six years before to Gilman, "I make the pretension to being the most thoroughgoing representative of ⌊the logic of science⌋ who as yet appeared." Convinced as he was (though ambivalently) of his own greatness, he was as curious to find out what he shared with other great men as he was to inquire into the nature of greatness in men generally. Peirce used contemporary biographies and worked out an elaborate series of questionnaires to apply to "an Impressionist List of 300 Great Men," whom he divided into three overlapping categories of feeling (first), action (second), and thought (third). Among those for whom specific questionnaires were prepared and, in some cases, answered were Pythagoras, Leonidas, Archimedes, Mencius, Ockham, Rabelais, Machiavelli, Michelangelo, Hobbes, Montaigne, Locke, and Gauss. The list was to be reduced to twenty-four after the application of statistical analysis to determine the general characteristics of each type. The study, never completed, may have been the first application of statistical methods to comparative biography. Peirce's 1901 paper "The Century's Great Men of Science," published by the Smithsonian Institution, was derived from these earlier researches done by him and his students.

Ever since 1880, when he had heard his father lecture on evolutionary cosmology, and with greater intensity since his father's death later that year, Peirce had been musing about the universe and process, in part because he knew that his father considered him his intellectual and spiritual heir. His thoughts about his painful predicament also drew him into speculation about the meaning of events. The beginnings of these remarkable musings appeared in an 1884 lecture given to the Johns Hopkins Metaphysical Club, titled "Design and Chance," which recalls the discussions of the Cambridge Metaphysical Club. As Nathan Houser has written:

> The lecture draws together a number of ideas that had become prominent in Peirce's writings and lectures. He had long been interested [in] the Darwinian controversy which had swept America after the first copies of *Origin of the Species* arrived in the fall of 1859, and as early as the following summer he was convinced that Darwin's theory, "which was nourished by positive observation," was destined to play a major rôle in the development of thought for years to come. Philip Wiener has suggested that Peirce saw in evolutionism, when welded to his "rigorous scientific logic," a way to "make room for freedom of the individual will and religious values," and Max Fisch has suggested that "Peirce had an ulterior interest in the logic of evolution as a weapon in his lifelong war against nominalism." But Peirce was also driven by the desire of the scientific philosopher to find things out and to bring whatever he could within the scope of explanatory hypotheses, and he was committed to the economy of explanation—he was a wielder of Ockham's razor—and always sought theories that represented the universe as parsimoniously as its richness would allow. In evolutionism he saw the prospect for a theory he could generalize and develop into a cosmological principle of the highest order.[45]

It was no doubt a relief for Peirce to consider the order of the universe when his particular world was so confused and painful. He became increasingly outraged as he worked harder and harder to vindicate himself, and he continued to berate Gilman and the trustees for the rest of the year with accusations of fraud and treachery. In fury and despair, he summed up his claims against the university in a letter written to the chairman of the executive committee, George W. Brown, in October, a month after his contract expired and he had given up all hope of continuing at Hopkins:

> I have in my possession a letter addressed to me last spring in reply to one of my communications to the Executive Committee, in which President Gilman assures me that he is confident the trustees will secure me

against loss in consequence of my being unable to get rid of the house . . . I had leased. I now write to ask your honorable body whether this assurance will hold good or whether it is only one of the promises made in air. . . . [Peirce then narrated the history of the events leading up to his dismissal and concluded that] he [Gilman] had acted most treacherously and falsely. . . .

When I asked him what were the causes of dissatisfaction, he said that my lectures had been irregular. . . .

There had been a little [of that] it is true. Namely, I was not present at three of my lectures. But the lectures themselves were read from my manuscript. . . .

The president gave a different reason in a letter to me. Namely, that while a good investigator, I was not a successful teacher. To this there are two replies.

1st. This year when I no longer lecture at the University, the students seek me out to get my private instruction.

2nd. My pupils have done some of the most import[ant] work of late years in advancing formal logic.

. . . The resolution of the Trustees was artfully framed to injure me as much as possible.

If it had named me, I suppose it would have failed to pass the board, for I hope you or somebody would have suggested that I be allowed to resign.

But it passed because it was expressed in general terms and extended to all the instructors in the department. Now all the others have been taken back, the disguise is thrown aside & I am spoken of as dismissed personally by the Trustees.

. . . I have thus been treated treacherously and unjustly. . . .

I now end by asking, as I began, whether the written assurance [citing Gilman's letter of March 11] of your President . . . that I should not suffer loss, is a valuable promise or whether it is merely something easy to say and convenient to unsay.[46]

Brown responded that if Peirce would be specific, he would do what he could to pay for his losses. Peirce responded with his bill for reparations the next day:

I hold that the University, having through its president recognized its obligation to do *something* for me in consequence of my having been led to take this house, it follows that what it is bound to do is to make me as well off as if I had not taken the house. [Peirce then outlined seven claims: (1) the house should be taken off his hands, (2) one-half of his expenses in painting, etc., should be paid, (3) the gas fixtures should be purchased at cost.]

4th. All the standing furniture, carpets, hangings, etc. should be purchased of me at 10 percent less than what I paid. This should be done, because these things are useless to me for the following reasons:

1). My wife's health already delicate, has been shattered by her strange experience of American dealings. I mean that line of conduct on the part of the University which has placed it under an acknowledged obligation of reparation. Consequently, she cannot keep house, and requires to be carried to the South. [In April, Juliette had ascribed her ill health to Charles's abusive behavior toward her.]

2). It is at this season impossible to get a suitable flat in Washington; and delicate furniture like ours cannot be stored without injury.

3). The furniture would be of no use, even if Mrs. Peirce had not sustained the shock mentioned, and we could get the flat in Washington, because the furniture is artistic, and money was paid to make it so; and this character would be lost if it were placed in rooms for which it is inappropriate, as it would be in a flat. Besides, apart from the question of taste, the pieces are much too large for a flat.

Ten percent is sufficient allowance for use during these months, because the furniture has been treated with exceptional care.

5th. All our expenses of travelling and transportation between here and Washington and hotel bills in Washington, incurred since the cessation of my connection with the University, should be defrayed.

6th. All expenses of bringing things from Washington, from the beginning, should be defrayed.

7th. The expense of packing and transporting to Washington everything in the house except what the University purchases should be defrayed, with an allowance of 15 percent on the value of the articles, for breakage.

Such are the assessable damages. The injury to my wife's health, the vexation caused by the bad faith of the University, cannot be estimated in money. Yet something should be allowed on this account, say the Doctor's bill, or ⅔ of it.

It would, however, be troublesome to enter into all the details above indicated, and therefore in lieu of everything, if all hesitation and haggling can thereby be avoided, I will accept one thousand dollars, and will, for the sake of terminating the business at once, call that sufficient and satisfactory, and will do what I can with the house and its contents.[47]

To protect himself from possible legal action, Gilman wrote a letter to the executive committee which concluded, after reaffirming his promise to meet Peirce's demands in a spirit of equity:

I think it will be clear

(1) that until near the close of December, 1883, I had no suspicion that

Mr. Peirce's relations to the University would be disturbed; gradually it became evident that they must be; & my change and bearing was undisguised, unequivocal, & so pronounced that he felt it keenly.

(2) That all my communications to Mr. Peirce after January 26, were under the authority of the Executive Committee. I was their agent. . . .

In conclusion, allow me to add that I know of no custom which should lead the Trustees to proclaim their reasons for terminating an annual engagement. . . . I am sorry that the desire to treat Mr. Peirce with consideration & equity & to attract as little attention as possible to his release from office should appear to him in such a different light.[48]

In a memorandum for the record written December 1, Brown reaffirmed Gilman's statement that he acted on the basis of information given him in late December 1883, and that "from that time onward Mr. Gilman's communications to Mr. Peirce were governed by the action of the Executive Committee and were taken in consultation with two members of that body."[49]

There is no official record of the way in which Peirce's claim was resolved, but the lack of further demands from him surely means that it was met. The settlement did not, however, mean the end of this embittered relationship.

Peirce had earlier asked Gilman for permission to take out as many books, mostly those he had sold to Hopkins, as he needed for his *Century Dictionary* project, and Gilman had instructed Browne, the librarian, to allow him to do so. Peirce made a practice of keeping them at his home for easy reference. When he left Hopkins, Peirce took the books, a substantial number, with him. He put off returning them again and again, pleading that he continued to need them for his work on logic. In 1887, he was so careless with some of them that at least two turned up at auction. Browne wrote Gilman:

> I have just received a note from Lowdermilk & Co., Washington booksellers, saying that among some books bought at a sale of unclaimed packages by the Adams Express Co., there were two with our label; and they give the titles. One of these is one of the books receipted for by Mr. Peirce, and the other I have suspected him of taking, though I had no evidence of it.
>
> I have asked L. & Co. what other booksellers were likely to have bought at the same sale. If I thought there was a reasonable probability of recovering our books, I would go or send to Washington. This whole thing has been a thorn in my flesh for more than three years.[50]

Gilman wrote to F. M. Thorn, then superintendent of the Survey, requesting that any books of Peirce's held there belonging to Hopkins be returned. Thorn then wrote to Peirce asking permission for Gilman to examine his boxes in Washington, which Peirce refused, saying that all the books were with him because a publisher had "induced me to resume my abandoned work [on logic]. . . . A limit of time was named and this has long been surpassed. My work is now ⅞ done, . . . " and Peirce wished to keep them until he was finished.[51] Peirce then offered to buy back for $1,000 the books he had originally sold to Hopkins. Gilman wrote to Brown, chairman of the executive committee, "I have conferred with Dr. Browne [the librarian], and we concur in thinking that it would be wise for the Trustees to accept Mr. Peirce's offer to pay $1000 for the books bought of him in January 1881."[52] By the end of May 1887, it was agreed that Peirce would keep the books he had and would be sent the rest of his books from Hopkins upon receipt of the four volumes in his possession belonging to Hopkins and $600. Peirce kept the books he had but never paid the agreed price, and so he never regained the remaining books at Hopkins. Twenty years later he tried without success to reopen the negotiation.

In time, Peirce's feelings about Gilman's treachery subsided; and his original respect for Gilman's idea and practice of a university returned. Ten years after his dismissal, Peirce wrote asking Gilman if he would object to having dedicated to him, as president of Johns Hopkins University, the twelve-volume work on philosophy which he planned to write.[53] Although Gilman replied that he would be gratified to have his name associated with the work and that he appreciated the spirit which had prompted the note, his agreeableness did not extend to his personal relations with Peirce.[54] When Gilman was in New York a year or two later visiting with Peirce's former student Christine Ladd-Franklin and her husband, Fabian Franklin, editor of the *Independent*, upon making the discovery that Peirce was also there, he took his leave, saying that he "would not stay under the same roof with so immoral a man."[55]

Thus ended Peirce's controversial connection with Johns Hopkins. Excepting those lectures given some twenty years before at Harvard and a course of lectures in Cambridge and one at Harvard University itself, both of which he was still to give under James's auspices, his time there was the whole of his academic career. Although the length of his stay was brief, its effects were profound on his few but exceptional students and, through them, on the course of logic and philosophy.

Peirce's disconsolate return to actual full-time duties with the Coast Survey in May 1884 was made slightly more palatable to him by a raise in salary to $3,000.[56] Hilgard and the other assistants, however, were aware that he had intended to leave the Survey and that he had little respect for the scientific abilities of his associates. Peirce commuted from Baltimore to Washington, where he worked at the Smithsonian pendulum station, avoiding his Survey colleagues. In July, Hilgard ordered him to swing pendulums at Fortress Monroe, Virginia, and then to reconnoiter the northern Appalachians for possible stations. Peirce spent the first half of September based at the Mountain Top Hotel in the Blue Ridge Mountains, where he had taken Juliette for a rest. Aunt Lizzie reported that Peirce "likes the Virginians *very* much—so much nicer than the 'pesky Yankees.' Juliette had been & was sick & suffering & Charley had her carried up in a litter to the top of a high & steep mountain."[57] Despite Juliette's frailty and frequent invalidism, she and Charles traveled almost everywhere together, an arrangement which seriously hampered Charles's professional life. Peirce's suggestion that he occupy the University of Virginia, among other locations, during the coming year suggests that he had hopes of employment there and had not yet given up hope of continuing in an academic career.

When the Peirces returned to Baltimore in October, Hilgard put Charles in charge of the Office of Weights and Measures, and in that capacity he traveled to Philadelphia, New York, Hartford, Providence, and Boston, where he met with electricians and manufacturers of gauges to help them meet higher standards of measurement. In Washington, he continued to work at the Smithsonian, mainly on overdue reports, of which there were many. At this point, Peirce had decided to regain his position and reputation in the Survey, and his work produced a flurry of publications on his pendulum researches, including the report, delayed since 1879, on "Methods, Results, Determinations of Gravity at Stations in Pennsylvania." In January 1885, he testified to Congress on the Office of Weights and Measures. In early March 1885, Hilgard ordered him to occupy Key West, where a series of unforeseen problems added costs and delayed work until April. Aunt Lizzie reported that

> Charles Peirce & his wife are away off at Key West on Coast Survey business—weighing the earth or something. The climate in Key West is delightful. It is an island about 5 miles long—the most westerly of some of the West Indian groups of Islands. It has not much to recommend it excepting the climate & cocoa nut trees. I should not like to live there even for a short time. There is an insect there called jiggers—a sort of flea—which gets under the flesh & there breeds a quantity of other jiggers which become very painful and troublesome & they have to be cut out. Now I must go up to dress.[58]

In Key West, Peirce had successfully conducted experiments in equal residual gravity in preparation for writing his major work on measurements of gravity along the eastern arc of the United States, the work for which had begun in the Hoosac tunnel in 1873.[59] On their return, with no stayover in Washington, the Peirces went directly to New York, arriving in late May.

Peirce did so in part to distance himself from the disarray in the Survey office, where Hilgard's drunkenness had become virtually public. In New York, he worked on several papers for publication in the Survey *Reports*, including a major one on procedures for determining gravity. Juliette continued in frail health, and Peirce informed Hilgard that he would reluctantly be obliged to give up the Office of Weights and Measures because he would be unable to leave her, but Hilgard refused to accept his resignation.[60] While in New York, Peirce spent much time at the Century Club discussing his future possibilities with his cronies. In June, while visiting his mother in Cambridge, he happened to see an announcement of Harvard courses for the following year and was pained to see that there was no logic course, except of the most elementary kind. Peirce, remembering the central position the discipline had held in his undergraduate days and hoping to breach Harvard's opposition to his teaching there, wrote of his feelings to his friend William James on June 20, offering to give twelve lectures in logic. The subjects constitute a summary of the work he had done at Hopkins:

Lect. I. Elementary ideas on the Theory of Cognition
Lect. II. Explanations of certain conceptions.
Lect. III. The Boolian Calculus
Lect. IV. Logic of Relatives
Lect. V. Logic of Second Intentions[,] Syllogisms of Transposed quantity, Fermatian Inference etc.
Lect. VI. Probability
Lect. VII. Induction & Hypothesis
Lect. VIII. Fair sampling.
Lect. IX. Predesignation.
Lect. X. Laws of Nature.
Lect. XI. A method for the discovery of methods.
Lect. XII. Transcendental Logic. [This is the first use of the phrase as his own in Peirce's correspondence.]

 I should take a pleasure & a pride in delivering these lectures gratuitously. Still, as I should lose $90 of my Coast Survey salary, I would not refuse to have that made up to me; at the same time I think it would be better that should not be done.[61]

James was intrigued and thought he might be able to convince Eliot to change his mind. Peirce wrote him again, summarizing his work at Hopkins on the subject and its importance:

 Of course, 12 lectures could give but a sketch of Logic; but still I am sure it would be a useful sketch (to a small number of persons,) because it would show what the true import is of writings which need such an explanation. It would open up the new formal logic, show its depth & importance, and also how to study it. It would outline a course of study in probability; and show what problems are merely special & what others are of the greatest utility. It would show, in regard to inductive reasoning, what the true rules of it are,—most important practically in carrying this method into a new field, & for want of appreciation of which most of such researches have suffered greatly; and it would also show the relation of the theory of induction to the theory of cognition. Finally, it would show how all these branches form one organic whole.

Thus, though a course of instruction in higher Logic cannot be given in twelve lectures, an outline & preliminary sketch might be given which I cannot help hoping would be found useful to three classes of persons, 1st, special students of philosophy, 2nd, students who may wish to take up some of the many new branches of what may be called special psychology, (such as my own study of Comparative Biography) and 3rd to those of you who are considering what instruction in logic ought to consist of.

P.S. I have not sent out any copies of my new memoir in the Am. Journal of Mathematics because the paper is not yet completed & the most important part of it is to come [in fact, it did not appear because the new editor, Newcomb, was to reject it]. But I consider it as the beginning of a new life for Formal Logic.[62]

James was unable to convince Eliot and the Corporation of the importance for philosophy and science of Peirce's offer, and nothing came of it.

On his return to New York, Peirce began to try to locate the Gautier pendulums he had left unfinished in Paris. Gautier had refused to send them uncompleted and was holding them for another destination, not having heard from Peirce for two years. The pendulums that Peirce was using were sufficiently flawed in workmanship that he considered it necessary to abandon further field work until receipt of those from Gautier. He suggested to Hilgard that he be ordered to Paris for three weeks to oversee their completion.[63] Hilgard refused, insisting that Peirce proceed with the field work without an assistant and with the pendulums on hand, and he blamed Peirce for having left Europe without the Gautier pendulums. Peirce then angrily decided to go to France himself:

> As I shall have, . . . to use the pendulums, and the satisfaction and reputation I shall derive from my work will depend upon their being properly executed, I will pay my own travelling expenses to Paris and return; . . . I shall certainly always feel that I have been treated with downright injustice, but not so grossly as you now propose.[64]

The next day he changed his mind, saying, "I do not think I could ask my wife to make two voyages at so short an interval without necessity, and I certainly could not leave her behind, so that I withdraw my proposition of yesterday."[65] Having backed down, Peirce made plans to occupy Ithaca, New York, Erie, Pennsylvania, Ann Arbor, Michigan, and Madison, Wisconsin, with three of the locations obviously offering the possibility of university employment. Four days before his arrival at Ann Arbor on July 29, which was to be his base of operations, the *Washington Post* had carried a story which stated that the Coast Survey had come under investigation by the Allison Commission because of "exorbitant expenditures," with the result that Superintendent Hilgard had been suspended, the assistant in charge, C. O. Boutelle, had been discharged, as had the disbursing agent, and Frank Manly Thorn, a Buffalo, New York, newspaperman and lawyer, then chief clerk of the Internal Revenue Bureau, had been appointed superintendent of the survey to "root out corruption."[66] Corruption there was, and Thorn eventually secured the restitution to the government of $4,600 from Hilgard and others.

The next day, the *Post* carried the following account:

> The Treasury officials . . . had come to regard the [Coast Survey] as a supercilious little aristocracy of scientists, who considered themselves an entirely self contained and independent organization, accountable only to Congress, the appropriations committees of which they could always control by bringing the influence of college professors to bear on them, and representing that science would suffer if the bureau was crippled by common restrictions or [ruled by other than] its own scientific heads. This attitude has become traditional in the bureau. . . . The men at the head of the service are a close set of old barnacles who have always tried to have things their own way, without any checks, supervisions or interferences; and having succeeded so long they are impatient under the present movement of reform.

On August 3, Peirce and two others were accused of appropriating Survey chronometers for their own use:

> It is true that gold chronometers purchased years ago for scientific use in the survey field, have cost from $100 to $300 apiece, have fallen into disuse of late in the bureau and have been appropriated to the private use of some of these officials. Prof. Pierce [*sic*], Mr. M. W. Wines, property clerk, and Prof Hilgard himself have found them worthy of being worn in their vest pockets.

Hilgard was given a summary dismissal on August 6, and the next day the *Post* carried the following headline:

INTOXICATED—DEMORALIZED
A Terrible Arraignment of Coast Survey Officials
Prof. Hilgard and Others Charged with Being Drunk in Office

The account went on to detail abuses of Survey funds, nepotism, and immoral conduct, and singled out Peirce as one of the worst offenders. Peirce was, in fact, the only assistant, other than Boutelle, the assistant in charge, accused of dereliction. By absenting himself from the Survey office in Washington because of his distaste for the mess there, he had left himself open to attack by those whom he had so often disdained. The Allison Commission's report, based upon Survey records prepared by Thorn's deputy, stated that

> for several years, beginning in 1873, C. S. Peirce, assistant, has been making experimental researches with pendulums, without restriction or limitation as to times and places; that since 1879 expenditures on account of those experiments, aside from salaries of chiefs and assistants, amount to about $31,000 [about $500,000 in 1990 dollars]; that the meager value of those experiments to the bureau have been substantially destroyed.[67]

Thorn was a high-minded Cleveland reform Democrat who believed in enforcing the distinction between theoretical and practical science by denying funding to the former. He immediately set about drastically reducing the salaries and operating expenses of the scientific staff, thus saving about $25,000 during his tenure, but gutting the Survey's scientific program, especially the kind of research done by Peirce.[68] Thorn, on taking charge, had immediately written to President Gilman to discover Peirce's schedule at Hopkins on the obvious and accurate grounds that his lectureship there had seriously detracted from his Survey responsibilities. This act changed the rule established by Patterson to relax demands on Peirce when no raise was given him, and which Hilgard had reluctantly adhered to, in part. Peirce's longtime assistant, Farquhar, testified that after 1876, Peirce had done very few of the pendulum experiments himself: one night's worth in 1877, two or three in 1879, only those for flexure in 1880. All the rest were done by Farquhar himself. When asked about waste, Farquhar said: "I can only record my general impression *one of prodigal extravagance.* An inspection of the room last occupied by him at this office No[.] 82 (usually locked) will speak more to the purpose than I can with voice & pen."[69]

Even though the charges against him were substantially modified by Thorn to extravagance and procrastination, the combined effect of Peirce's being dismissed from Hopkins and a year later being investigated by Congress for negligence was thoroughly damaging to his reputation. There is little doubt that his inability to obtain fitting employment after 1885 can largely be blamed on these two events. At any rate, from this time on, Peirce's reputation acquired more and more notoriety.

Peirce protested strongly that he was innocent of all charges, and he tendered his resignation from the Survey on August 9. With the resignation he enclosed a point-by-point denial of the charges against him, addressed to Secretary of the Treasury Daniel Manning.[70] He also circulated a pamphlet in which he denied categorically the charges made by the Allison Commission, which was successful in bringing the American Academy of Arts and Sciences to pass a resolution supporting him. Two days later he told Thorn that if the Survey intended to continue the station at Ann Arbor, another person should be appointed, "so as to avail himself of my knowledge of the subject. I do not think that any of the gentlemen on the Survey whom I know are fit to have charge of the work."[71] On August 14, Assistant Schott, of whom Peirce had said five days earlier that he "is personally inimical to me, as I have good reason to think," wrote Thorn's deputy, Colonna, that the acceptance of Peirce's resignation would result

> in a great loss to the higher scientific work of the Survey, and in particular since he has been able to build up, at home and abroad, a reputation of which the Survey may be proud.
>
> After experimenting, pointing out and removing, theoretically and practically, existing defects in earlier work he is now prepared to carry his experience into that regular and systematic work of the pendulum researches of which the C. & G. Survey now stands most in need. We cannot afford to lose all this experience *just at the eve* when the Survey can realize and be benefited by his earlier and necessarily costly labors. From a scientific standpoint and for the reputation of the Survey I could not but greatly regret if his connection with [the] Survey should be severed.[72]

But Peirce, who know nothing of Schott's letter, did not live up to these expectations, and Schott was assigned Peirce's gravimetric researches less than a year later. Peirce wrote Thorn that he had devised a new system for gravity work and that it might be best for him to contract with the Survey to carry it out, but he thought better of the suggestion and withdrew his resignation on August 15 by telegram.[73]

The complete disorganization of the Coast Survey brought about by the investigation resulted in Charles and Juliette's being stranded in Ann Arbor with neither funds nor equipment. Peirce complained bitterly to Thorn, who had counseled patience:

> The month is slipping by. I might be at work if I had the instruments. If I had a pendulum and head, only, I should be all right. Then our bed and

all our sheets and things are there [in Washington]. The consequent expo-
sure has I fear given my wife her death-blow. She is now very low, and
should she die I will have the heart's blood of the man, whoever it is, who
prevented those boxes from coming. I surely will. I can't find the beauty of
patience.[74]

The man whose heart's blood Peirce wanted was Benjamin Azariah
Colonna, whom Thorn had made his deputy in charge of Coast Survey
operations. Colonna was a blunt, brusque, Bible-quoting, incorruptible man
with little training in science, who had been in the Survey since 1870. He
was a partially crippled Civil War veteran, which may have added to the
harshness with which he dealt with those of whose morals he disapproved.
Colonna's disapproval of Peirce had nothing to do with Peirce's scientific
ability, for which he had the highest regard, but was founded on what the
Survey regarded as Peirce's principal defects: his extravagance and procrastination, to which was added the arrogance which he affected. Suggestions
have been made that Colonna was psychologically unfit to exercise authority, but there is no evidence of it, other than the accusations themselves.[75]

On September 1, Colonna wrote Peirce a letter in which he responded
to Peirce's complaints and tirades at length. Colonna had made some mistakes, and the tone of the letter was conciliatory. He reported that Peirce's
resignation was "not particularly sought and you are under misapprehension
. . . [which] in the interest of the Survey and of yourself I took the liberty of
withholding. Mr. Schott agreeing with my action." He then discussed his
report to the Allison Commission, which he enclosed for Peirce's information and comment. He apologized for mentioning Peirce in connection with
the Office of Weights and Measures, "that poorly organized establishment,"
because he had not known that Peirce had tendered his resignation from it
twice. Colonna went on to evaluate the various elements of the Survey,
frankly expressing his opinions of the condition of each one. He gave high
marks to only one office, computing, under the control of Assistant Schott.
The rest he considered to be in various stages of mismanagement, and he
said that the time for reorganization was long overdue. Of Hilgard, Colonna
wrote: "That the professor has proved a failure as Superintendent of the
Coast and Geodetic Survey, I do not hesitate to declare. He is dilatory and
vacillating, and addicted to drink, or some other habit, which at times much
impairs his fitness for duty. I believe him to be honest, but a much misguided man."

The report criticized the lack of restrictions on Peirce's research and the
high costs incurred. Colonna added an appendix for Peirce's examination
which showed the cited figures to be accurate and quoted Hilgard's testi-

mony: "I suppose Professor Peirce has failed to file the results of his pendulum experiments in original and duplicate. He usually carries the day & locates where he thinks best." Colonna commented that he did not believe Peirce's scientific reputation had been assailed—though his report had in fact called Peirce's results "meagre"—only Peirce's business methods and want of conformity with Survey regulations, which Colonna believed had been justly criticized. He also believed that "all hands" wanted Peirce to stay on, but that he would have to do so on the same terms as any other assistant. Colonna concluded:

> It is a rash friend but a true one who will venture to tell another the exact truth when it points out a fault but I feel that I would rather risk the loss of your friendship by this endeavor . . . than to retain it and allow you to injure yourself. . . . [Peirce commented in the margin: There is a general come down in the tone of this letter, which is virtually from Thorn. My letters to Thorn had been most plain in their tone to say the least. He could not him self give me the answer he wanted given.][76]

Two years later, Thorn wrote to Peirce, who continued to accuse Colonna of treacherous behavior:

> I do not undertake to answer for Mr. Colonna's sentiments, beyond the assertion of my belief in the rough-and-tumble earnestness of his purpose to correct abuses and promote efficiency in the administration of bureau affairs; but so far as yours relates to me or my sentiments toward you I am tempted to say that the entire screed is a spasm of ridiculous hysterics of which the exercise of a little of that "good sense" or "good feeling" which you commend to others will be pretty sure to make you ashamed.[77]

Peirce, for his part, was disgusted at being connected with the Survey, and he expressed himself characteristically to William James on October 28:

> I am very much obliged to you for your efforts in my behalf. This horrid & sickening business of the Survey makes me long intensely for University life. The villainous things which I hear whispered, the Vandal methods of trying to set things right, the accusations of which I have myself been the subject, combine to make me loathe the Survey so, that I would rather keep a pea-nut stand than stay in it one minute longer than my duty requires me to do.
>
> I think I have something of importance to say concerning methods of reasoning. . . . I think molecular science, for instance, cannot advance another step without the guidance of logic. But then if the world does not wish to hear what I have to say, my little dodge will be to find out what I am

wanted to do & to do it,—so long as it doesn't consist in remaining in the Service of the U. S.

I want to be appointed Professor of scientific Logic in the University of St. Helena. Could not some people be found who would subscribe something handsome to induce me to go there and never come back?

I wrote [E. L.] Youmans [editor of the *Popular Science Monthly*],—at his particular request,—a notice of Royce's book [*The Religious Aspect of Philosophy*]. I was a long time over the book & wrote I thought something really very good, for me; but Youmans wouldn't print it, i. e. he made such a wry mouth that I relieved him of it.

I have something very vast now. I shall write it for Mind. They will say it is too vast for them. It is, or within it has a part of it, an attempt to explain the laws of nature, to show their general characteristics and to trace them to their origin & predict new laws by the laws of nature. [Peirce outlined his cosmogony in Cambridge in January 1886, but it was not published until the *Monist* series in 1891–93.] The new philosophers will all say, "How crude"![78]

In Ann Arbor, Madison, and Ithaca, where he had the company of scholars and the possibility of academic employment to distract him from his increasingly distasteful Survey labors, Peirce took the time to work at his philosophy along the lines which he had announced in "Design and Chance" the year before at Hopkins. He raised two matters of interest in his letter to James. The first, his review of Royce, which he had retrieved from Youmans, represented a reexamination of the arguments against Berkeleyan idealism he had first presented in his review of Berkeley in 1871. In the process, he reexamined his own realist position, and this led him back to a closer consideration of the categories he had set forth in 1867 and, because of Royce's Hegelian sympathies, to Hegel's dialectic as a logically deficient predecessor of his own. Peirce was still so uncertain about the meaning of realism as a philosophical doctrine that as late as 1889 his entry for the word in the *Century Dictionary* was largely a quotation from Francis E. Abbot's *Scientific Theism*, and his definition of *realist* was limited to the logician as scholastic realist and the "philosopher who believes in the real existence of the external world as independent of all thought about it." This was the meaning he gave to Secondness, the indexical relation—the "Outward Clash"—which in 1885 he seemed to recognize for the first time as the key to his own doctrine that Apel calls "meaning-critical realism."[79] Peirce wrote a number of versions of "One, Two, Three" during his midwestern travels. In one he called them fundamental categories of thought and nature, in another Kantian categories, and in a third an evolutionist speculation. The second, his "attempt to explain the laws of nature," was a direct development of his "Design and Chance" lecture. There Peirce proposed a probabilistic physical universe which brilliantly anticipated the most recent cosmological hypothesis of some fundamental (or particle) physicists that the universe, including its laws, has evolved.[80] This prescience is the more remarkable because it derived not from an examination of physical laws, but from a questioning of the "exact truth of axioms," that is, from an analysis of the logic of science. Peirce questioned the axiom that nature is uniform:

> In order to explain what I mean, let us take one of the most familiar, although not one of the most scientifically accurate statements of the axiom viz.: that *every event has a cause*. I question whether this is exactly true. . . . may it not be that *chance*, in the Aristotelian sense, mere absence of cause, has to be admitted as having some slight place in the universe.
>
> Is this a mere idle doubt? . . .
>
> If we are to admit that every event has a cause, we are bound by every maxim of consistency to grant that every fact has an explanation, a reason. . . .
>
> Among the things that demand an explanation, then, are the laws of physics; and not this law or that law only but every single law. Why are the three laws of mechanics as they are and not otherwise? What is the cause of the restriction of extended bodies to three dimensions?
>
> And then the general fact that there are laws, how is that to be explained?
>
> The general idea of evolution governs science more and more; and every system of philosophy since Kant, however idealistic or however materialistic has strongly felt its influence. Evolution is the postulate of logic, itself; for what is an *explanation* but the adoption of a simpler supposition to account for a complex state of things. . . .
>
> A most important premise, playing a great part in the establishment of the Nebular Hypothesis [that the structure of the solar system can be accounted for by assuming its lawful evolution from a cloud of dense matter] or the Theory of Natural Selection, is that things must on the whole have proceeded from the Homogenous to the Heterogenous.
>
> Now the theories of evolution that have hitherto been set forth . . . all suppose essentially the same basis of physical law to have been operative in every age of the universe.
>
> But I maintain that the postulate that things shall be explicable extends itself to *laws* as well as states of things. We want a theory of the evolution of physical law. We ought to suppose that as we go back into the indefinite past not merely special laws but *law* itself is found to be less and less determinate. And how can that be if causation was always as rigidly necessary as it is now?
>
> . . . Explicability has no determinate & absolute limit. Everything being explicable, everything has been brought about; and consequently every-

thing is subject to change and subject to chance. . . . Chance will sometime bring about a change in every condition; or at least, this is as near a correct statement of the matter as can be readily drawn up, for quite correct it certainly is not.[81]

Peirce went on to suggest that in matter's fine grain, where "molecules are so inconceivably numerous, their encounters so inconceivably frequent, that chance with them is omnipotent," and that the

> feature of chance . . . although it can only work upon the basis of some law or uniformity, or more or less definite ratio towards a uniformity, has the property of being able to produce uniformities far more strict than those from which it works.
>   . . . Now I will suppose that all known laws are due to chance and repose upon others far less rigid themselves due to chance and so on in an infinite regress, the further we go back the more indefinite being the nature of the laws, and in this way we see the possibility of an indefinite approximation toward a complete explanation of nature.[82]

Despite its occasional strangeness, this extraordinary lecture, written during what was, for Peirce, a difficult and chaotic time, has great importance for understanding the uncanny accuracy of Peirce's thinking about physical reality in the light of modern discoveries. This prescience was pointed out in 1984, one hundred years after Peirce's lecture at Johns Hopkins titled "Design and Chance," by the Nobel Prize–winning chemist and one of the founders of the "new physics" of chaos, Ilya Prigogine, among the few modern theoreticians of science to have read Peirce. Prigogine showed how Peirce's view of time and the second law of thermodynamics anticipated the "new physics" which derives order out of chaos by means of the idea that very small, chance differences can quickly create "self-organized" large-scale uniform effects—that the physical world we perceive is characterized by extremely sensitive dependence on initial conditions, a fact which Peirce himself had pointed out.[83] Prigogine quotes a "remarkable passage":

> You have all heard of the dissipation of energy. It is found that in all transformations of energy a part is converted into heat and heat is always tending to equalize its temperature. The consequence is that the energy of the universe is tending by virtue of its necessary laws toward a death of the universe in which there shall be no force but heat and the temperature everywhere the same.
>   We may say that we know enough of the forces at work in the universe to know that there is none which can counteract this tendency away from every definite end but death.

But although no force can counteract this tendency, chance may and will have the opposite influence. Force is in the long run dissipative; chance is in the long run concentrative. The dissipation of energy by the regular laws of nature is by those very laws accompanied by circumstances more and more favorable to its reconcentration by chance. There must therefore be a point at which the two tendencies are balanced and that is no doubt the actual condition of the whole universe at the present time.[84]

Prigogine went on to state that " . . . Peirce's metaphysics was considered as one more example of philosophy alienated from reality. . . . Today, Peirce's work appears a pioneering step toward understanding the pluralism involved in physical laws."

The beauty and the distance of these extraordinary speculations from the everyday realities of his professional life provided him with a world of imagination fit to live in. He also diverted himself in the writing of entries for the *Century Dictionary*, finishing the words in E in 1885.

Although Peirce meant to leave the Survey, he had only limited financial means of his own and was used to living well. Juliette's persistent illness drew heavily on his time and resources, and, furthermore, she managed her income herself. For the first time, he realized fully that, despite his feelings about the Survey, he had no other source of employment, nor any prospect of any. The result was that Peirce stayed with the Survey, though he intended to leave it as soon as he could find the right way to do so. The realization of his dependency forced him for the first time to grapple, often unsuccessfully, with the bureaucratic details required of his position in the Survey, details he had usually left to his subordinates as he pursued his own philosophical interests. In his monthly reports he was required to give a daily account of his experimental and research activity. He was held accountable for the estimates he provided for the future occupation of pendulum stations. He was often short and paid for the shortfall out of pocket.

For the rest of 1885, Peirce continued pendulum observations at the universities of Michigan and Wisconsin and at Cornell University. Characteristically, after finishing at Madison, he was unable to travel beyond Niagara Falls on his way to Cornell before running out of money. He was forced to remain there for two weeks in November, begging Thorn and Colonna alternately for money: "I have already explained in a letter how unexpected demands just before leaving Madison and error in estimating expenses caused me to run short of cash at Niagara Falls, where I was unfortunately detained 15 days [during which time he gratefully pursued his own studies], until [the] check reached me from Washington."[85]

From Niagara Falls, Peirce remarked to Thorn that he might test the competency of his successor on some mathematical problems he had forwarded to Schott, as "I may perhaps be not much longer connected with the work. . . . "[86] He may have believed, wrongly as it turned out, that an appointment might be forthcoming at one of the three universities. While at Cornell in December, Peirce applied to Thorn for a leave of absence, saying that he had enough work to last him a year or longer without occupying any more stations, and that he was aware that there might not be funds sufficient to employ him for the remainder of the fiscal year. He proposed to work in New York under one of two alternative arrangements until June, when the report would be ready for publication.

When he finished at Cornell in late January 1886, the Peirces went to Cambridge to visit his family and to get the records necessary for his long gravimetric report. While there, Peirce enjoyed a philosophical interlude with his old friend William James and also shared his latest cosmological proposals in a lecture at his brother Jem's house, which was attended by James, Josiah Royce, John Fiske, Francis Abbot, and Ralph Barton Perry. With the probable exception of Royce, who was to make use of Peirce's triadic logic as the structure of his Christian idealism, they did not understand him. Abbot wrote in his diary what he thought of Peirce's "logical theory of evolution":

> Peirce begins with absolute or pure potentiality, with absolute Chance, or negation of all law, even logical, to evolve at last Absolute Being and Absolute Law—in fact, ingenious, and—impossible. Had a wine supper too, during which Charley continued to spin his glistering cobweb. Did not break up till near midnight, when I walked home with Fiske.[87]

Peirce returned to Washington in early February, where for the first time he was able to see Superintendent Thorn and talk to him about his future with the Survey. By this time Thorn had probably already decided that, except for a limited number of pendulum observations still to be carried out in Hoboken and Washington, Peirce would be given no further duties involving pendulum research until he had completed his long-overdue report on the gravimetric experiments carried out under his direction to that time.[88] This plan was complicated by numerous interruptions, both personal and professional, which delayed completion of the report indefinitely. It was still not finished when Peirce left the Survey in 1891. The decision by Thorn effectively removed control of the Survey gravimetric experiments from Peirce's hands and returned it to Assistant Charles A. Schott, who had been in charge of pendulum research until 1872, when Benjamin Peirce had transferred it to his son.

At the same time, Peirce, beside himself to protect his own scientific reputation, continued to press Thorn to obtain the Gautier pendulums which he had left behind in France two years before. He recommended again that he be sent to Paris to supervise their completion, so that the Survey could participate in the new round of experiments in England which he had managed to delay, but which were about to begin.[89] His facial neuralgia was plaguing him; as he wrote to Colonna, "Private . . . I am almost downright sick & in deep affliction & hence am a little confused about this business."[90] He continued to try and convince Thorn that the Survey ought to clear him of the charges against him:

> I tried to see you Saturday, before coming away [to New York] but could not do so. The doctor advised me I must bring my wife away without delay, so I was obliged to come. I fear you won]']t say what I consider satisfactory in regard to [the Allison Commission's accusation of] my going on "without restriction & limitation as to times and places." Can you not explicitly admit that the state of things described by me was the real state of things?[91]

In June, he telegraphed Thorn again, urging that he be allowed to go to England:

> Have received letter from [the distinguished British geodesist] Professor [George Gabriel] Stokes on part of Royal Society urging importance of my taking part in new operations in England this summer to connect with this country. Speed reply desired. I respectfully suggest . . . you then authorize me to accept.[92]

In August, he again suggested he be authorized to get the Gautier pendulums:

> If there is any way of getting these pendulums, that should be the very first thing done,—I say it most emphatically. And the Survey has so compromised me by its course in the matter, that I should only be too glad to be out of it at considerable expense to myself. . . .
>
> Of course it is impossible. I can only lament the unwisdom of the whole proceeding which will be more and more apparent as years go by. . . .
>
> I wish to be able in the future to show that I never ceased to urge the only sensible course. Therefore, notwithstanding all the rebuffs I have had, I am bound to recommend and do recommend emphatically, that I be immediately sent to get the Gautier pendulums, finish them, determine gravity in Paris, and then go to take part in the English work, the latter at my own expense or that of the British if you like.[93]

Thorn responded that he must disapprove the plan as impracticable. Peirce then went on to suggest an alternative and equally unlikely plan: that he go to Minneapolis or St. Paul, stopping in Buffalo for the National Academy of Sciences meeting to read a mathematical paper, then over the Northern Pacific Railroad to Portland, Oregon, Olympia, Washington, San Francisco and San Diego, and then over the Central Pacific Railroad to Salt Lake City, the Denver Railroad to Denver, and through Omaha back to St. Paul or Minneapolis, while throughout the trip occupying secondary stations and swinging pendulums. In response, Thorn asked (1) when the Hoboken work would be forwarded, (2) when the Kater pendulums (borrowed from the English geodesists two years before for purposes of comparison) would be returned to England, (3) when the reductions from Ann Arbor would be sent along, and (4) how long it would take Peirce to get himself, his records, and his equipment to Washington. Thorn added that he would tell Peirce about his future operations shortly.[94] For the remainder of his employment with the Survey, this embittered conflict dragged on between Peirce on the one side and Thorn and Colonna and their successors on the other. Peirce refused to send his raw data to Washington and continued to postpone his reports, saying that there were inaccuracies to correct to maintain the reputation of both himself and the Survey. Thorn, on the other hand, was in the position of being required by Congress to justify the $31,000 spent on pendulum experiments.

In addition, by October, the Department of the Army had been demanding for months that the Survey provide the results of Lieutenant Adolphus W. Greely's pendulum experiments made during his ill-starred expedition to Lady Franklin Bay, Alaska. Greely's expedition, one of two from the United States, was part of an international undertaking to conduct scientific experiments at polar stations established by the United States and ten European governments. The results were to be pooled, and all but those from Greely's pendulum experiments had been turned in. These had been in Peirce's hands for two years. It had been Peirce who carefully instructed Greely's astronomer, Sergeant Edward Israel, in the techniques of pendulum work. The hardships of the expedition had been so terrible that eighteen of Greely's party of twenty-five, including Israel, had died. Peirce pointed out difficulties in the computations caused by an unexplained loss of weight from the pendulum.[95] Greely and the survivors of the expedition were national heroes, and the weight loss was beneath notice. Thorn instructed Peirce to complete the work to prevent the army from complaining further and to prevent Congress from disallowing further pendulum experiments by the Survey. Peirce responded arrogantly, but accurately, with a new, large-scale plan: "If I were asked to advise a man about building a house, however eccentric I might know his ideas of economy were apt to be, I would never say that a ridiculously inadequate force of workman [sic] would do, that the masons could carry up their own brick, that the chimneys might be built of green wood, or anything of the kind."[96]

He went on to request, with a carefully considered assessment of the situation, not a year's appropriation but a general plan, including requisite instrumentation, standardization of methods, the occupation of extreme stations, and plenty of manpower to occupy stations in the south in the winter and in the north in the summer. He concluded that he realized this was much more than Congress would ever do, but it was the minimum. Thorn recognized the virtues of the recommendation, but after the Allison Commission report, Peirce's reputation made it impossible for him to consider. In December, Peirce triumphantly reported that he had finally succeeded in unraveling the Ithaca problems, a brilliant piece of applied mathematics:

> The new constants work equally well in all other cases. They will improve the agreement of all the work hitherto done with these [Peirce] pendulums. They will also materially modify the results at the different stations [including Lady Franklin Bay]. *This fact, be it noted, completely vindicates my refusal to publish any work with these [Peirce] pendulums before.* It also illustrates the truth of the practical maxim, which one would think every boy would see clearly the force of, but which seems to be too deep for the sublime wisdom which governs in Washington, that when you have entrusted so difficult and intricate a problem as gravity-determination *to a man*, you ought in policy and in fairness to do what *he* says ought not to be done (so far as means will allow) and not to insist on doing what *he* declares *ought not to be done*, until you lose confidence in him; and then you should entrust it to somebody *cleverer* [Colonna comment: and then more systematic].[97]

He went on to urge once again that the Gautier pendulums be gotten without delay, but regretted that it was too late to correct the Paris datum, so that the French

> will now make a point of decrying American science, which failed to discover the error! And they will be so far right that the sagacity of a seraph, if loaded down with the brutish stupidity with which I have had to contend, would be unable to reach good scientific results. However, this can last no longer. The time has come for the work to stop or be intelligently supported [Colonna comment: and systematically and thoroughly done].

Thus, Peirce tried constantly, in a manner thoroughly inconsistent with his professed desire to leave the Survey as soon as possible, to regain the control he had lost over the conduct of gravimetric research, but he was never able to do so. He went so far as to attempt Thorn's removal from superintendency of the Survey through political pressure. In September, he had written his cousin, then Representative Henry Cabot Lodge, that Thorn, "a perfect nincompoop, without sufficient force to prevent constant shindies in his office," had been placed in the Survey only to settle a political debt, and not, as Cleveland claimed, in order to benefit the public by reforming it.[98] In fact, the spoils system had introduced a bizarre form of confusion into the operations of the Survey. For eighteen months, malicious and quarrelsome Cleveland appointees had terrorized Survey headquarters by inventing stories and trying to make them a public scandal.[99] As Cleveland's political opponent, Lodge was interested, but Peirce was unable to produce any useful evidence, and the matter was dropped.

Despite their quarrels, Thorn and Peirce became cautiously cordial, principally because Thorn was able to retain his sense of humor where Peirce was concerned. Thorn was always aware that Peirce desired the superintendency of the Survey and accused him good-humoredly of the " . . . intrigues of a scientific Naboth":

> I presume you saw that Ahab [Peirce] was the covetous chap whom I was after and the Coast Survey was, during the long controversy, the Naboth's [Thorn's] vineyard [the Survey] after which he hankered.
> The substitution of the coy, and reluctant Naboth for the eager and avaricious Ahab was an instance of heterophemy to which I find myself becoming addicted since I became—what my children call me, in derision,—an "eminent scientist."[100]

Although there can be little doubt that he was unsystematic, procrastinating, extravagant, devious, and arrogant, when Peirce criticized the changes in the Survey for being against its best interests, there was justification for his position. The Coast Survey had completely changed from what the Washington Post had called a "supercilious little aristocracy of scientists" to a modern bureaucracy under the superintendency of Thorn, whose effective and efficient deputy was Benjamin Colonna. Up to the time of the dismissal of Hilgard, the Survey had been an organization in the old style: decentralized, informal, and casual. Finances were more often than not adjusted to meet conditions as they arose. All that previous superintendents had required of the assistants was their accountability in carrying out scientific work. The assistants had very general instructions which allowed them great latitude, and this was considered one of the advantages of being in Survey employ, considering the comparatively low level of salaries.

But the impetus to reform and reduced government spending which found limited expression under Presidents Arthur and Cleveland changed the government's attitude toward many of its departments, particularly those engaged in scientific work. The change which Peirce objected to and attacked had brought about the situation, so lamented by scientists in the twentieth century, in which the bureaucracy takes precedence over and judges all functions within it. In effect, the day of the sinecure, other than the political one, was over. No longer would a Joseph Henry, Alexander Dallas Bache, or Benjamin Peirce be able to treat his department as a means for developing free and disinterested researches, pleasantly spiced with the pleasures of personal privilege. Henceforth, the criterion of research would reflect the practical and immediate needs of politics.

Peirce wrote a long letter to Colonna in January 1887, in which he took a disagreement over the handling of boxes of his personal effects to be evidence of a conspiracy against him led by Colonna and Thorn, or perhaps others:

> Now you must have a singularly strong motive for behaving like this, and you had better tell me confidentially what it is. That some personal malice is somehow at work would seem probable. Or I can conceive that some powerful person, for some reason or other, good or bad, wants me out of the Survey, and you think that to avoid my resenting such action, the best way is to injure my reputation first. If so you make a wholly false calculation. There is nothing I desire so much as to get out of the Survey, and if you will show me an honorable and respectable way out, I shall be too glad to resign tomorrow. . . . I am now working for less than 2/3 the cost of my economical household, when if it were not for this damned incubus, my Coast Survey duty, the avenue to wealth is right open to me. . . .
>
> I can see that you and Thorn seem to be getting ready to make war at me. . . . I am for peace; and if you are wise you will be. . . . All I want is to get out of the Survey as soon as possible in a way honorable to me as a gentleman and as a man of science. . . . If you publish humbug results of gravitation work, it will be my direct duty to expose them, & I shall do so; otherwise, I wish you well with all my heart.[101]

Thorn responded three days later with some heat:

> As for my motives or purposes[,] I don[']t want to appear to "protest too much"; but it is my duty to say that no "person" is "powerful" enough to induce me to undertake to "get you out of the Survey" by indirection or other "damned diplomacy" . . . that I have not been, and am not now, "getting ready to make war upon" you.[102]

He went on to say that he had "a full appreciation of your great ability, in some special lines, and a genuine admiration of some traits in your character," but that funds were short and Peirce was well aware that it was impossible to continue with the occupation of more field stations until the money spent on them so far could be justified by his long-overdue reports. The battle over the boxes continued for two more months, and the reports remained overdue.

The "avenue to wealth" which Peirce mentioned in passing in his letter to Thorn, and a reference he made in a later letter to him that he had "advertised for scholars with a view to leaving the Survey," are allusions to the first of his many ill-conceived plans for quick wealth.[103] He explained the whole project to give the public the benefit of his pedestrianism to his cousin Henry Cabot Lodge:

My dear Cabot,

Will you lend me $500, $750, or $1000, for a short time, under the following circumstances?

I have long been dissatisfied with my Coast Survey place because I could not get Washington to conform to the conditions of effective work. They now refuse me the services of a copyist, and it is the last straw. I leave.

I have quite a reputation for my knowledge of the logic and methods of science. I have worked out a long series of practical exercises to teach the whole art of reasoning from beginning to end. There are throughout the country thousands of young men and women to whom these lessons would be of more real service than almost anything they could study.

The question is, first, how many of them I could teach? Now I have planned a system which I won't trouble you with, with passages written out answering every conceivable difficulty in the whole course, type-writers and assistants (upon whom I can lay my hands when I need them) by which I can write say 500 letters a day, or take charge of 1500 students. I propose to charge $30 in advance for 30 lessons, the entire course being about 200. Now how am I going to get before the public? The [New York] *Sun* has promised me a good editorial leader on the subject. The [New York] *Mail* & [New York] *Express* have partly promised. The [New York] *Post* & *Nation* with which I have relations [with editor Wendell Phillips Garrison] will do what it can I know. I am entitled to expect substantial aid from the Century Company. There are several other papers & magazines with which I am on very good terms. I shan't forget the religious press.

I propose to issue first a rather long circular. . . . I want to begin by sending out a hundred thousand in order to ascertain what number of circulars has to be sent to gain one scholar in the long run. I guess about a thousand. This first hundred thousand I think I can induce the *Century Magazine* to insert gratuitously between the leaves of the next issue. If the circulars pay, I shall send out others, as long as it seems to pay, perhaps up to a half a million or more. These will be sent five in a package to ministers of different denominations with a little address to the minister written in each case by a minister of the same denomination.

This scheme, or some modification of it which I will find, must pay.

My last year has not been a financial success & I have run two or three hundred dollars behind. Therefore, I am forced to borrow money to print my first hundred thousand circulars or so, to distribute them, & other preliminary expenses. The first payments of the first 20 or 30 scholars would repay this. Besides, I will pledge my books, which are worth $1000 [many of them still the property of Johns Hopkins]. . . .

My conviction is that this must in some shape prove a big thing, and I never shall be content till I have made it so. If my first anticipations prove deceptive, it won['][t take many scholars to keep my nose above water, until I can prepare a new coup. . . . I will send a copy of my first circular, as soon as I get one.[104]

Lodge did not lend him the money, and Peirce's anticipations proved entirely deceptive. He was never able to get more than a few students, and these did not keep his nose above water. Two letters from one of Peirce's few correspondence pupils stand as mute testimony to the impracticality of the venture, and Peirce did not resign from the Survey:

Dear Teacher:

I have spent about 4 hours on the Boolian Algebra. I didn't have much difficulty until I came to the Associative, Distributive, & Commutative Principles I haven't got beyond that yet I have enough to last until I hear from you I will report again at the end of two hours work.

Dear Teacher:

I haven't been able to go any farther than I mentioned in my last letter which is the reason I didn't report after two hours work as I promised I have spent 3½ or 4 hours on it since I last wrote.[105]

Although Peirce did not resign, Thorn was now ready to accept his resignation. He wrote to him on March 3:

References have not been altogether lacking in my presence to those personal characteristics which, in your case, tend to convert the hum drum routine of official intercourse into a series of lively episodes. . . . At the same time I must confess that your recent somewhat remarkable ignoring of official matters—and your refusal in response to courteous requests—even to acknowledge the receipt of such matters (which had been submitted for your official consideration and action) [particularly the Greely report] has for some time involved the question of my duty, in your case, in such embarrassment, as to entirely reconcile me now to the solution afforded by your proposed resignation.[106]

Among the reasons why Peirce did not respond to Thorn's official requests were his and Juliette's recurrent illnesses and their impending move out of New York City, but the main reason was probably that his time was completely taken up in finishing his definitions for the *Century Dictionary*, a project on which he had been working since 1883. To help him in this work, he depended for much of the research on Allen Douglas Risteen, who had been his computer and aide since January 1886. After February 1887, when Thorn had disallowed Risteen's continued employment, Peirce kept him on at his own expense, primarily because of the *Century* project, which Risteen had also been working on while an employee of the Survey. In the mid-nineties, Peirce asked him for help in making his proposed arithmetic text more readable, but Risteen found it beyond him. Risteen continued as Peirce's devoted friend and student for two decades. He studied under the physicist Willard Gibbs at Yale and wrote two books, one on the structure of molecules and the other on the second law of thermodynamics. In 1902, when Peirce was refused a Carnegie Institution grant, Risteen received one, for which Peirce had recommended him.

On April 22, 1887, Peirce wrote to Thorn that he and his wife were moving to Milford, Pennsylvania, and that he was putting off further work until the move was finished.[107] The register of the Hotel Fauchère in Milford shows April 28 to have been their first day there, although Peirce had visited the area before. Milford is located where the states of New York, New Jersey, and Pennsylvania meet at the Delaware River. When they moved there, it was still wild country, and a fashionable resort area as well. For ten years afterward, they also maintained an apartment in New York City.

The reasons for Peirce's choice of Milford as his permanent home are not at first evident. Most students of his life and thought have described the move as an escape from the tribulations of the world of affairs, but this reason, if valid at all, was minor. He had first seen the country in the company of two of his cronies at the Century Club, Edmund Clarence Stedman, the poet and stockbroker, and Persifor Frazer, a notorious atheist and a chemist, both of whom owned property in the area which they used in the summer. Another friend, the famed painter of majestic Western scenes Albert Bierstadt, spent time painting there.

The country had been settled principally by Huguenot families, whose French culture attracted Juliette. One of those families, the Pinchots, had settled there in the seventeenth century. The millionaire James W. Pinchot was a fine example of the late-nineteenth-century self-made man. He made so much money as a dry-goods merchant in New York City that he retired to the life of a philanthropist and a collector when he was forty-four. He built a Norman chateau overlooking the town of Milford which he called Grey

Towers. Mary Eno Pinchot, his wife and the mother of Theodore Roosevelt's chief forester, Gifford, had been a friend of Juliette's in New York City. Her father, Amos Eno, was a Manhattan real-estate tycoon whose Fifth Avenue Hotel sold after his death for the then-staggering sum of $7,250,000. Her brother, John Eno, absconded to Canada with several hundred thousand dollars from New York's Second National Bank, of which he was president. Charles and Juliette visited the Pinchot estate often and regularly, beginning shortly after their arrival in Milford.

Since Peirce had failed to breach the unyieldingly respectable wall of the academy and of upper-crust Cambridge and Baltimore society and now faced the collapse of his Survey career as well, the move to Milford represented the road to wealth and prestige through the patronage of the society of new wealth. The Peirces attended many lavish and festive social gatherings at the Pinchots' magnificent country estate in the company of Vanderbilts, Stuyvesants, Harrimans, Belmonts, and others, including European nobility. There exist in the Peirce papers at Harvard scattered and mostly incomprehensible drafts of correspondence between Peirce and some of these figures, such as Mrs. O. H. P. Belmont, the Vanderbilts, and the Harrimans, which had to do with the way in which Peirce intended to prosper as a consultant in practical scientific matters, at first—harking back to his father's advice twenty years before—as a chemist, but later in an array of enterprises. One such draft, written to Gifford Pinchot, to whom George W. Vanderbilt had given the responsibility of managing the forest on Biltmore, his 100,000-acre estate in North Carolina, illustrates the nature of Peirce's plan to use his inventive knowledge of chemistry:

> I would, for Mr. Vanderbilt, select the best apparatus now in the market [to extract wood alcohol and modified for greater production]. In doing so, I should be giving you the right to use processes upon which I intend to take out patents, and which I expect will have a decisive advantage over those now in use. . . .
>
> The advantages of my process are, 1st, that while [the competitor] only promises wood spirit to the amount of about 1 per cent of the dry wood . . . I should expect 2-1/4 per cent. Second, while the present processes give a spirit consisting of [40?] percent methylic alcohol, and 30 percent of acetone, with small quantities of several other substances, the mixture not being economically separable into its ingredients, my process would partially separate these things, and so give several articles each having special advantages for special purposes; and in the existing state of the law in this country, materially enhanced prices could be obtained. Third the amount of charcoal obtained by my process would be greater than others. . . . Fourth, the amount of fuel would be much less. . . .

> On the other hand, the plant I should recommend would cost a great deal more . . . .
>
> I should require a retaining fee of $1000 to begin with; and $50 a day for time occupied, my travelling expenses, and the value of all wood-spirit . . . in excess of 1-3/4 per cent of the dry wood. . . .[108]

A second reason for the move to Milford was the Peirces' desire to establish a household in keeping with Juliette's constant need for care and their luxurious style and inclination. Mary Eno Pinchot called on the Peirces for the first time at the house they were renting, until they could expand their own, on July 11, 1887, and her diary records twenty-three days between July and January 1888 spent in their company. Many evenings were spent at Grey Towers playing charades, capped with Peirce reading and reciting. In September, the Peirces wrote, produced, directed, and acted in a play which was given in the Pinchots' private outdoor theater on the estate.

A third reason for the move was Peirce's intention to turn his Milford estate, when built, into a summer school in logic and philosophy or, variously, into a summer institute to educate the wealthy and powerful in subjects appropriate to their responsibilities. The latter possibility was a reflection of his earlier comparative study of great men at Hopkins, which had led him to the conclusion that impractical cultural pursuits, such as philosophy, required powerful patrons, the major example for him being Alexander the Great's lifelong patronage of Aristotle. Peirce also, for a time, intended to use his land to support a number of manufacturing ventures, but these were dependent on a nonexistent railroad. Foolish dreams of sudden wealth such as these addled Peirce's mind until after the turn of the century. Juliette seems to have believed in them completely, at first.

Finally, Peirce intended to spend as much time as he could in writing out his philosophy in the study of his new home, filled with the books he had collected over the years to support that purpose. What he had intended, however, as a voluntary and partial seclusion among the elite of new wealth in which to pursue his original studies in logic became within ten years an involuntary exile which forced him to write as much for a bare living as for himself.

The contrast between these doings and dreams and Peirce's correspondence with the Coast Survey puts the life he desired in sharp relief. On June 9, he gave Thorn an estimate of the time it would take him to prepare his reports: at least 725 hours over four months to bring the existing total of seventy volumes in his possession into shape. Peirce added that he did not think his eyes could take it.[109] On July 29, he forwarded a table of contents of the long report.[110] On August 29, he submitted a monthly report with deep regrets that the report was unfinished and added, "My health has suffered this month from overwork, etc., but I have not lost a day."[111] For September, contrary to the spirit of Peirce's claim, Mary Pinchot's diary contains many mentions of the Peirces' presence in entries such as these:

⌊Saturday⌋ Sep 3 persuaded Mr and Mrs P to come up for Sunday. . . . We capped verses all eve & Prof P read and recited to us—Lord Ullens' daughter. The Starry Firmament.

Monday Sep 5 pleasant morning with the Pierce's ⌊*sic*⌋.

Tuesday Sep 6 Prof P. and I picked flowers in morning . . . read "the Sleeping car & Bat Ballads . . . ⌊Peirces⌋ went home at 6. . . .

Wednesday Sep 7 Eve Prof & Mrs ⌊Peirce⌋ to tea . . . later *charades.*

Friday Sep 9 Prof Mrs ⌊Peirce⌋ to tea . . . *Charades.* . . .

Sunday Sep 11 Prof & Mrs ⌊Peirce⌋ . . . called Eve Bible 20 Questions

Friday Sep 16 fine aft drove with Mrs ⌊Peirce⌋ Nettie & Children on Chucktown road—beautiful drive around by the old Buchanan place. . . . Mrs ⌊Peirce⌋ dinner & tea.

Monday Sep 26 Dr. Bidlark ⌊the tutor⌋ & Prof & Mrs ⌊Peirce⌋ here eve 12 meals

Tuesday Sep 27 fine busy preparing stages curtains etc—afternoon rehearsed with Dr. B . . . ⌊Peirces⌋ to dine . . . plus 15 meals

Thursday Sep 29 Messrs Stuyvesant Bidlark ⌊Peirce⌋, Brennan to dine—games after . . . plus 7 meals[112]

During the entire month, Peirce sent no communications to Thorn except a monthly report on September 29, which merely related progress and concluded: "I was suddenly called to the bedside of my nearest relative ⌊his mother⌋, and was thus absent 3 days this month; but as I have since made them up, and should be entitled to an absence with pay anyway, I have not thought necessary to mention this in my personal report."[113]

In late September, Peirce's mother, frail for the past ten years, began to fail. She died on October 12, leaving him an inheritance sufficient to buy up properties and begin building his country estate, both of which he did the following spring.

By November, Peirce had at long last completed his report on Greely's pendulum swings at Lady Franklin Bay, Alaska. By then, Greely was the army's chief signal officer and had been promoted to general. Greely took issue with some criticisms Peirce had made, and Peirce responded that he was surprised to find that you conceive that passages in my report imply blame of you or Mr. Israel. I assure you that this is neither the intention nor the effect of these passages [in which Peirce found significant weight losses affecting the results]. . . . Looking at the question from a purely impersonal point of view myself, and advancing my hypothesis as a means of strengthening, and not of weakening, the determination, I did not realize you would consider an accident, which in my opinion was absolutely unavoidable, as involving any imputation on you or Mr. Israel. . . .

For my part, I cheerfully accept my share of responsibility for the imperfections of the work; they are comparatively unimportant.[114]

On 29 December, Peirce wrote to Thorn: "I am not yet quite through with my report. It seems very slow work to myself, but I have been occupied with the utmost diligence upon it. It can't be much longer."[115] Thorn immediately and angrily responded that he had not received the information describing the amount of the reductions and other work that remained to be done, "and I will thank you to furnish me with this information as soon as convenient."[116]

Despite his bad relations with the Survey, the beginning of 1888, with its signs of a fine future in Milford, must have been festive for Peirce. He thought he would soon be quit of the Coast Survey; he had successfully entered the powerful world that surrounded the Pinchots; he was well on the way to acquiring a fine country estate; and he was confident that at least one of his many schemes would produce the wealth needed for his new life. As if to signal this new beginning, President Cleveland appointed him to the Assay Commission on the first day of the year.[117]

In March 1888, Peirce's maiden aunt Charlotte Elizabeth, his Aunt Lizzie, died, leaving him her excellent collection of French novels and a small inheritance besides. On May 10, using Charles's own and probably some of Juliette's money, the Peirces bought a farm of 140 acres for $1,000, upon which were a few buildings, with a lovely prospect on a slope bordering the western bank of the Delaware River about a mile north of Milford in what was called, after its owners, Quicktown.[118] In November 1889 they bought 1,200 acres of woodland, and the year after about 500 acres more, making altogether an estate of about 2,000 acres. All the land and other properties were placed in Juliette's name. After their first purchase, the Peirces immediately began designing the reconstruction of their house, built as a farmhouse in 1854, which, for the most part, they occupied during its construction.[119] Peirce expressed his enthusiasm to his correspondent Judge Francis C. Russell fours years later, after he finished the initial renovation made to his design of the house he called Arisbe, and which he covered with shingles in the New England style of a summer "cottage":

This valley of the Delaware where I live will compare with any country I have seen,—and I have seen many,—for picturesqueness. Moreover, the roads are set down by the bicyclists' guide-books as the best in the land. Moreover, there are many French settlers here, & especially *chefs*, and they have disseminated good cooking wonderfully. My wife and I own over two square miles in one piece nearly square; and I think that will be of value eventually. Outside of that we have two places. One is the small farm where we live, stretching a third of a mile along the river and reaching a quarter mile back. It is a most lovely spot, and never do I look out the window without refreshment. The house is a 2 story frame house of my design ⌊seventy-six feet deep by thirty-six feet wide with a front veranda eight feet deep⌋. . . . It is very pretty and very original, but the furthest possible from pretentiousness. The floors are mainly white ash waxed. The rest Georgia pine. There are eleven open fire places, some large; one you can stand up in. There is also steam heat throughout the house. A good cellar under the whole. Running water and all conveniences. The rooms are as follows:—

You enter at a *conservatory* or glass-gallery. . . . There you have three doors at Right (A), In Front (B) to left (C). Door A leads into my study . . . 3 windows, large open fireplace and an outer door. From the study you pass into the music room . . . , open fireplace, long windows opening upon verandah. . . .

Door B goes into the parlor . . . where is the big fireplace. This opens by wide doors into the Garden Room . . . with ⌊a⌋ large fire place. Two doors into ⌊the⌋ music room and ⌊a⌋ 9 foot glass door into flower garden. It ⌊the garden room⌋ opens by folding doors into Dining Room . . . with large fireplace & broad windows.

Door C goes into corridor (with large closet for coats, etc) leading into dining room and also having the staircase and leading into servants dining room. . . . It leads into the cook's room. . . . Has no steam-heat ⌊nor did any of the servants' quarters⌋. . . .

Going upstairs you find yourself in a corridor ⌊leading to the sitting room⌋ . . . fireplace, balcony with ⌊a⌋ beautiful view of the river.

From it you pass forward to a lobby with two doors . . . one leads into a chamber over music-room, with fireplace. . . . The other into chamber over study with fireplace.

From sitting room you pass into Mrs. Peirce's room . . . window seats extra space. Fireplace. From there into dressing room with 2 closets.

Thence into my room with fireplace . . . and closet. I go out of my room into corridor and opposite is a room we call the studio ⌊never finished⌋. . . .

There is also a bathroom . . . with four closets. . . . And a maid's room ⌊never finished⌋. . . .

Besides this, there is a cottage near by, very pretty with two rooms. We use it for servants. There are two barns, and various little buildings. ⌊The

Peirces also had two fine carriage horses, an elegant carriage, a wagon, apple and nut orchards, an old mill, a slate quarry, and other appurtenances.]

The 60 acres of land are worth $6000, the house, insured for $4500, is worth $6000, the other buildings $1000. My library, insured for $2500 is worth [sign for infinity over infinity]. Say in all $15000. Now I propose to put up three pretty cottages of about 4 rooms each, and make the house a sort of Casino for fashionable people of "cultural" tendencies, to spend the summer, have a good time, and take a mild dose of philosophy. There is now no railway through the valley. When it comes, as it will in a few years, values will be greatly enhanced, and my place, with the business I shall have built up will be worth considerable. My ultimate aim is to set going an institution for the pursuit of pure science & philosophy which shall be self-supporting.

Now I need to start $5000. . . . [120]

The Peirce domain was no "small farm." The estate quickly became more than the Peirces could manage or support. Within a few years it was encumbered with mortgages and suits for nonpayment of debts by their workmen and the servants who looked after them. Arisbe, intended, like its

Arisbe in its original shingle style, ca. 1900, before the addition of the third floor in 1907. Photo taken by Mrs. Quick. Courtesy of Houghton Library, Harvard University.

ancient namesake on the banks of the river Selleis in Asia Minor, to be a colony of Miletus, the Greek source of cosmology, philosophy, and science, became instead an overbearing burden and a reproach. Arisbe was itself the first of Peirce's disastrous ventures.

With a profound sense of betrayal and with work that showed uncharacteristic signs of carelessness, Peirce continued to labor at the long report on gravimetrics. His relations with the Survey deteriorated to such an extent that Colonna finally felt free to indulge in open sarcasm. The immediate reason for their worsening was that the Henry Kater invariable pendulums, extremely valuable for their long history as experimental instruments, which had been lent to the Survey two years before and used by Peirce for purposes of comparison, had been returned by him to England with certain irreplaceable parts broken. Thorn informed Peirce on January 24 that G. M. Whipple of the Kew Observatory had written that "the thermometers and barometers were broken, but Prof. Peirce informed Prof. Stokes that the damage occurred whilst the apparatus was in charge of the U.S. Survey Officers."[121] Thorn attached copies of signed sworn statements from the three officers, other than Peirce, who had handled the boxes in which the pendulums were packed, all of whom denied any damage at their hands. He concluded that Peirce had behaved disingenuously. Peirce admitted his responsibility, denied that he had anything to reproach himself with, and said that he assumed no charges would be made.[122]

More important, Peirce seemed not only incapable but unwilling to complete the long report on his pendulum experiments. On February 28, he wrote that it was almost done, and that it would take only four months more to prepare the stations of Montreal, Albany, Hoboken, Fort Monroe, and St. Augustine, all from 1883 to 1884, for the press. Thorn immediately brought him to task for the backwardness of his work. Peirce responded at length trying to explain the technical difficulties involved. Colonna made occasional marginal notes in red ink on the document. In the kind of experiments involved, Peirce insisted that he always had to be "on the look-out for the unexpected [Colonna: always found it]." Peirce said that he realized the enormous difference between his predictions and his performance and added, "but can you suppose that I do not look upon the labor of my life seriously? [Colonna: Yes.]" Peirce concluded with a plea:

> What with the overwhelming mass of the details, and the conviction which has settled on my mind under the last year's experience that were I to do my work with the ability of Newton at his best (I mean Sir Isaac), I should get mainly objurgations for it both from the official Olympus [Colonna: Who is he?] and from ordinary plain mortals and newspapers,—with all

this, I feel much discouraged; and that may tend to my doing much hard work without a tangible result.[123]

In the summer, Peirce sent in two short reports as pacifiers on aspects of geodesy that he found theoretically interesting, but he was unsuccessful. Schott advised Thorn concerning one of them:

> I would suggest that Asst. Peirce be asked to submit his report (complete) on the results of the pendulum observations at all stations occupied by him.
> The determination of the earth's compression from pendulum work is quite a distinct problem and it is not even desirable to have it mixed up with the preceding matter.[124]

Of the other, "On the Mean Figure of the Earth from Determinations of Gravity. Second Paper. The Formula for the Earth's Ellipticity in terms of the Variation of Gravity with the Latitude," Schott mentioned that it had "mere spelling errors, which are of no consequence," implying that it had not been proofread, and that the value derived for gravity was exactly that of another geodesist who used a variety of pendulum records, whereas Peirce used only those of the Kater pendulums.[125] Thorn, disturbed by the obvious implication of plagiarism, asked Schott about it. He was told that Peirce had used Stokes's formula, which F. R. Helmert had already used in covering exactly the same ground in his book *Geodasie*, which Peirce had with him at the time he wrote his paper.[126]

In late December, the time of Schott's indictment, Peirce informed Thorn that he intended to include the western as well as the eastern stations in his report, which would require that it be completely rewritten, and that he could be no more accurate about its completion than the next spring. He also expressed his conviction that "any flaws however trifling which might be detected would be husbanded to form material for an attack after the report was printed," which explained his reluctance to let the manuscript out of his hands.[127] On January 12, 1889, Thorn wrote Peirce that what he had so far sent in was largely unfinished, that the "utter paltriness" of his work was deeply upsetting to Thorn, and that he had "disgraced" the Survey by not providing Stokes with the information on the Kater pendulums he had requested. Peirce responded:

> The very tone of almost every communication from you or from the office,—varying from rude to insulting,—the matter of many of them, uncorrected by the slightest utterance to the contrary, have depressed my spirits, taken away my heart, poisoned every motive to exertion. . . . Could I have

hoped for anything like cordial appreciation of such good qualities as I might be able to impart to my work, I should have been more successful with it. But the only spirit I seemed able to discover was one of triumph at faults and of detraction for merits, of attention to the small and unconsciousness of the large. . . .

I am led to believe that you really hold that I have been of no service to the Survey at all, and that it had better never have seen me.[128]

On February, 18, 1889, Superintendent Thorn decided that he had had enough of scientists and announced his intended resignation from the Survey. He was unable to find a suitable successor until July, and in the meantime he showed his disappointment with Peirce, writing him first in late February:

[The reports] which in August 1886 you said required but a week's work to complete and which in January you said required but a week's work to complete, and for the transmittal of which you, three weeks afterward, requested an extension of time to Feb. 15th instant, have not come. What is the reason?[129]

On May 28, in a note to Colonna after Peirce wrote that he had a plan for the occupancy of pendulum stations, one a day, that would provide good results, Thorn said:

Ack. & remind him of various and repeated statements, during the winter, that his report, which he now promises to forward "shortly," would be done & sent during the *spring*—which has passed. It is desired that no other enterprise nor scheme be permitted to interfere with the prompt completion of that long delayed report, upon receipt of which your plan of daily pendulum stations will be in order for submission and consideration.[130]

Thorn's opinion that Peirce was engaged in projects other than his Survey work was justified by the appearance of the *Century Dictionary*, a project of sufficient size and difficulty that it must have taken much of Peirce's time over the previous six years, especially over the last three as the date of publication approached. Their mutual distrust and ill-feeling went so far that when Peirce reported that he had informed his former student Joseph Jastrow of the value of gravity for Madison, Thorn, unconvinced of either Peirce's accuracy or dependability and wishing to divorce the Survey from any responsibility for his findings, instructed his assistant to "inform Mr. Jastrow again so that he will be sure to be 'informed.'"[131]

During the spring Juliette had been increasingly sick with what appeared to Charles to be tuberculosis. At the end of May, he asked for and received two weeks' leave to take her to New York for diagnosis and treatment, which confirmed his fears. Tuberculosis, then a common affliction called familiarly consumption because it seemed to devour the sufferer from within, continued to affect Juliette off and on for the rest of her life. She returned to Milford a little better, where she spent an easy summer and fall, much of it in the company of Mary Pinchot. On November 21, the Milford *Dispatch* carried a notice that Juliette was "shortly to make a tour abroad and sojourn in Italy, in quest of health, during the winter." Charles put her on the steamer from New York a week later.[132] She returned much improved in the spring. The gynecological problems she had mentioned to Sarah and Aunt Lizzie in 1883 continued to worsen until surgery was required in 1891, and again in 1897. The inescapable burden of Juliette's illnesses together with his frustrations with his own health and the Survey often drove Charles frantic with anxiety.

In July 1889, Thorn was succeeded as superintendent by Thomas Corwin Mendenhall, who had been a student of Simon Newcomb, the man directly responsible for Peirce's dismissal from Johns Hopkins and thereafter his personal enemy in professional matters. Mendenhall had been professor of physics at the University of Tokyo and had directed pendulum research in Japan. Peirce took Mendenhall's appointment as a good sign and expected that the appointment of a scientist to the Survey would mean a renewed career for himself. Immediately after Mendenhall's appointment, Peirce wrote him a long letter explaining and exculpating himself from the charges made by the Allison Commission. He then gave a brief history of his work and went on to say:

> When Mr. Thorn came in, certain charges were made against me. Later, all these were retracted with the exception of one, which was a very vague one to the effect that I had not been under proper control and discipline. . . . Accordingly, to prevent my having 'my way' I have of late years been kept as far as possible ignorant of pendulum matters. I trust you will reverse this policy, and restore me to the charge of investigations into gravitation.
>
> I had charge of the office of weights and measures for a very brief period under Mr. Hilgard. When I came to realize what his habits had become, I declined to remain longer in Washington, although at his request I refrained from formally resigning the position. I think I have some claim to be considered in that relation, still.[133]

Mendenhall was, however, one of those modern scientists whose principal interest was administration of science and not its practice, a fact which Peirce soon discovered. After a long talk with him in New York in which

Mendenhall spoke feelingly of efficiency and other administrative virtues, motivated no doubt by Peirce's record of carelessness and procrastination, Peirce wrote him:

> I feel impelled to say that one or two things you said to me . . . appear to me quite wrong. You mentioned as almost culpable that every head of a bureau wants to set up an investigating laboratory of the branch of science which concerns him. The idea is, I suppose, that he mustn't try to do his work scientifically, because that might cost money. . . . That view seems to me in the first place to overlook the facts of human nature. If you pay a man a very low salary to begin with, and then forbid him to have any warmth or zeal in the conduct of his office, carefully remove all intellectual interest it might have and leave him nothing but the pure money to work for, and finally construct a series of fiscal regulations the main purpose of which seems to be to take up as much time with accounts as possible,—if you do all that you will have the heads of bureaus even worse than they are now. In the second place, it rather shocks me to hear *you* who know what a slough of materialism this country has sunk in, where nothing is considered as sacred except the holy, holy, holy dollar,—giving in to complaints against heads of bureaus that they are spending a little money in trying to advance science. . . . [134]

Peirce had a genuine basis for expressing himself so strongly, though his protest was vitiated by his record. Since the beginning of Thorn's superintendency in 1885, Peirce had spent four years devoted largely to inconsequential administrative paperwork of the most irritating kind. To a man of Peirce's impatience with such details, this type of work was insufferable, and it was only duty, buttressed by a profound lack of funds, which kept him in the Survey. The administrative requirements of the reformed Survey added considerably to his vexation, and when, because of severe cuts in the Survey budget, he was denied the use of a computer to do the routine calculations and administrative details which he considered beneath him, his anger turned to disgust. Almost all of the work required in the preparation of Peirce's long report was that of a computer: onerous, exacting, and pedestrian in nature in its many thousands of often intricate mathematical operations. To add to his burden, his sight was losing its sharpness. The result was to frustrate Peirce through and through. This angry frustration explains in great part the extreme delay in finishing the report and his concentration on the more interesting aspects of the logic of science involved in the research.

Peirce finally sent in the major part of his long-overdue report on the results of his pendulum experiments in final draft on November 20, 1889, more than three years after the latest date for which it had been promised.

Although the report covered only the stations at the Smithsonian, Ann Arbor, Madison, and Cornell, it contained all the parts of the report which set forth the theoretical and experimental issues involved. To follow "shortly" were reports covering Montreal, Hoboken, Albany, Fort Monroe, St. Augustine, and Key West.[135] Mendenhall, apparently thinking his knowledge insufficient for the task, sent the report for comment to his mentor Newcomb, who responded on April 28, 1890:

> In compliance with your request I have made a preliminary examination of the report on gravity, etc., sent with your note of the 24th. It gives me the impression of being in its main outlines a careful and conscientious piece of work, but its form and presentation are such as to make it impossible to pass a definitive judgment upon its value without a very detailed and minute examination. A remarkable feature of the presentation is the inversion of the logical order throughout the whole paper. The system of the author seems to be to give first concluded results, then the method by which these results were obtained, then the formulae and principles on which these methods rest, then the derivation of these formulae, then the data on which the derivation rests and so on until the original observations are reached. The human mind cannot follow a course of such reasoning in this way, and the first thing to be done with the paper is to reconstruct it in logical order. [For Peirce, the long report was his first chance to present a relatively complete application of the logic of science, organized in what he considered to be the right order to explicate the functions of hypothesis, deduction, and induction and their relations. This intention Newcomb missed completely.[I do not mean that, in printing, the great mass of original observations should be put at the beginning, but a summary should be given at the beginning and the mass placed at the end. Moreover the paper is still further confused by the insertion of various special investigations and explanations where they seem to have no logical place. For example in the description of stations are stated certain precautions which belong with the description of the observations themselves. Of the three papers entitled "Description of the Instruments" only a portion of the last is given to that subject, the two first being devoted to the discussion of different formulae, methods, etc., pertaining to pendulum work in general. Moreover what little description there is[,[is scarcely intelligible. The introduction of logarithmic seconds [a metric notation[seems to me productive of nothing but confusion to the reader. [These insertions were, for Peirce, entirely appropriate illustrations of the logic of science using such issues as error, probability, computability, the economy of research, and the interdependence of scientific disciplines.[The extraordinary discrepancy on page 130 between the results given by the four [Peirce[pendulums needs more investigation than the author gives it. On the whole the paper does not seem to me one which would prove useful scientifically or would redound to

the credit of the Survey if published in its present form. But in view of the evident amount of labor involved in making and discussing the experiments it seems to me that the best course is to have it reconstructed by one or more experts who have references to the original documents. It could then be determined whether any irreparable defects exist of such a nature as to destroy the scientific value and character of the work.[136]

The only copy of this letter exists in the records of the Nautical Almanac Office, which Newcomb headed. The letter may have been kept from Peirce, and he may never have realized Newcomb's part in his dismissal from the Survey. Newcomb's severe criticisms, which originated in great part from his ignorance, were directed at the only American geodesist with a well-established international reputation—certainly the ranking expert in the field—and they turned out to be ruinous for Peirce. Newcomb had no interest in the logic of science; in fact he was suspicious of it, and, like most "practical" scientists, he limited his thoughts to doing science rather than to thinking about it and believed that metaphysics, or anything smacking of it, was nonsense. Nor did he understand Peirce's innovative use of calculus. A fundamentalist in scientific matters, Newcomb was a fundamentalist as well in religious matters and believed, at least in Peirce's case, that what he perceived as Peirce's evil character infected the results of his science.

Obviously, Peirce's long report did not meet Mendenhall's expectations of a conventional, and to Peirce scientifically almost valueless, summary and reduction of his pendulum experiments. Peirce had seriously misjudged the caliber of his audience. Even so, it was precisely this report which became the modified text of Assistant Schott's highly respected gravimetric work "The Eastern Arc of the United States," for which, without giving credit to Peirce, he received the Wilde Prize in 1899.

While there are many reasons to believe that Peirce procrastinated, that he had poor judgment in the world of affairs, that he had become careless, and that he was extravagant, arrogant, and sometimes paranoid, there exists no convincing evidence that he was incompetent, inexpert, or a plagiarist. In retrospect (and at the time to the few who appreciated his work), the opposite was true. As a scientist, Peirce was remarkably able, profoundly knowledgeable, and a brilliant innovator. He was extremely unfortunate in the mediocrity and scientific literalness of those who judged his work.

Mendenhall took Newcomb's suggestion and convened a three-member panel, including Newcomb, to evaluate Peirce's report. It accepted Newcomb's judgment in a two-to-one vote. In July, Mendenhall sent Newcomb's criticisms to Peirce as his own and received in reply a strong defense which answered the objections point for point. Mendenhall had said that Peirce's system "does not appear to facilitate calculations in any way"; Peirce responded, "That is a big mistake, which yawns between your ground and the truth like a Colorado canyon," and explained why. Mendenhall then called Peirce's system of calculation obscure, to which Peirce retorted that

> In a Washington July a man is apt to find things 'nearly unintelligible.' At least, that is my experience. But just look at it. . . . [My system is to be] *used* chiefly by mathematical geodesists, men who have to deal with the most intricate parts of the calculus. . . . Say, if you please, that the American mind, at large, is too debilitated to adopt the metric system, which every other people has adopted,—so long as you don't ask me to agree with you; but do not say that mathematicians will find so simple an application of logarithms as my logarithmic seconds 'obscure.' . . . Having thus answered your objections and shown that my system *does* materially simplify calculations, that it is not obscure in any important degree, that its slight obscurity is not useless and is still less 'unnecessary' or uncalled for, let me present to your mind the advantages my system possesses.
>
> There is no universally used system of expressing relative gravity. [but my system makes that advance possible]. . . .
>
> In stating my reasons, I have used the directness of language with which a scientific man is entitled to be addressed. Had I been writing to an ordinary functionary, . . . I should have measured my language from that point of view. But I beg you will not think my warmth is beyond the bounds of decorum.[137]

Victor Lenzen, who in 1965 had written the definitive study of nineteenth-century pendulum research, in 1969 examined with great care Peirce's long report, which had been lost for eighty years. He agreed completely with Peirce and wrote, "It is my firm judgment that the experimental and theoretical work represented in Peirce's *Report on Gravity at the Smithsonian, Ann Arbor, Madison, and Cornell* was the best work of its kind in the nineteenth century."[138] It is obvious that neither Newcomb nor Mendenhall was sufficiently knowledgeable in either geodesy or mathematics to judge Peirce's work, with disastrous effects for him. Mendenhall wrote to Peirce on October 1 that he was contemplating the renewal of gravimetric researches on a large scale, but made it obvious that he was not considering Peirce in the matter except as a source of advice.[139] Peirce wrote a characteristically energetic letter explaining a new system he had developed for conducting rapid pendulum observations, about which Mendenhall, who seemed to rise to the bait, asked him to write in detail. Peirce submitted a thoroughly thought out proposal including sections on instruments, installations, procedures, stations (more where the error for value of gravity was great and fewer where the error was less), and explanations for each recommendation.[140] On the back of one of the pages of a Coast Survey Circular, a musing Peirce wrote hopefully (quoting Emerson):

[in red]That man and I have a splendid idea.
How doth the *little busy bee*
[in blue] Improve each shining hour
[in yellow]So fast eternity comes on.
And that delightful day.
[in brown] When all mortal hands have done.
[in green] God's judgment shall survey.[141]

But Mendenhall had no faith in Peirce's dependability and, thanks to Newcomb, was led to discount his competence as a scientist. Mendenhall was mainly concerned to show Congress that the many thousands of dollars spent upon Peirce and his pendulum experiments were justified by important results, but he did Peirce the courtesy of assuming that, given ample time and freedom from interference, he would finish his work. When, after almost a year had passed, the remainder of the report failed to appear, it was no doubt with some relief that Mendenhall asked Peirce for his resignation, effective December 31, 1891:

> Returning to my desk a few days ago after an absence in the West of several months I was somewhat surprised to learn that nothing had come from you in the way of a report upon the unfinished pendulum work on which you have been so long engaged, or anything showing that you were making any progress towards completing it. It is now about two years (I write without having the official correspondence at hand to refer to) since you assured me that the whole work would soon be completed. A partial report [the one criticized by Newcomb], referring to three or four stations was received last year, it is true, in matter and form very unsatisfactory and not in a proper condition for publication. . . . You will not deny that I have given you every opportunity to complete your work and I have scrupulously avoided any interference with it in any way which might . . . hamper or restrict you.
>
> I deeply regret to be obliged to confess that I was mistaken in assuming that if you were left thus free and untrammeled you would show a productiveness such as all friends of the Survey have a right to expect. I feel that I cannot justify, either to my own conscience or to any one who may investigate the expenditures of the Survey, your continued connection with it. I therefore deem it my duty to inform you by this personal communication that I shall ask that your services be discontinued after the 31st December next.

Thomas Corwin Mendenhall, superintendent of the United States Coast Survey, 1888–1894. Photograph courtesy of the Library of Congress.

I hope that before that time you will be able to turn the material in your possession into the office in such a condition that . . . we shall have the means of working it up. I trust you will understand that in taking this action I am influenced solely by what I believe to be my duty in the interests of the Survey and the Government; that I have not been unmindful of your long connection with the organization and of the high character of your services, and that the conclusion has not been reached without much deliberation and many efforts to continue a method of evading it.[142]

So ended a connection with the Coast Survey of more than thirty years' standing. It is obvious from the history of the last six years of his service in the Survey that Peirce expected the break to occur, although he had felt it necessary to remain for reasons of his reputation, his duty, and his shaky finances. The long series of pendulum experiments performed under Peirce's direction, together with all his unpublished reports, quickly became assimilated into the Survey. Peirce's feelings at the end of this long and troubled connection were clearly ambiguous: relief, anxiety, anger, shame, and a restive need for a new life. His reputation never recovered from the three blows of these years: his dismissal from Johns Hopkins in 1884, the accusations made against him and publicized by the Allison Commission report in 1885, and his forced resignation from the Coast and Geodetic Survey in 1891.

4

Paradise Lost

1 8 9 0 – 1 9 0 0   But man, proud man,
Drest in a little brief authority,
Most ignorant of what he's most assured,
His glassy essence, like an angry ape,
Plays such fantastic tricks before high heaven
As make the angels weep.

Shakespeare, *Measure for Measure,* II, ii, 117

The decade of Peirce's life, roughly 1890–1900, covered by this chapter is chaotic in the extreme. Its chronology is hectic and complex. I imagine him as a confidence man and prestidigitator—a frenzied juggler elegantly dressed in harlequin costume, on a flimsy but deceptively substantial stage of his own devising, gambling everything on keeping too many improbably seductive objects in flight, while trying to decide which one to snare. At the end, he stands there in tatters, surrounded by the melancholy debris of his life, contrite and apologetic, asking our—and especially his dearest friend William James's—indulgence. But all the while, this poor fool, behind the scenes and between the acts, has been building piece by piece the armature of a most marvelously intricate universe, so beautiful it transfigures him amidst the wreck of his afflictions, and we gratefully see the signs around us with new eyes.

During the year and a half between Juliette's return from Europe in the spring of 1890 and the end of his employment by the Coast and Geodetic Survey on December 31, 1891, Peirce had obviously been doing much more than preparing the long report. He was furiously but confidently preparing himself for the dramatically changing circumstances of his life.

A major project was to make their house the kind of place their ambitions and tastes required it to be, and by April 1891, the Milford *Dispatch* reported "a large and handsome addition to the residence of Professor C. S. Peirce in Westfall township this spring."[1] By May of 1892, the *Dispatch* reported, no doubt to the great satisfaction of both Charles and Juliette, that

> private enterprise has been lacking in the building of villas and cottages a la Tuxedo, but within the past year Mrs. Charles S. Peirce, wife of the eminent scientist, has brought her exquisite French taste and continental experience to the building of a picturesque villa. . . .
>
> The present need is for some enterprising society man . . . and some experienced hotel man . . . accustomed to meeting Metropolitan taste, to combine in developing other localities in Milford, as the Peirce estate, known as "Arisbe," has been developed.[2]

During this period, the Peirces spent much time with the Pinchots. Mary Pinchot was in Europe from May to September 1890, but thereafter, partly because Juliette remained ill, there are numerous entries of her visits at Arisbe. In early January, Juliette underwent surgery in New York connected with her gynecological problems and returned to Milford improved. The closeness of Peirce's connection with the Pinchots is reflected in an entry in Gifford Pinchot's diary for November 23, 1891: "Prof. Peirce read what little I have of the book [Pinchot's book on forestry]. Said it was first rate &c. Was not much delighted to hear him speak so well of it."[3] An interview with Pinchot by L. J. Henderson, then (about 1940) working on a Peirce memorial for the National Academy of Sciences, suggested that Peirce influenced Pinchot in his choice of forestry as a career.[4]

Because New York City was only about two hours by the Erie Railroad and ferry from Port Jervis, New York, a few miles north of Milford, the Peirces spent considerable time there at the apartment they maintained at 109 East Fifteenth Street. Mrs. Pinchot's diary recorded a number of expeditions to New York City with the Peirces, including the entry for Saturday, November 14, 1891, which reads in part, "G[ifford] arrived while we were gone to the theatre with Prof. P[eirce] to see Miss de Wolfe in Thermidor."[5] The outward conduct of their lives generally seemed to show that the Peirces had few fears for the future. These were the years Peirce later told James were the "palmy days" when he gave Juliette expensive gifts, including jewelry, high-fashion clothes, and bound books of French literature, mostly novels. They lived high, believing that great wealth was just beyond the next twist of fate. Arisbe provided the front which justified the appearance of the wealth that was soon to be actual. Peirce insisted on saving appearances long after it was beyond his finances to do so.

Ever since the year 1880, when his father had presented in Baltimore the series of lectures published the next year after his death as *Ideality in the Physical Sciences,* Peirce had been working steadily at analyzing the consequences of adopting the conception that ideas are real. An early and apparently unlikely manifestation of his musing about realism, also connected with his father's death, was a strong interest in the occult. This interest appeared, along with his speculations about the construction of the universe, in 1884 in "Design and Chance," where Peirce supported research into the "phenomena of spiritualism & supernaturalism" because it might "suggest the possibility of the relation between body and soul being different from what ordinary experience leads us to conceive it."[6] Peirce was interested in examining possible manifestations of the real, and ghosts were among them. He continued this inquiry into the meaning of realism in his far more serious cosmological speculations in "A Guess at the Riddle" during the next four years.

The first published précis of this musing inquiry appeared in the *Century Dictionary* in 1889, where Peirce defined his father's position (and his own by adoption) under the heading "ideal-realism" as consisting in "the opinion that nature and the mind have such a community as to impart to our guesses a tendency toward the truth, while at the same they require the confirmation of empirical evidence."

That his father's idea of a community of nature and mind, of *il lume naturale,* might be a genuine possibility first occurred to him in June 1879, as a consequence of his inexplicable ability to identify, "without the least scintilla of light," the thief of an expensive Tiffany lever watch bought for him by the Survey. In their article "You Know My Method," Thomas A. Sebeok and Jean Umiker-Sebeok artfully paired the detection of Sherlock Holmes with Peirce's account of this experience, called "Guessing," an examination of the nature of hypothesis as a reflection of the constitution of nature, which he did not write until 1907 and which was not published until 1929.[7] By 1888, Peirce had written most of what may have been intended as a memorial to his father, "A Guess at the Riddle." Although it was never published, its essential ideas appeared as a series of popular articles because of a letter he had received the year before, in January 1889, from a Chicago judge, Francis C. Russell, who had discovered Peirce through his own interest in logic.

On July 2, 1890, Peirce received a letter from Russell's friend Paul Carus, editor of the Open Court Publishing Company of Chicago, who was about to start a new journal, *The Monist.* Carus had written Peirce, at Russell's insistence, requesting contributions from "prominent American . . . and shall be greatly indebted to you for an article from you on 'Modern Logic' or . . . perhaps . . . 'Logic and Ethics.'"[8] In a second letter, Carus reported that "Judge Russell showed me your anonymous article [in the *Nation*] on Mr[.] [Herbert] Spencer. . . . I wish you would write an essay on Mr. Spencer's philosophy."[9] In the third, on August 3, Carus sent Peirce a check for $140 for the essay. So began the long and often angry but fruitful relationship between the two men that ended with Peirce's death in 1914. It produced from January 1891 to January 1893, as its first issue, the second series of the most well known of Peirce's writings.[10] Published in *The Monist*, these five essays set forth a very different metaphysical perspective than had the strongly positivist and anti-metaphysical first series which had appeared in the *Popular Science Monthly* under the title "Illustrations of the Logic of Science" in 1877 and 1878. The *Monist* essays forcefully and unexpectedly proclaimed an absolute idealist, as well as realist, metaphysics that seemed written by a different man. Each essay was devoted primarily to a single aspect of Peirce's cosmology, and each contained a brief but remarkably able intellectual history of the scientific and philosophical issues involved.

In the first essay of the series, "The Architecture of Theories," following Kant's proposal in opposition to the piecemeal approach of the English philosophers that systems ought to be constructed architectonically, Peirce

Charles S. Peirce, photogravure from *Sun and Shade*, August 1892, vol. 4, no. 12.

introduced in print the new form of his universal building blocks, the logical categories of Firstness, Secondness, and Thirdness (originally presented in "On a New List of Categories" in 1867 as Quality, Relation, and Representation), which "are conceptions so very broad and consequently indefinite that they are hard to seize and may be easily overlooked":

First is the conception of being or existing independent of anything else. Second is the conception of being relative to, the conception of reaction with, something else. Third is the conception of mediation, whereby a first and second are brought into relation. . . . The origin of things, considered not as leading to anything, but in itself, contains the idea of First, the end of things that of Second, the process mediating between them that of Third. . . . In psychology Feeling is First, Sense of reaction Second, General conception Third, or mediation. In biology, the idea of arbitrary sporting is First, heredity is Second, the process whereby the accidental characters become fixed is Third. Chance is First, Law is Second, the tendency to take habits is Third. Mind is First, Matter is Second, Evolution is Third.

Peirce then restated his father's evolutionary cosmology, introducing the Aristotelian notion of chance as the absence of cause:

Like some of the most ancient and some of the most recent speculations it would be a Cosmogonic Philosophy. It would suppose that in the beginning,—infinitely remote,—there was a chaos of unpersonalised feeling, which being without connection or regularity would properly be without existence. This feeling, sporting here and there in pure arbitrariness, would have started the germ of a generalising tendency. Its other sportings would be evanescent, but this would have a growing virtue. Thus, the tendency to habit would be started; and from this with the other principles of evolution all the regularities of the universe would be evolved. At any time, however, an element of pure chance survives and will remain until the world becomes an absolutely perfect, rational, and symmetrical system, in which mind is at last crystallised in the infinitely distant future.

That idea has been worked out by me with elaboration. It accounts for the main features of the universe as we know it,—the characters of time, space, matter, force, gravitation, electricity, etc. It predicts many more things which new observations can alone bring to the test. May some future student go over this ground again, and have the leisure to give his results to the world.[11]

Peirce greatly overstated his claims to having worked out this metaphysics. He spent the rest of his live gnawing away at it in the manner of the British philosophers and unpacking and classifying its elements, increasingly as a doctrine of signs. He never achieved his fantastic—and intoxicated—purpose of explaining the universe, material and immaterial, etc. He said more soberly ten years before he died that he was leaving the work about where he found it, but that was as greatly understated.

In the second essay, "The Doctrine of Necessity Examined," which appeared almost a year and a half after the first, probably because of his work on the long Survey report, Peirce attacked LaPlace's fantasy of a mechanical, completely determined universe.

> The proposition in question is that the state of things existing at any time, together with certain immutable laws, completely determine the state of things at every other time (for a limitation to *future* time is indefensible). Thus, given the state of the universe in the original nebula [chaos], and given the laws of mechanics, a sufficiently powerful mind could deduce from these data the precise form of every curlicue of every letter I am now writing.

Peirce went on to argue that the necessitarian position could not account for such major features of the universe as novelty, growth, complexity, consciousness, diversity, and irregularity, but that by invoking chance and spontaneity,

> I account for all the variety and diversity of the universe, in the only sense in which the really *sui generis* and new can be said to be accounted for.
>   . . . by supposing the rigid exactitude of causation to yield, I care not how little,—be it but by a strictly infinitesimal amount,—we gain room to insert mind into our scheme, and to put it into the place where it is needed, into the position which, as the sole self-intelligible thing, it is entitled to occupy, that of the fountain of existence; and in so doing we resolve the problem of the connection of the soul and body.[12]

Peirce's claim that he had solved the mind-body problem by means of the introduction of absolute chance, christened in the next essay in the series as "tychism," seems to be a statement of intent. He continued to think about chance (which he distinguished from probability) in various guises for the rest of his life. He never provided what he considered a final statement of this fundamental doctrine of spontaneity which allowed him to embody the universe out of nothing, or, as the theoretical physicist Alan Guth put it a century later when the idea reappeared as crucial to understanding cosmological beginnings, "It is often said that there is no such thing as a free lunch. The universe, however is a free lunch."[13]

Peirce began the third essay, "The Law of Mind," a portion of which was introduced earlier, with a sardonic admission of his true metaphysical colors:

> I have begun by showing that *tychism* must give birth to an evolution-ary cosmology, in which all the regularities of nature and of mind are regarded as products of growth, and to a [Friederich von] Schelling-fashioned idealism which holds matter to be mere specialised and partially deadened mind. I may mention, for the benefit of those who are curious in studying mental biographies, that I was born and reared in the neighbor-hood of Concord,—I mean in Cambridge,—at the time when Emerson, [Frederick H.] Hedge, and their friends were disseminating the ideas they had caught from Schelling, and Schelling from Plotinus, from [Jacob] Boehm[e], or from God knows what minds stricken with the monstrous mysticism of the East. But the atmosphere of Cambridge held many an antiseptic against Concord transcendentalism; and I am not conscious of having contracted any of that virus. Nevertheless, it is probable that some cultured bacilli, some benignant form of the disease was implanted in my soul, unawares, and that now, after long incubation, it comes to the surface, modified by mathematical conceptions and by training in physical investigations.[14]

Peirce left us to decide whether he was actually unaware of the long idealist (and realist) infection, or had simply been hiding it from the incredulous gaze of his nominalist and mechanist fellow scientists. The latter seems far more likely.

The essay introduces the principle of continuity, or as he named it, *synechism*, of which habit is a specialization. Peirce called it "the law of mind," for which he provided a formulation:

> Logical analysis applied to mental phenomena shows that there is but one law of mind, namely, that ideas tend to spread continuously and to affect certain others which stand to them in a peculiar relation of affec-tibility. In this spreading they lose intensity, and especially the power of affecting others, but gain generality and become welded with other ideas.[15]

In this objectively idealist universe, ideas degenerate by gradations. Logical inferences are more vital than habits; habits more vital than physical laws; and physical laws more vital than matter, which Peirce called "effete mind." Mind, the light of nature, pervades this hierarchy in an unbroken whole in a way reminiscent of the medieval vision of the "Great Chain of Being."

Peirce came to this idea of continuity by means of the concept of mathematical infinity, that between any two points an innumerable series of points may be taken, so that the universe of number is continuous. This continuity supposes infinitesimal quantities. Time and space are infinitesimally continuous in the same way, but for the law of mind time has a definite direction from past to future, unlike the time-reversible mechanics of Newton's physics. Thus, every state of mind is affected by every earlier state and has spatial extension. Since space is continuous, "there must be an immediate community of feeling between parts of mind infinitesimally near together." This is the "insistency" of an idea which is "habit, by virtue of which an idea is brought up into present consciousness by a bond that had already been established between it and another idea while it was still *in futuro.*" This affection of one idea by another is inferential; that is, "the affected idea is attached as a logical predicate to the affecting idea as subject." Mental law, therefore, follows the forms of logical inference, which are hypothesis, deduction, and induction, and these "correspond to the three chief modes of action of the human soul." By this argument, of which I have provided a mere précis, Peirce placed logic, ten years later called formal semeiotic, the study of signs or "the science of representation," at the center of inquiry. He summarized the thrust of this doctrine he called synechism under the heading "Communication":

> Consistently with the doctrine laid down in the beginning of this paper, I am bound to maintain that an idea can only be affected by an idea in continuous connection with it. By anything but an idea, it cannot be affected at all. This obliges me to say, as I do say, on other grounds, that what we call matter is not completely dead, but is merely mind hide-bound with habits. It still retains the element of diversification; and in that diversification there is life. When an idea is conveyed from one mind to another, it is by forms of combination of the diverse elements of nature, say by some curious symmetry, or by some union of a tender color with a refined odor. To such forms the law of mechanical energy has no application. If they [the forms] are eternal, it is in the spirit they embody; and their origin cannot be accounted for by any mechanical necessity. They are embodied ideas; and only so can they convey ideas.[16]

Peirce concluded the essay by pointing out that synechism carried along with it three doctrines: "1st, a logical realism of the most pronounced type; 2nd, objective idealism; 3rd, tychism with its consequent thoroughgoing evolutionism. We also notice that the doctrine presents no hindrances to spiritual influences, such as some philosophies are felt to do."

While synechism may appear very distant from physics as it has developed since the discovery of Einstein's relativity theories and of quantum mechanics (about which Peirce could have known nothing in 1892), the contrary is true, at least for some modern theoretical physicists. David

Bohm, who apparently had no knowledge whatever of Peirce's writings, has written of fundamental physics in a way so similar to Peirce's that to read his work gives one an uncanny sense of déjà vu. The title of his 1980 book *Wholeness and the Implicate Order* is itself a rewording of synechism. Bohm summarized his thesis, but not as clearly as Peirce, thus:

> Throughout this book the central underlying theme has been the unbroken wholeness of the totality of existence as an undivided flowing movement without borders.
>
> It seems clear . . . that the implicate order is particularly suitable for the understanding of such unbroken wholeness in flowing movement, for in the implicate order the totality of existence is enfolded within each region of space (and time). So, whatever part, element, or aspect we may abstract in thought, this still enfolds the whole and is therefore intrinsically related to the totality from which it has been abstracted. Thus, wholeness permeates all that is being discussed, from the very outset.[17]

Some other modern theoretical physicists, such as Robert Feynman, Freeman Dyson, and John A. Wheeler, have written in the same vein as Peirce. Most others retain their allegiance to mechanism.

The most startling, scientifically, in this new series was the fourth essay, "Man's Glassy Essence," an application of the previous doctrines to biology which seemed to Peirce's former student Christine Ladd-Franklin to be clear evidence that he was losing his mind.[18] Peirce wrote:

> [Protoplasm] not only feels but exercises all the functions of mind. . . .
>
> If consciousness belongs to all protoplasm, by what mechanical constitution is this to be accounted for? The slime is nothing but a chemical compound. . . . Protoplasm certainly does feel; and unless we are to accept a weak dualism, the property must be shown to arise from some peculiarity of the mechanical system. Yet the attempt to deduce it from the three laws of mechanics, applied to never so ingenious a mechanical contrivance, would be obviously futile. It can never be explained, unless we admit that physical events are but degraded or undeveloped forms of psychical events. . . .
>
> It may be well here to reflect that if matter has no existence except as a specialization of the mind, it follows that whatever affects matter according to regular laws is itself matter. But all mind is directly or indirectly connected with all matter, and acts in a more or less regular way; so that all mind more or less partakes of the nature of matter. . . . Viewing a thing from the outside, considering its relations of action and reaction with other things, it appears as matter. Viewing it from the inside, looking at its immediate character as feeling, it appears as consciousness.

. . . a general idea is a certain modification of consciousness which accompanies any regularity or general relation between chance actions.

The consciousness of a general idea has a certain 'unity of the ego,' in it, which is identical when it passes from one mind to another. It is, therefore, quite analogous to a person; and indeed, a person is only a particular kind of general idea. Long ago, in the *Journal of Speculative Philosophy,* (["Some Consequences of Four Incapacities"] Vol. II [1868], p. 156), I pointed out that a person is nothing but a symbol involving a general idea; but my views were, then, too nominalistic to enable me to see that every general idea has the unified living feeling of a person.[19]

What is expressed in this passage is virtually mystical doctrine: that the suprasensible is mysteriously and paradoxically represented in the sensible. It is no wonder that Ladd-Franklin, with her commitment to positivism, thought it showed, in a scientist, a mind gone askew. What Ladd-Franklin saw as madness may have been the intoxication of discovery (and of alcohol and drugs) reflected in the grandiosity of Peirce's claims, but not in the doctrines, which are ancient in their origins. At the time, Peirce did no more than admit very indirectly the connection between his position and the *philosophia perennis.*

The fifth and last essay of the series, "Evolutionary Love," was, as the title suggests, Peirce's adaptation of Christian theology. In its execution, it is the least interesting of the group. It begins with a thoroughgoing and millennial condemnation of the Gilded Age, with its massive greed, social Darwinism, and inhumane social values expressed by late nineteenth-century political economy:

The reign of terror was very bad; but now the Gradgrind banner has been this century long flaunting in the face of heaven, with an insolence to provoke the very skies to scowl and rumble. Soon a flash and quick peal will shake economists quite out of their complacency, too late. The twentieth century, in its latter half, shall surely see the deluge-tempest burst upon the social order,—to clear upon a world as deep in ruin as that greed-philosophy has long plunged it into guilt. No post-thermidorean high jinks then![20]

The essay continues with a discussion of three forms of evolution which embody his categories: that by fortuitous variation (Darwinian), that by mechanical necessity (Hegelian), and that directed toward an end (Lamarckian). Peirce identified Lamarckian evolution, none too clearly, with evolutionary love, "the action of love" which "must embrace what is most opposed to it, as a degenerate case of it," and so give the universe life. Peirce then provided a confused account of the intellectual history of the West using these three evolutionary forms. Indeed, the entire essay seems unfinished and shows evidence of the intervention of personal misfortune. Peirce ended it on an uncertain note: "If thinkers will only be persuaded to lay aside their prejudices and apply themselves to studying evidences of this doctrine [evolutionary love[, I shall be fully content to await the final decision."

These five essays, written during an intensely promising and frustrating time, present a magnificent universe dramatically infused with mind and lovely in its form. The essays were mostly misunderstood in his time or else thought to be the eccentric musings of a mind in decline. They did not bring him the audience he hoped for, nor did they repair his badly damaged reputation.

Peirce's professional life during this period was directed especially to the expansion of his relations with periodicals, such as *The Monist*. It was through writing book reviews, obituaries, and some articles for the *Nation*— for which he had been writing occasionally since 1869, but with increasing frequency beginning in 1890, when he began his long and demanding friendship with its editor, Wendell Phillips Garrison—that he both made money and stayed in touch with the world of learning through the books that Garrison constantly sent him for review. He wrote for money for other periodicals as well, such as the *Open Court*, the *Independent*, the *American Historical Review*, and various newspapers.

He continued to put out feelers for academic employment. In July 1890, he wrote to ask his current defender, former colleague, and winner of the position in philosophy at Hopkins, G. Stanley Hall, now president of Clark University, if he might be able to lecture there, but Hall thought not, even though " . . . such a course as you outline . . . would interest & stimulate every man on the grounds in a most admirable way."[21]

In late December 1891, Peirce wrote Newcomb to ask his assistance in receiving a grant and in getting a position at Stanford University. Newcomb responded bluntly on the day before Christmas:

> As to getting a grant of money for the purpose you mention, it seems to me the difficulties are insuperable. . . . It is, I believe, unusual, if not unprecedented, to pay an investigator to do a work of his own out of trust funds for the advancement of science, at least among us. I do not know where to look for funds to do this with.
>
> As for the Stanford University, I have never been in any [way] consulted respecting it, and in fact know nothing about it, except what I have seen in print. I do not, therefore, feel able to do anything in that direction.[22]

Also in December, Peirce was recommended by George Ferdinand

Becker, a friend from his Harvard days and a member of the Geological Survey, to the Lowell Institute as an excellent lecturer on the history of science. The series of twelve lectures was given in Boston the following winter and probably formed the outline for a history of science he projected for Scribner's in 1898.[23]

Finally, Peirce hoped to be able to complete his pendulum report for the Survey on a contract basis, and to that end he asked his cousin, Representative Henry Cabot Lodge, to use his influence in Washington. Although Lodge wrote to Mendenhall urging this project and later went to speak to him, sentiment against Peirce was so strong that it prevented his proposal from being seriously considered.[24] When Peirce tried again to get Survey employment with a later superintendent, the response was the same.[25]

As Peirce was soon to discover, the ending of his Survey salary was a serious matter. Despite the many schemes he poured his energies into after leaving the Survey, only a very few were successful, and those did not produce enough money to support the life he insisted on. Because of the welter of unfinished plans and projects, the years 1890–1900 are a tangle that almost defies unraveling. At first, Peirce retained his characteristically misguided optimism and usually blamed others, almost always wrongly, for his failures. He never seemed to guess the extent of Newcomb's enmity, nor did he, with a few

Peirce's classmate and fellow outcast Francis Ellingwood Abbot, Harvard Class Album, 1859. Photograph courtesy of the Harvard University Archives.

exceptions, ever admit to himself in these years the part he himself had played in his own ruin. As the decade progressed, his projects for financial success became increasingly extreme, desperate, and ill-considered, until by its end he was bankrupt and heavily in debt, and several times had threatened suicide. Arisbe, of which he and Juliette were so proud, steadily drained their uncertain resources. They had all their assets tied up there and could not sell except at a loss, which they refused to do until it was far too late. When he was so poor that he actually reached the edge of starvation and was stealing food to survive in 1897, he was almost sixty years old, so that his age, as well as his reputation, stood squarely against him. By 1898, he had settled unwillingly into the life of a recluse and was forced to reexamine his past with a harshly critical eye. He came to believe that his only redemption lay in the sacrificial pursuit of philosophy to the exclusion of everything else but Juliette.

But in November 1891, still sanguine, he went to the rescue of a fellow philosopher who was caught up in the nastiest—and most absurd—philosophical dispute to take place in the United States in the late nineteenth century. It began with a "professional warning" made by Josiah Royce in the pages of the *International Journal of Ethics* accusing Francis Ellingwood Abbot, member of the original Metaphysical Club, author of *Scientific Theism*, and an outsider like his friend Peirce, of purveying philosophical fraud and plagiarizing indirectly (presumably from Royce) from the works of Hegel in a pamphlet entitled "Way out of Agnosticism."[26] Earlier Abbot himself had privately confided his low opinion of Royce to his diary:

> Attended, on summons, a meeting of the "Haunted Houses and Apparitions" committee of the Psychical Research Society, at the rooms of Richd Hodgson, Sec'y, 5 Boylston Place, at 8:30 P.M. Nobody there but Royce and Hodgson. What a farce! We talked over the trash, and adjourned to a restaurant for a glass of whiskey! Royce is all gas: Hodgson is more practiced. But what *could* come from such attempts to sift a fog?[27]

Peirce went quickly and strongly to his old friend's defense anonymously in the columns of the *Nation*. To a great degree, he saw Abbot's situation as his own. After pointing out that Royce had actually warned the public against Abbot, "unequivocally and fully conscious of what he was about," Peirce continued:

> The next question is whether it is so plainly true that Dr. Abbot is a blatant and ignorant pretender & in philosophy that it is impossible competent men should think otherwise. So far is that from being the case that philosophers of the highest standing, such men as Churches in Germany, Renouvier in France, and Seth in England, have drawn attention to the

remarkable merit of his work. I am not personally intimate with Dr. Abbot, and am far from being a partisan of his doctrines, but as an humble student of philosophy, endeavoring to form my estimates with the eye of truth, I recognize in him a profound student and a highly original philosopher, some of whose results are substantive additions to the treasury of thought; and I believe that the prevalent opinion among competent philosophers would be that Prof. Royce's warning is an unwarranted aspersion. Next, what excuse was there for such conduct, what motive prompted it? Prof. Royce and Dr. Abbot have their rival ways out of agnosticism. Both start from the same premise to come in the main (at least, so Royce says) to the same conclusion. Shall we say, then that a passerby cannot loiter near Dr. Abbot's shop, attracted by the placard, "The Way and The Truth" without Prof. Royce's rushing out and shouting from across the street that he can offer the same article at a lower figure? . . . Prof. Royce's article was written with the avowed purpose . . . of ruining Dr. Abbot's reputation. . . . Thus it was a brutal, life and death fight from the first. Prof. Royce clearly perceived this, for he ends his article *by saying that he shows no mercy and asks none!* That's ethics. . . . It is quite impossible not to suppose that Prof. Royce conceived it was his duty thus to destroy Dr. Abbot's reputation, and with that the happiness of his life.[28]

William James, who was friend to both Peirce and Royce, and who thought that Abbot was "simply *insane* in all that touches on his philosophic or personal pretensions," wrote Peirce the day the letter appeared:

I have been somewhat amused and somewhat made sorry by your letter in the Nation about Abbot-Royce. If you knew Royce as I do, and had seen the whole evolution of his side of the business as I have, you would see how simply comical is the notion of there being any element of intellectual rivalry with Abbot in his attitude. The animus of his article was *objectively philosophical*; but being a man of mass, he can't do a thing briefly or lightly. . . .

He went on to describe the bitter wrangling that had accompanied Abbot's threatened suit for libel, pointed out that his critical reviews were mixed, and concluded:

His philosophy surely must seem to *you* the scholastic rubbish [Peirce, to the contrary, greatly admired the scholastics, especially Duns Scotus and Ockham] which it seems to me and which it seemed to Royce. . . .

In short as a hyperaesthetic human being, Abbot deserves our pity at being so handled without gloves. But as a philosopher I can see no ground for complaint on his part; what are philosophers for but to fight with each other? On the whole, I wish you had let the thing die away in silence, and not propagated a new series of undulations from the Nation's columns.[29]

In contrast to James's damning opinion of Abbot, this insightful and friendly characterization of James was written by Abbot three years earlier:

> Prof. Wm. James dined with us today, at 6:30 P.M[.], and spent the evening. We discussed the outlines of my system in the "Philosophemes" and the four "Analyses", but not altogether satisfactorily; he lacks the systematic mind, and seems to be in a state of philosophic bewilderment. His nature is essentially dominated by feeling rather than by thought, and his "Principle of Ease" is the genuine expressions of it: that is, he chooses his beliefs according to their capacity of gratifying his emotions. Such a mind is radically non-philosophical; and it amuses one to see him in the unnatural position of a professor of Philosophy. But he is charmingly genial and friendly: I *like* him immensely.[30]

Abbot seems never to have changed either his opinion concerning James's philosophy or his liking for him. Peirce and James continued to correspond about the matter, and, although James wrote a last soothing letter for the *Nation* before the controversy ended in December, Peirce seems to have closed the matter effectively when he wrote to James:

> your treatment of the principal question, that of the propriety of criticism like Royce's, I will say to you in secrecy that it seems to me a little sophistical. And sophistry upon a highly important question of right and wrong is hurtful and blamable. Such remarks I keep for the ear of my friend. . . .
>
> Philosophy has not reached the position of an exact science where being in the wrong is somewhat of a reflection upon a man's competence. Even in physics, Magnus does not come forward to warn the public that Tyndall is a fraud, or precisely stated, that he is 1st ignorant, 2nd blatant, 3rd pretentious. In philosophy, unfortunately, we are all probably pretty far wrong so far, . . . Plato, Aristotle, Aquinas, Descartes, Leibniz, Kant, Hegel, Mill and all are generally acknowledged to have been radically wrong. That hardly affects our estimate of their merit as thinkers, of the usefulness of their thought. . . . Under those circumstances, to say a man's philosophy is wrong is no worse than to say he parts his hair on the wrong side. . . . Now Royce was plainly, overtly, trying to injure Abbot and take away his bread and butter. . . . [Royce] repeatedly adverts to his pretentiousness. He practically accuses [Abbot] of ignorance in philosophy. His *general tone*, which cannot be denied, is that of contempt. That there may be no mistake after *much* of this he at length says he 'warns the public' against him! What can that mean? He *professionally* warns. That is, he plainly says Abbot ought not to be reckoned as among those who are to rank as serious students of philosophy. Finally, he says, he shows no mercy and asks none.
>
> Now *will Royce say he did not mean this?*[31]

Although Abbot printed privately a pamphlet accusing Royce of libel, and a long and bitter lawsuit seemed inevitable because Royce never expressed anything like an apology, the event faded into silence. Within a decade, Peirce and Royce became close philosophical allies, with Royce as Peirce's student of logic.

The defense of the outcast, Abbot, by the pariah, Peirce, has a pathetic resonance which is echoed in Abbot's letter of thanks to his defender and friend Charley Peirce:

> Every advantage of position is on Royce's side; I am out of the professorial ring, hold no office which commands the respect of our toady press, and have nothing in the world but naked justice and truth on my side. All the more do I feel the nobility of spirit which moves you to strike a brave blow for me for that reason.[32]

In 1886, Abbot had written in his diary about Peirce:

> The *Nation* today has an article, by Prof. C. S. Peirce, I see also stumbling over the book [*Scientific Theism*] very blindly. But there is no ill nature in it. Strange that there is so little real philosophic insight or originality in America—not even keen or valuable criticism! *That* would be instructive and helpful to me.[33]

In May 1892, six months after the fracas, he wrote approvingly that he had heard Peirce give "an able paper on 'Syechism,' his new system of philosophy" to some twenty graduates and friends at his brother James's house in Cambridge and then invited him to dinner. The next entry said that "Peirce sent a note of regret—had a headache, and could not dine here. Sorry."[34]

The similarity between the two men is striking in many respects. Neither was able to keep a job equal to his talents. Each one, from his place outside the world he wanted to join, wrote dozens of letters to the editor, trying somehow to make an impression that would give him recognition. In the end, Peirce died in abject poverty supported by a dole provided by friends. Abbot committed suicide upon his wife's grave. The pathos of their lives is bitterly evident in the comments written by Abbot on a clipping of a review of Royce's great work *The World and the Individual*, which appeared in the *Nation* in 1902, a year before Abbot killed himself. The part of the review underlined by Abbot reads:

> As a first serious attempt to apply to philosophical subjects the exactitude of thought that reigns in the mathematical sciences, and this, *not on the part of some obscure recluse whose results do not become known to the public,*

but on that of an *eminent professor in a great university, to whom the world is disposed to listen with attention.* Royce's 'The World and the Individual' will stand a prominent milestone upon the highway of philosophy.[35]

Beside this clipping Abbot wrote, "Is there here an oblique reference to me? I think so—I am sure of it." And then in his diary he wrote:

> The lines marked tell the *stern truth*, little as my children and friends are disposed to admit it. I am still toiling to finish my great work, yet with no hope of a hearing, now or after my death. I do it just to acquit myself to my Master, whose business, and not mine, is all disposition of the results. I cannot die in peace with my conscience till I have done my task—yet hopeless work in ceaseless pain is a heavy load. Thank God, I am already nearing the goal—and then——[36]

The sharp irony in this situation was that the review was written anonymously by Peirce, and the "obscure recluse" was, of course, Peirce himself. The greater part of Abbot's confession of despair might well have been written by Peirce, though in his less heavy style, as this letter of Peirce's to James written five years later shows:

> Nobody understands me. . . . America is no place for such as I am. . . . I detest life, & just as soon as I can frame a plausible excuse to my-self—in about a fortnight I hope,—I shall follow Frank Abbot's example,—except that I shall leave no unreadable book behind me. No! no![37]

The year 1892, the first without Charles's Coast Survey salary, was to end with the Peirces close to bankruptcy, although he was able, because of his two inheritances and Juliette's income and by writing for *The Monist* and the *Nation*, to keep out of other than minor debts. The ruinous but characteristic thing about Peirce's handling of money was that he had always refused to adjust his style of living to his income. The loss of his Survey salary seemed to change nothing. The Peirces were both extravagant. He and Juliette proceeded with the work on Arisbe. To go with it they bought two fine horses and an elegant carriage. They also maintained an apartment in New York City and went there often. When in New York, Peirce frequently stayed at the Century Club and Brevoort House, both expensive. He traveled often to Boston and down the East Coast. He did show some concern about money to his cousin Henry Cabot Lodge in a letter written from the Century Club on February 8, 1892:

> I was gratified at your speedy admission to this Club, where I trust we may often see you. It is still very agreeable, though of late much changed.

I am just now in an impecunious condition, though I have plenty of things on hand which promise to be very profitable before long. Meantime, I am almost tempted to borrow money on my real estate, all of which is entirely unencumbered. The difficulty is that there is no bank in the country. . . .

But what I would rather do is sell a nice square lot of about 1850 acres of woodland, with a good deal of good timber, well watered, two bluestone quarries, not yet opened, a large clearing, two log houses, plenty of deer and small game. I would take $4000 for it. So large a square lot is not easy to get. It is very accessible.

I hear the Boston Public Library wants a librarian. Now I have always been a great student of books. Could you not try to get me the place? . . .

Have you, perchance, any work of looking anything up, or bibliographic list or anything you would like done in a library? I would work for you for $1 an hour. For anybody else for $2.50 an hour.

I am going to give some Lowell lectures next season, on the history of science from Copernicus to Newton, and to write them, I must frequent a library a good deal.[38]

Peirce gave no indication of how he intended to care for an ailing Juliette, keep up his estate, and work in Boston, all at once.

In May, Peirce was considering, because of James's recommendation, the idea of employment at the newly founded University of Chicago, but his reputation with Presidents Eliot and Gilman convinced Chicago's President Harper not to make the offer.

What Peirce really wanted to do, however, was to find a wealthy and powerful patron and protector to subsidize him indefinitely in his philosophical investigations. In a draft letter in mid-January to an unknown correspondent, he wrote, with an almost complete sense of identification and longing, of an ancient such relationship:

In the enclosed notice of the Calendar of Great Men [a project that Peirce was touting at the time], I have expressed the *belief*, that is my word, that Aristotle without Alexander would scarcely have been heard of. This is not an entirely gratuitous opinion. In the first place, that Alexander was very generous to Aristotle is quite beyond doubt. That Aristotle was extravagant & early spent nearly all his father left him is stated on good authority & is confirmed by his going to live on Hermeias. He could not have saved much on the downfall of that tyrant, it was too sudden. Therefore, he was probably at first dependent upon the aid of Phillip and Alexander. He spent vast amounts, we know, on books and other things necessary to his studies. He must have worked very calmly and with an easy mind to have produced such vast works which were *never published at all*. There is no reason to suppose his school was very profitable. Without Alexander's vast aid he would have done much less, very much less; and he just escaped oblivion as it was.[39]

Peirce's major hope for a patron centered on Edward C. Hegeler, a German immigrant and wealthy Chicago businessman who had founded the Open Court Publishing Company and *The Monist* to promote a Buchnerite monotheism. Hegeler was to play the role of Alexander to Peirce's Aristotle. Peirce had already become a major contributor to *The Monist* through the good offices of his fervent admirer Judge Francis Russell, whose friendship with Paul Carus and assiduous praise of Peirce's greatness to both Carus and Hegeler brought about their invitation to Peirce to visit Chicago in February 1893, a month after the appearance in *The Monist* of "Evolutionary Love."[40] Hegeler seemed deeply impressed by Peirce's metaphysics and also seemed to feel that Peirce's religious views would add to the high purpose for which his publishing ventures had been founded. Since Hegeler had already invested about $1,200 in the *Monist* series and two articles, "Dmesis" and "The Critic of Arguments," published in the *Open Court*, Peirce had high expectations for their meeting. They discussed several projects for the printing of Peirce's work, but apparently concentrated on two, "Illustrations of the Logic of Science" in book form and the arithmetic textbook he had been working on since 1888, which James Pinchot had said would be "better than Butler's iron mine," a forecast that Peirce believed completely. As late as 1906, with no basis beyond his confidence, Peirce proclaimed his arithmetic "worth a half million."[41]

Peirce also expressed his strong desire for editorial responsibility, but in this he was disappointed, because he ran immediately into resistance from Carus, who wanted no interference from a dangerous competitor such as Peirce. Carus had married Hegeler's daughter and, probably accurately, tied his future as Hegeler's editor to the success of his role as the defender and illuminator of Hegeler's confused theology. Carus's jealously was strong enough that when Peirce and Hegeler came to have serious misunderstandings, Carus used them to reduce, for most of a decade, Peirce's publications in the two journals to a very few.

Hegeler lent Peirce $1,750, to be paid over a year in seven monthly installments of $250, for the textbook on arithmetic. In return, Peirce was to repay the loan at six percent interest from the future profits of his arithmetic books.[42] But Peirce had already approached Appleton and Company, the publishers of his father's texts, to see if they were interested in his arithmetic text. They were interested not only in the arithmetic, but also in an elementary geometry. Appleton also controlled the copyright on his "Illustrations." Hegeler wrote Peirce:

I request that you write me a memorandum of all our arrangements to avoid misunderstandings. Concerning the books, Dr. Carus made the remark yesterday that he thought the logical papers would best appear . . . in one volume. . . . I must say that my impression was . . . that the papers to be published were principally logical papers. I never closely examined the list.

For the publication on my part of the papers that appeared in the Pop Sc M. the permission of the firm "Appleton & Co." in writing is necessary.[43]

Carus was easily able to convince Hegeler that Peirce's religious views were antithetical to his own, in large part because of Peirce's fatal attraction to controversy. By the end of February, Hegeler had made clear to Peirce the distinction between the Open Court Press and *The Monist*: the latter was to remain the vehicle for views allied with his own, so that while they might choose to publish articles by Peirce, they reserved the right, exercised by Carus, to agree or disagree with them. Peirce found this restriction insulting. On the other hand, Hegeler wanted to proceed with the publication (including the "Illustrations" if the copyright problem could be settled) of two volumes on logic by Peirce with the Open Court Press. Hegeler continued to be concerned enough about Peirce to ask how much it would cost to send the ailing Juliette and Charles to visit with her family in France.[44] By May, Hegeler's letters began to show concern over Peirce's procrastination:

I have to give a negative answer to what you say about a sojourn in France and for the present also to what you say about the rewriting of your papers for publication in book form.

I think you should concentrate yourself totally on the completion of the arithmetic. I request for your report of the status of this matter. It is a large sum of money that I am to invest therein.[45]

Peirce then offered to put up his library (still owned in part by Johns Hopkins) as security, and Hegeler asked for a catalogue of the books. When Peirce, having promised to provide it, failed to do so by July 29, Hegeler withheld the last installment of his advance on the arithmetic.[46] Peirce finally provided a complete list on August 29, with the promise of a complete bibliography when he had time, and Hegeler sent him the final payment of the advance.[47] From this point on, Hegeler refused to deal directly with Peirce. Eisele has shown that the evidence concerning Peirce's relationship with Hegeler over the arithmetic is confusing. There is reason enough to doubt that Peirce ever sent the manuscript to Hegeler, although he certainly told Russell that he had. The whole manuscript, reconstructed by Eisele from the table of contents Peirce had given to Hegeler in May 1893, exists among the Peirce manuscripts at Harvard.[48] How it returned to Peirce's hands, if it had ever left them, is a mystery, because he never had the $1,750 to repay Hegeler's loan, the condition for its return to him.

In the meantime, Peirce had been criticizing Carus's criticisms of his articles in a way that Peirce immediately apologized for as being "exaggerated in tone" as well as "hastily written." He suggested new articles, such as "Philosophical Reflections on Table Turning," "Immortality in the Light of Synechism," and "What Is Christian Faith."[49] Peirce had also been attacking Hegeler in letters to Carus, who responded:

> You will confer a favor on me by omitting all remarks on your relation to Mr. Hegeler, such as made in your letter of July 4th. I must leave many of your remarks unanswered (for instance your reflections on the distinction between seminary-bred and laboratory-bred). If I do not answer them do not take my silence [as indicating] assent. This is especially true [of my own] attitude toward Mr. Hegeler for I look at [the matter] in a different light than you do.[50]

Here the correspondence with Carus lapsed, with a few exceptions, until a year later. In the interim, the depression of 1893–94, one of the most serious in the country's history, had devastated the Peirces' slim resources. Carus wrote Peirce on July 16, 1894:

> I handed your two letters to Mr. Hegeler and also informed him of the Mss which you offer for publication, . . . When I advised him of the emergency in which you were at present, he handed me for your immediate needs a five-dollar bill which is here enclosed at his request. Under these circumstances I must return your Mss and can do nothing except to hope that you will pull through.[51]

Nevertheless, later the same month Carus accepted an article, "The Marriage of Religion and Science," and paid Peirce the piddling sum of $27.50 for it.

In a draft letter to Russell written in late August, which demonstrated some rare insight into his own character, Peirce reflected on his relationship with Hegeler, which Russell had questioned him about:

> I don't know now what the matter with Hegeler is. It is quite clear to me that his state of mind is entirely different from what you suppose it to be, that for some reason or other he is violently inimical to me [the phrase that appeared as a warning of impending disaster in every controversy Peirce became involved in]. I dare say I may be greatly at fault in some way, &

probably more than you seem to think, or more than you say. But how I am so, I really don]'[t comprehend. . . . Hegeler never wanted me to publish my papers. He reluctantly consented for a while then objected & finally talked to reporters about 'heading' me 'off.' As for Carus, I think if it were not for Hegeler, he would give me some aid to say my say,—at least, he wishes me to think so. . . .

I don't know that it ever occurred to me Carus was jealous of me. I don]'[t rate Carus very high certainly. I don]'[t think him or Hegeler either at all 'liberal,' if you mean broad and tolerant. I think them very narrow, as all Buchnerite sects are for the most part. . . .

I have a very high respect a sort of veneration for Hegeler. I think his ideas are admirable & the whole morale of the man high, though he is too arrogant and too little aware that truth is not something to be pushed like a business. I think he says to himself 'Now here is this Peirce. Judge Russell and others say that I could do the world some good by helping him. Besides, he is rather an interesting man, I can see. I will see if I can't help him.' But for some reason or other, perhaps because he has made up his mind my philosophy is pernicious, he is now only anxious to put me down.

That I am extravagant & heedless about money to put the thing in its mildest terms I must acknowledge. Neither do I for a single instant feel anything but a heavy load of obligation toward Mr. Hegeler. I certainly have not the slightest desire to have him do anything more for me in a financial way. On the contrary, the thing which is driving me crazy is how I can ever get clear of the situation. . . .

If you can talk Hegeler around, why you may be sure, that I shall be as grateful as I can be—In point of fact there are some features of my philosophy which chime in remarkably with his views on immortality. . . . But what I would like would be to have an Article in every Monist (or every other one) until I can sketch my whole system. . . .

This is what I tried to bring about through Carus some time ago; but for some reason it did not work. Hegeler was just as insulting and disagreeable as Prussian resources in that line enabled him to be. If you can manage it, as I shouldn't wonder, it would be a great help; for till my books are out I am quite strapped. In fact, there is hardly enough food to keep body & soul together & I am considerably weakened by it. I don]'[t suppose the state of things will last very long; but it don't take long to finish a man.[52]

In several letters he did send Russell from September 5 to 8, Peirce expressed his bitter resentment of Hegeler and chronicled the depth of his misery. He promoted himself, with no experience, as the equal of Garrison to be editor of a national literary magazine and described his fears of a mysterious conspiracy against him:

It is difficult for me to conceive the state of mind of a person who wants to have their errors go uncorrected. . . . But when I see person's of that absurd temper pretending to be *philosophers,* my contempt is very deep. Now when I had a very exalted idea of Hegeler, I could not conceive that setting up to be a bit of a philosopher, he should look upon philosophy as a *contest,* where your triumph consisted in not having your errors exposed. Consequently, I soon mortally offended him, by pointing out that he was wrong about something, a thing which anybody doing for me has always endeared himself to me. Of course, in this respect I have a small opinion of Hegeler. I came here and found all my pipes frozen, the house uninhabitable, the railway blocked, & in this neighborhood one can never get work done in time. There was a great delay during which it was impossible to advance my work much. . . . My arithmetic was, however by that cause, and also because of certain domestic events upon which I could not calculate unavoidably delayed. If Hegeler would have advanced me a small additional sum, that would have been all right; but as he would not, & *I had to live,* the only thing I could do was to give it up, go to New York & live on my earnings. Even then, I should have been all right, if I had not been awfully swindled; and then I should have been all right if it had not been for certain treacherous friends who contrived to play me a bad trick. But I still should have come out all right, if it had not been for the terrible times. And even as it is, though it has been a terrible squeeze, I shall soon be in condition, I believe, to repay all I owe to Hegeler, pack up the books & send them to him, and go about my proper business of making the exposition of my philosophy. . . .

Of course, the *Open Court* is so badly conducted at present that I really believe Carus couldn't do worse if he were trying to scuttle it. It will be a damned shame; for the paper is a splendid monument to Hegeler. If I had hold of it, I would make it rival The Nation on the literary side and on the scientific side the best thing in the country. . . . I would have ten to fifteen thousand subscribers at $3 for an increased size of the paper & a valuable line of advertisement. . . . [53]

I happen just now to be off the *Nation* for the time being, owing to my striking [in fact, Garrison, the editor, had suspended him], although they really pay me at a very high rate as newspapers go. The thing will be adjusted soon and a new agreement made. Meantime I am free to make a suggestion which I shall not remain long free to make. . . .

Now if the *Open Court* were made as large as the *Nation,* a first rate critical journal, advocating Mr. Hegeler's views of Religious matters, & moderately but distinctly republican in its tone, giving attention also to Science, to Intellectual Amusements, theatres, chess, whist, etc. and paying also more attention to *the tastes of women,* there is no doubt in my mind its subscription list would equal or surpass the *Nation*'s very soon. . . .

If I were offered a responsible position on such a journal, I would endeavor to bring capital into it, and no doubt should succeed in doing so.

Of course I would accept no other than a responsible position. . . . My writing of advertisements, by the way, has been repeatedly praised by men at the top of *that* profession. . . . I should then be in the best possible situation to get out my philosophy. . . . But I know the stupid German ire too well to expect anything from the suggestion.[54]

I repeat that I have not the least hope that you will be able to arrange anything. He [Hegeler] will act as before, pretend to agree to it in the hope of getting me into further difficulty & turn round at last & show his animus. 'Kiss it,' he'll say. Kiss what? I shall ask? 'My animus,' he will reply.[55]

Now I have an idea. I must have some immediate cash or [I go] to smash. Suppose I assign you the copyright of this work as collateral security for a loan of $250. . . . I enclose an agreement to do so. . . . [56]

Here Peirce appended the outline of a long manuscript, entitled *The Art of Reasoning,* a later version of *Grand Logic,* completed in 1893, probably for Hegeler, but never published. Despite the near impossibility of concentrating on the intricate distinctions of philosophy amidst the exacting and poignant chaos of his life, Peirce managed to do it in every spare moment by taking small pedestrian steps within the larger vision of his still-vague system. The way in which the evidence of new philosophical work appears suddenly and unexpectedly in odd places, such as this and other personal letters, is uncanny. The manuscript whose outline Peirce sent to Russell included both reworked old essays and new material:

Chapter 1. *What is a sign?* My old theory, but entirely newly written & one of the clearest pieces of analysis I have ever made. Likeness, Indices, Symbols, more clearly discriminated than ever before, especially the last, which had been a little hazy.
Chapter 2. *The Materialistic Aspect of Reasoning.* My old theory, newly written out, & somewhat elaborated.
Chapter 3. *What is the Use of Consciousness?* New. Questions the assumption that it is one thing to *see* red or green & another to *look* red or green. Empedocles a little pirated here.
Chapter 4. *The Fixation of Belief.* My old piece. Improved in parts, adhering to the same inflated style. The *a priori* method much better treated & enforced by criticisms of Descartes, Kant & Hegel.
Chapter 5. *Of Inference in General.* This is a new work, largely occupied with discussion of terminology.
    "Simple Apprehension, Judgment, & Reasoning"
    "Term, Proposition, Argumentation"
    Understanding, Verstand, *intellectus.*
    That most languages have no nouns, at least not so radically separated in the minds of those [who] use them from verbs as are ours. . . .

Onslaught upon grammatical terminology in general & upon the Procrustes bed into which European grammarians force languages. . . . [Peirce here examines elements of a number of languages, including Egyptian, Latin, Greek, German and Eskimo.]

The kind of language that reasoning demands. How each kind of sign is required shown more clearly than ever before. The psychology of languages. . . .

Chapter 6. The Algebra of the Copula. This difficult subject is here perfectly cleared up and systematized for the first time, and made to lead directly to the Boolian algebra.

History of the principles of identity, contradiction, and excluded middle.

Chapter 7. The Aristotelian Syllogistic. Aristotle's formal logic shown to rest on his doctrine that we cannot know anything unless it be a uniformity. . . . This chapter presents the ideas of my paper on the classification of arguments in greatly improved form. . . .

Chapter 8. The Quantification of the Predicate. Refutation of Hamilton.

I then consider De Morgan's propositional scheme from two points of view, which I call *Diodoran* and the *Philonian*, with reference to a celebrated controversy between Diodorus and Philo. . . .

Chapter 9. Logical Breadth and Depth. This is my old paper worked over. Breadth & Depth *in relationem.*

Chapter 10. The Boolian Calculus. I show that the rules of the non-relative algebra may be immensely simplified by dropping all connection with arithmetic & I show that arithmetic itself dictates this . . . I then pass to the *Logic of Relatives* which I now bring to a much more perfect and interesting form than before & greatly simplify the proceedure [*sic*]. The student will work it practically with facility and advantage. I show that it is necessary to learn to think with it, and that is the chief use of it. . . . I have a formula which embraces Hegel's [logic] as a particular case. I do not pretend, however, to be able to work it out from my *Icheit*. I don['][t believe any mortal can. Yet theoretically it might be done.

Chapter 11. Graphs and graphical diagrams. Shows the value and limitations of the geometrical way of thinking.

Chapter 12. The Logic of Mathematics. This is I think the strongest piece of logic I have ever done. It analyzes the reasoning of mathematics by means of the Calculus of Relatives. I don['][t see what loophole there is to escape my conclusion as to the nature of Mathematics, that it is merely tracing out the necessary consequences of hypotheses.

Chapter 13. The Doctrine of Chances. The worst chapter in the book. A mere revision of my Popular Science Monthly article. . . .

Chapter 14. The Theory of Probable Inference. My old essay. . . .

Chapter 15. How to Make Our Ideas Clear. Old article

Peirce said that he intended two more chapters, "The Law of Continuity" and "Logical Recreations and Exercises," plus a "Glossarial Index." He then outlined a "more Radical revision of it," which would restrict the volume he had outlined to "Necessary Reasoning and make a separate book about Probable Reasoning, and a third about Objective Logic." The letter immediately continued to describe how desperate was his situation:

> My dear friend. The crops have utterly failed. No hay. No oats. Not even the seeds back. Three magnificent horses I have advertised all around, but though willing to sell for a song cannot because of the ruinous price of hay & the failure of oats etc. In Europe last year's drought, this year's wet, and certain special circumstances reduce my wife's income to *below her taxes*.
>
> My Geometry promised to be so profitable (& I don't think it can fail) is *nearly ready*. My arithmetic is *out of my hands*. If I could only borrow enough on the copyright of my logic to carry me along awhile I should be all right. I don't want to force myself on Hegeler who *don't want* my writings. He has shown that clearly enough. But perhaps you can show him that he is harsh in his judgment of me. I *can't*, because I can get no inkling of what he thinks of me. . . . I know I have one of the most powerful men in Europe as enemy who will leave & has left no stone unturned to make people act in a way really ruinous to me. Contrived to cause people to give my wife such advice as nearly landed me in a madhouse—& how can I guess what has been said to Hegeler? I know [Ogden] Rood and others (how influenced I don't know) have joined in a regular hounding of me. I believe I shall come out on top; but I don't know *why*. I guess you can influence Hegeler if anybody can, but his animosity is nasty. Try to get me scholars to have me invited to give lecture or readings.
>
> Above all, don't lose time. . . . don't wait. If you can't raise all at once, raise a part and send in haste. I need it & my wife needs it even more. . . . My two brothers are both abroad. There is nobody to whom I [dare] make my condition known.[57]
>
> I don[']t care a straw what you do about Achilles [Hegeler]. . . . I don[']t know where anything to eat is to come from tomorrow. In the last 24 hours one cracker and a little oatmeal—my wife will go very soon.
>
> My wife cannot live unless we get away at once—Now if the University of Texas would ask me down there to give some lectures *at once* & pay expenses, i.e. journey & hotel bill for self & wife, that would suit nicely![58]

Afterward, although Peirce hated Hegeler, his failed Alexander, he never admitted it to him because he still continued to hope for his patronage. Because of Russell's insistence, Carus remained inclined to help Peirce and continued to print articles and occasional reviews by him until 1910.

As the depression deepened in the three years following 1893, Peirce's fortunes reached their lowest ebb. Even as early as the fall of 1893, his financial straits were so obviously desperate that his brother James Mills, now dean of the faculty at Harvard, took it upon himself to write to President Gilman of Johns Hopkins, pleading with him to employ his brother as lecturer. He pointed to his well-received Lowell Lectures on the history of science, which "should rather have been 'some Chapters in the Early History of Science,'" and mentioned his brother's real need. He concluded by recognizing that a real favor was involved, but that it would be greatly appreciated.[59] Of course, Gilman refused.

The *Nation*, another principal source of income for Peirce in the years after he left the Survey, was, in the person of Wendell Phillips Garrison, its literary editor, much more sympathetic. In fact, Garrison allowed himself to be swayed by his concern over Peirce's condition into advancing him so much money that in the summer of 1894 he felt obliged to refuse to accept any more manuscripts from him until the balance of unpublished manuscripts which he had already accepted and paid for were in print. This situation was resolved in 1895, and Garrison remained a loyal patron until he resigned from the *Nation* in very bad health in 1905. Altogether, Garrison gave Peirce at least 230 books to review. At an average payment of $40 dollars each, high for the times, Peirce's income from the *Nation* was about $9,000 from 1890 through 1906. Peirce reviewed a remarkable breadth of subject matter: geodesy, metrology, physics, chemistry, radioactivity, astronomy, optics, aeronautics, history of science, mathematics, logic, philosophy, ethics, biology, psychology, sociology, economics, history, archeology, literary criticism, dictionaries, grammar, education, biography, autobiography, gambling, wine, fine food, and charades. A very short list of the writers he reviewed would include William James, Josiah Royce, John Fiske, Andrew Carnegie, Simon Newcomb, Santayana, Herbert Spencer, Locke, Nicholaus Lobatchewsky, Spinoza, Edward Everett Hale, Sir Walter Scott, Darwin, Hegel, Boethius, Mendelejeff, Leibniz, and Kant.

Many of these persons were his American and European contemporaries, and because all of Peirce's reviews were anonymous, and because the complaints about them, of which there were many, were directed to Garrison, he was in the delicious position of being able to criticize their work with impunity and, perhaps, even to affect their reputations. A fine example is Peirce's review of Victoria Welby's minor work *What Is Meaning?* together with Bertrand Russell's *The Principles of Mathematics*, in which he compared Russell unfavorably with her.[60] The use of this hidden power, of which Garrison was complicitly aware, undoubtedly tickled Peirce's well-developed sense of irony. At the same time, Peirce, often isolated in Milford by poverty and unable to buy his own books, was dependent on the vagaries of Garrison and other editors for the books he received to review. This frequently meant that he was unaware of major work being done in a number of fields that interested him. This ignorance of the work of others important to him, especially logicians and mathematicians, explains why so much of Peirce's own work was idiosyncratic, but it does not explain how Peirce was able, as isolated as he was after 1898, to anticipate the direction and often the very elements of entire disciplines, semeiotic being perhaps the major example.

Garrison liked and pitied Peirce and took a personal and somewhat clinical interest in his and Juliette's life; he also funded it in an insufficient (about $600 per year) but indispensable way. Garrison's letters are filled with personal inquiries, comments and advice, and instruction in the writing of reviews:

⌊5/18/1893⌋

It is a long time since you vanished clean out of sight, & my inquiry of your brothers has not shown them to be any better informed about you than myself. I hope you are well & that some of the objects of your Western journey ⌊to meet with Hegeler⌋ have been attained.

⌊7/19/1893⌋

Speaking of lectures, have you ever lectured before the Peabody Institute in Baltimore ⌊one of the last places Peirce would consider⌋? . . . They pay pretty well. . . .

⌊8/4/1893⌋

. . . I can only sift you in with the rest ⌊of the twenty members of his staff⌋, and give you a very precarious assistance. To no one else would I have given the license to buy foreign books to review. . . .

⌊11/15/1893⌋

Your discursiveness is often very piquant, & suggestive & enlightening, but it is always in danger of resembling the pin-wheel which has got off the stick. Contributors who abound in *obiter dicta* are a great trial to me.

⌊11/29/1893⌋

Not to spoil your Thanksgiving. . . . I send you herewith the desired check for $100. At the same time I think it salutary to produce a reckoning that we may see just where we stand. . . . There is a clear ⌊owing to advances⌋ $200 against you. . . . This seems to me as much as I ought to carry for the good of either of us. . . . I am now forwarding a parcel which will show the amount of risk I boldly incur. It contains a collected volume of Huxley's & the letters of Walter Scott. . . . I hope you will justify my boldness.

⌊12/3/1893⌋

A happy thought just occurred to me. Every well conducted paper keeps a "graveyard" of obituary notices of eminent personages against their decease. . . . Will you nominate some? Tyndall is just gone. Do you feel competent to do Huxley? Helmholtz? We pay pretty well for this sort of work—and don't wait till the subject is dead either.

⌊1/18/1894⌋

. . . I oughtn't to have sent you the book ⌊Scott's letters⌋ as I said when I did send it. Whether you can recover . . . I don't know. If you do, it will be by taking the *literary* view of the subject. . . . ⌊You are not making any attempt⌋ to reduce the large sum to your debit. . . . I am open to reason if I appear niggardly or short-sighted, but in truth I have never done as much (editorially) for any one as you, & I am chargeable with my conduct of the *Nation*'s literary expenditure.

⌊1/30/1894⌋

. . . I was rather surprised that you bespoke the review ⌊of *Funk & Wagnall's Dictionary*⌋ knowing that you had not the apparatus for comparison at hand. In this light you were an unfit man at Milford who would have been the fittest man in N.Y. . . . Be assured that your straits are never out of mind, & that I regret my own closeness of living as incapacitating me from rendering any personal assistance.

⌊5/18/1894⌋

Though I ought, as custodian & trustee of other people's money, to be insensible to your letter just received, I cannot be, & I have just telegraphed you that I have deposited $100 to your credit. . . . I can say nothing of your affairs, for I am dumb with affliction myself whenever I view affliction that I cannot help.

⌊7/23/1894⌋

There has been no other change in our arrangements, as you allege, & it is not becoming—or modest, if you prefer—to stigmatize my editorial judgment as a whim. I have always paid you promptly and generously, on the assumption that you were giving me not waste paper but *Nation* matter *in my judgment*. . . . The result is that your debit is $400. . . . I submit that if there is to be any concern of mind or any coolness, it should be on my part rather than yours. I notified you long ago that you were leaning on me (*i.e.* the *Nation*) too heavily; this fact ought to have prevented your taking—or giving offence.

⌊12/14/1895⌋

It surprises me less that your Milford paper ⌊the Port Jervis, N.Y., *Gazette*⌋ went back on you than that it offered to print your 'caviare to the general' ⌊Peirce's popularization of his metaphysics⌋. I must say, too, that as a scheme for revenue it seemed to me very unpromising, like that project of a great work [to publish twelve volumes of Peirce's philosophy by subscription] which you advertised some time ago in the *Nation*. They are not means adopted to the end. I shall be glad enough when your life falls into the humdrum which affords no material for a novel.

[2/18/1896]

I am sorry to hear you have been ill. From what your wife told me, I feared you were overworking yourself.

[2/21/1896]

I do not wish to discourage you in any effort to get out of your present difficulties, but your twelve volume scheme appears to me more likely to involve you further than to help you out. To become a teacher is certainly more reasonable, but does not your advertisement propose too much?

[3/4/1896]

It has heretofore seemed to me useless to make any comment on the despairing tone of your letters so far as they touch upon your personal affairs; nor am I now sure that I am doing wisely to notice them. What has brought you to your present straits is beyond my knowledge, and I have no impertinent curiosity. Defective judgment in worldly matters such as I have observed in you would account largely for your failure to make a permanent place for yourself. . . . Far be it from me to reproach you for what you were born with, but if you could become conscious of it, the world would perhaps not seem so entirely to merit your reproaches.

[3/22/1900]

I am going to offer you an aside which I think will interest you . . . *Confidentially:* The *Evening Post* is undertaking a special Supplement for the end of the year, reviewing the century philosophically. . . . Pay will be liberal and not delayed till publication. . . . The subject I propose to you is an appreciation of the century's contribution to the great men of history— the intellectual "summits" [published January 12, 1901, by the *New York Evening Post* as "The Century's Great Men in Science" and reprinted in the *Annual Report of the Smithsonian Institution*]; and I think you can do it in fine style if you hold yourself in.[61]

Because Peirce complained to James about Garrison's treatment of him, it has sometimes been maintained that Garrison was a poor friend to Peirce. But it would be hard to find another man, other than James himself, who so consistently, and often against his better judgment, went out of his way to help Peirce as Garrison did. During this disastrous decade, the work Garrison sent him was often all that he had, as Peirce himself admitted. When Garrison left the *Nation* in 1905, the one source of income on which

Peirce could depend virtually disappeared, and in less than a year he was almost without any income whatever.

Peirce tried to expand the number of publications accepting articles by him and wrote to the editors of *Scribner's Magazine,* the *Independent,* and a number of others. Generally he was unsuccessful in these efforts, although a number of articles were published in this way. For example, in December 1893, he published a study of Napoleon in the *Independent* as "Napoleon Intime," in two parts after an argument over its considerable length. Peirce also suggested himself to its editor, Kimley Twining, as science editor, who replied: " . . . I am afraid you do not examine our issue very often. We have a scientific column edited by as good a scientific man as we know, and I find on talking to Dr. [Lester Frank] Ward that neither he nor I feel that we ought to do anything to disturb the arrangement as it exists in its present form."[62]

Peirce might have broken into the lecturing circuit. Certainly his flair for dramatic declamation suited him for it. M. E. Waring, owner of the Atlantic Lyceum Bureau of Baltimore, wrote him, at the suggestion of someone who had heard him lecture, requesting a list of topics and descriptions, which Peirce sent him. Waring was interested and asked him for the Lowell Lectures, and for one of which Peirce was particularly proud, entitled "Embroidered Thessaly, found among the papers of an attorney recently deceased." In it Peirce imagined himself as born in the course of a wild flight to the hospital in the wilderness of New York State. His mother's and his lives were saved by Thessalian gypsies near Watkins Glen. Her stories of the adventure made him want to go to distant Thessaly. The lecture begins, "A good many years ago, before the face of the world had all its wrinkles smoothed out by modern bards, it happened that this writer, then a young man, landed on a bright summer's morning from an Aegean steamer at a little town of Thessaly, Bolos . . . ," which Peirce had visited twenty years before during the eclipse expedition of 1871. The lecture contained highwaymen, maidens in distress, and other standard elements of melodrama. Nothing came of Waring's interest.

On January 20, 1894, the *Publisher's Weekly* carried an advertisement for two prospective works, one in philosophy and the other in medieval science:

> Charles S. Peirce, Milford, Pa., has in preparation a work in twelve volumes, each distinct, the general title of which is "The Principles of Philosophy, or, logic physics, and psychics, considered as a unity, in the light of the nineteenth century." The first volume, which is ready for the press, will be "A Review of the Leading Ideas of the Nineteenth Century."

Mr. Peirce also issues a prospectus of a limited edition, now in course of printing, in two colors of hand-made paper, at the De Vinne Press, of "The Epistle of Pierre Pelerin de Maricourt to Sygur de Fouacucourt, Soldier, On the Lodestone." The original treatise dates from 1269, and "occupies a unique position in the history of the human mind, being without exception the earliest work of experimental science that has come down to us." The transcript of Peter Peregrinus's text has been made afresh from the contemporary MS. in the Paris Library, and is reproduced in black-letter together with a translation and notes.[63]

The prospectus itself was extraordinarily grand in its ambitions and stated, in part:

> This philosophy, the elaboration of which has been the chief labor of the author for thirty years, is of the nature of a Working Hypothesis for use in all branches of experiential inquiry. Unmistakable consequences can be deduced from it, whose truth is not yet known but can be ascertained by observation, so as to put the theory to the test. It is thus at once a philosophy and a scientific explanation of observed facts. . . .
>
> Both logically and dynamically the whole doctrine develops out of the *desire to know*, or philosophia, which carries with it the confession that we do not know already. . . . Nothing can be more completely contrary to a philosophy the fruit of a scientific life than infallibilism, whether arrayed in its old ecclesiastical trappings, or under its recent 'scientistic' disguise. . . .
>
> The principles supported by Mr. Peirce bear a close affinity with those of Hegel; perhaps are what Hegel's might have been had he been educated in a physical laboratory instead of in a theological seminary. . . .
>
> The entelechy and soul of the work, from which every part of its contents manifestly flows, is the *principle of continuity*, which has been the guiding star of exact science from the beginning. . . .
>
> The principle of continuity leads directly to Evolutionism, and naturally to a hearty acceptance of many of the conclusions of Spencer, Fiske, and others. Only, Matter, Space, and Energy will not be assumed eternal, since their properties are mathematically explicable as products of an evolution from a primeval (and infinitely long past) chaos of unpersonalized feeling. This modified doctrine, so much in harmony with the general spirit of evolutionism, quite knocks the ground from under both materialism and necessitarianism.
>
> In religion, the new philosophy would teach us to await and expect definite and tangible facts of experience, actually undergone. While details of dogma are beyond its province, it would favor rather old-fashioned Christianity, than any attempt to make a christianoidal metaphysics serve in lieu of religion. . . . It distinctly upholds a *Christian Sentimentalism*, as contra-distinguished from a gospel of salvation through intelligent greed.

[Peirce then outlined the twelve volumes, of which only the titles are given here, many of which are familiar from earlier compilations.]

Vol. I (Nearly ready.) *Review of the Leading Ideas of the Nineteenth Century.*
Vol. II (Substantially ready.) *Theory of Demonstrative Reasoning.*
Vol. III. *The Philosophy of Probability.*
Vol. IV. *Plato's World: An Elucidation of the Ideas of Modern Mathematics.*
Vol. V. *Scientific Metaphysics.*
Vol. VI. *Soul and Body.*
Vol. VII. *Evolutionary Chemistry.*
Vol. VIII. *Continuity in the Psychological and Moral Sciences.*
Vol. IX. *Studies in Comparative Biography.*
Vol. X. *The Regeneration of the Church.*
Vol. XI. *A Philosophical Encyclopedia.*
Vol. XII. *Index raisonée* of ideas and words.[64]

The volume from this list which stands out is that on the regeneration of the church, not a subject to which Peirce had given prominence before. The reason for it appeared a year later in a letter to a Roman Catholic churchman, Father Searle, who had written a book aimed at non-Catholics centered on the doctrine of papal infallibility. This doctrine was anathema to Peirce, and he put forward against it the doctrine of "contrite fallibilism," that mistakes are a necessary and inescapable part of the search for truth. Peirce began by saying that he would join the church of Rome if he could, but that the logic of science forbade it. He pointed out that no conceivable argument could support metaphysical infallibility, "for it is a long journey but to a certain end, that of metaphysics, namely,—it is bound to reach a conception different from that assumed at the outset":

> Were your Church only to reflect that if it could gain a power over the human heart equal, say, to the horror against *incest,* it would have power enough, and that nobody ever has *proved,* or is likely within, say, a century to prove, that incest is contrary to rational principles of conduct, but that we all fully accept the judgment of common sense against it, without in the least pretending that common sense is infallible in anyone . . . but simply that *practically* the dicta of the human heart ought to be accepted *practically* as infallible, then, i.e. if Rome were content with as much authority as *that,* and it is mighty, there might be a strong probability of her uniting the entire *christendom.* In short, the great foe to Rome is metaphysics. It is her malady.[65]

Peirce sent out announcements for his magnum opus to eminent intellectual figures of the day, including, among many others, William James, Simon Newcomb, John Fiske, Francis Abbot, G. Stanley Hall, Josiah Royce, Samuel P. Langley, Paul Carus, and Oliver Wendell Holmes, Jr. He also included the prospectus in issues of the *Nation* and volumes of the *Century*

Dictionary. He hoped, in this way, to get sufficient subscriptions to have the work published. Peirce had already tried to interest a number of major publishers in such a series, including Henry Holt, who responded using inconsistently the approved spelling of the Philological Society:

> [I] am positiv that if you think you coud "do it without a publisher and sell 500 copies", that is by all manner of means the wisest course. . . .
> To a publisher, the matter would not take an aspect of very great *business* importance, . . . and as far as I am concerned, the older I get, the more reasons I find for doing what litl that cums in my way . . . to do in aid of 'the things of the spirit,' outside of business. If the two ar mixt, they hurt each other.[66]

Other publishers, although they all favored the idea, were equally unwilling to take on a work which their experience led them to believe could end only in financial loss. Garrison sent in a subscription, but thought the project both too large and unsuited to its purpose. In fact, only about thirty subscriptions came in on this first attempt. James wrote more gently:

> I hope that subscribers to your magnum opus come in. It may be that if the more distant thunder had been held in reserve and the first 3 volumes alone announced at present, the circular would have met with a better response, but it ought to be responded to as it is. In case of a renewed circular with such letters as mine printed, might it not be well to draw a line between the earlier and later volumes, expressing the later as something hoped for and conditional upon the success of the former? People are afraid of schemes too vast and ambitious—and also threatening to be too expensive. *I* hope for the whole set, but all men are not as I! [James appended this note of support for Peirce to use.]

Harvard University

My dear Peirce,
I am heartily glad to learn that you are preparing to publish the results of your philosophizing in a complete and connected form. Pray consider me a subscriber to the whole series. There is no more original thinker than yourself in our generation. You have personally suggested more important things to me than, perhaps, anyone whom I have known; and I have never given you sufficient public credit for all that you have taught me. [Four years later James did so in his California Union Address, where he attributed the origination of pragmatism to Peirce.] I am sure that this systematic work will increase my debt.

Always faithfully yours,
William James[67]

In what he hoped would turn out to be an additional source of funds for the publication of his magnum opus, Peirce had arranged with an art press of the time, the De Vinne Press, to print with his translation and commentary, also on a subscription basis, Peter Peregrinus writing on the lodestone.[68] Although the reaction to these projects from his friends was heartening, there were far too few subscribers to finance the venture, and this means of publishing his philosophy was given up. As for the De Vinne Press project, it is not even known what happened to Peirce's manuscripts.

Peirce was heavily in debt by May 1894, and in his letters to Garrison, Carus, and others, he continued to press for work and for loans. He was able to borrow fifty dollars from his cousin Lodge, offering land (already mortgaged) as collateral. This and other loans made to him by his relatives and friends always seemed justified to Peirce by his perennial and unfounded confidence that one or another of his many schemes would pay off.

By this time, probably through James Pinchot, he had become acquainted with George A. Plimpton, the New York publisher and collector of antique manuscripts. Peirce considered him a good candidate to be his new patron, Hegeler having failed him. The two men had originally been brought together because of Peirce's bibliographical knowledge, and Plimpton employed him as a consulting librarian and advisor concerning his extensive collection of mathematical works, but eventually gave the permanent position to someone else. In May, Peirce's financial condition led him to presume upon Plimpton for money, and he suggested a detailed and grand scheme for replacing *Roget's Thesaurus* with *Peirce's Logotheca*. Peirce would have based the *Logotheca* upon the pragmatic and semeiotic principle that all conceptions can be infinitely extended, expanding from the simplest conceptions to the most complex and abstract. He intended to derive the classes of terms from his newly developed phenomenology, a development of his categories. In a letter to Plimpton, Peirce wrote in part:

> The problem of how to make a really good book like Roget's Thesaurus is one I have had in mind for nearly forty years. . . .
>
> [My plan is] to begin with the simplest, most sensuous, most ordinary ideas, for which we have generally direct names not reposing on any metaphor. I first take the names of sensations: colors, sounds, tastes, smells, feelings, etc. Then, simple actions, walk, strike, eat, etc. Then, common things, etc. I then take mathematical & physical ideas. Then the simplest relations of life. Finally, the fine and complex ideas which are only expressed by words originally metaphorical. Under each of these, besides words the words peculiarly appropriated to them, I mention . . . metaphors that are usual; as, for instance, under *cunning*, a fox. Under *altruism, elevation, height*. Under *learning*, depth, etc. This saves much space & improves

the Index. Besides my own arrangement, I would furnish a Hegelian classification, and several others. The book would thus be useful to people of
diverse ways of thinking.[69]

Plimpton was fascinated and asked Peirce for a plan to get it into shape.
Peirce eagerly replied:

> The first thing in making a new work would be to form a new provi-
> sional scheme of pigeon-holes or classes. This I have [but it needs revision
> which will take twenty days]; . . . It would still be provisional, and would
> only contain about a thousand classes. . . . It would next be necessary to go
> through a good dictionary, say the Century Dictionary. Only about 50,000
> words would be wanted; . . . But many words have several meanings &
> have to be entered in several places. . . . [To experiment to find out how
> long each word would take, say from 1½ to 2½ minutes, depending on the
> talent of the assistant] . . . would be a year's work there. . . . I should pre-
> fer to do the work somewhat on this plan. Your firm to furnish the capital
> including pay for my work.
>   . . . supposing it proved to be what I now estimate, I would be satisfied
> with $250 a month, and a proviso that I should finish in 16 months. After
> it was out, the capital should be repaid out of the profits with 10 per cent
> interest. After that, I think you ought to let me in for half the profits. . . .
>   the utility would be very great. It could not be superseded; because very
> peculiar powers and accomplishments are required for the work of classify-
> ing ideas. In my opinion it would be an extremely profitable thing. Roget
> would be not only left in the cold; but almost everybody who has Roget
> would want to get this. . . .
>   [It will be] the 12th volume of my great work on Philosophy.[70]

In the end, Plimpton did not think the project feasible. Peirce tried other
publishers, who liked the idea but asked for a more complete proposal,
which he never provided.

Peirce added another source of income in the spring of 1894, through
his long friendship with Samuel P. Langley, the newly appointed secretary of
the Smithsonian Institution. Langley, one of those men in positions of authority who went out of their way to help Peirce, sent him for translation as
many European scientific publications as he felt he could afford to do, paying a higher rate than usual.[71]

In the June term of 1894 came the first of a long series of suits for
nonpayment of debts that had been brought against Peirce in the Milford
County Court. These debts came almost entirely from charges for work done
on Arisbe, work which was going on at the very time Peirce was being sued.[72]
On July 26, the Milford paper carried a note to the effect that Peirce was

making decided improvements on his house.[73] At the end of July, Garrison wrote Peirce that the debit of his account with the *Nation* was $400, and by September he refused to raise Peirce's indebtedness any further. As if to heighten the contrast between Peirce's hopes and the reality, Juliette and he spent many afternoons and evenings at Grey Towers enjoying the rich hospitality of the Pinchots, who were spending July and August in Milford.[74] On September 8 Peirce wrote Russell saying, "I must have some immediate cash or [I go] to smash," and suggesting he turn over to him the rights for his *Art of Reasoning.* He went on to detail the failure of his crops, his inability to sell his horses, the insufficiency of his wife's income, and his deep-seated belief in the existence of a national and international conspiracy directed against him. He described his poverty: "Need can not be more extreme. There is nobody to whom I [dare] make my condition known." Less than a month later, the Milford paper again carried an account of improvements to the Peirce property, this time an expensive rerouting of the main road by his house.[75]

Peirce seems to have had no understanding of the part he played in his own destruction; he could find no reason for his failure except the faults or ill-will of others. The way in which he continued to involve himself, against all good sense, in large expenditures in connection with his property, which he justified by the necessity to present the facade of wealth, shows clearly that he was unwilling or unable to face the facts of his condition. Instead, he convinced himself that he did have, through his Working Hypothesis, the categories, an experimental (and therefore testable) knowledge of the real workings of the universe. When, in spite of this superior knowledge, nothing turned out his way, he invented a mysterious, omniscient national and international conspiracy of evil and powerful men—none of whom he identified with the names of those who, like Newcomb, actually did act against him—intent upon destroying him and his mysterious Juliette as well.

One of the more unattractive personal traits which Peirce indulged during these hard times is well illustrated in his attitude toward relatives and friends. His estimate of the worth of those who were close to him was often determined entirely by the use to which he could put them. He really did believe that his value for humankind was sufficiently great for him to impose indiscriminately upon whoever would accept the burden. It appears that he repaid only a very few of his debts. The remarkable thing is not so much that Peirce was a consistent practical failure despite his great talents and immense labors, but that his friends and patrons almost always freely acknowledged his genius and did what they could for him.

Peirce wrote Garrison in November out of desperation and asked him to reopen his credit, which had been closed for several months. Garrison replied:

My long silence was not intentional in the beginning, but it comes about naturally, & I concluded that the practical thing to do was to print your store of notices, as rapidly as I could, & then make a new footing. The more you wrote (so long as I advanced anything) the deeper we seemed to get into the mire. I am, as always, extremely sorry for your straits, but I have stretched my privilege to an extreme in striving to lend you a helping hand. It may be that we can arrange a system of half pay, or there can be some obituaries to prepare.[76]

Out of money and with his food supply reduced to "one cracker and a little oatmeal," Peirce may well have been considering who would be given the task of writing his own obituary.

Fortunately, Langley of the Smithsonian telegraphed one hundred dollars in time to stave off starvation.[77] But the result of malnutrition was to make Peirce very ill. Somehow or other, through small amounts of money for translations paid by Langley, and small amounts from friends and essays for periodicals, Peirce managed to continue through early February 1895, when debts of various kinds, but principally those incurred in improving Arisbe, were pressed through the courts for payment, and he stood to lose everything. At this time, his elder brother, James Mills, stepped in just in time to save what he could. The court had ordered a sheriff's sale of Peirce's library to pay off some of his debts. This magnificent collection was described in the sheriff's report as follows:

> Historys, Cyclopedias, Treatise on Philosophy, Proceedings of London Mathematical Society, The History of Napoleon, The Dialogues of Plato, Bismarck in the Franco-German War, Life of Oliver Goldsmith, The Puritan in Holland, England and America, French Revolution, Sir Thomas Browne's Works, Walks in Rome, on Geometry, Cyclopedia of Anatomy and Physiology, . . . 29 Vols Philosophical transactions of the Royal Society of London, Cowpers Works, Shakespeare's works, Robert Browning Poems, and thousands of other books making up the whole of aforesaid library, and all Stationery, Tables, Cases, and Instruments.[78]

James Mills bought the library, equipment, and instruments for the low figure of $655.25 and returned them to his brother. He then arranged a $1,000 mortgage, which, together with the price paid for the library, settled a $2,000 debt connected with work on Arisbe. He also paid the first five installments, the initial one on February 15. The bank, fearing, with good reason, that the Peirces might be unable to pay, required as a condition of granting the mortgage that the house remain tenanted at all times. If it was left unoccupied, the bank could foreclose. The Peirces defaulted payment in December 1896, but the bank chose not to foreclose and stayed payment of

James Mills Peirce, ca. 1895.

the debt until December 1899, provided they did not default again (they did) and that they insured the house for $1,000.[79] This aspect of the mortgage was not discovered by the Peirces until 1897, after they had lived more than a year in New York City. Fortunately for them, there were no buyers for the property during that time.

James Mills, finally realizing the true state of his brother's circumstances, tried to help him in a number of ways. He asked Ginn and Company, the publisher of their father Benjamin's geometry text, to agree to publish both Charles's arithmetic and the reworking of their father's geometry textbook. This was to be a joint effort, largely to take advantage of James Mills's sober and responsible reputation. Early in the relationship, Edwin Ginn wrote James Mills thanking him for a letter "concerning your brother's book. It is gratifying to us that it meets with your approval and that you will be willing to aid in the revision of it. . . . and there can hardly be doubt but that we shall want to publish it. If it were not in some respects a matter of form we would settle the question now."[80] But by March, Ginn was writing that they were interested in publishing only Book V, "Metrics," which they considered a good revision of Benjamin's textbook which could be made "suitable for the use of schools and colleges. . . . We would say that it [the whole text] seems to be in two parts, one a sort of mathematical philosophy, and the other more properly a text-book. Now the mathematical philosophy would meet with hardly any sale. . . . "[81]

Charles wrote a reply to Ginn explaining his rationale for his version of the text:

> Nevertheless, although my experience of teaching is that the worst results are obtained by beginning with metrics & the best by taking topology, graphics, metrics in that order, yet, after all, I want the book to sell, & if you think the old stupid way, which makes a large percentage of the scholars dunces, is the best way to sell the book, I consent reluctantly to the excision of the facts you do not like. . . .
>
> Now I leave you to make such decision as you like. I dare say J. M. P. [James Mills] would lend his judgment if desired.[82]

In the end, neither text was published. Eisele tells the story in detail in her *Introductions to the New Elements of Mathematics*.[83]

James Mills also did his continuing best to have his brother appointed to an academic position. He gave his own explanation of Charles's failures and expressed his great concern to William James on February 7, 1895:

> It is certainly amazing that with all Charlie's power of doing work of high ability, scientific, literary, philosophic, & his devotion to work, he commands no public & offers his wares in vain. Admitting all that is erratic in his judgment & temperament, all that is rebellious against the commonplace in his personality, I must think it a glaring proof of the want in our country of the sincere love of intellectual truth, & of even the ordinarily current respect for intellectual standards that we see in Europe, that nobody cares even to render a formal encouragement to one who shows intellectual originality without popular gifts. I do think that it is primarily C's originality of mind which wrecks him. That is not a quality that commends itself to the American newspaper reader.
>
> He is preeminently suited to a university lectureship somewhere. He has things of real value to say to scholars. He needs the freedom of mind which only a salary can give.
>
> He has for months been toiling at work [on the mathematics texts] that he fancied more saleable than a volume of his projected Philosophy could be. But he seems to have toiled in vain. The little that he can pick up by a notice here & there has been his sole support. He has been & is much out of health. I fear a total breakdown. His little property is so involved that I fear he will lose it (even his library) without saving a penny from the wreck. And what then? I can assure you the case is one of real urgency & which I can do but little to relieve.[84]

Acting upon James Mills's suggestions, James wrote President Eliot, who was then vacationing in Egypt, recommending Charles in the most persuasive terms to give a new course in cosmology:

> Now I want to propose to you no less a person than Chas. S. Peirce, whose name I don't suppose will make you bound with eagerness at first, but you may think better of it after a short reflection. He can easily be got for one year now, being in hard pecuniary straits. He is the best man by far in America for such a course, and one of the best men living. The better graduates would flock to hear him—his name is one of mysterious greatness for them now—and he would leave a wave of influence, tradition, gossip, etc. that wouldn't die away for many years. I should learn a lot from his course. Everyone knows of P.'s personal uncomfortableness; and if I were president I shouldn't hope for a harmonious wind up to his connexion with the University. But I should take that as part of the disagreeableness of the day's work, and shut my eyes and go ahead, knowing that from the highest intellectual point of view it would be the best thing. . . . It would also advertize us as doing all we could and making the best of every emergency; and it would be a recognition of C.S.P.'s strength which I am sure is but justice to the poor fellow. I truly believe that the path of (possibly) least comfort is here the *true* path, so I have no hesitation in urging my opinion. A telegraphic answer to *me* will be understood: "*yes*" for invite him, "*no*" for let the matter drop.[85]

As expected, Eliot refused to consider Peirce, saying that he was " . . . very sorry to dissent from C. S. Peirce, particularly because that dissent cannot but grieve J. M. Peirce. All that you say of C. S. Peirce's remarkable capacities and acquisitions is true, and I heartily wish that it seemed to me possible for the University to make use of him."[86]

As Garrison refused to give him more than a minimum of work, and Carus was accepting nothing from him, and there was but little translating work to be done for Langley, it was fortunate for Peirce that a friend, probably George F. Becker of the Geological Survey, recommended him to the distinguished civil engineer George S. Morison, who also became Peirce's patron. Morison wished Peirce to help him with the theory, design, and mathematical analysis of stress and other factors for a suspension bridge to span the Hudson River from New York City to New Jersey, a project which fifty years later, under different auspices, became the George Washington Bridge. The connection between the two men began in March, and by August, when Peirce finished the calculations, Morison had paid him a thousand dollars. Thereafter, Morison joined the small group of American men of wealth who did what they could to help their erratic and increasingly vulnerable friend.[87]

This respite was marred by a court action in Milford which began in April, when Peirce's servant Laura Walters charged him with committing aggravated assault and battery two months earlier and sued him for damages. He was freed on $500 bail.[88] This was not the first such case in which Peirce had been involved. His lifelong proclivity toward violent behavior was greatly intensified by the repeated defeats and ignominies of his life and by the constant and inescapable burden of Juliette's illnesses. The miseries and afflictions he endured sometimes caused him to explode in fury, especially toward his servants and workmen. Fortunately, such eruptions were usually limited to sarcasm and other verbal attacks. On some occasions, however, he became physically violent. In July 1889, he had pleaded guilty to one count of assault upon his servant Marie Blanc.[89] Five years before that, in Baltimore, Peirce had been involved in a battle with his cook. A newspaper clipping preserved by Gilman as an example of what went on in Peirce's household reported:

> Benefit of the Doubt—Margaret Hill, an old lady, was charged with assaulting her employer, Dr. Pierce of Calvert Street, with a brick. . . . Her counsel, pleaded strongly that a doubt existed in her favor. Judge Duffy—'It is only on that doubt that I act. I strongly suspect that the woman struck the man with the brick, but I give her the benefit of the doubt. Not guilty.'[90]

The affair in Baltimore had been resolved in his favor, and Peirce was able to escape by paying a fine of $25 and costs in 1889. However, his financial straits were such in 1895 that he felt he could not afford to let the case come to trial for fear of losing his home. He managed to have the Laura Walters case continued repeatedly from session to session until it was settled out of court in February 1897.[91] Several other cases were brought against him for nonpayment of debts, but only one was serious. In this one, brought on November 14 by Leo, another member of the Walters family and one of the workmen employed by the Peirces, an unusually high bail ($1,000) was set in absentia, and a warrant *capias ad respondum* was issued for Peirce's arrest. Five unsuccessful searches were made for him in Milford between November 1895 and January 1897.[92] The Leo Walters case was also settled, along with that of Laura Walters, in February 1897. Because Juliette's health required hospital care, the Peirces left Milford in August 1895 for New York City before the Laura Walters case came to trial. In November, with the issuance of the warrant for Charles's arrest, they became fugitives from the law. Thereafter, only Peirce himself returned for brief visits, often incognito, until the suits against him were settled with the help of Morison and Plimpton, and he returned in December 1897 to bring the house back into livable shape and make arrangements for tenancy. He did not return permanently until May 1898, and Juliette not until two months after that.

Charles and Juliette were both well-connected in New York City. Charles had been a member of the exclusive Century Club since 1876 and was at first a conspicuous and later a disreputable figure in the society of the city's old-line upper crust. In 1895, he was still a regular and respected contributor to the city's scientific associations. His working relationship with Garrison of the *Nation* assured him of entry into the broader intellectual life of New York. Wealthy patrons such as James Pinchot, Morison, and Plimpton continued to use their influence in his favor. Juliette was herself a creature of high society, moving easily in the increasingly cosmopolitan sphere of great wealth and the arts. She had been an amateur actress of note and enjoyed the company of the more bohemian practitioners of the arts, as did Charles, probably through his friend and crony Edmund Clarence Stedman. Stedman was a notorious figure in the New York literary world. As a young man, he fell in love with a girl from his neighborhood, and they toured New England as a brother-and-sister act, an escapade for which he was expelled from Yale. He later became a poet, publisher, and stockbroker and was probably among the most esteemed and popular members of the post–Civil War New York literary scene. The Peirces also knew a number of prominent theatrical figures, such as Steele and Mary McKaye, and acted occasionally in amateur theatrical events, including a performance of Legougé's *Medea*, which he and Juliette translated into English.[93] These and similar connections made it possible for the Peirces to survive their three-year New York City ordeal, but their experience of life had not prepared either of them for the harsh world of urban poverty into which they were plunged.

New York City, the "New Cosmopolis," invented itself haphazardly in the late nineteenth century out of a social chaos presided over by the Irish politicians of Tammany Hall. By 1895, it had become the ethnic stew called by Israel Zangwill the "melting pot," but that transformation had taken place remote from the notice of the older population:

> Immemorially cosmopolitan, it yet possessed a tribal core that recent immigrant strains had scarcely weakened, so that one could still speak of the New York of the Knickerbockers as one spoke of the New Orleans of the Creoles or of Quaker Philadelphia or Puritan Boston. This quintessential provincial town, the heart of the spreading world-city, was all but unaware of its own East Side, as it was hardly aware of the West and, except in Wall Street circles, virtually ignored the country beyond the Hudson. Its horizon was bounded by Trinity Church, the Knickerbocker Club, the Res-

ervoir, the Astor Library and the Academy of Music, though its brownstone uniformity was yielding here and there with the coming of the Western millionaires. French Chateaus had begun to appear with copies of ancient manor-houses filled with loot from England, Italy and Spain.[94]

The slums, when first discovered by this insulated elite, were romanticized even in their degradation as "the worst hell known to man." The association of romance and magic with slumming in the Lower East Side began to wane after the coming of the reformers.

> But before the rise of the settlement houses there was still a quality of the Arabian Nights in this "region of socialistic rainbows," . . . when one could play the disguised sultan and sally forth with a favorite vizier at eve from Park Row in pursuit of strange adventures. It was an adventure in itself to slink down some sinister alley that was full of Chinese and American tramps, and there, amid thrilling encounters and escapes, one could take part in anarchist meetings and rejoice, at Bohemian tables, in true Pilsner beer [and delight] . . . in the contrasts of this East Side world where sweat-shop workers and push-cart pedlars were sometimes Talmudic scholars and poets as well.[95]

Police reporters such as Lincoln Steffens and Jacob Riis provided a different and graphic picture of misery and human waste, and with it introduced a different attitude. In 1890, Riis wrote *How the Other Half Lives*, a description of the three-fourths of the city who lived in the slums, in decrepit old buildings without sanitation, with dangerously rickety staircases and filthy yards, in damp basements and leaky garrets, all breeding dysentery, typhus, tuberculosis, and smallpox. They slept often fifteen or more in a room on straw pallets overrun with rats. Five hundred thousand poor immigrants from southern and eastern Europe and Ireland were crammed into the Lower East Side. They were often drunk and violent. Thousands of prostitutes, burglars, pickpockets, confidence men, and criminals with many other skills ranged much of the city. Gangs, usually Irish, but representing every ethnic group, ruled the slums. The most violent gang was the Irish Whyos, who would accept no new member unless he had killed at least once. They advertised their services openly in handbills passed out in most of the city. A price list from 1884 proclaimed:

Punching	$ 2.
Both eyes blacked	4.
Nose and jaw broke	10.
Jacked out (blackjacked)	15.
Ear chawed off	15.

Leg or arm broke	19.
Shot in leg	25.
Stab	25.
Doing the big job (murder)	100. and up.[96]

It was common practice for the wealthy to hire bodyguards when they went about the city. These bodyguards as often as not came from the gangs or the police, whom the gangs paid off. The Irish of Tammany Hall used both the gangs and the police to ensure their winning elections by means of the immigrant vote, to enforce their decisions, and, when necessary, to threaten the old-line elite and the new wealth, both of which became increasingly reform-minded as a result, but also at the same time more willing to deal with Tammany behind the scenes in their own interests. The political machine constructed out of these disparate elements lasted from the time of the Tweed Ring in the 1860s to the election of Fiorella La Guardia in 1933, founding its great popularity with the city masses on what George Washington Plunkitt, one of the more thoughtful Tammany henchmen, called "honest graft"—the providing to the poor immigrants of much-needed social services in exchange for personal fortunes robbed from the public till.

Peirce knew virtually nothing of this world, and what he did know of it, especially of the Irish, he strongly disapproved, but his poverty and Juliette's need increasingly forced him to live by his wits. How deeply he was forced to enter into the city's underworld is unknown. One factor, however, is clear. His income from free-lance writing was far too small to support them, and he refused to use Juliette's income, which anyway had declined drastically during the depression. Peirce was reticent and indirect in his references to how he survived this period. No doubt he resisted outright criminal acts as long as he was able by cadging food and by means of the loans he seldom, if ever, repaid. But at times he was so poor that he did not eat for days and had no place to sleep, spending days and nights wandering the city. Sometimes he may have been reduced to stealing what he needed to survive. Whether he actually joined "the poor" and learned compassion from them is also unknown, but it is likely that he did so in spite of his strong social prejudices.

In August 1895, Juliette fell gravely ill, probably with gynecological problems, and Peirce took her to a hospital in New York. He was so short of funds, however, that Juliette was turned out because he was unable to pay the fees. He wrote to Russell:

> My wife was turned out of the hospital, as I supposed. I paid them the next day. But she is now in imminent danger. I do not leave her bedside for over half an hour at a time; & as I am the only nurse, am pretty thoroughly done up. Still, I write my logic, just the same. I lost some 300 acres of blue

stone quarries owing to want of cash; and I fear I have lost my house. But I have had no positive information. I had arranged another way of getting the money in time; but being obliged to say whether I wanted it or not, said no, counting on the Monist money, which I was not able to get till yesterday.

In the same letter, Peirce bitterly attacked Carus for not sending him the money which he thought was owed him:

> This was a disgraceful treacherous performance. Now if he does the like this third time, I shall act in a way which will injure his reputation for fairness,—[i]f he has any,—and show that the code respected by all American editors of standing condemns him. . . .
>
> At the same time, having been handsomely paid by the Monist, I wish to offer him the best I can do.

The letter continued with Peirce's usual misplaced confidence that he would soon be in receipt of large sums of money from an invention. In the meantime, however, he was short of cash and wanted to sell a picture.

> I have a picture by Alfred Bierstadt about 2½ x 3½ feet with a handsome frame outside of that measure. He gets $2500 for such a picture. There is a mountain with snow in the background, towering up high. It is big, solid, cool, calm. In the foreground large trees rocks, etc. I came within an ace of selling it to a bank for their ladies' room. I shall be content to get $1250 for it. I think I shall probably sell it before long; but being unable to leave my wife's chamber, have not done so yet. Do banks in Chicago hang up such things? If you can get a purchaser for $1500 or more, I will give you half the excess above $1000. . . . It is a fine picture, with great technique, and very natural. But there is no passion or sentimentality about it. It is a thing calculated to make people who look at it, especially women, calm and reasonable, and to suggest ideas of greatness, reliability, etc. That is why I thought of a lady's room in a Bank; & I should have sold it. Only the President said, 'You are so persuasive, I don't dare to trust myself '.[97]

Peirce had long believed that his great avenue to wealth lay in his practical knowledge of chemistry and physics. His first speculative venture of this kind was his development, in 1892, of an invention for electrolytic bleaching, which he expected would make him millions, and there seemed some prospect that it might succeed. In letters to Russell and Ferdinand Becker, Peirce said that he had been swindled in 1892 so effectively that his capital was wiped out. The only venture of any importance in that year was the bleaching process, so his reports of being swindled were likely tied up with it. In June, Peirce wrote a Wall Street businessman, T. J. Montgomery, apparently at the suggestion of a friend, about his bleaching process.[98] This approach must have fallen through, for there is a letter from the Peter Cooper Glue Factory of New York, sent to him at the suggestion of his brother James Mills in Boston while he was there delivering the Lowell Lectures, which offered an outlet for his invention.[99] Peirce ordered a boiler to try out his process, but there the record of his first disastrous failure as a scientific entrepreneur ends.[100] Peirce wrote of it indirectly in the *Monist* article "Evolutionary Love" of 1893:

> So a miser is a beneficent power in a community, is he? With the same reason precisely, only in a much higher degree, you might pronounce the Wall Street sharp to be a good angel, who takes money from heedless persons not likely to guard it properly, who wrecks feeble enterprises better stopped, and who administers wholesome lessons to unwary scientific men, by passing worthless checks upon them,—as you did, the other day, to me, my millionaire Master in glomery, when you thought you saw your way to using my process without paying for it, and of so bequeathing to your children something to boast of their father about,—and who by a thousand wiles puts money at the service of intelligent greed, in his own person.[101]

This failure only whetted Peirce's already sharp appetite to succeed as a capitalist inventor and man of science. In the eighties and nineties, New York City was filled with eager self-appointed entrepreneurs. Indeed, some of the most eager ones were members of the Century Club. It was the day of the Dandy, and aspiring millionaires went to job interviews and business meetings in tails and top hat. Like Peirce, they were almost as intent on sartorial smartness as they were on grabbing the main chance. Many enjoyed Peirce's company and included him in vast and vague plans for quick wealth. The invention which Peirce expected next to bring him wealth became the basis for one of the thousands of similar speculations which failed in the days of the Robber Barons. It was a sophisticated design to produce cheap domestic lighting from acetylene gas. It was probably no more unlikely than Thomas Edison's equally shoestring electric lighting venture, the success of which was a matter as much of skillful promotion as of technical potential.

Connected with Peirce in the venture were a small group of men considerably more colorful than Jay Gould, J. P. Morgan, or John D. Rockefeller, all of them soberly greedy. The undertaking had its genesis at the Century Club, perhaps in the mind of Edmund Clarence Stedman; he, Peirce, and Alfred Bierstadt decided to try and make their fortunes together. In addition there were Nelson Easton, a broker and friend of Peirce's father who wrote the first history of the stock exchange, and a fortune-hunting French nobleman, John Edward, Count d'Aulby del Borghetto and Prince of Montecompatri and Monteportium. D'Aulby had married the daughter of Adelaide

Lunt, a family friend, and as punishment for marrying beneath his station had been largely disowned, but he had been able to hold on to a collection of masterpiece paintings. Each man had a specific function in the enterprise. Easton, through his connections, brought a New York financial house, Stewart and Company, into the venture, and dealt with the details of organization. Bierstadt was to bring in some of his many European and American connections. Count d'Aulby was to be the European representative as well as assist in raising cash through the sale of his collection of masters, which was said to include Rembrandt, Raphael, Titian, Guido Reni, Velásquez, and Murillo. Peirce provided the necessary inventing power and scientific sophistication and was, as well, expected to obtain political influence and additional funds through his cousin Senator Henry Cabot Lodge and his connections with Pinchot, Plimpton, and Morison.[102]

Originally, the entire venture was centered on the development of cheap lighting from acetylene gas, the key to which was a necessary element in the acetylene gas generator, invented and patented by Peirce. In this, the undertaking was in competition with Thomas Edison's electrical solution to the same problem. At a later stage in the developments, the enterprise was expanded to include a hydroelectric generating plant. Things probably happened more or less as follows: Peirce heard about a new light powered by acetylene, and discovered a fault with it which he could correct. Through Easton, he was put in touch with Stewart and Company, who asked him to write a complete report of the possibilities. This he did, pointing out a more efficient way to derive acetylene gas from ore. For his share, Peirce and his partners were given the European rights for the sale of the acetylene lamp and a chance to buy stock in the pool which was eventually funded. While examining the site of the carbide mine near Massena in upper New York State, Peirce discovered that it would be an excellent location for a hydroelectric generating plant because it offered naturally the long drop necessary for the tailraces of the generators. Engineers were brought into the project, and perhaps, after a favorable report, such names as Harriman and Vanderbilt, though this is speculation based on cryptic references in the Peirce manuscripts. The operation was thus three-sided, having the capability of selling carbide, acetylene lamps, and electric power. It seems that the only reasons Peirce did not succeed in this venture, since the hydroelectric plant was indeed (eventually) built, were his gullibility and poverty.

By the late fall of 1895, Juliette was out of the hospital somewhat improved, and she and Charles, having lost their fine brownstone, took the first of several small places and later hotel rooms in the city. They did not return to Milford because of her state of health, which remained precarious well into the next year, and because of the outstanding warrant for his arrest in Milford. Peirce took an office in the Commercial Gas Company at 40 Wall Street, around the corner from the Stewart and Company offices at Broadway and 41st Street. During 1896, Peirce worked frantically to stave off starvation and make a success of acetylene speculation. To earn money, he worked on a book translation for Appleton and Company, wrote more extensively for the *Nation* and *The Monist,* and did two reviews for the *American Historical Review,* with which he became characteristically embroiled when payment was not immediately forthcoming.[103] As the year progressed, Peirce became more and more desperate. His life, which Garrison thought would make excellent "material for a novel," took on the cast of a nightmare in which, as it seemed to him, no matter what he did, because of some demonic influence he was bound to fail. Throughout 1896, like a kind of infernal chorus, the case of assault and battery and the suit for nonpayment of debt in Milford were continued from one session of the court to the next, as each search for Peirce proved unsuccessful. He retained a tenuous hold on his Milford property, which remained unsold only because no one wished to buy it.

By March 1896, Peirce had written a series of despairing letters to Garrison, in the last of which he threatened suicide. Garrison replied,

> You ought not to have communicated to me your intention, in a certain contingency, to make away with yourself. Such confidences belong to your kindred, if to any one. And innocent men have been known to go cheerfully to prison. Two of my ancestors had this distinction and are well remembered for it.[104]

But Peirce's condition was worse, if anything, in October when he wrote Russell:

> My dear Judge:
> This is merely to say good bye. If it is to be good bye. I have been tramping about night & day in the rain & am ill & can't hold out any longer
>
> very faithfully
C. S. Peirce[105]

Peirce felt the more bitter over his failures because in the middle of the summer he had come to believe that the venture in which he was engaged might make him a millionaire, and at the same time, his poverty prevented his taking advantage of that opportunity. He had tried desperately to raise money, using all his influence with Russell to have Carus accept an article or two at this crucial time. He tried to involve Russell himself, but with no success, since Russell had no money to spare:

Now if you want to go in, I will take you in on the ground floor: . . .
There will be four millioris of shares & two millions of 5 percent bonds. . . .

Not a share will ever be given to the public, it will be a close corporation. I want you to be in it. But don]'[t talk about it, either now or later.
. . .

This brilliant prospect does not prevent my being on the verge of
starvation for want of cash.[106]

He tried to bring his cousin Lodge into the venture and wrote him in
great detail, explaining that the site would make a superb location for a
hydroelectric generating plant, as it was uniquely located on the south bank
of the St. Lawrence River near Massena, New York. He claimed that the
company, the St. Lawrence Power Company, had

favorable reports of the greatest hydraulic engineers of the country. Its
ultimate capacity is at least 5 times that which has hitherto been got at
Niagara. In one year from now we shall have twice what Niagara has given.
In place of the tremendous outlay for tail-race that they have there, we have
our tail-race perfected by nature. Our head-race is almost made by nature.
An expenditure of $750,000 will set up in operation. There will be no long
shafting as at Niagara; but the mills will stand directly down at the tail-race
on bedrock foundations. No ices can interfere in winter. We are a hundred
miles nearer New York than Niagara; and ocean-going vessels can load up
right there. We have our company formed. We have the broadest charter
with one exception that has been granted by the state of New York for
many years. We have, of course, rights of eminent domain. But we also have
options on all the lands needed, 1500 acres, at moderate prices, $40 to
$100 an acre, except one farm of 200 acres. I have inquired into the general
character of the titles and find that they are particularly simple, being held
by descendants of the settlers who received grants from the state a century
ago. . . . The rock is suitable for making a richer carbide than pure [cal-
cium[carbide. . . . Niagara charges $18 per horsepower, [but we can sell
for $14[. . . .

[I am allowed[to purchase any amount of stock for cash up to
$100,000. They will let me in on the ground floor, and *into the pool,*—
which last privilege will never be given to anybody except those who have
the right to it. It lets us into the profits of the carbide business, the acetylene illuminating business, and every development.

This stock is to remain hypothecated to you, on these conditions; that
you are to be at liberty at any time to give me half of it and retain the other
half in payment of principal and interest, and that I am to have the right, if
you do not avail yourself of your right, to sell within three years but not
before fifteen months one half the stock or enough to pay the principal and
interest and thus free the other half. Your investigations, if you look into it,

will absolutely convince you it is as safe an investment as any speculation can possibly be, and that you are morally certain in this way to triple your money, at least.

If you say so, I will sign the contract, if you will go in for $100,000 . . . and will then carry you to see the reports, plans, charter, the people connected with it, the engineers, etc., will then take you to the ground, and show you everything there, and finally go to Cincinnati (if you care to go) to see the Morley [acetylene] light in operation. When I say no contract is needed for less than $100,000 I speak of the guarantee pledging my country estate. Of course, I don't mean to dispense with the subsequent contract about the stocks. If you would like a few 5% bonds, I think I could get them, but I am not sure.[107]

In January 1893, some months before he began to design his great coup with his Century Club cronies, Peirce had written in *The Monist* in answer to Andrew Carnegie's essay "The Gospel of Wealth," which had appeared in the *North American Review* in 1889:

The *Origin of Species* of Darwin merely extends politico-economical views of progress to the entire realm of animal and vegetable life. The vast majority of our contemporary naturalists hold the opinion that the true cause of those exquisite and marvellous adaptations of nature for which, when I [w]as a boy, men used to extol the divine wisdom is that creatures are so crowded together that those of them that happen to have the slightest advantage force those less pushing into situations unfavorable to multiplication or even kill them before they reach the age of reproduction. Among animals, the mere mechanical individualism is vastly reënforced as a power making for good by the animal's ruthless greed. As Darwin puts it on his title-page, it is the struggle for existence; and he should have added for his motto: Every individual for himself, and the Devil take the hindmost! Jesus, in his sermon on the Mount, expressed a different opinion.

Here, then, is the issue. The gospel of Christ says that progress comes from every individual merging his individuality in sympathy with his neighbors. On the other side, the conviction of the nineteenth century is that progress takes place by virtue of every individual's striving for himself with all his might and trampling his neighbor under foot whenever he gets a chance to do so. This may accurately be called the Gospel of Greed.[108]

No one urging these innocent and vulnerable views could succeed in the competitive maelstrom of New York City, except by blind luck. By 1896, despite his Christian convictions, Peirce was so "crowded together" that he was taking whatever slight advantage came his way and was as intent on success as any Robber Baron. Lodge was far too aware of his cousin's reputation to stake his money in such a speculation, and he was later to remark to

Gilman about Peirce's "infirmities of temper which have stood in his way in life."[109] As it turned out, the St. Lawrence Power Company was absorbed in 1903, and the hydroelectric venture, under different auspices, was financially extremely successful and still ranks as a brilliant feat of engineering. This was no comfort to Peirce's dream of "an Arabian Nights' cave of wealth."

The acetylene lamp venture, for which they had the European rights, was still thought to be worth developing by Peirce, d'Aulby, and Bierstadt. They decided that, in order to raise cash, d'Aulby would try to sell a few of his paintings in America, but he considered the prices as insultingly low as American culture. D'Aulby then went to England to interest English financiers in the commercial possibilities of acetylene gas light there.[110] D'Aulby wrote that he was succeeding in placing a loan, and in January 1897, Bierstadt said that the three of them would soon receive at least $30,000 each, which raised what proved to be false hopes.[111] By July 1898, d'Aulby took control of the European venture, cutting out Peirce completely.[112] All that remained was the virtually worthless American stock, for which Nelson Easton tried to make a market, unsuccessfully.[113] With that failure, Peirce's fevered dream of wealth faded forever.

Christian J. W. Kloesel opened the way to a public examination of this long-suppressed side of Peirce's life when he pointed out in 1988, seventy-four years after Peirce's death, a parallel that Peirce himself had drawn. In the summer of 1913, less than a year before he died, Peirce discovered a devastating, but in his view entirely accurate, portrait of himself in the protagonist of the French novel *La Grande Marnière* (The Great Marl Pit). The Marquis Honoré de Clairefont was an inventor who, as its author Georges Ohnet put it, "shamefully squandered and lost all" because of his "hazardous speculations," "most unreasoning caprices," and "blind, relentless egoism." "Astride his fantastic hobby, in his pursuit of the impossible," the Marquis "has pursued shadows and given way to false hopes" and still "has confidence in his dreams," which are "the very essence of his life, his unique element of happiness." He is always "on the eve of realizing important sums." On the title page of the book, a gift to Juliette, Peirce wrote, "The Marquess of Clairefont is C. S. P. to a dot."[114]

In this context, a description given by John Jay Chapman of an evening he spent with Peirce in the summer of 1893 at the Century Club takes on depth of meaning:

> I am too tired to write. Went to the Century [Club], where I happened to sit down next to Charles Peirce, and stayed talking to him ever since, or rather he talking. He is a most genial man—got down books and read aloud. He began by saying Lincoln had the Rabelais quality. It appears he

worships Rabelais. He read passages in Carlyle in a voice that made the building reverberate. He also read from an Elizabethan Thomas Nash—a great genius whom he said Carlyle got his style from, but he is wrong. Nash is better. I almost died over the language of this Elizabethan—he is a gargantuan humorist of the most splendid kind, as good as Falstaff, and Peirce read with oriflamme appreciation. He then talked about—plasms—force, heat, light—Boston, Emerson, Margaret Fuller, God, Mammon, America, Goethe, Homer, Silver, but principally science and philosophy—a wonderful evening. It was ask and have, and, but that he talked himself positively to sleep with exertion, he would be talking yet, and I have many more things I want to ask him. . . . He is a physical mathematician mechanician, that sort of a man of a failed life so far as professional recognition goes, but of acknowledged extraordinary ability, and is positively the most agreeable person in the city. He is a son of old Professor Peirce, is about 55 and is like Socrates in his willingness to discuss anything and his delight in posing things and expressing things.[115]

In another context, that of meetings of the American Mathematical Society, the mathematician Thomas Fiske remembered that

conspicuous among those who attended the meetings of the Society in the early nineties was the famous logician Charles S. Peirce. His dramatic manner, his reckless disregard of accuracy in "unimportant" details, his clever newspaper articles (in *The Evening Post* and *The New York Times*) on the activities of the young Society, interested and amused us all. He was the adviser of the New York Public Library for the purchase of scientific books, and wrote the mathematical definitions for the *Century Dictionary*. He was always hard up, living partly on what he could borrow from friends, partly on what he got from odd jobs like writing for the newspapers. He seemed equally brilliant whether under the influence of liquor or otherwise. His company was prized by the various organizations to which he belonged; and so he was never dropped from membership even though he failed to pay his dues. He infuriated Charlotte Angus Scott by contributing to the *Evening Post* an unsigned obituary [written for Garrison] of Arthur Cayley, in which he stated, upon no grounds whatsoever, that Cayley had inherited his genius from a Russian mother [she was English, and had lived for some years in St. Petersburg, but Peirce was intent on demonstrating the truth of biological determinism].[116]

In 1896 in New York, Peirce, living hand to mouth and often without food or shelter for days at a time, tried with desperate ingenuity to find some way to make enough money to feed and shelter the two of them and to provide care for Juliette. One unsuccessful idea, probably proposed by his friend Bierstadt, was to obtain the job of English-language correspondent in

Paris for the New York *Tribune*. He confided one of his many schemes to Russell:

> The idea which occurs to me is this. Bierstadt has invented a car which opens out into a room 27 feet wide. The Russian & German governments have taken it up; the N.Y. Central people are about to go into it. It is a very practical thing. It goes about like a car, and then can be transformed in a few minutes, by lifting the roof and drawing up sides for part of the roof and by letting down inner sides for a floor and other movements, into a chapel, or a theatre, or a picture gallery, or a shop, etc.
>
> I believe a car costs $8000. It is quite cheap. Now let Hegeler pay me $2000 and I will get him the right to build a number of such cars for Sunday or other lectures on the Religion of Science, which being sent about the country & free sermons & lectures given, & would distribute the Open Court and raise that to a satisfactory paying basis. The lecturers (preferably two) would sleep and eat in the car, and their expenses would be light. If it would add to the inducement I will give 100 lectures.[117]

In the midst of all these unsuccessful promotions, Peirce was also trying to arrange a way to review in *The Monist* the third volume of *Algebra der Logik,* by his friend the German logician Ernst Schröder. They had never met, but they had corresponded since about 1879, sharing their ideas about various aspects of logic and their mutual need for money to finance their books. Peirce had told Schröder about his troubles getting published in *The Monist* and about his battles with Carus. Schröder wrote in an appealingly fractured English that he had in six pages exhausted his eloquence trying to convince Carus that he was incompetent to review his book, and that

> I most seriously assured him, that however ungrateful your countrymen and contemporaneans might prove, your fame would shine like that of Leibniz or Aristoteles into all the thousands of years to come, and that he could do no better than openly to join your banner (however: no difference of opinion as to necessitarianism allowed); pointing you out as the one most, if not only, appropriate for undertaking the task of the criticism, and laying stress on the fact that *your* doing so would evidently lie in the interest of the Monist itself; advised him to ask, and offer you a good salary for the contribution. Should he therefore (as I hope, but with regret cannot help doubting somewhat) come to meet you, then build him a golden bridge!

Peirce was trying to arrange for the review he had written of Part One of the third volume to appear under Russell's name. All three plotted at length to bring their "secret" plan to fruition. In the end Carus relented and allowed the review to appear under Peirce's name.[118]

Sometime in the midwinter of 1896–97 Juliette, who for years had suffered from gynecological problems, underwent a hysterectomy, life-threatening surgery at the time. Peirce wrote his friend Schröder, "My wife is dreadfully ill. The doctor says to me brutally. 'We think the thing to be done is to extirpate womb & ovaries.' A pretty speech!"[119] His single paying student, F. W. Frankland, wrote Peirce in May 1897, "I am truly glad that Mrs. Peirce is recovering."[120] But it was not until October that Juliette was finally well enough recovered that Garrison could write: "Your wife brings me, in her face & in her words, most welcome news of the great physical change which surgical science has wrought in her. She also gives me good tidings of yourself and your joint prospect of a return to Milford."[121]

The house to which they were to return the next year had gone badly downhill in the two years since they had left it. A friend who had visited the area around Milford the year before wrote Peirce a description of Arisbe in decline:

> It is a rather coincidence that on the day your letter was written . . . I should have paid my first visit, (after so many years) to your beautiful little

Ernst Schröder (1841–1902).

cottage. I had left Philadelphia that morning with Herzog [a painter to whom Peirce had hoped to rent his house] to make a bicycle trip through the valley. We reached Port Jervis at half past four, and halted for dinner at Yorick's "Hickory Grove". While the pheasant was roasting we rode further, hoping to find you at home. Of course we were disappointed in this, but it recalled pleasant memories to see the house again.

As it was after sundown we did not dismount; but the next day we returned and made a nearer inspection of the place and its improvements noting also with deep regrets the evidences of its owner's absence, in rusting hinges and fallen shutter, and neglected garden. Through the side door I saw the lozenge mirror, and hall furniture, and through the slats of the front blinds your work-table and books as you left them. The contrast with the picture memory painted made me very sad, and I should have written to you at the earliest opportunity [even] had there been no letter from you.[122]

The improved state of his wife's health seems to have brought Peirce into a more balanced state of mind during late 1897, though he may simply have begun the process of resigning himself to the truth of his situation. George F. Becker had provided him with work for the Geological Survey for the first few months of the year.[123] In March Peirce was able to arrange for a tenant for Arisbe and to lease the land for pasturage.[124] He wrote William James a long letter from his Broad Street office (where he slept on a cot borrowed from Bierstadt). He began by thanking him for the dedication of *The Will to Believe*, calling it a masterpiece. James had written "To My Old Friend, CHARLES SANDERS PEIRCE, to whose philosophic comradeship in old times and to whose writings in more recent years I owe more incitement and help than I can express or repay." Peirce went on to examine, now in calmer retrospect, his last two desperate years in New York City and their effects on his thinking:

> That everything is to be tested by its practical results was the great text of my early papers; so, as far as I get your general aim in so much of the book as I have looked at, I am quite with you in the main. In my later papers, I have seen more thoroughly than I used to do that it is not mere action as brute exercise of strength that is the purpose of all, but say generalization, such action as tends toward regularization, and the actualization of the thought which without action remains unthought.
>
> I have learned a great deal about philosophy in the last few years, because they have been very miserable and unsuccessful years,—terrible beyond anything that the man of ordinary experience can possibly understand or conceive. Thus, I have had a great deal of idleness & time that could not be employed in the duties of ordinary life, deprived of books, of laboratory, everything; and so there was nothing to prevent my elaborating

my thoughts, and I have done a great deal of work which has cleared up and arranged my thoughts. Besides this, a new world of which I knew nothing, and of which I cannot find that anybody who has written has really known much, has been disclosed to me, the world of misery. It is absurd to say that [Victor] Hugo, who has written the least foolishly about it, really knew anything of it. I would like to write a physiology of it. How many days did Hugo ever go at a time without a morsel of food or any idea where food was coming from, my case at this moment for very near three days, and yet that is the most insignificant of the experiences which go to make up misery! Much have I learned of life and of the world, throwing strong lights upon philosophy in these years. Undoubtedly its tendency is to make one value the spiritual more, but not an abstract spirituality. It makes one dizzy and seasick to think of those worthy people who try to do something for 'the Poor', or still more blindly 'the deserving poor'. On the other hand, it increases the sense of awe with which one regards Gautama Booda [sic]. This is not so aside from the subject of your book as it might seem at first blush, because it implies that much [h]as led me to rate higher than ever the individual deed as the only real meaning there is [in] the Concept, and yet at the same time to see more sharply than ever that it is not the mere arbitrary force in the deed but the life it gives to the idea that is valuable.

As to 'belief' and 'making up one's mind,' if they mean anything more than this, that we have a plan of proceedure [sic], and that according to that plan we will try a given description of behaviour, I am inclined to think they do more harm than good. 'Faith,' in the sense that one will adhere consistently to a given line of conduct, is highly necessary in affairs. But if it means you are not going to be alert for indications that the moment has come to change your tactics, I think it ruinous in practice [written, no doubt, with his recent failed venture in mind]. If an opportunity occurs to do business with a man, and the success of it depends on his integrity, then if I decide to go into the transaction, I must go on the hypothesis he is an honest man, and there is no sense at all in halting between two lines of conduct. But that won't prevent my collecting further evidence with haste and energy, because it may show me it is time to change my plan. That is the sort of 'faith' that seems useful. The hypothesis to be taken up is not necessarily a probable one. The cuneiform inscriptions could never have been deciphered if very unlikely hypotheses had not been tried. You must have a consistent plan of procedure, and the hypothesis you try is the one which comes next in turn to be tried according to that plan. This justifies giving nominalism a fair trial before you go on to realism; because it is a simple theory which if it don't work will have afforded indications of what kind of realism ought to be tried first. . . .

I do not think suicide springs from a pessimistic philosophy. Pessimism is a disease of the well-to-do. The poor are ready enough to concede that the world in general is getting better, which is the best conceivable world, far better than a 'best possible' world. But men commit suicide because they are personally discouraged, and there seems to be no good to anybody in their living. There was Mrs. [Adelaide] Lunt [mother-in-law to d'Aulby] who drowned herself in a well. I often talked to her when she was coming to that resolution. It wasn't the universe that she thought intolerable, but her own special condition. . . .

Religion *per se* seems to me a barbaric superstition. But when you come to Christianity, or as we ought to call it Buddhism, for surely the Indian Prince was an incomparably more perfect embodiment of it than the miracle monger of the synoptic gospels, if that is to be called religion,—and the distinguishing feature of it is that it teaches the degradation of all arts of propiating [sic] the higher powers, which I take to be the definition of religion, that seems to me essentially the deepest philosophy, having the virtue of *living*. The clergymen who do any good don't pay much attention to religion. They teach people the conduct of life, and on the whole in a high and noble way.

As for morality, it is not a bad thing, taking it in the true evolutionary sense. But it is not everything that evolution results in that is good. Evolution has two results. One is the realization of the dormant idea. That is good. The other is the variation of types. That is indifferent. There really is no evolution in the proper sense of the word if individuals can have any arbitrary influence on the former [the realization of the dormant idea]. If they could it would fully justify Napoleon's remark to Josephine 'Madam, the rules of morality were not meant for such men as I.' Even as it is, there is some truth in it. The philosopher is considerably emancipated from morality. I, for example, often say to myself 'Your disgust at sports of killing, is really contrary to the traditional morality. You can't be wiser than the experience of the race on a complicated question you have not studied?' But I should think Gautama quite absolved from such a moral law.

I am much encouraged by your thinking well of 'tychism.' But tychism is only a part and corollary of the general principle of Synechism. That is what I have been studying these last fifteen years, and I become more and more encouraged and delighted with the way it seems to fit all the wards of your lock. It was a truly sweet thing, my dear William, to dedicate your book to me.[125]

In this letter Peirce identified the lesson he had learned from his afflictions as that which brought him "to rate higher than ever the individual deed as the only real meaning there is [in] the Concept, and yet at the same time to see more sharply than ever that it is not the mere arbitrary force of the deed but the life it gives to the idea that is valuable." One way of putting this shift in his philosophical perspective would be to argue that in the logic of science, the conception of conceivable results was a sufficient standard for the conduct of life, but in the moral life of a person, it was necessary to act out the idea in order to embody it in the world. Peirce here began to recognize that the moral dimension of his metaphysics was fundamental. Shortly he would write that logic was founded on ethics, and later, with some surprise, that ethics itself grew out of aesthetics. These shifts brought him back philosophically to his freshman year at Harvard, when he and his friend Horatio Paine intensively studied Schiller's *Aesthetic Letters* and were fascinated by his concept of *Spieltrieb,* in Peirce's phrase, "the play of musement." By 1897, Peirce was refounding his philosophy and logic on the lesson taught by affliction.

In a letter written to James the following December after James had arranged for his lecture series at Harvard, Peirce wrote, "I am all alone in the house here [Milford] & have spent some of the quiet hours over Substance & Shadow & in recalling your father [its author]. My experiences of the last few years have been calculated to bring Swedenborg home to me very often."[126] Peirce's return at this time to the ideas of the mystic Swedenborg were a continuation of his examination of the meaning of ideal-realism in the sense that it proclaimed the real as both immanent and transcendent in the community of nature and mind. This recognition of his concern with mystical doctrine he also associated with his experience of misery, specifically the anguish he had suffered since the publication of "Evolutionary Love" in January 1893. It was expressed in the March letter by the replacement of the revered Christ of the Gospels of the *Monist* series with the "miracle monger of the synoptic gospels," on the one hand, and the substitution of Buddha, the master of suffering of the Eightfold Path, for the "monstrous mysticism of the East," on the other. Peirce had also come to a resolution of his difficulties with nominalism by asserting its great, if not in fact necessary, instrumental value for getting at the root of things in the form of Ockham's razor.

In early June, however, his finances were still desperate, and he was able to arrange a loan of $218 from Morison using his land as collateral. Morison already had his Bierstadt landscape as collateral for another unpaid loan.[127] In August, he interested Benjamin Eli Smith, his former editor at the Century Company, in his *Logotheca,* about which Smith said, returning the manuscript, that if it were completed "it would receive very favorable consideration," but that in its current form it was too vague and "the practical experience of this office in such matters has shown the wisdom of caution."[128] In December, J. Franklin Jameson of the *American Historical Review* requested that Peirce review Bacon's *Opus Majus.*

In May, he had heard from Carus that James was trying to get him an opportunity to teach logic in Cambridge, and he wrote his friend from New

York City, saying, "If I were to have such a charge, I ought to spend every moment from now till October in preparing the first part of my course. Therefore, I beg you to let me know what the prospects are," and suggested a fee of $900.[129] It was not until December that James responded with the good news that a course of eight lectures was scheduled for February 1898, but that the fee would be $350 plus almost a year of weekly payments to Juliette. Peirce commented at some length on these arrangements, which were a forerunner of the Peirce fund:

> As to the ten dollars a week for 45 weeks to be presented to my wife, I cannot regard in any other light than as alms from totally unknown persons. Clearly it is not payment for my lectures. I shall not tell my wife how I look upon it, for we are in truth very poor, and she is ill, and if she sees her way to accepting it, I shall simply take care it is spent on her personal comfort. . . .
> But now she wishes me to ask you to send me an advance of $100.[130]

Peirce reported Juliette's reasons: (1) that he was ill and that they were forced to maintain two households to prevent the sale of Arisbe without notice if it was not tenanted; (2) he should be in New York City, where negotiations were under way for a position for him at Cosmopolitan University (the forerunner of the City University of New York); (3) the roof was leaking, and he had to pay cash to fix it because two men were coming to inspect the house, one to buy and the other to consolidate three mortgages totaling $2,500; and (4) "She wants me to have decent clothes for the lectures [the Dandy had become sadly shabby]. . . . Also that as things stand now, I should neither be able to leave here, nor have the money to go to Cambridge, or if I did go there might perhaps be too ill to give the lectures."[131]

Peirce and James argued about the content and the style of the lectures. The original title proposed by Peirce in December was "Eight Lectures on the Logic of Events," which was to include:

> 1. *Logical Graphs.* A novel method of treating formal logic . . . two systems, Entitative Graphs & Existential Graphs. . . .
> 2. *Lessons of the Logic of Relatives.* Showing the erroneousness of current logical notations, due to the particular nature of non relative logic. Also, exhibiting the generalizations of logical conceptions obtained by the logic of relatives. Here I might have space to say something of Duns Scotus & how I interpret him differently from Royce.
> 3. *Induction & Hypothesis.* Though not very fresh indispensable to comprehending my kind of objective logic
> 4. *The Categories:* Quality, Reaction, Mediation or Representation

5. *The attraction of Ideas.* Generalized law of association of ideas to which the cerebral anatomy is adapted. Perhaps 4 & 5 in one lecture
6. *Objective Deduction*
7. *Objective Induction and Hypothesis.*
8. *Creation.* or the earliest steps in the evolution of the world. Perhaps 2 lectures.[132]

Originally, Peirce had thought that these were to be technically advanced lectures which would embody the philosophical labors he had carried out in the depths of his despair and misery. James, however, had ten to fifteen students (and himself) in mind with a general interest in such ideas as tychism and synechism, so Peirce wrote out a new series "'on separate topics of vital importance.' I feel I shall not do it well; . . . Your Harvard students of philosophy find it too arduous a matter to reason exactly."[133] These became "Detached Ideas on Vitally Important Topics." On January 29, 1898, Peirce forwarded two urgent requests to James to send fifty dollars to Juliette in New York, which he did.[134] On February 14, James wrote his brother Henry: "Have just been 'raising' 1000 dollars to pay Chas. Peirce for a course, he being destitute, and that has begun too."[135] The final title of the lectures, as advertised by the Cambridge Conferences, was "Reasoning and the Logic of Things," and they included "Philosophy and the Conduct of Life," "Types of Reasoning," "The Logic of Relatives," "The First Rule of Logic," "Training in Reasoning," "Causation and Force," "Habit," and "The Logic of Continuity." Garrison wrote him, "At last you are the right man in the right place, & I am heartily glad to hear that you are speaking *ex cathedra* in Cambridge. . . . Enclosed is a check for all your notices in type or in print since my last accounting."[136]

Peirce gave these lectures in a private home in Cambridge from February 10 to March 7, 1898. The home, at 168 Brattle Street, belonged to Sara C. Bull, widow of Ole Bull, the Norwegian violinist and collector of Norse melodies, who opened her house for university events. James made the usual arrangements to use it.[137] James had asked the Harvard Corporation to allow Peirce to lecture on campus, but permission was denied. James may have hoped that by thus cracking the door at Harvard a little ajar, he might well be able to get Peirce in; after all, almost twenty years had passed since the scandals of the early 1880s, and a new spirit of tolerance could be called upon. At the time Peirce was in Cambridge, James's friend Josiah Royce tried to send work his way. D. C. Heath and Company had asked Royce to prepare a textbook on logic, but he had declined and suggested Peirce do the job. After considerable correspondence with Peirce, Heath remarked, "From your description of your work it is evidently scholastic and belongs to a period of thought which rather antedates the present . . . ," and nothing came of it.[138]

Heath's remark illustrates the remarkable degree to which Peirce was isolated, not by the outdated quality of his work but by the degree to which his thought—and not merely in logic—was ahead of its time. The more he worked along his pedestrian way, the more he outdistanced his world. At the same time, the more he moved away from nominalism and mechanism to-ward ideal-realism, the more soft-headed he appeared to his scientific and philosophic contemporaries, who were moving eagerly toward modern posi-tivism in one of its several forms. James himself was a nominalist and scarcely understood Peirce's philosophic intent, much less the exact distinc-tions of his innovations in logic. While James had indeed dedicated his book *The Will to Believe* to Peirce, in 1907 he dedicated the more important work, *Pragmatism,* "TO THE MEMORY OF JOHN STUART MILL FROM WHOM I FIRST LEARNED THE PRAGMATIC OPENNESS OF MIND AND WHOM MY FANCY LIKES TO PICTURE AS OUR LEADER WERE HE ALIVE TODAY." In his preface, James did not mention Peirce in his list of references for further reading, though he did mention Dewey, F. C. S. Schiller, Papini, and several others. Mill was a thoroughgoing and uncompromising nominalist. Royce, the Christian idealist, did understand and approve Peirce's philosophic purpose, but he was a rare exception and clearly was himself far removed from the mainstream of positivist science. Peirce called Royce the only true American pragmatist, other than himself to be sure. But Royce was also a novice in logic, as Peirce knew, and Peirce believed this to be the major defect in his philosophical work. This fact and the similarity of their objective idealisms made them, during Peirce's last sixteen years, almost co-workers as philosophers. Royce, with Peirce's help, was able to master the logic of relatives, including its mathematical aspects, and to apply it directly to his philosophy (for example, in the second volume of his late work *The Problem of Christianity*).[139] Royce gave Peirce his deep thanks. Even now, it is difficult for most students of Peirce to appreciate the necessary connection between his suspect metaphysics and the precision of his logical system, the semeiotic.

Also in February, Peirce was given a real opportunity to publish a work up to his standard. At the request of a friend and former student, the psy-chologist J. McKeen Cattell, he was to undertake a volume in a scientific series projected by G. Putnam and Sons. Cattell was the editor for the project and quickly realized that Peirce's contribution, which was to be the history of science, would require two or more volumes. The contract stipu-lated that Pierce would complete the first volume by December 1899.[140] His friend William James agreed to use the work as a textbook in one of his courses, and Peirce wrote to Putnam's that he expected that this would lead to its general utilization.[141] George Putnam thought the first chapter was impressive, and Cattell, on reading the same material, indicated that he would like to publish some parts of the projected book as articles in *Science*.[142]

In May 1898, Peirce moved back permanently to Milford; Juliette followed him in July. With the coming of spring and the outbreak of the Spanish-American War, Peirce, still the irrepressible inventor, wrote his cousin Senator Lodge that his " . . . ingenuity ought to be made serviceable. . . . I could make a machine which would write a cipher dispatch, as secure as a combination lock . . . and a companion machine would translate it as fast as a stock-ticker,—every dispatch a different cipher which the machine itself would discover. This would be valuable to merchants in war times."[143] He also poked fun at his cousin's blatant imperialism, saying, "I have from boyhood been taught by all our Massachusetts Statesmen the U.S. ought to possess Cuba."[144] Two years later, Peirce expressed himself on the matter of American imperialism more succinctly in the syllogistic form:

William James (*left*) and Josiah Royce at Chocorua, New Hampshire, ca. 1900. Photograph courtesy of the Harvard University Archives.

All men are entitled to life, liberty, and the pursuit of happiness
No Phillipino is entitled to life, liberty and the pursuit of happiness
Hence, No Phillipino is a man.[145]

Sometime in September, Peirce became seriously ill. By mid-October his condition seemed improved, and Garrison wrote Juliette, "I hope he has no touch of typhoid fever, which some of my friends near Milford have reported to be prevalent."[146] In late October, Peirce suffered a relapse and was unable to undertake even a review of Darwin's *Tides* for Garrison.[147] Still, he tried to work, including further studies for Morison's suspension bridge. Morison and Plimpton also helped the Peirces with their finances during this period, which at times were reduced to Juliette's income and the $10 a week provided by James, but the mortgage was reduced to $1,000 from $2,500. Both men had accepted Peirce's land as collateral. Morison had also accepted Peirce's water power stock and taken Juliette's jewels, including a large canary diamond, as further collateral for a loan designed to give Peirce working money for a year, which would be repaid by his completion of Morison's suspension-bridge work.[148] Mary Pinchot helped with food and money. On December 8, the Milford *Dispatch* carried the report that Peirce, "whose serious illness was noted some time ago, improves very slowly." By spring he was fairly well, but he never fully recovered from this attack of what was probably typhoid. His poor health prevented him from finishing even the first volume of his history of science for Scribner's.

On April 20, 1899, there was an announcement made of a forthcoming examination for the post of inspector of standards, and Peirce applied immediately. To get the political lay of the land, he wrote an old friend in the Coast Survey, E. J. Sommer, who had been fired under Thorn's administration and reinstated under the current superintendent, Henry S. Pritchett. At the time, the Office of Weights and Measures, soon to become the Bureau of Standards, was still under the Survey. Sommer wrote in mid-May advising Peirce to get recommendations from the scientific world rather than from members of Congress, except where the latter could influence Secretary of the Treasury Lyman Gage. He suggested Lodge as the most likely senator to be able to help, venturing that Pritchett probably had someone already in mind and that Peirce would need "pull."[149] Peirce requested letters of recommendation from five scientists with appropriate experience and credentials, including Simon Newcomb, a member like himself of the National Academy of Science's committee on weights and measures. Peirce provided Newcomb with a brief summary of his major—and important—contributions to the field, including his successful experiments to improve accuracy in measuring the meter using a wavelength of light. All answered with strong letters of support except for Newcomb, who wrote from Maroja, Switzerland:

> I do not see how I could say anything of real value about your "scientific administrative qualifications & experience." Your work was done for the Coast Survey and its records are there, and tell their own story. The Superintendent has at his command all the data for reaching a conclusion and nothing I could say could add to his knowledge of the subject.
>
> It is very clear to me that persons to whom the C[ivil] [Service] Comm. should apply are those who have made a more careful study than I have of your work or have had occasion to examine it [both of which Newcomb had, in fact, done for Superintendent Mendenhall, who had used Newcomb's evaluation to fire Peirce from the Survey eight years before]. These are best to be found among the C.[oast] S.[urvey] and other pendulum experts.[150]

Newcomb's obvious implication that his Survey record would be used against him motivated Peirce to write his cousin Senator Lodge and ask him to apply pressure in such a way that the results of the examination, and not other considerations, would determine the choice of the position of inspector. Since Lodge was in Europe, he was unable to do more than write a letter to Superintendent Pritchett, which had no practical effect, but did elicit in reply, on September 14, five days after Peirce's sixtieth birthday, the information that the job had already been offered to "a wellknown physicist [S. W. Stratton] of large practical experience and conditionally accepted."[151]

A month later, another job announcement for the examination appeared, which made clear that its purpose was to give the appearance of a competitive search. At the same time, Peirce received a letter from Pritchett saying that his application would receive proper consideration, a statement which admitted both Pritchett's duplicity and the accuracy of Sommer's forecast to Peirce in May. Peirce's copy of the examination, which exists in his papers, is brilliant. On November 15, Pritchett wrote to James Mills, who had asked him to explain the failure to appoint his brother, clearly the American scientist most knowledgeable in the field:

> I have considered the matter with great care. As you know, I have had occasion to know closely of his work in the Coast Survey and elsewhere. . . . notwithstanding the high scientific qualifications of your brother, it did not seem to me that he possessed those qualifications in such a degree as the place required. I regret that I have been unable to carry out your wishes in this matter.[152]

Peirce informed George A. Plimpton of this turn of events, who thereupon wrote not only to Superintendent Pritchett and Secretary of the Treasury Gage, but also to President McKinley in the strongest of terms in Peirce's support.

None of these efforts had any effect, and Peirce turned to an offer of Plimpton's to sell the *Cyclopaedia of Practical Information,* a multivolume hack encyclopedia peddled from door to door. He wrote to Plimpton:

> You think the best course is to organize a corps of 25 road agents. So do I. . . . I think too that would be highly successful, if I train them & arranged their work. Please send me a few agents outfits,—specimen books. . . . At any rate, I will at once begin the work. They will insist on 40%, though I shall struggle to make them take a round dollar and freight fee. I am assuming the price is to be $3 a copy. You will fix my commission or share or discount, whatever you call it. I want also 30 days credit, and a little more in the beginning.[153]

Not only was the plan humiliating and unlikely, but Peirce's age and health and Juliette's delicate condition made it utterly impractical.

In November 1899, Plimpton recommended Peirce to Walter Hines Page, then connected with development of *McClure's Encyclopedia,* as the best possible editor for its scientific section.[154] Langley also strongly supported Peirce for the position, but this possibility fell through as well, as did an attempt by Plimpton to place Peirce as the librarian of the Grolier Club in New York City.[155]

The absurd and sardonic cap to Peirce's sixtieth year arrived in the mail at Arisbe about Christmastime. It was the report from the Civil Service Commission containing the inspector of standards examination, stating that his score was 96.00, the highest, and that he was therefore eligible for the position.

5

Endgame

1 9 0 0 – 1 9 1 4   I am nothing but a farmer living in the wildest part of the Eastern States; although our National Academy of Sciences has most indulgently honored me with one of its chairs.

CSP to Georg Cantor, 1900

As the century turned, Peirce estimated with remarkable prescience that he had about thirteen years of life remaining in which to finish his philosophical labors. He passionately believed that only by carrying on with his original inquiry into "the laws of thought," for which he knew that he had unique and remarkable God-given talents, could he atone for the disastrous mistakes of his life. The foolish confidence of the past decade in schemes that would produce millions from his inventions had—almost—vanished. He knew that both his and Juliette's health was bound to decline, perhaps to the condition of invalidism. In 1909, adding greatly to the affliction of neuralgia, he was to be diagnosed as having cancer. He was very poor. Arisbe, mortgaged beyond their ability to redeem and a constant struggle to keep habitable, especially in wintertime, was now the only place they had to live. Both he and Juliette loved it, and he could work there in relative peace in the company of his books and papers. All Peirce needed to keep them going in Milford was fifty or so dollars each month added to Juliette's small income. But, with the exception of the Pinchots, they were thoroughly isolated there from friends and from the world of intellect and art only a few hours away. Had Peirce been able to sell his house and lands, he would have done so and returned to New York City, where life was much easier, their illnesses could be better looked after, and he could find work with the help of his patrons. Within five years, he was desperately trying to get rid of Arisbe, but there were no buyers for it until it was sold at auction after

Juliette's death in 1934. Consequently, they stayed on there hoping that, one way or another, they could not only survive the next threatening winter but come to live modestly comfortable lives without the humiliation of depending on the charity of others. Peirce still fervently believed that he would be able to reconstruct his life and become the success he and his father had always believed he should be.

At first, it seemed that things might work out as they hoped. In 1902, Peirce's long-time dream of being provided a stipend to complete his life's work became a real possibility. Peirce's loyal friends James, Garrison, Langley, Plimpton, Pinchot, Cattell, and Morison and his brother James Mills sent his way whatever odd jobs they could find for him to do, so that he and Juliette never lacked the necessaries of life. All tried with varying degrees of energy to find him some kind of regular work which he could do and enjoy, but they all failed, even when the signs seemed right. When Peirce could not, they paid his taxes, his dues, his mortgage payments, and other small bills.

A summary of some of the events of 1900 will serve to characterize these last years. In February, James Mills Peirce wrote E. C. Pickering, director of the Harvard Observatory, to find out if his brother might be employed to complete under contract his earlier pendulum work done there. Pickering answered that this would be impossible because the material concerned was at the Coast Survey, but that he would write his friend Superintendent Pritchett and try to arrange employment through him for Peirce.[1] Although Pritchett promised to do what he could, he let the matter drop.[2] Both James Mills and Lodge reopened the request with Pritchett's successor, O. H. Tittman.[3] Peirce himself had written E. D. Preston, the Survey's editor of publications, who said that even though two of his papers had not been published, he could do nothing unless the superintendent submitted them.[4] All these efforts came to nothing.

Garrison substantially increased both the number of reviews for the *Nation* and the payment for them. He continued this policy until his retirement in 1905. He expanded the range of the subject matter greatly, sending Peirce in 1900, for example, not only Funk and Wagnall's dictionary (his review of which included a charge of plagiarism against Nicholas Murray Butler from definitions in the *Century*), science, logic, and mathematics, but also Marco Polo for children, poetry, gastronomy, and wines. A new source of income during these years came from articles and reviews printed in journals of which J. McKeen Cattell was editor: the *American Journal of Psychology*, *Science*, and the *Popular Science Monthly*. Peirce wrote to his friend Secretary Langley of the Smithsonian, asking for as many jobs of scientific or philosophical translation from French, German, and Italian as possible from the Smithsonian or any other agency in which he had influence.[5] Langley responded by sending him at least a half-dozen scientific works for translation each year for several years, including, for example, Poincaré's paper "Relations entre la Physique Expérimentale et la Physique Mathématique."[6] More requests for translations and articles came from Carus of *The Monist*. In this way, though dependent on the whims of his editors. Peirce was haphazardly able to keep abreast of his interests. Peirce had written in part of a draft fragment to Carus:

> Of late years I have suffered extreme adversity & affliction. . . .
> I have found immense help from certain other reflections. Such as this. "If," I would say to myself, "[by] voluntarily enduring what I am forced to bear I could further certain objects I had at heart, would I not do so and more? And if I could comprehend the purposes of God, would I not give an absolute preference to these purposes over the objects I actually have at heart,—which indeed I only now prefer as being [as near as I] can make out the objects it is God's will I should pursue? Since then God is doubtless using me, so far as I can be of use, to promote his own purposes which should I not be content?
> Why should I not feel particularly honored that I have been selected to undergo all this agony?"[7]

In March, Garrison offered Peirce the job of writing a special supplement for the New York *Evening Post* "reviewing the century philosophically. . . . The subject I propose for you is an appreciation of the century's contribution to the great men of history."[8] This history was published in the *Post* in January 1901, as Part IV of its "Review of the Nineteenth Century," and reprinted by Langley in the *Annual Report . . . of the Smithsonian Institution* for 1900 as "The Century's Great Men of Science." Between April 19 and September 10, Garrison paid Peirce $192.75 for his *Nation* work. On April 2, Garrison wrote him, "I am sorry enough that sickness still reigns in your home. . . . I hope you will soon be well enough to get to work on the Century's greatest men, though our need is not urgent."[9] Later in the month, Peirce did a review for the *Bookman* on George A. Coe, *The Spiritual Life*, and Frank Thilly, *Introduction to Ethics*, which paid him $10.00.[10]

In May, Peirce wrote Cattell to congratulate him on his editorship of the *Popular Science Monthly* and to offer to write for it. He suggested, among other projects, bringing "Illustrations of the Logic of Science" up to date as a magnum opus, written in his new, more readable "Berkeleyan style, fitted at once to gain the ear and the interest of a large public, and, at the same time to place the rationale of reasoning in so clear a light as to make it really serviceable in reference to living questions of science."[11] He went on to inquire about his chances at McClure's and to report that he was writing an editor's manual on hyphens, punctuation, and spelling to be completed soon.

In June, Peirce again wrote his former Johns Hopkins colleague President G. Stanley Hall of Clark University to discover if, with the death of its founder and his disapproval of Peirce, there was the possibility of a position. Hall responded, "You certainly do not overestimate my high appreciation of the value of your own work or of the very great interest I have always felt in everything you write and of your power to inspire students"; however, until the details of Clark's will were settled, he could not give Peirce a definite commitment.[12] Instead, Hall did try, in January 1901, to get Peirce an appointment at Worcester Polytechnic Institute, but this failed as well, though Hall reported that he had "had the great pleasure last Sunday week of expressing to your brother at my house my own sense of the value of your work & what I owe to it."[13] Also in June, Peirce was negotiating with Mighill and Company to act as a sales representative for them for their book *The Popular History of the Presbyterian Church*.[14] On June 12, *Cosmopolitan* paid him forty dollars for his article "Our Senses as Reasoning Machines."[15]

During the year, Mary Pinchot visited the Peirces at least twice a month with food and other help. In August, another side of the Peirces' life was briefly illumined when the Milford *Dispatch* carried an article entitled "Mother Goose Bazaar," a paragraph from which reported:

> The next booth bore a large placard announcing "Modern Telepathy." In the interior amid oriental furnishings was Mlle. LeNormand, the most famous of all fortune tellers, trusted by the Empress Josephine . . . and Czar Alexandre. Her seances gave general satisfaction and this booth was liberally patronized. The Mlle., was impersonated by Mrs. C. S. Peirce.[16]

In September, Plimpton sent Peirce a check for $50.00 to pay the mortgage and asked him for the receipts "for the payment of taxes, etc."[17] He had earlier written that the *Cyclopaedia* project was a "dead dog," that Peirce's editor's manual would not be considered by Ginn and Company, and that there was no cataloguing work for Peirce to do because his house was closed. In October, Juliette was in New York City visiting, and Garrison wrote Peirce that he had "added a little to her purse as you requested."[18] At the same time Peirce received a letter from Cattell informing him that his review of "Pearson's Grammar of Science" had arrived too late for inclusion in the *Psychological Review*, but might be included in the next issue of the *Popular Science Monthly*. On October 31, Peirce received from Langley $33.07 for a translation of Count Zeppelin's report of the flight of his airship, *Ballon*. In mid-December, Peirce wrote to James Mark Baldwin that he was enclosing " . . . a letter I started to write you a fortnight ago; but violent neuralgia, putting me back in every way, and especially depriving me of the power of normal judgment, prevented my finishing it."[19] Peirce was suffering more from the disease with each passing year, sometimes for days at a time. It usually left him badly confused for several days after each attack. In the same month, Peirce was considered for the position of mathematics editor of the forthcoming *International Encyclopedia*, among whose editors was President Gilman of Johns Hopkins. By February 1901, it was plain that Peirce asked too high a price for his services, and negotiations were broken off.[20]

Beginning late in 1899, George A. Plimpton had moved to help Peirce sell his woodland acres of land along the Delaware River. By February 1900, he had put Peirce in touch with J. T. Rothbrook, superintendent of forestry for Pennsylvania, and a sale seemed imminent at $2.00 per acre.[21] The negotiations dragged on for the rest of the year, and finally, in January 1901, through Plimpton's intervention, the land was sold at $1.25 an acre to the Commonwealth of Pennsylvania, for a total of $1,144.56.[22] Although the sale did not resolve the Peirces' financial problems, it did ease them considerably and allowed them as well to lower their mortgage and indebtedness to Plimpton and Morison.

As the last years of Peirce's life ran out, the tempo slowed. The constant grinding poverty, the recurrent ill health that plagued both Charles and Juliette, the steady, pedestrian labor demanded by his work on logic, the unmet deadlines and continuously unsuccessful efforts by Peirce, and by his patrons, to find him work—all of these things clearly took their toll. Yet, in many years at least one opportunity for a genuine rebirth of his career appeared to brighten the grotesque routine of his life, only to fade maddeningly away.

One such possibility occurred in late October 1900, when Peirce received an urgent request from James Mark Baldwin, the psychologist and newly appointed chief editor of the *Dictionary of Philosophy and Psychology*, to write the definitions in logic for that volume. It was at this time that the exchange between Peirce and James on the origins of pragmatism took place. Peirce wrote on November 10 that Baldwin "arrived at J in his dictionary, suddenly calls on me to do the rest of the logic, in the utmost haste, and various questions of terminology come up. Who originated the term *pragmatism*, I or you? . . . What do you understand by it?"[23]

James responded by postcard that he had given Peirce full credit for the invention of pragmatism two years before in his California Union Address entitled "Philosophical conceptions and practical results," two unacknowledged copies of which he had sent to Peirce.[24] Peirce's failure to claim pragmatism for himself in 1878, when he had defined it in "How to Make Our Ideas Clear" without using the word itself, remains an enigma. Why he never used the word in subsequent publications or correspondence (until 1900) is equally puzzling. Obviously, he did not then think the word important. Perhaps he thought it merely a label, without realizing the impact both the concept and the term would have on his philosophical contemporaries, and therefore, ironically, did not realize its significance as icon, index, and symbol. His only explanation was that, "As late as 1893, when I might have procured the insertion of the word pragmatism in the *Century Dictionary*, it did not seem to me that its vogue was sufficient to warrant that step."[25] Once the importance of this oddly diffident oversight became clear to him, Peirce began to write his various and charming accounts of the Metaphysical Club, in which his claim to the invention of pragmatism would be made clear to all. More important by far, this newfound fame drove him to reexamine pragmatism, not from the limited perspective of the maxim proposed in 1878 for the clarification of concepts, but in the light of his later realist metaphysics and cosmology and his semeiotic. This retrospection showed him just how foreign in important ways his earlier work in the logic of science had become. He soon coined the term *pragmaticism* to set his views apart from those of the "kidnappers."

Peirce quickly realized that the work on Baldwin's dictionary was beyond him. He had neither the mental stamina nor the scholarly resources to attempt it. His solution was to engage his friend and former student Christine Ladd-Franklin to do much of the work under his supervision. He thereby retained the credit for the sections on logic, but Ladd-Franklin soon took charge because of Peirce's disabilities and found herself pushing him to finish his parts of the dictionary. Among the terms known to have been defined by Ladd-Franklin were *proposition, syllogism, symbolic logic, signification*, and *transposition*. Some subjects she refused to undertake:

> I should not think of writing (as you suggest) the article on Relative Logic! A Logic-Dictionary without an article from you on that subject would be a dictionary with Hamlet left out.
>
> Why are you so remiss as not to write a big book? What's a Dictionary, with its contracted little articles?[26]

When Peirce suggested that they write such a book together, she quickly refused, although she continued to urge him to do so.[27]

Newcomb was the contributor of, among many other terms, *energy*. Peirce wrote to Baldwin, who sent it on to Newcomb, a very strong criticism of the entry, in which he said in part:

It is a violation of scientific ethics to use the term otherwise [than is accepted usage] and a violation of pedagogic ethics to put a wrong definition in a dictionary. The writer must be perfectly aware that he is not conveying information as to the received meaning of the term. . . . I do not think the article is as instructive to students of philosophy as it ought to have been made. S. N. is too far from them to appreciate their needs, of which they are not themselves distinctly conscious.[28]

He went on to make a more general condemnation:

Newcomb's articles are excessively bad. His notions of philosophy are such as an intellectual person about Cambridge, not a special student of philosophy, would pick up about 1855. They have not progressed. He is not a mathematician, or at any rate has only become so late in life,—he is only a mathematical astronomer. He is therefore very narrow both on the philosophical & on the mathematical side, and I propose from this [time] on to pitch into his articles and try to render them serviceable to students of philosophy. A few years ago he was engaged in writing for the [Funk and Wagnall's] "Standard" Dict'y. Like all writers for that work he simply revised & condensed the articles in the Century Dict'y. He wrote to me and said my views about limits were 40 years behind the time. The correspondence which followed showed he had not read any of the remarkable works on the logic of mathematics of late years & in short what it came to was that I was returning to a view which the nominalism of forty years before had persuaded him was wrong & he had not advanced a step since that time. Now, you know, no amount of vigor of intellect will make a man an up to date philosopher; and ideas current in Cambridge 40 or 50 years ago and those now held by advanced thinkers are as far apart as South Africa and Berlin.[29]

Whether Peirce actually rewrote any of Newcomb's entries is unknown, but it seems unlikely. Peirce's credited contributions to the dictionary amounted to more than two hundred, a few of which were jointly credited to Baldwin. On the basis of the evidence in the existing correspondence between Peirce and Ladd-Franklin and that in the *Collected Papers*, it appears that more than half were actually written by her.

Peirce had promised Cattell the first volume on the history of science by December 1899. In March 1901, Putnam's wrote him that they were pleased that the first volume was practically completed and that they would wait to hear of his further progress during the year.[30] In his letter of response, Peirce urged Cattell, soon to become a member of the National Academy of Sciences, to put up William James for membership. "Surely, we all who are at all in the psychological line would wish to put him forward. I most of any & I must be your ally in the Academy until you get in others."[31] James was admitted within the year. Two years later, in March 1903, Cattell again asked about the progress of the manuscript.[32] In December 1903, G. P. Putnam himself, after Cattell's resignation as editor, made the final inquiry about Peirce's progress on the volume, at the same time that he refused to publish Peirce's Lowell Lectures of that year.[33] Peirce never completed the history of science manuscript.

On April 3, Secretary Langley reported that he intended to reprint "The Century's Great Men in Science" in the Smithsonian *Annual Report* as part of his effort to publicize Peirce and his work. He went on to say:

> I take the occasion to say that I still remember with pleasure my read-ing of your first paper on "The Fixation of Belief", in the Popular Science Monthly of nearly 25 years ago. . . .
> P. S. Would you care to write an article of one, or at most, two thou-sand words, on the "Laws of Nature," as understood by Hume's contempo-raries . . . with special reference to his argument on miracles; write it, I mean, in the untechnical speech which is so lucidly clear in the article I have just referred to?[34]

Peirce was immensely gratified at the Smithsonian's printing of his arti-cle and by the invitation, to which he responded with three drafts within a few weeks. He intended the paper to be an elucidation of his own ideas, in the context of Hume's essay, about hypothesis, deduction, and induction. In a draft letter, he wrote Langley that deduction is a necessary inference re-lated to an ideal state of things in which premises are absolutely true, and that deduction may relate to probabilities, but that it

> can never ascertain what a probability really is, but only calculate what it would be, supposing certain other probabilities are so and so. . . .
> Induction consists in taking samples of a genus and observing how many fall into a certain species, and thence concluding the probable and approximate value of the probability that in that genus any given individual will belong to that species. It supposes that there is a certain *course of experience*. . . .
> Hypothesis is guessing, or if you please starting a question. A phenom-enon is observed having something peculiar about it. Rumination [*Spiel-trieb*, the play of musement] leads me to see that *if* a certain state of things existed, of whose actual existence I know nothing, that phenomenon would certainly occur, or, at any rate, would in all probability occur. I say, By George! I wonder if that is not the very state of the case! That is hypothesis.[35]

Apparently, Langley did not find the final version of Peirce's essay on Hume appropriate to the audience he had in mind, for it was not published even though it was paid for.[36] Peirce's thanks to Langley for even this miscarried opportunity were effusive and were addressed to Langley's other help as well:

> I beg you, my dear Prof Langley, to understand that I fully appreciate the great kindness and friendliness with which you treat me, and that I am deeply grateful for the material succour which it brings and of which I am very much in need, indeed. My wife whom I sent to N.Y. to see the doctors came back with their verdict that a second great operation *has to be* performed just as quick as she can be brought up into condition to undergo it.[37]

A month later, in May, Juliette was still sick, and Morison wrote, "I am sorry to hear of Mrs. Peirce's illness; her former operation was so successful that a second one must be less appalling than to many people."[38] Morison misunderstood the nature of her ailment, which this time was a severe recurrence of tuberculosis, and the surgery being considered was the removal of a lung. The surgery was never done, and Juliette continued as before, suffering recurrences once or twice a year.

In January 1902, Peirce wrote confidently to his friend Cattell that he was engaged in writing out his logic in full:

> It involves a complete construction of the whole subject from a certain point of view. I have my doubts as to whether thought or reasoning is, properly speaking, an operation of the soul. At any rate, whether it be so or not, it is the business of logic, as I conceive it, to treat it just as if it were not. Now since I am not by any means a mere formal logician,—holding formal logic to be nothing but a useful mathematical adjunct to logic proper,—to make a completely satisfactory account of reasoning in all its elements without saying one word about mental operations is a work never done & a very large job. There is no part of logic which I do not consider in a fundamental manner, both the stechiology [from W. Hamilton's *Logic* of 1860: "in its Stoicheiology or Doctrine of Elements, Logic considers the conditions of possible thought"] & and the methodeutic, as well as objective logic. It is therefore a very large & very laborious business, notwithstanding that my 40 years of close study have shaped my doctrines in almost every detail. There are also an infinity of objections small & great which have to be examined, critcisms [*sic*] of me that must be answered, and historical notes to be made.
>
> I cannot possibly complete this work, whose great utility impresses me more and more, unless I have aid. I must have sustenance for self and wife

while it is doing, or it must go undone. And now I am at the very height of my philosophical powers, & am also in admirable trim for work. But I am getting along in years [sixty-two] & every day must now be turned to account & no time lost. Now this new Carnegie Institution seems to have been created just to meet such cases as mine. I think it will be long before they get another chance to spend money to such good effect as in furthering the completion of my logic. I want you kindly to write to Gilman [its president] & to Carnegie and urge upon them the doing of what is necessary to that end.[39]

In the newly organized Carnegie Institution, Peirce saw clearly his last chance to write and publish his life's work in philosophy. A grant of Carnegie funds would free him from financial worries and give him the uninterrupted time that he desperately needed to devote exclusively to his work. Peirce began to marshal all the influence at his disposal to help him achieve his goal. He wrote to Plimpton, to Morison, to his cousin Senator Lodge, to Langley, to James, in fact to all those who he thought might influence the decision in his favor. Plimpton wrote to Gilman:

> George S. Morison, the great bridge-builder and engineer, met me some time ago, and said that he would be glad to be one of twelve to give $100. a year each to Charles. S. Peirce, provided he would finish his book on logic; that he considered that book of very great importance. Now, why is not Peirce just the sort of man to benefit by the Carnegie Endowment? I should think if he had enough to pay for his bread and butter, he would work like a Trojan on this book until it was finished. He has his peculiarities, but so have all other geniuses that I have ever struck. I wrote to his brother, James Mills Peirce, of Harvard, and possibly you may have heard from him in regard to the matter. I have seen a good deal of Charles S. Peirce, because he has worked for me in my mathematical library, and he is a genius, if there ever was one.[40]

On April 12, Peirce wrote to Gilman, as president of the Carnegie Institution, a letter in which he developed at some length his fear that the institution's high purpose to support science would be endangered by conservatism in following and encouraging only the "long approved sciences":

> If by a science we understand a study which has reached that stage of maturity at which the fundamental methods are undisputed by serious students, then logic and metaphysics are not yet sciences, although both are apparently rapidly approaching that condition, logic being in advance, as it must be, since metaphysics necessarily is based upon the theory of logic. . . . [I believe that] energetic encouragement of a study should commence as soon as it begins decidedly to approach the scientific stage. This is the

moment in the history of a science when the bold, originating genius is of inestimable service.[41]

It was obvious from the beginning of his campaign that Peirce's case would be a controversial one, and that his own statements would do nothing to make it less so. Opinion as to his merits was divided among three groups: the first, represented by Gilman and Eliot, recognized his genius, despised his morals, and feared that his instability would prevent his completing the work; the second, represented by Newcomb, considered Peirce debauched and something of a charlatan and were opposed to giving him a grant; the third group, represented by his friends James, Plimpton, and the rest, were convinced of his genius and were strongly in favor of his receiving a grant, in spite of his peculiarities. Thus, it seemed that Peirce had a good chance of success with Gilman, president of the Carnegie Institution, provisionally favorable, and with so much support from reputable men of science and of affairs. But Peirce was by no means satisfied that his chances were good, and thus he was not always straightforward in his campaign. He had written Mary Putnam Jacobi, the publisher's daughter, asking her if she might use her influence with J. S. Billings, who as a member of the executive committee of the institution would vote upon his grant. According to a letter from Mrs. Jacobi to Peirce, written June 4, Billings said that

> he knew all about you, and your name was one of those now under consideration by the Committee. . . . I am now writing to Dr. Billings to urge your cause. But it is evident from this that you have yourself already made an application which is of course exactly what you should have done. But why did you not tell me that you had done so? I always am confused by the lack of frankness in both you and Mrs. Peirce. I do not see any reason for it. It do hope you can profit by this Carnegie Institution, for it seems to me you are fairly entitled to its largess.[42]

Shortly afterwards, Billings wrote to Mrs. Jacobi that he knew both Peirce's professional and personal reputation and that "in making the selection there must be considered . . . the probability that the person who asks the assistance will do it especially if the money is to be paid in advance." Mrs. Jacobi enclosed Billing's letter and wrote Peirce that "the suggestion made by Mr. Billings that there would arise the question whether a given beneficiary would really continue and complete his work,—seems to be very pertinent."[43] Billing's comment seems to have been the most common caution regarding Peirce's suitability in the minds of those responsible for dispensing the institution's funds, and there existed among some of those who would vote on his application, including Newcomb and Gilman, a direct knowledge of Peirce's past procrastinations and unreliability.

These comments put Peirce into a deep depression, which he expressed to James:

> Knowing Billings from watching his behaviour in meetings of the [National] Academy [of Sciences], I feel that this means that he has made up his mind to fight any grant to me to the extent of his power and energy. . . .
>
> If the Carnegie Institution will do nothing, my duty will be to continue to endeavor to do the work I seem to have been put into the world to do; and when the moment arrives at which there seems to be no rational hope of making my life useful, my duty, as I see it, will be to treat my life just as I would an aching tooth that there was no hope of making useful. I will have it out.[44]

Nevertheless, on July 15, Peirce sent a long application to the executive committee of the institution, proposing that he be aided in drawing up "some three dozen memoirs, each complete in itself yet the whole forming a unitary system of logic in all its parts," to include both his logic and his metaphysics. The original of this application no longer exists in the Carnegie Institution's archives, though the records show that a typewritten copy was returned to Peirce by its secretary in December 1902.[45] The draft (or copy of the original) list is appended here, with some of Peirce's comments about it, because it represents the only complete outline of his system of philosophy extant. Almost all the subjects are familiar from his past work, though sometimes their titles were rephrased. Many had already been published, but required revision:

No. 1. *On the Classification of the Theoretic Sciences.*
No. 2. *On the Simplest Mathematics.*
No. 3. *Analysis of the Conceptions of Mathematics.*
No. 4. *Analysis of the Methods of Mathematical Demonstration.*
No. 5. *On the Qualities of the Three Categories of Appearance.* . . . The list was first published by me in May 1867. . . . The categories were originally called Quality, Relation, and Representation. . . . I am inclined to call them Flavor, Reaction, and Mediation.
No. 6. *On the Categories in Their Reactional Aspects.*
No. 7. *Of the Categories in their Mediate Aspects.*
No. 8. *Examinations of Historical Lists of Categories.* My list differs from those of Aristotle, Kant, and Hegel, in that they never really went back to examining the Phenomenon to see what was to be observed there [Peirce questioned the presumed immediacy of sensation and perception and

maintained that perceptual judgments are hypothetic inferences[; and I do not except Hegel's *Phenomenologie* from this criticism. . . .

No. 9. *On the Bearing of Esthetics and Ethics upon Logic.*

No. 10. *On the Presuppositions of Logic.* . . . The true presuppositions of logic are merely *hopes*; and as such, when we consider their consequences collectively, we cannot condemn scepticism as to how far they may be borne out by facts. But when we come down to specific cases, these hopes are so completely justified that the smallest conflict with them suffices to condemn the doctrine that involves that conflict [compare Karl Popper's doctrine of falsification]. This is one of the places where logic comes in contact with ethics. I examine the matter of these hopes, showing that they are, among other things which I enumerate, that any given question is susceptible of a true answer, and that this answer is discoverable, that *being* and *being represented* are different, that there is a reality, and that the real world is governed by ideas. . . .

No. 11. *On the Logical Conception of Mind.* The logicians concept of mind must be different from the psychologists.

No. 12. *On the Definition of Logic.* Logic will here be defined as *formal semeiotic.*

No. 13. *On the Division of Logic.* . . . Stechiology, Critic and Methodeutic.

No. 14. *On the Methods of Discovering and of Establishing the Truths of Logic.* . . . The one universally valid method is that of mathematical demonstration; and this is the only one which is commonly avoided by logicians as fallacious.

No. 15. *Of the Nature of the Stechiologic* [Hamilton's coinage for conditions of possible thought].

No. 16. *A General Outline of Stechiologic.*

No. 17. *On Terms.*

No. 18. *On Propositions.*

No. 19. *On Arguments.*

No. 20. *Of Critical Logic in General.*

No. 21. *Of First Premises.* My position on this subject comes under the general head of sensationalism; but I contend that criticism is inapplicable to what is not subject to control. Consequently, not sensation nor even percepts are first premises, but only perceptual judgments.

No. 22. *The Logic of Chance.*

No. 23. *On the Validity of Induction.*

No. 24. *On the Justification of Abduction* [Retroduction, Hypothesis].

No. 25. *Of Mixed Arguments.*

No. 26. *On Fallacies.*

No. 27. *Of Methodeutic.*

No. 28. *On the Economics of Research.*

No. 29. *On the Course of Research.*

No. 30. *On Systems of Doctrine.*

No. 31. *On Classification.*
No. 32. *On Definition and the Clearness of Ideas.*
No. 33. *On Objective Logic.*
No. 34. *On the Uniformity of Nature.*
No. 35. *On Metaphysics.*
No. 36. *On the Reality and Nature of Time and Space.*

With care and patience, this outline and the whole application can be used—as Eisele used Peirce's outline of his arithmetic for Hegeler as the basis for her reconstruction of his arithmetic in her work *The New Elements of Mathematics by Charles Peirce*—to reconstruct Peirce's system from the scattered elements of it he had written out by 1902. That part of his system which now became for him the crux of his life's work, logic (the categories) conceived as semeiotic—"the science of representation"—he developed in depth for the most part after he made application to the Carnegie. The integration of that material would not require a reorganization of his architectonic, but would subtly shift its perspective because his late phenomenology insisted that perceptions are inferences.

Since a great part of this application was written as an apology for his life, it deserves to be examined in some detail. He began in a familiar vein:

> I imbibed from my boyhood the spirit of positive science, and especially of exact science; and early became intensely curious concerning the theory of the methods of science; so that, shortly after my graduation from college, in 1859, I determined to devote my life to that study; although indeed it was less a resolve than an overmastering passion. . . . Owing to my treating logic as a science, like the physical sciences . . . and making my studies special[,] minute, exact, and checked by experience, and owing to the fact that logic had seldom before been so studied, discoveries poured in upon me in such a flood as to be embarrassing.

Much of what he wrote was an able defense, the justice of which must be admitted. He asked the executive committee if it would not be a waste to let his work of a lifetime go unpublished, and he mentioned Julius Wilhelm Richard Dedekind and his friend Ernst Schröder as major figures in mathematics and logic who had praised and made use of his work. He pointed out the complete dependence of all the sciences on logic:

> It is my belief that science is approaching a critical point in which the influence of a truly scientific logic will be exceptionally desirable. Science as the outlook seems to me, is coming to something not unlike the age of puberty. Its old and purely materialistic conceptions no longer suffice; while yet the great danger involved in the admission of any others, ineluctable as

such admission is, is manifest enough. The influence of the conceptions of methodeutic [the methodology of hypothesis, deduction, and induction] will at that moment be decisive.

He tried to ward off the criticisms he knew would be leveled against him. Concerning the professional jealousies and rivalries of which he considered himself the object, he claimed that

> any man over 60 years of age who is endowed with reason, is a better judge of his own powers and of the utility of his performances than other people can be expected to be. Particularly is this true when the man has accumulated a large fund of unpublished results. Yet as soon as such a man assumes the attitude of seeking recognition for the utility of his work, suspicions as to the candour of his appreciation may be suggested by those who, for any reason, are unfavorable to the action he desires.

Some of what he wrote, however, was angry special pleading of a kind utterly inappropriate in such an application, and so defensive in tone that it undoubtedly made its readers, all of whom knew one version or another of the story, uncomfortable, if not deeply embarrassed for him:

> I have a reputation of not finishing things. I suppose there is some basis of truth beneath it; but it has been like every evil reputation, exaggerated out of all semblance of truth by calumny. . . . the most bare-faced calumny invented by the intriguers of the Coast Survey. I have three voluminous memoirs completed. They refused to print them, and the consequence was that I lost interest in the work very largely and became absorbed in my logic. I have several times offered to see those memoirs through the press; but the offers have always been refused, probably on the utterly mistaken notion that I wished to interfere with the Survey. . . . and then I was accused, vaguely and in intangible forms, of not getting my work ready for publication. For the truth of this (except that the accusations were made) I stand responsible.

There is little in the documents of the Coast Survey that supports anything like the intrigue he claimed had been mounted against him, although there was considerable dislike and professional jealousy evident, as well as the demoralizing influence of President Cleveland's political appointees and the disastrous effect of drastically reduced funds. The three memoirs which Peirce claimed to have completed were not in the finished form that his statement implied. He had put off turning in the long gravimetric report on the eastern arc of the United States, for whose development he had been responsible for fifteen years, for three years past the date he considered the latest possible. Three superintendents criticized this failure, but kept him on in the hope that he would finish. The last of these, Mendenhall, who did receive the report in 1889, did not have the competence to appreciate its high value, and Peirce was entirely correct in stating that its handling of theoretical issues was publishable in the form he gave it.

In view of the fact that Peirce's original appointment was considered by him and his father to be the kind of career that would leave him time to pursue his interest in logic, and was thought by both a poor second to the academic career he really desired, and that the resulting strain upon his loyalties led a number of times to serious lapses in his duty to the Survey, Peirce's defense of his actions while employed there was disingenuous. No doubt his desperation for the grant in the face of Newcomb's and Gilman's profound disapproval of him led Peirce to these humiliating disclosures. He proposed a number of ways in which the Carnegie might be satisfied that he would complete the work, and then went on to outline his claim to a Carnegie grant in a manner very likely to put its readers off with its queerly antagonistic humility:

> A man has put nearly fifty years of single-minded endeavor into a work of benefit to science. He has a sort of claim,—vague only in being addressed to no particular party, that he should be rewarded for what he has done. But the only reward which would be a reward would be that of being enabled to complete his life-work. . . . Should it seem to you to be true that the duties of an "exceptional man" [quoting the application] in the department of logic have to be borne by me, then it will become one of your duties to aid me in the performance of mine to make the work for which this man "seems specially designed his life work." I am frank to say that the idea that phrase embodies has long impressed me; namely, that men seem to be specially designed for various kinds of work, and that, if it be so, the work for which I seem to have been designed is that of working out the truths of logic.

Peirce also described, in a manner not likely to inspire his readers' confidence in his dependability, his passionate dedication to logic as being derived from "an uncontrollable impulse. . . . it has been necessary for me at all times to exercise all my control over myself, for fear that my mind might be affected by such unceasing application to a particular subject."[46] This description is accurate. Peirce sacrificed everything to his lifelong and all-consuming passion to solve "the Riddle of the Sphynx": health, inheritance, family, profession, and, on more than one occasion, sanity. He paid a terrible price in mental and physical agony, poverty, ostracism, and the corrosive effects of an evil reputation. Such extremes of sacrifice carried little weight in his favor with the men of solid reputation who judged him. To the contrary, it counted heavily against him with most of them, to whom his life represented a fanaticism too dangerously out of control.

Marcus Baker, assistant secretary of the institute, replied enthusiastically to Peirce's application, saying that he had read the letter,

> some of it twice, and I assure you, with the keenest satisfaction. Like you, however, I can only guess at the attitude of the Executive Committee, but, as for me, I say by all means, support this application. *How* to do it best, may produce diverse views. It had occurred to me that a good way would be to pay you a comfortable salary, to live in Washington, near the great libraries, to work at the Institution and to enter upon the printing one by one under your own eye of these memoirs. . . . Try your logic on me.[47]

Baker went on to say that Secretary Walcott was about to return from Woods Hole and would then direct the disposition of Peirce's application, and that the executive committee was to meet in August and the trustees in September. Through the summer, letters continued to come into the institute supporting Peirce's application. The first meeting of the executive committee to consider his application deferred action until September because two of its members, Gilman and Elihu Root, were in Europe. In the meantime, Peirce's income had deteriorated to the point that he was forced to sell some belongings: three first-class folding beds, a parlor mantelpiece of carved *gallo antico* marble, an enameled sink, and four old Santo Domingo mahogany folding doors. That fall, Peirce advertised for the first time such produce as his place supported: cider vinegar, Northern Spies apples on the trees, nuts, and hay.[48] By November 1902, the great anthracite coal strike was at its height, adding to the other hardships from which the Peirces already suffered. At the end of November came the news that the executive committee had decided to defer action on Peirce's application again. Peirce wrote bitterly to James:

> I cannot tell you what balm to my heart there is in the mere sight of your handwriting, condemned as I am to live in a world where nobody can understand the intensity of my desire to do the work God put me into the world to do.
>
> The Carnegie Institution have given me my answer at last, a refusal of all assistance. The wording is that the committee has 'decided to defer action upon your application for the present.' I had not thought just that possible; I see now that I had not, by the shock it gives me. Still, the relief from the painful tension is great.
>
> I shall keep right on doing the work as well as adverse circumstances will permit.

Meantime, with a dwindling wood-pile, with my furnace out of order, with an income from my present earnings, barely sufficient for meagre food, I would accept any employment in which I could give satisfaction.

One such situation would be that of a professor of logic at Columbia or elsewhere.[49]

Marcus Baker was not as pessimistic as Peirce and wrote: "I can only guess what will finally result from your proposition about the Logic. Personally I have convictions on the subject and have frankly spoken them to the Secretary. The effect of this will be, I hope, to hasten a decision though I cannot guess what the decision will be."[50] Peirce thereupon marshaled more supporters to write the Carnegie, including Benjamin E. Smith, chief editor of the *Century Dictionary*, and the mathematician William Pepperell Montague. In the meantime, Cattell had been trying to get Peirce a position as lecturer in logic at Columbia University, where he was chairman of the department of psychology. Peirce had written Cattell in response to his queries about what he proposed to teach, in addition to a description of classes, that

> Pragmatism [one of the few appearances of the term in Peirce's personal correspondence since his letter to James in 1900] is the life of my teaching; that is, logical questions are to be decided by simply noting what *purpose* is concerned. . . .
>
> I should ground my class so in the *rationale* of reasoning that they could not fail to see the weakness of agnostic doctrines nor fail to recognize that anthropomorphic conceptions are the proper ideas for us to trust to.[51]

President Nicholas Murray Butler, whom Peirce had accused of plagiarism in his review of the Funk and Wagnall's dictionary, did not "regard it as feasible."[52] Then, in January 1903, Cattell wrote Secretary Walcott of the Carnegie Institution suggesting a new possibility for the handling of Peirce's application, which he and the other Peirce supporters hoped would resolve the doubt in the minds of many of the trustees that Peirce could not be depended upon to finish the work:

> Mr. C. S. Peirce is one of the few men of genius of the country. His originality, his knowledge and his power of expression are of the highest order. He might do work for science entirely out of proportion to any appropriation that the Carnegie Institution could make to assist him. He has certain peculiarities, as is not uncommon in men of genius, which make desirable the plan adopted by the British and American Associations for the Advancement of Science. This is to appropriate money to a committee under the direction of which research is conducted. If a Committee were

appointed on logic and scientific methods that would supervise the work and defray the living expenses of Mr. Peirce as he proceeded, I believe that results of the greatest importance for science would be obtained. As I said to you[,] Professor Royce of Harvard, Professor Dewey of Chicago and Professor Fullerton of Pennsylvania would be a suitable committee for the purpose.[53]

Peirce's brother James Mills wrote Newcomb a long and forceful letter asking his assistance with Cattell's plan.[54] Shortly afterward, Peirce's younger brother, Herbert Henry Davis, wrote him that he was confident Cattell's plan would be put into action, and for that purpose he needed some of Charles's finished manuscripts, "the larger the volume of these manuscripts the better . . . only put in my hands without loss of time anything you have ready which you feel worthy of yourself." He cautioned Charles, "don't write to anyone but me,—or to Jim [Cattell] on the subject. Let me deal with these people as I know how."[55] On January 12, President Theodore Roosevelt, whom Peirce's cousin Senator Lodge had fascinated with the tale of Peirce's life, expressed himself in favor of a grant to Peirce in a letter to the Carnegie's President Gilman.[56] Lodge also influenced Secretary of War Elihu Root to hold off deciding on Peirce's application until Root could be present to vote in favor of it. By May, the earliest time which Root could be present, Peirce had submitted a long manuscript, probably the first of the thirty-six memoirs, "On the Classification of the Theoretic Sciences," which Walcott, the Carnegie secretary, fatefully submitted to Simon Newcomb for examination, "with a view of ascertaining whether it is worth publication. . . . The Committee wishes to get at the actual cash value. As you are probably aware, there has been great pressure brought to bear upon the Committee to make a grant to Professor Peirce."[57] In his report to the executive committee, given March 13, 1903, Newcomb said:

> so far as I have been able to see their purport, they appear to consist of discussions and reviews pertaining to the definitions and fields of various logical subjects, and the merits and demerits of different views that may be taken of them, rather than well-reasoned scientific development of any one subject. Quite likely such developments may be contained in the papers, but, if so, they are buried so deeply in the mass of preliminary discussion that it is difficult to exhume them.
>
> It does not appear to me that discussions of this class belong to the class which the Carnegie Institution should publish.[58]

So much, from the eminent astronomer's viewpoint, for Peirce's brilliant development of the logic of science. At the vote in May for which Root was present, it was decided on J. S. Billings's motion not to act on Peirce's application. There seems to be no doubt that Newcomb's report had been the principal factor in their denying Peirce a grant, for the institute files noted, "Not recommended by Newcomb, H. H. D. Peirce to be notified."[59]

In Newcomb's steady and unmerciful opposition to him lay the justification for Peirce's conviction that he was the object of a vindictive and secret association to destroy him. Newcomb had informed Gilman of the facts of Peirce's adulterous liaison with Juliette, which led to Peirce's being dropped from the Johns Hopkins faculty in 1884. When he succeeded Sylvester to the editorship of the *American Journal of Mathematics* in 1884, Newcomb rejected as nonmathematical the second half of Peirce's groundbreaking essay "On the Algebra of Logic," the first half of which Sylvester had already accepted for publication with the intention of publishing the second, knowing of its major importance for logic. Newcomb, in 1889, by giving his strongly adverse and hostile judgment of Peirce's gravimetric report to Superintendent Mendenhall of the Coast Survey, had been the major cause of his subsequent dismissal from that organization after more than thirty years' service. In 1899, when Peirce had requested Newcomb to recommend him for the post of inspector of standards, Newcomb had refused, while at the same time implying that Peirce's record with the Survey stood against him. Lastly, this eminent and politically powerful astronomer had, through his influence with the trustees of the Carnegie Institution (from which he himself had just received a grant), prevented Peirce from receiving what was to be his last chance to publish his life's work in philosophy. Newcomb seems, however, to have been motivated by nothing more baleful than a sincere disgust for Peirce's morals and a jealous and ignorant misunderstanding of his work, not by the vindictive, conspiratorial malice Peirce believed was aimed at him by persons unknown. Peirce must have been profoundly shocked when he learned from his brother Herbert that his longtime correspondent Newcomb, who had been one of his father's favorite students and for years a welcome guest in his family's home, was the author of his humiliating defeat at the Carnegie.

The fact that Peirce was refused a grant even though Carnegie himself, the president of the United States, various other politically prominent men, and a majority of the leading members of the scientific community favored it, was due largely to the nature of his evil reputation, some of it well deserved, and the power of the self-righteous men who controlled the politics of American science in the late nineteenth century. They considered Peirce morally degenerate, mentally unstable—perhaps insane—arrogant, and irresponsible, a man of broken and dissolute character. Even those sympathetic trustees, if they knew of Peirce's neurological affliction and its effects, including the use of drugs, would have found it hard to support his fitness for a grant. The effect of Newcomb's adverse report must have had a heightened effect, especially since none of the trustees and members of the executive committee knew that Newcomb simply was not competent to judge Peirce's work. The conclusion which these factors support is that the executive committee, faced with Newcomb's influential opinion that Peirce's work was of no value, added to their already established concerns about his fitness, decided it would be a waste of their limited resources to support Peirce. Even Plimpton, Morison, and the ten other wealthy men who had been willing to aid him substantially in writing his logic withdrew their support after the Carnegie decision.

It is probably unlikely that he would have been able to carry out his grandiose plan. By 1903, his pedestrianism had produced thousands of mostly unorganized elements of his architectonic, for which he had no adequate index. He himself was unsure that he could find his way through the plethora and thought it would be impossible for anyone else to do so. His health deteriorated more rapidly after the Carnegie's refusal, but he continued doggedly, until he could no longer put pen to paper, to pursue the work he believed that God had graciously given him to do. Between 1884, when he left Johns Hopkins, until his death in 1914, Peirce probably produced the great majority of 80,000 unpublished handwritten pages. Almost all of those relating to pragmaticism, critical common-sensism, the categories, phenomenology, aesthetics, ethics, and semeiotic were written after his return to Milford in the spring of 1898 following the collapse of his extravagantly foolhardy ventures in New York City.

By February 1903, Peirce was again in such hard financial straits that Garrison paid his annual dues of five dollars to the National Academy of Sciences.[60] In the same month, Peirce's loyal friend James once again broached the subject of Peirce's lecturing at Harvard. He wrote to President Eliot:

> You may remember that some 5 years ago I asked the Corporation whether, in case I raised the money, they would appoint Chas. S. Peirce to give a short course of lectures on Logic.
>
> The Corporation declined, and the lectures were given at Mrs. Bull's in Brattle Street, and were a great success, so far as arousing strong interest in advanced men went. Peirce wants to devote the rest of his life to the writing of a logic which will undeniably (although in some points excentric [sic]) be a great book. Meanwhile, he has apparently *no* means. I am willing to help financially again, & venture (since the Corporation has partly changed its composition) to renew my old question. My class in Phil. 3 has this year been dosed with some of Peirce's ideas at second hand, and is (I

Charles William Eliot, President of Harvard University, in 1904. Photograph courtesy of the Harvard University Archives.

know) full of curiosity to hear his voice. I can't imagine the possibility of a personal clash with the authorities here, in case he lectures. He is one of our 3 or 4 first American philosophers, and it seems to me that his genius is deserving of some official recognition. Half a dozen lectures, at 100 dollars a piece, would seem to me about right.

Can't the Corporation change its earlier mind?

Respectfully *its*
/s/ William James[61]

The Corporation gave its approval, the money was again privately raised, and Peirce gave a series of lectures on the Harvard campus for the first time since 1870. The seven lectures—"On pragmatism and the normative sciences," "On Phenomenology, or the Categories," "On the categories," "The Seven Systems of Metaphysics," "On three kinds of goodness," "On three types of reasoning," and "On pragmatism and abduction" (an eighth, "Multitude and Continuity," may have been given as well)—were presented between March 26 and May 17 in Sever Hall, and the Peirces stayed on in Cambridge afterward for two pleasant weeks, during which Charles indulged his frustrated longing for philosophic controversy with his friends.

Most of his hearers, including James but with the surprising exception of George Santayana (Royce was away), found the lectures obscure, if not unintelligible, because they were so deeply embedded in his largely unpublished theory of categories. James was unable to abstract even a semblance of pragmatism as he knew it from the material Peirce presented, which included such confusing concepts as the Firstness of Thirdness to mean a vague perception of the general in the particular. He therefore strongly opposed publication of the lectures. The following October, Peirce wrote of his disappointment to Christine Ladd-Franklin:

> In the spring of 1903 I was invited, by the influence of James, Royce, and Münsterberg, to give a course of lectures in Harvard University on Pragmatism. I had intended to print them; but James said he could not understand them himself and could not recommend their being printed. I do not myself think there is any difficulty in understanding them, but all modern psychologists are so soaked with sensationalism that they can not understand anything that does not mean that, and mistranslate into the ideas of Wundt whatever one says about logic.[62]

In these lectures, Peirce returned to the issue he had first raised in 1868–69 as the key question of philosophy, and for which he had proposed a preliminary answer in 1892 in "The Law of Mind"—how knowledge as experience is possible at all; that is, how does independent, intractable nature, both within and without us, enter into logical discourse? He answered that it enters by means of the abduction (hypothetic inference) which mediates between the percept and the perceptual judgment, between, for example, the color perceived by the eye and the perception of space inferred from it. Peirce explained:

> But the sum of it all is that our logically controlled thoughts compose a small part of the mind, the mere blossom of a vast complexus, which we may call the instinctive mind [a synonym for Peirce of the continuity of mind and nature], in which this man will not say that he has *faith*, because that implies the conceivability of distrust, but upon which he builds as the very fact to which the whole business of his logic to be true.[63]

Where James could find nothing familiar, Royce later found the logical basis for his idea of an unlimited community of interpretation.

Santayana had attended the third lecture, "On the categories," which dealt with Peirce's semeiotic, and later reported to Justus Buchler:

> I heard one of [Peirce's] Harvard lectures. He had been dining at the [William] James's and his evening shirt kept coming out of his evening

waistcoat. He looked red-nosed and dishevelled, and a part of his lecture seemed *ex-tempore* and whimsical [Santayana elsewhere called Peirce bibulous and a drunkard]. But I remember and have often used in my own thought, if not in actual writing, a classification he made that evening of signs into indexes and symbols and images [icons]: possibly there was still another distinct category which I don't remember.[64]

It would be wrong to say that Santayana was a pragmatist, but that he was something approaching a pragmaticist in some respects seems true.

The correspondence with Victoria Lady Welby, which eased to some extent the hardships of Peirce's last years with the palliatives of praise and comradeship, began in the spring of 1903. It also provided Peirce with a receptive and intelligent audience to whom he could expound his ideas and with whom he could argue on equal terms without too much pretense. Lady Welby, a minor figure in English philosophy and letters, wrote a series of books on some aspects of meaning whose simplicity and charm so attracted Peirce that he took the trouble to write a review of one of them in which he compared Bertrand Russell adversely with her. Lady Welby thereupon wrote to thank him, and so began this sometimes delightful, and at other times saddening, correspondence in which Peirce played the great philosopher and country gentleman with pathetic and disarming earnestness. The correspondence, edited by Charles Hardwick, is one of the better introductions to Peirce's philosophy, especially his semeiotic.[65]

Peirce spent the summer preparing his third series (the first was given in 1866) of Lowell Lectures for a popular audience on his philosophical system. W. T. Sedgwick, the Lowell Institute's curator, had arranged for him to give eight lectures that winter between November 23 and December 17, entitled "SOME TOPICS OF LOGIC ON QUESTIONS NOW VEXED." The lectures would have been easily mastered by someone who had heard and understood those given there almost forty years before, and, unlike those given at Harvard, these were well received. In them Peirce introduced "A System of Diagrams for Studying Logical Relations," the first public appearance of his existential graphs, in which "his objective was to have the operation of thinking literally laid open to view—a moving picture of thought. He believed that these existential graphs would allow logical relationships to be displayed in such an iconic way as to yield solutions to problems that had defied analysis through algebraic logic."[66] For the lectures he had prepared a printed syllabus, primarily a description of his classification of the sciences, copies of which he distributed to James, Cattell, Royce, Newcomb, and others. Peirce stayed happily discoursing in Cambridge until after Christmas, dining at least once with the Jameses and talking at length with Royce, who understood him so well that Peirce was to call him America's greatest pragmatist.[67] James, who attended Peirce's lectures, said in the first of the eight Lowell Lectures he gave on pragmatism three years later:

> I have heard friends and colleagues try to popularize philosophy in this very hall, but they soon grew dry, and then technical, and the results were only partially encouraging. . . . The founder of pragmatism [Peirce] himself recently gave a course of lectures at the Lowell Institute . . . ,—flashes of brilliant light relieved against Cimmerian darkness! None of us, I fancy, understood *all* that he said—yet here I stand, making a very similar venture.[68]

In January 1904, Peirce wrote Newcomb after hearing that he had been elected as Foreign Associate to the French Academy of Sciences, an extraordinary honor for an American. Peirce proposed to review his *The Reminiscences of an Astronomer*, just published, and to describe the importance of his election to the French Academy (the same institution that Peirce felt had humiliated him in its anterooms thirty years before) for the *Nation*. Garrison, who admired Newcomb as a public man, agreed.[69] Peirce had already arranged for the publisher G. H. Putnam to act as middleman, so that no one could accuse Newcomb of being so gauche as to conspire in his own glorification.[70] Peirce wrote a review of Newcomb's autobiography and a history of the French Academy, both of which were flattering to Newcomb far beyond what Peirce believed was his actual worth as a scientist. In March, the first appeared in the *Nation* and the second in the *Post*. Since Peirce knew of Newcomb's decisive part in his rejection by the Carnegie (and probably by this time had strong suspicions of Newcomb's part in other similar events), it is difficult to imagine his motive in arranging so carefully for such adulation for his enemy, unless it was calculated. Perhaps Peirce thought that by so praising him, he could later influence Newcomb to use his great prestige to his advantage, which, indeed, he and Juliette tried to do two years later.

By February, both Charles and Juliette were very sick. Peirce wrote James about the prospect of James's visit to Milford in March, a visit that did not take place:

> But we have had a disastrous winter; & that is the reason I have not known what to write you. The bridge between us and Port Jervis, our base of supplies, was carried away in October with some loss of life & a ferry that was established was wrecked with further loss of three lives & thus we were prevented from getting coal or using our steam furnace. Then the cellar was so cold the pipes froze [as happened many winters] & I have not yet been able to put them in order. However, I hope to do so soon. Besides that my

Juliette in her bedroom at Arisbe during an illness, ca. 1900.

wife was ill in bed for five weeks & does not yet leave her chamber. Part of the time it was very immediately alarming. She is of course very weak. . . .

I think I have been ill for three or four days,—one of the feverish attacks that I don't understand but that once in two or three years I am subject to. . . . I said I did not understand my illnesses. But this much I *do* understand. Namely, that though my constitution is very strong my emotional system is such slush that to see my wife suffering & particularly to see her power of bearing it, which completely transcends my impotence before suffering, let me steel myself against my feelings & dominate them as I may, they make me sick. They put me into a stupor and a fever. And I mention it because if I have any message for the world, it must be given while my wife lives. For having only her & having this poor paste of an emotional nature should she go I would be gone. Therefore I think I must formulate what I can in S. M.—short metre,—& put it out for whatever it may be worth. . . . Anyway, much or little, the duty has to be done. . . . Peu m'importe, à moi, personellement, si ce que j'ai a dire vaut grande chose ou peu de chose. Ce qui m'importe, c'est que j'aurai fait mon mieux. So come up and see our waterfalls. Therein is peace.[71]

By August, Peirce was forced to borrow money again from his brother James Mills, to whom he said, "I am duly grateful for the loan which was more needed than I care to say."[72] Like the other such loans from his relatives, this one was not repaid. To supplement his trickle of an income, Peirce again resorted in the fall to the sale of furniture, apples, nuts, and hay. Although Lady Welby several times asked the Peirces to visit with her in England for an indefinite period, perhaps even permanently, such a trip was not only far beyond his means but beyond their abilities. They were both too sick. It was all he could do to earn money enough for food, and as he explained to Lady Welby on December 2, "I am dangerously fatigued from overwork. . . . A man of 65 ought not to work through two consecutive nights and three days as I have done; but the work is pressing."[73] Lady Welby responded by encouraging them to come and visit her, to use her home as a central headquarters while he scouted for a suitable position. She also offered to make her extensive library available for him to use. Peirce wanted more desperately than ever to escape the prison Arisbe had become and was fancifully placing all his hopes in the possibility that his brother Herbert could arrange a consulship for him in Ceylon, a frontier post at best, the long journey to which could easily kill them both. He wrote her on December 16:

> Certainly dear Lady Welby we must accept your ladyship's kind hospitality; and it is an immense pleasure to do so,—would be so, even if I could not accept. But it is by no means an easy thing to sell this place & that I must do; for I could not be worried with it. I am very sorry to do so, too; because the house is a work of art of my wife's decoration. We planned it, together. I was my own builder, hiring the workmen direct & buying the materials that I could not have procured easily. My wife is a true artist in decoration. Everything is exquisitely soft without the faintest suggestion of ambition. The house is entirely unlike any other & breathes a spirit of deep peace. I am sorry to lose it. . . . So, though we are putting the price very low indeed,—needlessly, perhaps,—still one cannot [easily] sell a place so out of the social world. . . . Besides, I haven't received my appointment yet. I am a friend of Roosevelt's of many years. My brother is Assistant Secretary of Foreign Affairs (of "State", as we call it) and has all matters connected with consuls under his special charge. All appointments are made by the President, ordinarily at my brother's recommendation, and have to be confirmed by the Senate, this last step being by no means a matter of form. One of the most powerful Senators Cabot Lodge of Massachusetts is a cousin of mine and his wife is a specially intimate cousin of mine, too; and in the Senate, "courtesy" is a very great consideration. Besides all that, I have personal claims to some rewards or recognition. Therefore, I do not

think there will be any difficulty in my getting the consulate,—a minor one,—which is to be vacated; but it is impossible to be sure, for I have powerful enemies. . . .

Mrs. Peirce wanted to add something in her hand to this letter. But writing occasions her so much pain, not merely while she writes, but for a long time after, that I would not permit her to do it. She is one of those persons whose energy far exceeds their strength, and is really in a most precarious condition, the reflection of which poisons my life.[74]

Peirce spent more and more time on the edges of a world of fantasy such as the one exhibited in his letters to Lady Welby. Still, he managed to pursue his logic with remarkable insight and precision. When James suggested that he send a short version of "How to Make Our Ideas Clear" to Frederick J. E. Woodbridge's new *Journal of Philosophy, Psychology and Scientific Matters*, Peirce, who had just taken three bad falls, wrote him the day after his letter to Lady Welby:

By one of those freaks of luck for which Fortuna has always been noted I lately had three bad knock-outs. It was odd that any one had not killed me. The last has so disabled my brain, as the first had my writing arm, that I can't write. However, Woodshed [Woodbridge] or whatever his name is, has been so markedly rude to me, as if I needed to be kicked to take a hint, that I certainly will never write to him under any circumstances. Besides, interest seems to be growing in Firstness, Secondness & Thirdness, & I do not think my idea of pragmatism can be understood from the article you mean by itself without the previous one ["The Fixation of Belief"]. My [1903] Harvard Lectures were chiefly devoted to bringing out the point [the inferential character of perceptual judgments] which you seem surprised I should attach any importance to. However, I shall have a chance to set myself right if the Monist sends a proofsheet.[75]

The final sentence refers to Peirce's reopened dialogue with Carus and *The Monist* through the good offices of Judge Russell, who was now a member of its editorial board. Peirce was to write a series of four or five articles developing his own version of pragmatism, now called "pragmaticism," the completion of which was prevented by an unusually severe nervous collapse, reminiscent in its intensity and character of the attack of conversion hysteria he had suffered in Paris in 1875–76. In mid-April he wrote Lady Welby: "Early in February I was suddenly collapsed with nervous prostration. After more than two full months I find myself able to do half a day's work, but all my engagements are thrown back, [and] a great printing establishment [*The Monist*] is put to inconvenience."[76] To James he wrote, " . . . I was so ill that that whole month was ever after blotted out. . . . "[77] As a result, only three of the proposed five *Monist* articles appeared from April to October: "What Pragmatism Is," "The Issues of Pragmaticism," and "Prolegomena to an Apology for Pragmaticism." Peirce basked in the publicity generated by the first paper, writing to Lady Welby, "A platoon of philosophers from Eastport Maine to San Diego Cal. has me under fire at the moment . . . anything stimulating, especially anything antagonistic, that may occur to you to say would be a help to me."[78]

On April 12, Peirce received a letter on this reconsidered version of his thinking about pragmatism from his old classmate and friend Thomas Sargeant Perry:

Dear polypragmatic C. S. P.!

Many thanks for yr. defense of yr. position in the *Monist*. It convinces me that I too am a pragmatician & have been one always without knowing what was the matter with me—as the hypochondriac is afflicted by all diseases he reads about.—I agree with those who, of all things, never argue with one another. That is because I am like the village idiot & am the prey of any evil wind that blows. Luckily you have filled my tyres with sound learning & I am now able to look with scorn on those who assault the True Faith. As I read, you appear to me to speak words of wisdom & that they are clear is proved by my thinking that I follow you.

I used to think that pragmatic meant *cross* & was a term of abuse, but see how refining & elevating is divine philosophy, it now means a person who knows the truth. This knowledge may (a) or may not (b) make him cross, but the attention of the by-standers is distracted from the study of his moods to admiration of his stores of learning. This shows how useful philosophy is. I can now *see* what I had often been *told*.

I am also very much interested in another philosopher, Nietzsche, who, other philosophers tell me, is no philosopher. Never mind he died too young to profit fm. the lessons of Pragmatism, but he was very clever, very poetical, eloquent & unhappy. I wouldn't give a damn for his philosophy, but the way he says things & the things he says, delight me.

Yours ever
T. S. Perry

Peirce answered playfully in a characteristic burst of clever burlesque:

Dear Perry

I am under the fire of a platoon of philosophers reaching from you and your B. I. G. neighbor in the Museum to Berkeley, Cal.; but I shall devote my next article to replying to your strictures by showing that *pragmatical* does not mean 'cross' since the final *Al* is not at all the symbol of Aluminum! It is simply the word 'haul' and with the preceding C = carbon implies a person disposed to haul others over the coals for not managing their private affairs after his notions. Now the less 'crossly' and more obtrusively tactfully and diplomatically this is done, the more *pragmatical* it is. And this explanation is proved by the circumstance that if the *hauling* is eliminated, as in 'pragmatic sanction,' one still meddles with other people's intimate concerns, but only at their particular request. The idea of *ought to be* which is here expressed by the close conjunction of the *tic* to *pragma* (for a poor rag mattress *ought to* have a tick) is removed if we substitute 'tis! giving *pragma-'tis-tic* and quite reversed if we make it 'tis, is't? with the emphasis on the is't—*pragma-'tisis't-ic* where I heap another atom of C on the objector's head in the spelling pragmaticistic, or PrAgMaticistic as much as to say, 'Praseodymide of Silver and Magnalium, 'tis is it,—hic?' The notion that *Pragmaticism* is 'A poor rag, but its his, mum' is phonetically impossible and scarce deserving of notice.

C.S.P.

If you had suggested your 'poly' in time I might have called it Polly-Peirceism. Its mere Peirce-istence now.[79]

What Peirce attempted in this fifth and final set of representative articles was to unite the logic of inquiry of the "Illustrations of the Logic of Science" of 1877–78, the logical realism of the categories as developed from "A New List of Categories" of 1867, and the objective idealism of the evolutionary metaphysics and cosmology he had first formed twenty years before in "Design and Chance." He did so from the "hard" scientific perspective. His strategy was to give a brief history of the way in which the term arose, to present the ideas of pragmatists such as James, Ferdinand C. S. Schiller, and Papini, and then to distinguish the ways in which his own version of the doctrine differed essentially from theirs in its logical realism:

> That which any true proposition asserts is *real*, in the sense of being as it is regardless of what you or I may think about it. Let this proposition be a general conditional proposition as to the future, and it is a real general such as is calculated really to influence human conduct; and such the pragmaticist holds to be the rational purport of every concept.[80]

Referring to his cosmological articles in *The Monist* of 1891–93, he went on to summarize the idea he had introduced there that continuity is an indispensable element of reality and that it is expressed in logic as generality, the essence of thought, and that reality consists in

> something more than feeling and action could supply, inasmuch as the primeval chaos, where those two elements were present, was explicitly shown to be pure nothing. Now, the motive for alluding to that theory just

here is, that in this way one can put in a strong light a position which the pragmaticist holds and must hold . . . namely, that the third category—the category of thought, representation, triadic relation, mediation, genuine thirdness, thirdness as such—is an essential ingredient of reality, yet does not by itself constitute reality [as he put it in his 1902 application to the Carnegie, "being and being represented are different"], since this category (which in that cosmology appears as the element of habit) can have no concrete being without action, as a separate object on which to work its government, just as action cannot exist without the immediate being of feeling on which to act. The truth is that pragmaticism is closely allied to the Hegelian absolute idealism. . . . For pragmaticism belongs essentially to the triadic class of philosophical doctrines, and is much more essentially so than Hegelianism is.[81]

In June, Peirce was writing additional entries for the 1906 supplement of the *Century Dictionary* at the request of its chief editor, Benjamin E. Smith. Among others, he wrote entries (for which Smith had asked John Dewey's assistance) for *pragmatic, pragmaticism, pragmatism, pragmatist,* and *instrumentalism.* He wrote Smith that he was going to propose in his paper for the October issue of *The Monist,* titled "Issues of Pragmaticism," a new philosophical term of sufficient importance to include in the supplement, called *critical common-sensism,* and also included a new version of *common-sensism,* the term from which it was derived. The *Century* already included his definition of *common-sense,* which mentioned Aristotle and Kames and Reid, and a definition of critical philosophy, which referred to Kant's critics of reason. Smith, by this time unsure of Peirce's philosophic competence, refused to include Peirce's proposal to join these two approaches to inquiry in what Apel has called "meaning critical Realism," and which he argues is the sound starting point for a modern logic of science:[82]

> *common-sensism,* n. The doctrine that every man believes some general pro-
> positions and accepts some inferences without having been able to genu-
> inely doubt them, and consequently without being able to subject them to
> any real criticism, and that these must appear to him to be perfectly satis-
> factory and manifestly true.
> *Critical common-sensism,* [n.] a kind of common-sensism which is distin-
> guished from the Scotch philosophy of common sense in maintaining the
> following six positions: 1st, that there are not only uncriticizable proposi-
> tions, but also uncriticizable inferences; 2nd, that while there is a body of
> propositions and inferences which are uncriticizable by the ordinary trained
> and well-matured minds of one generation, and while these are, in the
> main, the same for generation after generation, yet they are not quite the
> same for all generations nor for every individual mind without exception

even within a given field of civilization; but on the contrary signal changes have taken place in history; 3rd, that all uncriticizable beliefs are vague, and cannot be rendered precise without evoking doubt; 4th, that uncriticizable beliefs resemble instincts, not merely in the vague sense in which they were so-called by the Scotch philosophers, but also in relating to matters of life, in being beneficial, especially for the stock, in coming up into consciousness only on occasions of applicability, in being accompanied with deep unaccountable feeling, in often involving singular details, and in other respects; 5th, that many dubitable propositions are only so if a carefully followed and elaborate plan for attaining a state of doubt be followed out, so that, in this sense, the uncriticizable beliefs ought to be severely criticized, while, on the other hand, there is in many cases great danger of counterfeit doubts being mistaken for genuine doubts; 6th, that the position of those philosophers who profess to doubt uncriticizable beliefs are to be carefully examined, and especially that of those who propose to base logic and metaphysics on special sciences, whether on psychology, history, etc on the one hand, or on physics, biology, etc on the other [should be carefully examined]; and that the precise errors of Kant ought to be specified, and that it should be shown that his philosophy, after the correction of its errors agrees with the doctrine of critical common-sensism.[83]

This characteristically dense précis of his late argument against Descartes again reached all the way back to his introduction in the late 1850s and 1860s to Kames, Reid, and Kant, and more specifically to his 1877 paper "The Fixation of Belief," first read in draft to the Metaphysical Club in 1872, which he had come to believe was too dependent on a psychological basis for the acceptance of beliefs. His reintroduction here of the idea that uncriticizable beliefs are an example, in their instinctual aspect, of the community of nature and mind is part of his attempt to specify the nature of his logical realism, as is vagueness, a sign of the reality lurking in things.

In a letter to Russell written at this time, Peirce summarized for him the essence of his logical realism:

> Nominalism introduced the notion that consciousness, i.e., percepts, is not the real thing but only the *sign* of the thing. But as I argued in the Pop Sci Monthly for Jan. 1901 ["Pearson's Grammar of Science"], these signs are the very thing. Reals *are* signs. To try to peel off signs & get down to the real thing is like trying to peel an onion and get down to [the] onion itself, . . . If not *consciousness* then *sciousness*, is the very being of things; and consciousness is their co-being. . . .
>
> Lately, when I was suffering at every mouth through which a man can drink suffering, I tried to beguile it by reading three books that I hadn't

read for a long time, three religious books; Bunyan's Pilgrim's Progress, Boethius's Consolations of Philosophy & Hume's Dialogues concerning Natural Religion. The last did one most good owing to the utter blindness of the man. Man can naturally get but a vague idea of the *all* of things; and a vague idea is always open [to] being driven into contradictions. But man will never find a doctrine of the all nearer than theism.[84]

Peirce was slowly moving toward an empirical justification for religion, called by him *theism* (and, in fact, very closely related to Abbot's "scientific theism"): the nonpantheistic doctrine that an all-pervading divine presence can be experienced in a manner no different in the strength of its authority than the verification of any hypothesis—the doctrine of mysticism that the suprasensible real mysteriously exists in the sensible as a community of mind and nature. In a letter to James, who was suffering more and more from heart trouble, Peirce wrote consolingly on July 26:

> Forgive me for harping on the subject of theism. It would indeed be most ridiculous for me to think I could say anything to make you better, but living in this beautiful country, I cannot but be overwhelmed with the lovableness of the universe, as everybody is. Every mortal who stops to consider it is penetrated with love. It is irresistible.[85]

This letter, which argues informally for the priority of aesthetics over ethics—a position he was already developing formally in drafts of "A Neglected Argument for the Reality of God"—was written shortly after Peirce discovered that a position to lecture at a summer school in the Adirondacks, upon which he had counted, had fallen through. In commenting upon this blow, he wrote James:

> I have for a very long time been puzzling over a practical question. Certainly, if there were the smallest real prospect of my having an opportunity to teach Logic even to one capable person, I should not allow *anything whatever* to interfere with that duty, because I certainly was put into the world to stand ready to do that thing whenever called upon. It is the duty that transcends all others. On the other hand, I can & must not allow a fantastic possibility without any real likelihood to obstruct my performance of a plain duty. That duty is not to allow myself to be a burden upon everybody and a simple nuisance, as I must soon become, even if I have not already become so. It is my duty to get out, to make away with myself. I have considered the question maturely. It is plain that a man was made to judge of his own duty as best he can; and to my apprehension nothing is clearer to me than that a man who can render no service whatever, but is simply a bore and a nuisance ought to begone. That is one reason why I

desire early intelligence of any chance to teach logic, because other considerations become more and more pressing. My wife, especially, must not be
made to endure her martyrdom longer. If I had two years occupation, I
could put my Arithmetic on a paying basis on which she could live. (It
would be no excuse for *my* living longer that I could pay my way.) C. S. P.[86]

James responded:

> . . . I read your long notice [in the *Nation*] of Wundt [*Principles of Physio-
> logical Psychology*] a fortnight ago with admiration at its cleverness. You
> have the journalistic touch very well now and in addition to that your
> articles always contain some original thought or bit of learning. . . .
>
> When you wrote of the "Summer School" I tho't you meant either
> Harvard or Chicago. It appears you meant this place [Adirondack Summer
> School, Hurricane, N.J.]. Have no regrets. I have given two lectures, to
> about a dozen auditresses, flabby boarding house old maids, two "settle-
> ment" jews from NY. & two men who can understand philosophy. It's
> lamentable; and the cash would doubtfully cover your journey. Shed no
> tears for that! . . .
>
> I'm awfully sorry, dear Charley for your hard plight. Isn't it time now
> for some systematic aid from your relatives? I of course can take no
> initiative.[87]

Garrison resigned in bad health from his editorship of the *Nation* in
mid-year, and Peirce expressed his warm appreciation of

> . . . the truly extraordinary skill that Garrison shows in conducting the
> journal. However little acquaintance he may have with a subject, his *flair* is
> such that before he sends out a book he knows pretty accurately what its
> value is. His "graciousness," for which we all feel, as we ought, so warmly to
> him, ought *besides* to command respect as an essential element of his ability
> to gather and keep such contributors as he does. Every head of a works, to
> ensure his success, must have a genuine sympathy with his workmen; but
> there is no other class so difficult to deal with as those who are skillful with
> the pen. The immense influence of the *Nation*, far beyond its subscription
> list, has been exercised with amazing sagacity and directed to the best
> ends.[88]

Garrison did not have so high an opinion of his contributor. He wrote
to the Boston historian William Roscoe Thayer that he chose his philosophers on the basis of their knowledge and judgment, not the camp of their
opinion:

> In philosophy I go much further than my natural inclination, which would

be to shut the door in the face of metaphysics. I affect to regard it as of importance, and do the best I can in choice of reviewers; but I sometimes control these (not in advance, but in editing the MS.). James's vivacious intellect I highly esteem, ranking it much above his brother's; but his "Will to Believe" I have the least possible sympathy with. With X [Peirce], I could never come in rapport. Since Z. has ceased to write for me, I hardly know what he is doing; but his life-work *ex officio* seems to me barren of profit to mankind.

Nous sommes des animaux;
Voilà mon système.[89]

Garrison's resignation left Peirce virtually penniless because, although almost thirty more of Peirce's reviews written for Garrison were still to be printed in 1905–1906, all payment for them had already been advanced. The ensuing poverty affected him profoundly, as he described wryly in a letter to James apologizing for some unknown presumption in January 1906: "Let a person go half fed for many months, fearing to take food out of another's mouth & one's mind will suffer confusions & one will do & say things one ought not to have done, & expose oneself to severe judgment from the righteous."[90]

The Peirces seem to have existed during this period through gifts arranged by William James and help from Mary Pinchot. Peirce commented on the last:

> When I was so ill that a whole month was ever after blotted out, Mrs. Pinchot came to my wife and thrust a fifty dollar bill into her hand. . . . As soon as I was well enough to be consulted, we sacrificed something & the money was paid back with a handsome present. . . . Long after, I learned that it was currently said in the village that the Pinchots supported us.[91]

That James arranged for substantial assistance is obvious from the evidence, one example of which is this letter to him from his friend C. A. Strong, written in July 1905:

> I hope that Mrs. Peirce has not been starving while I have been dallying. I think her case would come within the limits of those my wife desires to aid, & I send you a check for a hundred dollars, to be dealt out at your discretion, & only asking you not to reveal the identity of the giver. (I will try to send you a larger check in the fall, for general uses.)[92]

It is probably impossible to determine just how early aid began to be given to the Peirces, and in what amounts. The problem is complicated by the fact that Juliette had some small income of her own. Those who gave money naturally wished to have that information kept secret, which makes the task even more difficult. Donations of cash to the Peirces from James, the Pinchots, and a few others likely began in an unorganized, informal manner as early as 1898, when James arranged part of the payment for Peirce's lectures to be disbursed over a year to Juliette.

The year 1906 brought deeper poverty than ever. There was only occasional work from the new editor of the *Nation*, Paul Elmer More, and other editors, even Carus of *The Monist*, were not sufficiently interested in Peirce to extend their aid as had Garrison. The last and utterly improbable scheme to obtain a suitable position for Peirce was the result of Juliette's belief that she could convince Newcomb to put her husband forward as the candidate to replace Samuel P. Langley as secretary of the Smithsonian Institution. Both she and Charles believed in her powers of persuasion, and Juliette, knowing with certainty that Charles had the fatal gift of genuine originality, loved her difficult and outrageous husband so deeply and was so incensed about his evil treatment by the world, especially by Newcomb, that she insisted on taking that world on by herself. Charles prepared for her a list of men who might be helpfully influential and a carefully worked-out script, which included a brief biography and the insistence that she was acting on her own, but that if offered the job he would "think it his duty to take up the work for a few years at least."[93] Juliette made two appointments with Newcomb at the Cosmos Club, on January 15 and 22, but there exists no record of the conversations in Newcomb's papers, only the record of the meetings.[94] That the possibility of Peirce's appointment to the Smithsonian was seriously considered is made clear from a letter to Cattell, written in an uneven hand:

> My delay in considering your letter has not, you may be sure[,] been due to any lack of cordiality. On the contrary, if you are to be secretary of the Smithsonian [the position went to Charles D. Walcott of the Geological Survey], you may rest assured that you will have no more earnest nor more loyal friend of your administration than I.
>
> You are quite mistaken if you suppose that such a place would be particularly to my taste. My wife wanted me to have it; and reflecting that I could do a certain service to science and to mankind, if I had charge of the Smithsonian, which would be a real benefit and that nobody could do as well as I could, I was compelled to tell her that, in case it were offered to me, I would accept it for a term of three years. I am very poor; and that equally forbade . . . me to lift a finger to secure it.[95]

Charles's brother James Mills, who had helped him out so often and had tried his unsuccessful best to work with Charles to bring his geometry and arithmetic into publishable form, died in mid-March, leaving little more than his collection of books, which were sold at auction. By October, Peirce wrote James that he "possess[ed] 29 cents, am too ill to write successfully, & there is one can of beans in the house & nothing more. If you could spare me a loan even if only five dollars. . . . "[96] As a last resort, he put some of his more valuable books up for sale, using James as his agent, but with little success. In late November, he and Juliette went to Cambridge so that he could attend the Boston meeting of the National Academy of Sciences as the reporter for the New York *Post*. By December 13, Juliette had returned to Milford, but Charles moved into a rooming house called Prescott Hall, at 472 Broadway, Cambridge, to work on his report. There he ran out of money, after living for a week on a loaf of bread and $1.70. He wrote Russell on December 28 in a spidery hand:

> Believe me I haven't forgotten the article on religion. But I really have not had any time. When I have been forced to take a little rest, I have been so overwhelmed with worry that I am in danger of serious illness,—very serious, & the temptation to give up & commit suicide when I find my mind weakening under worry & starvation is great.[97]

Within a few days of this letter, Peirce was found by James's student Henry Alsberg, who told this story:

> One day, the landlady asked him to come into one of the rooms to see an old gentleman, who had been ill and was very likely dying. When he went in, he saw a sick, worn body of a man obviously suffering from under-nourishment and lack of care; and when he asked his name, he was told, 'Charles Peirce.' In a wild confusion of emotions, Alsberg and a friend went to find William James, and caught him coming out of class. James listened to their story. 'Why,' he said, his face changing, 'I owe him everything!' and swung them into a cab to call for Peirce and take him home, to the house he had left with the few cents he had in his pocket.[98]

This was in early January 1907, and it was obvious that Peirce could no longer support himself. William James then organized the fund for Peirce's support, the details of which he explained in a letter to Henry P. Bowditch:

> The time has come to recognize that he [Peirce] *can't* make his living. The makeshifts of the last few years are played out, and he must be kept going by friends & relatives.
>   I am representing the friends and trying to get enough pledges of a certain sum *yearly* to make in the aggregate 400 or 500 dollars ('Yearly' means for as long as not too inconvenient—nothing binding!). A small

number of 50 dollar subscriptions would do the job. I myself pledge 50. If the relatives do as much, the relief will be immense, for *Mrs.* C.S.P. is a first rate economist, and living as they do in the country, they get along on little.

The plan is to guard against waste (for Charles is unfit to handle money, having no notion of the difference between a dollar and a hundred), by appointing a bank-cashier to receive the subscriptions and send them a fortnightly remittance, never to be exceeded.

Will you kindly send this to your brother Charles, and possibly, in memory of auld lang syne and in consideration of C. S. P.'s genius (if not of his character) add your own name to the subscribers?[99]

The evidence naming those who supported the fund is incomplete, but there were sufficient contributors among friends and relatives to raise yearly about $1,000 from between fifteen and twenty-five subscribers (the actual number is uncertain, since some, such as Pinchot, Lodge, and Strong, gave at least $100). Some difficulties arose concerning the administration of the fund. Juliette was very proud and refused at first to have anything to do with it, but finally agreed to handle the money if it was made clear that all funds were meant for the support of her husband.[100] Since Juliette handled all the money, Charles often found himself short, and there were some petulant letters to James motivated by pangs of hunger.[101] There are also a number of ungracious letters from Peirce in which he inquired disingenuously about the identity of the subscribers who wished to be anonymous.[102] On the whole, however, the arrangement worked to the evident satisfaction of all concerned with it.

Peirce stayed on in the Cambridge rooming house, acting as tutor for an old friend and admirer, until July.[103] Still dangerously depressed, he threatened suicide in a letter to James written June 13:

> My dearest William:
> I am not in a position to teach young men anything; and in this worm-eaten university I am happy to think that I should be even more out of place than you; but if I had some young philosophers to aid, I should certainly hold myself up as a warning against withholding publication until one can be quite satisfied with his expression. The result is that I am so hemmed in with analyses upon which I labored until they are brought to a presentable finish, that I am completely cut off from the mass, even of the philosophical world.
> Nobody understands me. You balk at the distinction of denotation and connotation as something utterly incomprehensible. . . . America is no place for such as I am. . . . & just as soon as I can frame a plausible excuse to myself—in about a fortnight I hope,—I shall follow Frank Abbot's example,—except I shall leave no unreadable book behind me. No, no!

Peirce and Juliette in front of the well at Arisbe, ca. 1907.

With best regards to Mrs. James & your family & I am the same old sixpence,

C S Peirce[104]

In early July, after giving two lectures on "Logical Methodeutic" to the Philosophy Club, his last at Harvard or anyplace else, he returned to Milford to join Juliette, where they became one of the more interesting charities of the Cambridge elect.[105]

In September Peirce wrote his will, which left everything to Juliette, but in case she predeceased him, "I give all to the eldest son of my friend Professor William James, the psychologist of renown. . . . "[106] In October, Newcomb angrily complained of Peirce's review of the collected works of the mathematician George William Hill, and Peirce answered with unusual straightforwardness. He began by saying that the science of celestial mechanics, Newcomb's field, was not a method for discovering new truths but merely a method of calculation, and continued:

I never cast any slur on the men who do this sort of thing. I said they must have peculiar minds. . . . That you & Hill & other theoretical astronomers find in the afternoon of life that their own successes have rendered their science uninteresting to most people,—even to most mathematicians, is distressing; but it is a fact.

. . . that which my article contained that was disagreeable was due to my expressing truths that may be unpleasant to a man like you, but are truths just the same for all that.[107]

Newcomb, his nemesis, was dead two years later.

Despite his steadily declining health and increasingly undependable mind, Peirce continued until the last few weeks of his life to work doggedly and surprisingly fruitfully on his great undertaking, now called a "system of logic defined as formal semeiotic." This dry description meant far more than a change in name. Between about 1900 and 1912, Peirce transfigured his entire architectonic on the basis of a transcendental doctrine of signs that had been present in kernel in 1867. With it he transformed pragmatism, the original conception of a normative, methodological logic of inquiry proposed in 1877–78, into pragmaticism, a cosmologically oriented, synechistic metaphysics justified by critical common-sensism and the realist theory of universals, the whole of which he contrasted sharply with the nominalist, individualist pragmatism of James and others.[108]

For Peirce, a sign "is something by knowing which we know something more." It constitutes a pragmatic instruction to interpret. Peirce named three kinds of signs, corresponding to the three categories: icon, index, and symbol. Sebeok explained that a "given object can, depending on the circumstance in which it is displayed, momentarily function, to a degree, in the role of an icon, an index, or a symbol. Witness the Stars and Stripes":

> 1. iconicity comes to the fore when the interpreter's attention fastens upon the seven red horizontal stripes of the flag alternating with six white ones (together identical with the number of founding colonies), or the number of white stars clustered in a single blue canton (in all, identical to the actual number of States in the Union);
> 2. in a cavalry charge, say, our flag was commonly employed to imperatively point, in an indexical fashion, to a target; and
> 3. the debates pursuant to the recent Supreme Court decision on the issue of flag burning present our banner as an emotionally surcharged emblem, being a subspecies of symbol.[109]

Semeiosis, the activity of using signs, involves three elements, a sign, an object, and an interpretant. For the semeioticist and novelist Umberto Eco, the universe of semeiosis is the labyrinth of human culture, which is itself a virtually infinite network of interpretants whose order is, at most, a shared way of using signs.[110] About 1909, Peirce identified three such universes as familiar to us, which are exemplars of the categories:

> the first comprises all mere Ideas, those airy nothings to which the mind of the poet, pure mathematician, or another *might* give local habitation and a

Peirce's representation of the labyrinth of signs. Photograph courtesy of the Harvard University Archives.

The Quincuncial Map Projection invented by Peirce in 1876.

name within that mind. Their very airy-nothingness, the fact that their Being consists in mere capability of getting thought, not in anybody's Actually thinking them, saves their Reality. The second Universe is that of the Brute Actuality of things and facts. I am confident that their Being consists in reactions against Brute forces, notwithstanding objections redoubtable until they are closely and fairly examined. The third Universe [is the semeiotic one, which] comprises everything whose being consist[s] in active power to establish connections between different objects, especially between objects in different Universes. Such is everything which is essentially a Sign—not the mere body of the Sign, which is not essentially such, but so to speak, the Sign's Soul, which has its Being in its power of serving as intermediary between its Object and a Mind. Such, too, is a living consciousness, and such the life, the power of growth, of a plant. Such is a living constitution—a daily newspaper, a great fortune, a social "movement."[111]

For Peirce, any person is a sign, and "even plants make their living . . . by uttering signs."[112] His universes were prodigally rich in utterances, speaking to him of the Real. The world as we perceive it is, therefore, an infinite string of signs, each of which imitates, points to, and symbolizes something more than itself—the Real. Semeiotic is still, despite the vast literature associated with it, a vexed field of inquiry which cannot approach answers to such fundamental questions as how meaning occurs or how meaning is anchored. It is very likely in Peirce's brilliantly original and pioneering work in semeiotic as the foundation and armature of his architectonic, most of which was done in the last fourteen years of his life and almost none of which was published or understood in his lifetime, where his greatest fame rests.

Peirce continued his skeptical interest in ghosts, partly to please his friend James, who found the field fascinating, and wrote a correspondent who concerned himself with psychical research: " . . . there is *something* in the spiritualist theory. There is *some* life after death, at least for some people, though it may be a brief butterfly life. All I have ever seen of manifestations was odious beyond words."[113]

In 1908 and 1909, in what was intended by him as an interlude in the *Monist* series begun in 1905 and never completed, Peirce published the "amazing mazes" series. These were a development of his 1903 Lowell Lectures and had the same purpose, to expose to a popular audience the visible skeleton of logical form—"a moving picture of thought." Earlier, he had begun writing a series of articles on religion, a subject about which he had mused steadily for a decade, for *Hibbert's Journal*, but only the first of the series was published, in 1908. The paper, "A Neglected Argument for the

Reality of God," set forth three arguments whose effect was to clothe in the pragmatistic mode his father's informal argument from beauty and experience which ended with the exclamation, "Gentleman, there must be a GOD!" The first argument was what he called the "Humble Argument," which depended on a wide-eyed, even childlike, free play of musement (*Spieltrieb*) about the world around us. Once the idea of God appeared, the muser "will come to be stirred to the depth of his nature by the beauty of the idea and by its august practicality, even to the point of earnestly loving and adoring his strictly hypothetical God. . . . "[114] The second was that the justification of the "Humble Argument" lay, not in the fruitless enterprise of criticizing this impossibly vague proposition, but in the immediate aesthetic attraction of the idea of God itself, both as an explanation of the nature of things and as a source for ideals of conduct. It was in this manner that logic grew out of ethics and aesthetics, since it expressed at root a loving hope for the truth. The third was a statement of the ideal-realist doctrine that nature and the mind have such a community as to impart to our guesses a tendency toward the truth: " . . . because the discoveries of science, their enabling us to *predict* what will be the course of nature, is proof conclusive that, though we cannot think any thought of God's, we can catch a fragment of His Thought, as it were."[115]

Together, the three arguments, corresponding to Firstness, Secondness, and Thirdness, described Peirce's theism. The entire argument in favor of a "strictly hypothetical God" was put forward as empirical in a scientific sense:

> Where would such an idea, say as that of God, come from, if not from direct experience? Would you make it a result of some kind of reasoning, good or bad? Why, reasoning can supply the mind with nothing in the world except an estimate of the value of a statistical ratio, that is, how often certain kinds of things are found in certain combinations in the ordinary course of experience. And scepticism, in the sense of doubt of the validity of elementary ideas—which is really a proposal to turn an idea out of court and permit no inquiry into its applicability—is doubly condemned by the fundamental principle of the scientific method—condemned first as obstructing inquiry, and condemned second because it is treating some other than a statistical ratio as a thing to be argued about. No: as to God, open your eyes—and your heart, which is also a perceptive organ—and you see him.[116]

The direct experience—the vision—of which Peirce wrote was that of scientists standing outside the phenomena they observed. It was not that of the mystic. Peirce was never able to realize, despite a life spent obsessively and ingeniously tracking the clues leading to it, the end which his ideal-realist doctrine required: to move beyond the sign, thoughtless, into the experience itself. This point is made in a vivid anecdote about the Sufi mystic Rabi'a:

> Into the house she came and bowed her head.
> And it was Spring. "Come out," her servant prayed,
> "Rabi'a, come out and see what God has made."
> "Come in and see the maker," Rabi'a said.[117]

For a time in 1909, Peirce seriously considered again an offer of Carus's to revise his old *Popular Science Monthly* "Illustrations of the Logic of Science" for publication by the Open Court Press, but the revisions were never completed.[118] Peirce never gave up his attempts to earn money, with a view to repaying the James fund if he could. He had written James two years before, "The will-power to work to pay old debts is rare, & I can only hope that I may learn to practice close economy for that."[119] In early December 1909, he wrote of their latest plan to James:

> we hope to do enough . . . in early spring to enable us to rent the house and put up a small bungalow for ourselves out of the first year's rent, then out of the *second* year's rent to put up a little farmhouse, so as to be able to *rent the farm*. . . . Meantime some kind of a railway will certainly come ere long. . . . That railway will enable us to **Sell Lots** and when we can do that,—having the finest site in the whole valley—we can begin to think of reciprocity. Meantime, the house is more habitable than it was & I indulge in hopes of pulling Juliette through the winter alive,—a dream that would have been madness before. If I do what rejoicing there will be along about Decoration Day![120]

Some improvements were made to the house to make it more attractive: two large verandas with concrete floors and a pebblestone facing for the ground floor. But by Christmas Day, Peirce was sunk in despair and remorse, perhaps intensified by cancer. He wrote in a painfully forced hand in a letter begun on Christmas Day:

> Dec. 28 I have been suffering horribly for 2 days & am now like a drowned rat. Juliette was also ill last night & it sometimes seems all but hopeless to keep her alive through the winter if it is going to keep on as it has begun—50 [degrees] F[ahrenheit] only attainable for a couple of hours. My ink will freeze in a few days & then what shall I do, I wonder. . . .
> You tell me I don't deserve Juliette. But so far as there is any real meaning in [just] desert, I know but too bitterly,—and it is a bitterness

Peirce's cartoons of Juliette as the bourgeoise Athena. Photograph courtesy of the Harvard University Archives.

that I love,—that I fall further short than any man if possible of deserving any good at all; and I cannot protest against any condemnation that may be visited upon me. . . . I am accustomed to hear and read upon countenances that when I speak of religion people say I am a sham. I am supposed to be a cold blooded hypocrite of the lowest and most disgusting order, but I hardly expected as great a student of psychology & of Religious experiences as you are to class me so. I think there is too much about *desert* in the New Testament. In that respect I can't help thinking that the mother of christianity, Buddhism, is superior to our own religion. . . . [There follows a discussion of the papers James thought were Peirce's best, those on "the Evolution of the Laws of Nature."]

Now I will tell you why I set down all this boastful stuff. It is because I am not only over 70 years of age, but my powers are waning, and my health presents alarming features as to the continuance of sanity; and if I should be cut off before I had done anything to repay all the money that your genius for sympathy and unspeakable goodness has collected for us,—although if Juliette should pull through this winter & complete her work on this house, I firmly believe that will suffice ultimately to refund the money,—yet it is a reason for wanting my system of Logic to pay & . . . there is enough prospect of my book paying for me to wish that there should be something for my friends to say[,] especially if I am dead[,] that will help its sale. . . .

Dec. 30

. . . I am frightfully done up not having had a wink, not a wink of sleep the last two nights, couldn't lie still, bursting with intense disappointment at the results of a sale of books,—books that I loved—but whose sale I hoped was to facilitate Juliette's task of getting the house in disposable condition. It makes me sick, it drives me crazy! I can't dismiss it for an instant. Worst of all, after I had got together all the books I could possibly spare, my poor little girl put in some that I had given her in palmy days, French literature with extravagant bindings. . . .

. . . Indeed I have no employment in writing at all & shant have for 2 years. So it is no wonder that Juliette heartily agrees with you in the matter of my not deserving her. She says that if she has to pick out another husband, it will be *surtout pas un logicien*. And she adds that in this country it ought to be against the law for a young man to take up such a *folâterie de profession* unless he can satisfy the directors of the Society for the Prevention of Cruelty to Donkeys that he has money enough to hold out till he is 90 & at any rate he should be debarred from wedlock and be 'exilé à une léproserie jusqu'à le rétablissement de sa santé morale!'[121]

William James died in August 1910, leaving Peirce without the company of his one great friend, although James's goodwill lived on in the Peirce fund, which went on without him. Peirce had taken the name Santiago (St. James) in May 1909, and thereafter often styled himself Charles Santiago Sanders Peirce.[122]

Peirce's terrible remorse led him, in his last few years, to a search for the causes of his self-destruction. His search focused on the type of biological determinism proposed by Cesare Lombroso and Francis Galton, in their time considered revolutionary in their social reform programs. In 1892, he had written that the evidence of Lombroso's "and a half dozen physiologists'" experiments clearly established that criminality was inherited and that, in the sensational case he referred to, the criminal

cannot be made to suffer. He is incapable of any but a low degree of that sensation. It is only his poor mother & sister that this insensate rage of the million really reaches! These poor women, who have been able to resist the poison of hereditary criminality,—why should the howling mob of New York trample over their hearts? If ever there was a case calculated to bring home to a tender and Christian heart the iniquity of our punishments, it is this one. . . . [123]

Three years before his death, it was to the poison of biological inheritance that Peirce looked in large part to find the causes for his own flaws. Where Lombroso looked for heavy brows, prognathous jaws, lowered ears, and other evidence of atavisms, Peirce searched his ancestors and found evidence of "three mental twists": an unusual number of mathematicians, a characteristic which he felt led to unorthodox religious views; a fatal attraction to violent controversy, of which he found several extreme examples among his ancestors; and an exaggerated sensibility, for which he blamed his failure of moral self-control.[124] He tried to find out if mathematicians showed an unusual propensity for insanity. Lacking from this account (which is, however, truncated in the original), and all the other attempts he made to explain himself to others, his family and James excepted, is mention of his battle with trigeminal neuralgia, which, because his father suffered from it, too, Peirce probably believed was inherited. Lacking as well is any mention of his left-handedness, to which he attributed "one of the most extreme and most lamentable of my incapacities . . . my incapacity for linguistic expression."[125] That Peirce should seek genetic flaws to explain his wrongheaded behavior was consistent with his view of instinct as a physical expression of the community of mind and nature, but it is also characteristically lacking in moral and psychological insight. He probably thought so badly of himself that, for him, the only adequate explanation for his consistent and disastrous failure of moral self-control and lack of common sense, despite his best intentions, was the poison of biology.

It was two years later, in the summer of 1913, that Peirce, as he bleakly surveyed the accusing wreck of his life, wrote on the title page of the novel *La Grande Marnière* that its hero, the reckless inventor Marquis Honoré de Clairefont, who had so "shamefully squandered all" and brought his family "to the verge of utter ruin," was "C. S. P. to a dot."

In the same year, Royce gave a series of four lectures on Peirce's philosophy, the outcome of his intense study of the papers of 1867 and 1868, called "Perception, Conception and Interpretation," "The Will to Interpret," "The World of Interpretation," and "The Doctrine of Signs." These were included in the second volume of *The Problem of Christianity*, which Royce sent to Peirce late that summer as an expression of his sense of fellowship and respect. Royce was brought to Peirce's triads because of his lifelong study of Hegel:

> Peirce's concept of interpretation defines an extremely general process, of which the Hegelian dialectical triadic process is a very special case.

Hegel's elementary illustrations of his own processes are ethical and historical. Peirce's theory of comparison is quite as well illustrated by purely mathematical as by explicitly social instances. There is no essential inconsistency
between the logical and psychological motives which lie at the basis of
Peirce's theory of the triad of interpretation [firstness, secondness,
and thirdness] and the Hegelian interest in the play of thesis, antithesis,
and higher synthesis. But Peirce's theory, with its explicitly empirical origin
and its very exact logical working out, promises new light upon matters
which Hegel left profoundly problematic.[126]

Peirce was deeply grateful for this extraordinary and knowledgeable
praise from his one real student. He replied in a letter which Royce received
in time to read to his seminar with a pride that his students and colleagues
could not have understood, and to report what few of Peirce's peers were
ever able to claim: "my interpretation of him gained, on the whole his
approval."[127] That fall, between October 14 and November 16, Peirce, still
moving along his pedestrian way though deeply depressed and a little awry
and petulant with age, wrote the historian Frederick Adams Woods, author
of *Heredity in Monarchs*, a long letter in a spidery hand about the
methodeutic of history, himself, his system, and, again, instinct as biologically determined. He asked why we should have faith in our beliefs and
pointed in answer, as he had done now for ten years, to the instinct of
guessing:

> Any race of animals that has subsisted for ten millennia or more must
> have had instincts of reasoning that have been marvellously near right so
> far as their purposes were guided by them in reference to matters vital to
> them.
> Therefore, since animals themselves cannot discern the strangeness of
> their own instincts, and must regard the dictates of their own instincts as
> matters of course, it would be the height of folly for them to try to act
> contrary to their impulses even if they could. Of course, they never can; but
> equally of course they must, all of them, exercize a certain amount of self
> restraint,—though probably the lower races are not conscious of doing so.
> Such animals as the horse and dog and various birds plainly are conscious
> of it. That is what we call 'conscience.'
> Their instincts however become modified by experience and man's
> most rapidly.
> The sexual instinct has evidently been much weakened in human be-
> ings and is destined to become in time quite an exceptional passion. The
> suffragette movement is an evident sign of this; for what real womanly
> woman would not prefer her way of ruling to theirs?
> But what concerns the present study is that our instinctive guesses

must be presumed to tend toward the fulfillment of the ends of our being (whatever that instinctive phrase may mean, since otherwise, . . . we cannot escape our doom.[128]

Between 1911 and 1914, in a desperate and pathetic effort to make Arisbe more salable as a "fashionable inn, clubhouse or sanitarium," the Peirces added a rickety, gable-roofed third story, which was never finished in Charles's or Juliette's lifetime, though she did eventually make the exterior weathertight. The addition lacked room partitions, floors, or ceilings, but it was very large, and in property descriptions it was represented as suitable for a ballroom or a solarium.[129]

During the last few years of Peirce's life, Mary Pinchot and her son Gifford did as much as they could to make life easier for them, as this letter of Peirce's to Gifford shows, written in December 1913:

> My dear Gifford:
> If I would not too seriously interfere with your purposes, you would do Juliette and me whatever benefit there may be in prolonging our lives if you could let us have Myer, the carpenter for a few days, not more than a week. I want to get us into well-warmed rooms; for it has suited certain persons to prevent our getting workmen; and our best man died suddenly, after we had waited long for him. Juliette is in consequence in a dangerous condition, and I get incipient pleurisy at every cold snap. . . . [130]

Peirce's last letter was written on January 7, 1914, to thank Mary Pinchot for a Christmas basket of food:

> Your magnificent present gladdened us greatly. The basket itself was a delight to her; for she always had a passion for beautiful baskets, and this was a stunning one, and in really good taste. As for the contents, though the few days have not sufficed for sampling yet any large part of it all, we can only say that we have, each of us, found what was most delightful in it. She has found some specially fine prunes; and I have been in a state which nothing could seem so good as peppermints of which there are a large box on which I have made inroads with benefit. . . .
> The progressive movement has, at least, had a very salutary effect on the Republican party,—and a much needed one. It seems that Roosevelt's South American trip must do good. As for the President [Wilson], he has done much better than I anticipated. In *principle*, I am a strong Democrat but the actual party is awful. I wish there were some way of diminishing the actual number of absolutely silly votes.
> As for female suffrage, no doubt women are about as fit for it as the men,—or say, no more unfit. . . . But I don't believe that, in the mass, they desire it, or ought to desire it; and in this country I think they have all the

influence they need desire. In the great mass your sex is so much better than ours, and does what it undertakes in so superior a fashion, that the only question to my mind is whether it will ever desire to cast votes. . . . [131]

On March 15, he wrote the last fragment of his semeiotic, still intent on the expiation of his sins by doing the work God gave him to do:

The doctrine of reasoning here outlined is the result of an inquiry conducted most carefully during more than 50 years of the author's life.

Like every other person who has made any considerable contribution to Logic, the science of reasoning, I have found it practically impossible to convey a clean cut idea of my results without some modifications in the meanings of some of the received terminology on the subject. . . . [132]

With a distant grief, I muse about this tragic life—about the pain; the folly; the failed great ambitions; the immense and exacting labors; the unrelenting search for truth; the great loyalty of his friends; the blindness of his enemies; the power, the prescience, the care for truth, and the startling beauty of his philosophical creation. I wish to believe that, at the end, Peirce experienced for himself that community of nature and mind, *il lume naturale*—the direct experience of the "triune Real"—that his doctrine of ideal-realism made the real test of his lifelong passionate search, but I think not; he was too filled with pain, remorse, and despair. Charles S. Peirce finally grew silent at 9:30 on the evening of Sunday, April 19, 1914. His body was cremated, and the ashes were placed in a silver urn that Juliette kept on the drawing-room mantlepiece until her lonely death twenty years later in circumstances her doctor described as "not suitable to sustain life or dignify death."[133] His nephew Benjamin Peirce Ellis wrote on a newspaper clipping of Peirce's obituary, published in Boston on the following day, "He loved & hated & quarrelled with almost everyone he came in contact with, wives, relatives, & associates."[134] His brother Herbert wrote their sister Helen two days later about "Charley's native sweetness and great ability" and recalled "that life which had so great promise but the memory of what it might have done. Of the sweetness of his nature and his affectionate impulses you and I almost alone can have any very close associations."[135]

Juliette did not immediately retire into the life of a recluse. She and Royce together arranged for the gift of Peirce's papers and books to the Harvard department of philosophy, for which she received a few hundred dollars. During the First World War and immediately thereafter, she became much involved in activities supporting the cause against the hated *Bosch*. Mary Pinchot died during the war, leaving her without the company of her closest friend. The Milford *Dispatch* reported on July 18, 1918, that

Charles Sanders Peirce in his deathbed, April 19, 1914. The portrait on the wall is of their favorite dog, Zola. Photograph courtesy of the Pike County Historical Society.

Mrs. Juliette Peirce of Westfall Township is again in Port Jervis telling fortunes with the famous pack of cards that belonged to one of the ladies of Napoleon's court and will be located at the store room near the entrance to The New Theatre, for a limited time, as her services are in much demand in other places. Every cent received goes for war relief work. Mrs. Peirce last year told fortunes with her unique cards here and in Port Jervis and realized a substantial sum for Red Cross work. The past winter she spent in Cambridge, Mass., as the guest of Mrs. William James, widow of Prof. James of Harvard University, who was a close friend of the late Prof. Peirce. While in Cambridge, she told fortunes for the benefit of war relief work, and was very successful, so much so that there is a strong demand for her return. One of her patronesses in Cambridge was Mrs. Frances Sayre, daughter of Woodrow Wilson.

Although Juliette continued to visit her few friends, such as Alice James (who died in 1923), very occasionally and to involve herself more and more eccentrically in Milford affairs until two years before her death, within a few years heart trouble and her own wish kept her in the house filled with the memories and mementos of her beloved and brilliantly failed husband, the tragic man who had so fascinated her and whom she had always loved to distraction. She continued to build onto Arisbe according to his plans, never finishing what she began, and tried without success to interest Yale University in taking on the house after her death, perhaps with the touching fantasy of making it a monument to Charles. By the time of her death on October 4, 1934, the condition of the house and grounds had so degenerated that there were no sanitary facilities, no running water, and no heat. The trees and shrubs around the house, many of them French lilacs, had grown into a high and tangled thicket so dense that the house could not be seen from the county road fifty feet away, as if conspiring to hide Arisbe and its ruined hopes from the world forever. Juliette was buried with her husband's ashes in the Milford graveyard.

Juliette died intestate, though she intended to leave everything to Gifford Pinchot, who with his wife Cornelia had been considerate and helpful to her over the years since her husband's death. Pinchot arranged for an administrator and paid for her funeral and debts. His attorney wrote Yale, Harvard, and Columbia, with negative responses, to discover if they had any interest in Peirce's remaining books, papers, and instruments. The attorney also arranged for an auction on November 27, 1934, of the belongings; he expressed his surprise at the emptiness of the house, which contained, with the exception of the two fully furnished living rooms, in addition to a few other pieces of furniture and a set of china and silver, only what remained of Peirce's instruments, books, and papers in the library. The second and third floors were almost completely empty. The library contained "two or three cases of French novels and standard works and two or three cases of his scientific works. . . . There are also quite a number of scientific instruments," all of which were reserved, along with the silverware (marked "P") and a portrait of Peirce, from public sale.[136] At the auction, Pinchot bought a few odds and ends and the French novels, which were taken to Grey Towers, for $50. The residents of Milford bought the china, the furniture, and whatever miscellaneous items appealed to them, including what is known as the Cuddeback Letter Book, a small but tantalizing collection of Peirce's correspondence from 1859 and 1860, which contains letters from his early loves and is now in the collection of the Pike County Historical Society in Milford. The house then stood vacant for two years and was thoroughly vandalized before it was auctioned at a sheriff's sale for $3,600 in 1936. The new owner, after trying to interest whomever he could in what was left of the debris of the Peirces' life, burned it all in the front yard.

6

The Wasp in the Bottle

Josiah Royce called him "poor Peirce," and it is easy to understand his pity. At the same time, Royce admired Peirce deeply for his philosophical accomplishments and contributed, along with James, Pinchot, Lodge, and others, to the Peirce fund. None of these men could fathom Peirce's character, and Peirce, too, found himself mysterious. He drafted a letter in November 1904 for Judge Francis Russell of Chicago, his most fervent admirer and promoter, in which he tried to explain himself. It was Russell who, in the summer of 1890, had convinced Paul Carus, editor of *The Monist*, to solicit papers from Peirce for that journal, thereby initiating a fruitful but turbulent twenty-year connection. At the time of the letter, Russell was on *The Monist*'s editorial board and had arranged for Peirce to write five articles on pragmaticism, his revised version of the pragmatism of the "Illustrations of the Logic of Science" published in the *Popular Science Monthly* a quarter-century before. Because of Peirce's illnesses, only three of the five appeared, from April to October 1905. This intriguing, diffident, but entirely serious assessment of his intellect and work is one of very few such thoughtful self-examinations; it is more perceptive than most and, consequently, is worth analyzing at length:

> As to what you say about me, pretty seriously, strictly *sub rosa* I hold that a man of 65 well read in philosophy & a thinker himself must be a precious fool or be able to place himself better than anybody else can do, and I place myself somewhere about the real rank of Leibniz. Of course, Leibniz had the advantage of coming to a field into which no reapers had come. But what I want to say which is more practical, is that I am by nature most inaccurate, that I am quite exceptional for almost complete deficiency of imaginative power, and whatever I amount to is due to two things, first, a perseverance like that of a wasp in a bottle & 2nd to the happy accident that I early hit upon a METHOD of thinking, which any intelligent person could master, and which I am so far from having exhausted it that I leave it about where I found it,—a great reservoir from which ideas of a certain

kind might be drawn for many generations. It is a pity that necessities have prevented my leaving a scholar to take up this method. . . .

P.S. Add to the elements of whatever success I have had that I have [been] always unceasingly exercising my power of *learning new tricks*—to keep myself in possession of the childish *trait* as long as possible. That is an immense thing.[1]

Peirce's letter is particularly important because it was written at a crucial time in his intellectual explorations, when he was more convinced than ever of the extraordinary value of his discovery "by happy accident" almost forty years before of a "METHOD" of thinking which would form the basis of an architectonic system with the power to transfigure philosophical inquiry for generations. At the same time, he was desperately aware of the brief time left to him, at most ten years by his estimate, a time made even shorter by what he knew to be signs of the deterioration of his mind. A year and a half before, in March 1903, the Carnegie Institution had denied his application for a grant to complete and publish his life's work. Two months after that, James used his influence with the Harvard Corporation to enable Peirce to present the outline of his system to a group of interested philosophers in a series of lectures on pragmaticism. That fall, Peirce gave his Lowell Lectures on the same general topic. Either of these exposures might have been the means to bring Peirce into a dialogue with the mainstream of American philosophy, but they did not. James, by his influential disapproval, effectively prevented publication of the Harvard series, and the Lowell Lectures did not mend Peirce's isolation from his peers, because of their oddity to conventional thinkers. This outcome depressed Peirce powerfully. In the early spring of the same year, Peirce had taken two bad falls and was partially paralyzed for a time. A year later, he was so sick "with nervous prostration" that a "whole month was ever after blotted out." Juliette was constantly ill, and they remained very poor. He became steadily more despairing. In the summer of 1905, he wrote James that he was considering suicide because "It is my duty to get out, to make away with myself. . . . a man who can render no service whatever, but is simply a bore and a nuisance ought to be gone."[2]

At the same time, he knew that he was in the midst of the great work of his life, the God-given duty to bring together and justify his immense philosophical labors. In his thoroughgoing realist reconstruction of his system, he rid his early pragmatism of the "baleful influence" of nominalism which was "false in all its shades and degrees," and he also undertook at the same time what he believed to be the proof of pragmaticism.[3] Closely connected to his revision of pragmatism was his reconstruction of Kant's *Kritiks* in his own *critical common-sensism*. In the letter to Russell, he had also written that he was sending on "his latest on the classification of the Sciences," a project which he believed would provide the structure of the whole of inquiry. He was deeply involved in the study and clarification of phenomenology (which he named *phaneroscopy*, from the Greek for "evident" or "manifest"), an analysis of "prelogical notions" that he had begun in 1902 in his "Minute Logic." He was exploring the possibilities of tychism, the operation of chance; of synechism, the idea of the continuity of the universe; and of "A Neglected Argument for the Reality of God," his justification of scientific theism. Most important, he was bringing his whole system within the framework of his "System of Logic considered as Semeiotic," the realist, triadic, and diagrammatic doctrine of signs, which in our times comes more and more to be judged a profoundly original and important creation. All of these ideas had been with him in some form since 1867 and even earlier. Nor were these a majority of the difficult subjects with which he wrestled fruitfully in these years.

It is in the context of this teeming and germinal universe of signs that Peirce's ranking of himself with Leibniz—and Aristotle—must be considered. Ten years before, the German logician Schröder had written to Carus that Peirce's "fame would shine like that of Leibniz or Aristoteles into all the thousands of years to come."[4] Almost thirty years before, the British mathematician W. K. Clifford had ranked him with Aristotle and Boole.[5] In 1909, five years after his letter to Russell, Peirce expanded on his own assessment of his worth in a draft letter intended perhaps for President Abbott Lawrence Lowell of Harvard University, writing that it had become a

> matter of so much concern to me to know just what my comparative powers of logic are that I have taken the utmost pains to estimate them correctly, and neither too high nor too low. Now I am well acquainted & deeply read in the whole literature of the subject in the widest sense & have so carefully studied the question that personally concerns me, that I feel sure I can have made no great mistake about it; and the only writers known to me who are in the same rank as I are Aristotle, Duns Scotus, and Leibniz, the three greatest logicians in [my] estimation, although some of the most important points escaped each. Aristotle was a marvelous man in many other directions; a great writer, a great zoologist, a great psychologist, a profound sociologist, and a very able practical politician. I only compare myself to him in respect to logical powers. Leibniz, too, was a sublime mathematician, as well as very able in all that concerns politics and jurisprudence. But I consider him only as a logician.[6]

Clifford, Schröder, and Peirce himself all limited their evaluations to Peirce's work in logic. While this narrow appreciation of his work was appropriate, it is misleading. For Peirce, logic, or semeiotic, was the means to meaning, the logic of science. It was the structure of thought, since all thought is in signs, and all knowledge was represented by it, regardless of the field of inquiry. Peirce could, therefore, present himself as modest—"I only compare myself to him [Aristotle] in respect to logical powers."—while hiding his mature purpose and ambition, as he had expressed them when approaching fifty,

> to make a philosophy like that of Aristotle, that is to say, to outline a theory so comprehensive that, for a long time to come, the entire work of human reason, in philosophy of every school and kind, in mathematics, in psychology, in physical science, in history, in sociology, and in whatever other department there may be, shall appear as the filling up of its details.[7]

Peirce believed that he accurately stated the worth of his pioneering voyages across the abstract worlds of thought. He *did* rank himself with the greatest philosophers of the past, while he freely admitted that he was "a backwoodsman" cutting out a clearing in the seldom-explored universe of signs.[8] His placing himself close to Leibniz had a special meaning. As Fisch has pointed out, Leibniz was an important part of his education in mathematics and logic supervised by his father, and equally important in his development as a thinker.[9] It was probably Leibniz who, though a nominalist himself, led Peirce to realism by way of his idea of mathematical continuity. In two reviews for the *Nation* in 1899, Peirce characterized Leibniz as a philosopher always in process and, like himself, "a writer of papers and not of books":

> The Columbus of the subconscious mind, the discoverer of mechanical energy, the joint discoverer of the differential calculus, and, more than all of these, the great promulgator of the law of continuity (understood by himself to include historical continuity, and, as he was dimly aware, supposing an evolution of all things and all laws from a primal chaos), is a figure to excite the curiosity of thinking men of the present day.[10]

In the second review, Peirce wrote that "Leibniz had more sides than one" and distinguished the extreme nominalism adopted in the *nouvelle monadologie* from the direction later suggested in his differential calculus and writings on continuity. He wrote:

> in philosophy we must regard the law of continuity as most Leibnizian. This principle would at once do away with the isolated monads, and render the extravagant and unverifiable hypothesis of preëstablished harmony superfluous by directly solving the riddle of the transitivity of causation, while it

would form the basis of a philosophy in deepest unison with the ideas of the last half of the nineteenth century.[11]

In a draft of what would become his third essay in the 1905 series for *The Monist* on pragmaticism, Peirce underlined his identification of himself with Leibniz when he pointed out that Leibniz had written his most nominalistic piece at the same age, thirty-eight, that he had written "How to Make Our Ideas Clear," whose "principal positive error is its nominalism."[12] Fisch wrote that,

> while accepting without change scarcely any of his positive doctrines, Peirce identified himself more closely with Leibniz than with any other thinker; that among the many grounds for the identification was that Leibniz alone of the great philosophers was mathematician, logician, historian, and physical scientist as well as metaphysician; and that not the least ground was that Peirce saw prefigured in Leibniz, as in no other philosopher, his own progress from nominalism to realism.[13]

While Peirce saw himself as the equal of Aristotle in his claim to the authorship of a great realist system of thought, he saw himself as Leibniz's close, even intimate, philosophical kin. In his careful criticisms of them both and of Duns Scotus and Kant, Hegel, Berkeley, and Reid, all of whom he considered his most important predecessors, lay his claim to the superiority of his own work to theirs. However, insisting as he did on the vitality of the community of inquirers, he was careful to point out all the ways in which his work grew out of theirs and would have been impossible without it. While Peirce's claim to rank with Aristotle as a systematic thinker remains (and will remain) controversial, his identification of himself with Leibniz as a thinker of the same sort and rank is unassailable.

Peirce placed the origin of his own achievement in the happy accident of his early hitting upon "a METHOD of thinking." At first glance, the method he referred to was pragmatism, the method for the clarification of concepts, but on second thought the matter is not so simple, because Peirce wrote that he had come to pragmatism " . . . from a logical and non-psychological study of the essential nature of signs."[14] This description of the method's origins leads to the year 1867, ten years before the announcement of the pragmatic maxim (without the label), and to his "central achievement, the paper of May 14th of that year, 'On a New List of Categories.' "[15] The three categories, quality (later flavor), relation (later reaction), and representation (later mediation), provided the ground for his division of signs into three kinds, icons (at first, likenesses), indices, and symbols. These three categories became the basis for the hierarchical generation of further triads of signs, each of which embodied the characters of the first three categories. That this dialectic of the hierarchies of signs was continuous, Peirce made clear in another paper of the same year, "Upon Logical Comprehension and Extension," when he wrote, "A philosophical distinction emerges gradually into consciousness; there is no moment in history before which it is altogether unrecognized, and after which it is perfectly luminous."[16] Such a description appears distant from the pragmatic notion "That everything is to be tested by its practical results [which] was the great text of my early papers."[17]

Just what, then, did Peirce mean by his method of thinking "which any intelligent person could master . . . a great reservoir from which ideas of a certain kind might be drawn for many generations"? First of all, it was not so easy to master, a fact which puzzled him and often misled him into believing that his readers would have no difficulty in following his arguments. Such was his mistake in assuming in 1887 that his correspondence school in logic would be a great moneymaker. He continued, as well, to insist, despite its consistent rejection by publishers, that his arithmetic—his "new Math"— would make him and his heirs millionaires. Even his beloved and only true friend, William James, himself no slouch as a philosopher, never understood him and remarked, characteristically, of the Harvard lectures given in 1903:

> They are wonderful things—I have read the second one twice—but so original, and your categories are so unusual to other minds, that, although I recognize the region of thought and the profundity and reality of the level on which you move, I do not yet assimilate the various theses in the sense of being able to make use of them for my own purposes. I may get to it later; but at present even first-, second-, and third-ness are outside of my own sphere of practically applying things, and I am not sure even whether I apprehend them as you mean them to be apprehended. I get, throughout your whole business, only the sense of something dazzling and imminent in the way of truth ["flashes of brilliant light relieved against Cimmerian darkness"!]. This is very likely partly due to my mind being so non-mathematical, and to my slight interest in logic; but I am probably typical of a great many of your auditors . . . —so my complaint will be theirs. You spoke of publishing these lectures, but not, I hope, *tels quels*. They need too much mediation, by more illustrations, at which you are excellent (non-mathematical ones if possible), and by a good deal of interstitial expansion and comparison with other modes of thought. . . . [18]

Thirty-five years before, James had expressed the same kind of confusion about Peirce's *Journal of Speculative Philosophy* articles, writing, "They are exceedingly bold, subtle and incomprehensible, and I can't say that his vocal elucidations help me a great deal to their understanding, but they nevertheless interest me strangely."[19] James was right when he said that few thinkers understood Peirce, and that they, by implication, were probably mathematicians and logicians. Yet the latter, who were impressed by his mathematics and logic, did not comprehend and generally were not interested in his philosophy. When Royce, who was neither, finally understood what Peirce was about at the turn of the century, it was because he had returned to Peirce's papers of 1867 and 1868 and found there the mathematical and logical basis of Peirce's dialectical system. Unlike James, Royce was able to learn his way around in Peirce's architectonic and to transform his own late work with that knowledge. He was probably the only philosopher to so grasp the kernel of Peirce's method of thinking in Peirce's lifetime. In the letter to Russell, Peirce wrote, "It is a pity necessities have prevented my leaving a scholar to take up the method." By happy accident, because of his life-long study of Hegel's triadic dialectic and his recognition of its great problems, Royce became that single scholar, whose sense of the great value of Peirce's philosophy and of his own indebtedness to Peirce led him to arrange for the transfer of Peirce's manuscripts and annotated and interleaved books to Harvard University and so to save them from oblivion.

Also in the letter to Russell, Peirce stated that he was "by nature most inaccurate," and that he was "quite exceptional for almost complete deficiency of imaginative power." This description of himself was constant, beginning with his youthful characterization of his method of thinking as "pedestrianism," which he defined at twenty-five as the reduction "of all our actions to logical processes so that to do anything is but to take another step in the chain of inference."[20] Of this sort of thinking, James wrote Peirce, "Your mind inhabits a technical logical thicket of its own which no other mind has as yet penetrated."[21] At the same time, James also judged Peirce's thinking as "so original" and as moving on a level of profundity and reality. Peirce resolved the apparent contradiction by characterizing the effect of his left-handedness as giving the impression of originality, while it was in fact a neurological peculiarity that "betrays itself also in my ways of thinking. Hence, I have always labored under the misfortune of being thought 'original'. . . . my mental left-handedness makes me express myself in a way that to a normal mind seems almost inconceivably awkward."[22] Tied to this diagnosis that he did not use his brain the way the mass of people do because of his left-handedness was his conviction that it also was the cause of "One of the most extreme and most lamentable of my incapacities . . . my incapacity for linguistic expression."[23] At the same time, his highly developed talent for diagrammatic expression was demonstrated throughout his work and especially in his existential and other graphic representations, whose purpose was to present a moving image of thought. His writing was the medium in which he awkwardly and laboriously embodied the abstract world he constantly explored. Because his "METHOD" was so clear to him, he never understood why others could not master it.

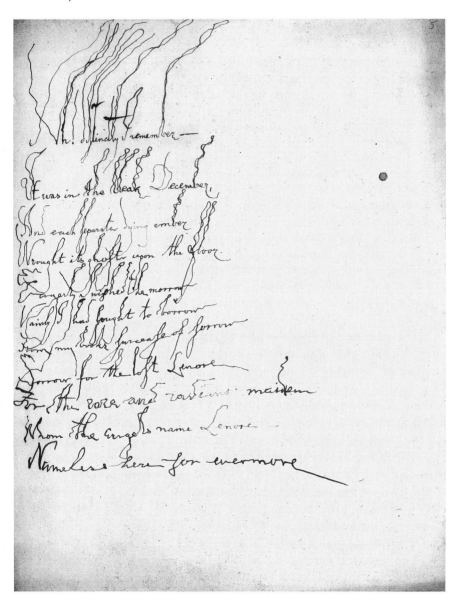

An example of Peirce's chirography: Poe's "The Raven." Photograph courtesy of the Harvard University Archives.

Peirce was not being modest when he claimed to be devoid of "imaginative power." One side of this apparently eccentric assertion is that he knew he did not possess the poetic imagination exemplified by Shakespeare or Rabelais, two of the men of letters he prized most. Peirce did try his hand at verse occasionally; this punning sonnet, perhaps a description of a marine painting by Whistler, is interesting only because Peirce wrote it:

No mental eyes of erst e'er hads't thou shone;
Thy entailed gnomon had not splayed as prone;
Not, at all, fact borne ideas sprayed as grown,
Nor Man as halo'd tower of nature Known.
Thy fearful lift's bed rock stepped arbor type—
Sight bearing wake's upholding spinelike gripe,
In the last inhauling hall o' the endstead, down
Where glues the gloomy swipe of night's tar frown
And stays the rathe of day's eclipse, where lone,
The moon gropes round in purblind monotone,
For there her tender stars are dark as stone—
Now from that indrawn earth's sky-gauging billow
Sees out about, through art tied back, they cone,
Whose spread of insight beam far round out-thrown
With wake each slippery rising peak doth crown
Pale as the pallors tip this pile o' pillow.[24]

The other side of Peirce's claim to lack imaginative power was a consequence of his theory of hypothetic inference, or abduction. When Peirce said that he was "always unceasingly exercising my power of *learning new tricks* to keep myself in possession of the *childish* trait as long as possible," he was referring to what he called the Play of Musement, and what Schiller had called *Spieltrieb*. In this play, the Muser does not create by the force of imaginative power but, instead, experiences an aspect of reality represented in a sign and guesses at its meaning by means of the instinct of hypothesis embodied in the community of mind and nature. Hypothetic inference, born in the Play of Musement, with its subsequent deduction of conceivable consequences and the testing of these by means of induction—the logic of science—is a strong candidate for the "METHOD of thinking, which any intelligent person could master." Certainly, James understood that method clearly enough, and that was not the source of his problem. That lay in "the technical logical thicket . . . into which no other mind has as yet penetrated."

There, too, lies the "METHOD of thinking" where Royce found and mastered it in Peirce's papers of 1867 and 1868. What follows is a brief summary of the "thicket," intended to demonstrate just how difficult it is to penetrate and know. Peirce held that all thought is in signs and capable of being diagrammed, and his categories may be taken to constitute what he considered to be the essential diagram of reality, the mathematics of experience. Because of his father, Benjamin's, convictions about reality, from Peirce's youth onward, mathematics and logic were intimately related as disciplines, with the former holding the status of the most fundamental science. At first, his father's definition of mathematics as the science of drawing necessary conclusions sufficed for him, but by the time of his letter to Russell, he had broadened his definition to mean that mathematics was the science of what is true of hypothetical states of things reduced to forms of relation which are themselves abstractions: that is, to diagrams such as $1 + 1$ (without the apples). As Houser has pointed out, so broad is this definition that it will include *any* attempt to find deductively what follows from a given hypothesis as a mathematical inquiry, so long as it is abstracted from all accidental attachments.[25]

Abstract forms of relation are objects of a mathematical inquiry called the logic of relations (or relatives), which Peirce began to examine in 1870 with his "Description of a Notation for the Logic of Relatives." By 1885 he had proposed, in what Hans Herzberger has called "Peirce's remarkable theorem," that there are only three fundamental kinds of relations: monadic, dyadic, and triadic; that by combining triads, all relations of a greater number than three can be generated; and that all those of a greater number than three can be reduced to triads.[26] Since, in addition, triads cannot be reduced to dyads, nor dyads to monads, monads, dyads, and triads constitute the fundamental categories of relations. At the same time, triads are made up of dyads and monads, and dyads of monads. Hence, in logical order, monads are first, dyads second, and triads third, which gives a second group of relations: first, second, and third. Hypostatic abstraction provides a third group of relations: firstness, secondness, and thirdness, which contain first, second, and third, which in their turn contain monads, dyads, and triads. Altogether, these elements constitute the abstract, formal mathematical categories and relations that constitute the elements of thought.

These mathematical relations themselves underlie the "New List of Categories," quality, relation, and representation (mediation), which provide the basis for Peirce's division of signs into icons, indices, and symbols; of symbols into terms, propositions, and arguments; and of arguments into hypothesis (abduction), induction, and deduction. Each triad manifests the original relations. Peirce generated many more such trinities, of which the following are a further illustration of his architectonic: of semeiosis (sign function) into sign, object, and interpretant; of semeiotic (equivalent to logic, since all thought is in signs) into speculative grammar, critic, and methodeutic; of philosophy into phenomenology, normative science, and metaphysics; of normative science into aesthetics, ethics, and logic; of consciousness into feeling-qualities, sense of reaction, and sense of generalization; of cosmogony into mind, matter, and evolution; of evolution into chance, law, and habit-taking; and of metaphysics into Firstness, Secondness, and Thirdness, representing the three universes of Idea, Brute Actuality, and the Sign's Soul. Several times Peirce thought he must be mistaken in his commitment to the triadic structure of thought, admitting that he suffered from "triadomany," and tried to disprove the reality of the categories, but he was brought back each time ineluctably to his trinities.[27] Here, indeed, is the "technical logical thicket" into which James and many others have never yet penetrated.

The "METHOD of thinking," then, is the generation of other relations from the three original relations so that their distinct characteristics remain manifest in each subsequent appearance. An impression of the characteristics of these relations may be given by simple diagrams. A dot [.] will constitute firstness, two dots [•—•] secondness, and three dots [△] thirdness, so that the single dot represents the monad or quality, the two dots represent the dyad or relation, and the three dots the triad or mediation. Complexity can be expressed in terms of the triad by taking each dot to represent firstness. Then as, say, three people look at one another, each is simultaneously first, second, and third, depending upon the point of view. Peirce's claim that all relations greater than these can be reduced to or generated from triads may be illustrated by adding dots indefinitely to the triangle [. •—△, etc]. Thinking then takes on the quality of an infinite dialectic reminiscent of that of Hegel.

The effort to understand Peirce on the categories sometimes gives one the giddy feeling of learning how to waltz—ONE, two, three; ONE, two three; ONE, two, three. . . . The broken repetition of rhythm also resembles the mechanical gait of an insect (perhaps a wasp?). But, finally, the sheer beauty of the dancing categories evokes nothing so much as the chaotic and recursive fractal images of Benoit Mandelbrot plunging deeply into the microcosm and always reflecting lovely and minutely differing variations of themselves. There is also a close similarity to the dancing trinities of Christian and Hindu theology, a connection which Peirce recognized. For example, in the Christian Trinity, God the Father is Firstness, God the Son is Secondness, and God the Holy Ghost is Thirdness.

Peirce had realized ten years before James complained about the "technical logical thicket" that he was not creating an audience for his ideas. His *Monist* articles of 1891–93 were designed to remedy that lack by presenting them in a popular and literary manner. In "The Architecture of Theories," he gave dramatic guise to the triad of metaphysical relations he there called Firstness, Secondness, and Thirdness. Although Peirce was no poet, he was a dramatist whose imagination was profoundly influenced by Shakespeare, and he set forth his metaphysics as vast cosmological theater. Of interest to the biographer, he also found characteristic qualities of human behavior in the categories which embodied the everlasting struggle to overcome the hard resistance of events with rational purpose. Peirce stated his definitions simply and elaborated them vividly:

> First is the conception of being or existing independent of anything else. Second is the conception of being relative to, the conception of reaction with, something else. Third is the conception of mediation, whereby a first and second are brought into relation.[28]

Firstness is the chaos of sense experience before it is thought about. It is original, fresh, immediate, spontaneous, and it cannot be articulately thought or asserted, since articulation implies otherness and assertion implies negation of something else.

> Stop to think of it, and it has flown! What the world was to Adam on the day he opened his eyes to it, before he had drawn any distinctions, or had become conscious of his own existence—that is first, present, immediate, fresh, new, initiative, original, spontaneous, free, vivid, [un]conscious, evanescent. Only, remember that every description of it must be false to it.[29]

Firstness is monadic, and it is necessarily a vague concept. How can we be anything but vague about what cannot be thought? By vagueness, Peirce meant lack of definition or the quality of unformedness, and specifically denied that by Firstness he meant the One:

> By the First, I do not at all mean the One, of which Parmenides spoke, which is a synthetizing unity or whole. I am thinking simply of what presents itself as first, immediate, fresh. . . . The moment that freshness is distinctly asserted, it has lost its innocence.[30]

Firstness can only be known to have been experienced, and Peirce did not tell us how we can recognize it, only that we do.

Secondness is existence independent of oneself, otherness, opposite, the dyad; it is the necessary quality in existence which brings about struggle. Peirce called it "Brute Actuality":

We find secondness in occurrence, because an occurrence is something whose existence consists in our knocking up against it. A hard fact is of the same sort; that is to say, it is something which is there, and which I cannot think away, but am forced to acknowledge as an object or second beside myself, the subject or number one, and which forms material for the exercise of my will.[31]

Fate with its sure result is second; *chance* with its irregular manifoldness is *first*. Conflict involves a second; *duel* is dual. So with negation, as a kind of conflict; and lying *(duplicity)* as a negation of truth.[32]

While the monadic quality of Firstness is mere potentiality of what could be and is without existence, the dyadic quality of Secondness is mere individual fact which has no generality. Thirdness gives generality by mediating between a first and a second. It is the category which gives meaning and is meaning itself. For the pragmaticist, the meaning of a first and a second is constituted as Thirdness. Meaning is, therefore, purposive because something *will* happen when a first meets a second. Words to describe Thirdness are *mediation, purpose, generality, order, interpretation, representation,* and *hypothesis.* While the absolute present and immediate, unthought, unconscious experience describe Firstness, and existence and the compulsion of external reality, of brute fact, of the blank resistance we find everywhere in our experience—the Outward Clash—describe Secondness, Thirdness is that which mediates between the two and gives meaning, order, law, and generality. Thirdness is the category which brings intelligibility into the Peircean universe by showing where it leads. Thirdness is pragmatism reformed in its real purposiveness by the expulsion of nominalism. It is the idea that Mind moves toward concrete reasonableness in the long run. This brief illustration shows how Peirce's triadic architectonic ranges seamlessly from the most minute to the most immense concepts.

In his letter to Russell, Peirce gave two reasons for his success as a philosopher: one was a METHOD of thinking and the other was "a perseverance like that of a wasp in a bottle." The image he created of himself as an angry wasp trapped in a bottle (perhaps a nearly empty wine bottle) seems wonderfully apt as a description of the Secondness of Peirce's experience of life, but it also has broader meaning. The image clearly expresses the human condition: we are trapped behind a pane of metaphysical glass which we can see through darkly by means of the senses, but which distorts the reality we see glancing beyond it. Peirce's picture of himself as the furious wasp buzzing ominously but impotently about the cramped confines of his pellucid bottle, futilely jabbing at the slick glass with his stinger, pragmatism, in a lifelong attempt to penetrate the riddle and escape with the secret of the universe, only to die humiliated and unrewarded, seems to be no more than a metaphor for the unreasonable state in which we find ourselves. And so it is, but the truth is, too, that the bottle—not the glass—was of Peirce's own manufacture, and his frustration, remorse, and despair were predominantly self-inflicted. His remarkable inability to deal with practical problems, his disastrous relationships with reputable men, his wildly speculative ventures, his adulterous affairs, his misreadings of the intentions of his friends, his failure to publish any major philosophical work in a form other than popular articles (with the single exception of the *Studies in Logic* published jointly with his students at Johns Hopkins in 1883)—in fact, most of the significant events of his life (outside his achievements in science and logic) tend to support the idea that Peirce acted on the basis of misperceptions of a fundamental sort.

I used Baudelaire's concept of the Dandy as that man who heroically creates himself as a perfectly unique being as an aid in understanding Peirce's character. The meaning of the Dandy is identical with the definition of Firstness, for the Dandy is what he is regardless of anything else. He is irresponsible, indifferent of consequences, and impulsive, and his life will show an originality deriving from such qualities. In one place, Peirce defined Firstness in a way reminiscent of the unreasonable and inscrutable Calvinist God:

> It would be something *which is what it is without reference [to] anything else* within it or without it, regardless of all force and of all reason. Now the world is full of this element of irresponsible, free, Originality. Why should the middle part of the spectrum look green rather [than] violet? There is no conceivable reason for it nor compulsion in it. Why was I born in the nineteenth century on Earth rather than on Mars a thousand years ago?[33]

We would expect (though to Peirce it seems to have been a surprise, a form of Second) that the Dandy, mirroring only himself, in his free and irresponsible course would meet with resistance from the external world and experience "Brute Actuality." Peirce met with just such resistance from Eliot, Gilman, Newcomb, Thorn, and other respectable and powerful representatives of conventional society. That part, then, of Peirce's life in which he met with failure after failure was the experience of Secondness. As Peirce wrote, about 1887–1888, with knowing and melancholy introspection:

> In youth, the world is fresh and we seem free; but limitation, conflict, constraint, and secondness generally, make up the teaching of experience. With what firstness
> 'The scarfed bark puts from her native bay;'

with what secondness
'doth she return,
With overweathered ribs and ragged sails.'[34]

The original is from Shakespeare's *The Merchant of Venice:*

All things that are,
Are with more spirit chaséd than enjoyed.
How like a younker or a prodigal
The scarféd bark puts from her native bay,
Hugged and embracéd by the strumpet wind!
How like the prodigal doth she return,
With over-weathered ribs and ragged sails,
Lean, rent, and beggared by the strumpet wind![35]

Peirce's Dandyism was especially manifest in his marriage to his beloved mistress Juliette and in his move to the isolated resort of Milford to establish Arisbe, his 2,000-acre estate, the facade behind which to court his intended patrons, James Pinchot and his Robber Baron cronies, and to convince them to fund his inventions and so make him a millionaire scientist and philosopher. With their fateful collapse, these foolish and reckless actions destroyed the possibility of his leadership in American philosophy and his world leadership in logic, both of which were within his grasp.

Peirce's remarkable achievements in science and philosophy provide a startling contrast to the failures of the Dandy. In his scientific ventures he was remarkably disciplined and productive. In logic he was a self-controlled master. His hypotheses in every field of inquiry were exceptionally original and fruitful. He was a broad-reaching polymath who easily occupied the fields of chemistry, physics, astronomy, geodesy, metrology, cartography, psychology, philology, the history of science, and especially mathematics, phenomenology, logic, and metaphysics. In his 1867 and 1868 papers he was the inventor of a semeiotic whose essential ideas he developed fruitfully over a lifetime of labor and which is still being found to be rich in potential. In these parts of the universe Peirce was at home and powerful. It was in his application of his method of thinking to life that he went awry, in part by confusing the controlled conditions of the laboratory with the chaotic context of the everyday world, but primarily because of his moral blindness. Ironically and unexpectedly, Peirce's blindness lay in his idea, set forth in the "Illustrations," of the practice of science as a community of inquirers using a method that would, "in the long run," approach closer and closer to the Truth. Peirce both formalized what has become the characteristic isolation of science from the great issues of moral life (excepting truth) and expressed the belief in science of its practitioners that it is a special and sacred calling.

For the Peirce of the "Illustrations," the contrast between those within the sacred precincts and those without is even sharper than that dramatized in C. P. Snow's essay *The Two Cultures and the Scientific Revolution*, which described a closed community of scientists whose universe was limited in its consideration of values to that of truth, and which created a scientific culture closely similar to what Apel called Peirce's "logical socialism," in which "the social principle is rooted intrinsically in logic."[36] Individuals, distinct from the community of inquirers, are, for Peirce, unable to find truth in the long run because their mental evolution is simply too short. Furthermore, individuals have no virtue apart from the community of inquirers. In 1868, Peirce had said that "The individual man, since his separate existence [separate from the community of scientific inquirers] is manifested only by ignorance and error, so far as he is anything apart from his fellows, and from what he and they are to be, is only a negation."[37] This drastic denial of the estranged individual's moral authority gives an unexpectedly Calvinist ring to Peirce's ideas about ethics during much of his life, for he believed his own and anyone else's behavior as an individual separate from the congregations of science to be incorrigible. His mother complained of his contempt for convention, but she misunderstood the depth of his alienation. Believing himself incorrigible—like Baudelaire, who knowingly debauched himself, and like the Antinomians of the Reformation, who absolved themselves from God's moral law because all was predestined—he acted as he wished, "indifferent of consequences." And like his Puritan and Quaker ancestors, but with a different moral ideal, at the same time he devotedly and passionately pursued Truth in the company of the elect of the sacred congregations of science, past, present, and future, in their countless generations. Well into his sixties, Peirce was a deeply divided being, unable to unify his Manichaean life because of his insistence on the communal basis of scientific ethics.

Peirce's moral blindness also derived from another source, perhaps even more unexpected—the influence, dating back to his college days, of Henry James, Sr., and his Swedenborgian characterization of evil in *Substance and Shadow*. In 1893, Peirce had already written that it is love's part in the evolution of the universe to overcome evil, and that hatred is misdirected and imperfect love. By 1905, building on the theatrical Swedenborgian universe where God lovingly created evil, Peirce proclaimed as truth the idea that evil must be regarded as one of the "perfections" of the universe, that "God delights in *evil per se*," and that sin itself is God's own creation.[38] Of his own afflictions, he believed that God inflicts pain as a "warning," so that its existence "harmonizes beautifully" with the idea that our universe is one that is very gradually being "worked out."[39] Peirce believed, in a paraphrase of Alexander Pope, that "Whatever is is best" *in the long run.*[40] In 1905 he wrote this opinion of what St. John and the elder James meant for him:

> Thus, the love that God is, is not a love of which hatred is the contrary; otherwise Satan would be a coordinate power; but it is a love which embraces hatred as an imperfect stage of it, an Anteros—yea, even needs hatred and hatefulness as its object. For self-love is no love; so if God's self is love, that which he loves must be defect of love; just as a luminary can light up only that which otherwise would be dark. Henry James, the Swedenborgian, says: 'It is no doubt very tolerable finite or creaturely love to love one's own in another, to love another for his conformity to oneself: but nothing can be in more flagrant contrast with the creative Love, all whose tendernesses *ex vi termini* must be reserved only for what intrinsically is most bitterly negative and hostile to itself.'[41]

This resolution of the problem tended to justify Peirce's Dandyism by trivializing evil. If, as he believed, God loves evil and evil is a necessary part of the working out of the universe by giving love something to do, then doing evil (as well as fighting it and doing good) is justified and necessary. In this uncanny world, it is impossible to decide what good and evil may be or how they might be distinguished. That being so, the moral classification of any action will be ambiguous, since every action is perceived as furthering the evolution of the good. Together with his belief in the moral incorrigibility of the individual acting outside the elect of the congregations of science, this vision of a universe which requires evil to realize itself in the long run is a most intriguing creation, since deceit is necessary for the evolution of the universe toward concrete reasonableness, Peirce's highest goal. Instead of a universe evolving toward a more and more refined *summum bonum,* we find good and evil working harmoniously together in just the way we find them in the evolution of life: a world in which camouflage, mimicry, masquerade, artifice, trickery, snares, and lures provide the guarantee of survival for a multitude of life forms quite as much as does altruism. Ironically, this world is ethically indistinguishable from the tangled bank of Darwinian evolution which Peirce had attacked because it created a world in which "mere mechanical individualism is vastly reenforced as a power for good by the animal's ruthless greed. As Darwin puts it on his title-page, it is the struggle for existence; and he should have added for his motto: 'Every individual for himself and the devil take the hindmost!' "

A metaphysics which encompasses and justifies in one perfectly harmoniously evolving universe the pink crab spider camouflaged in the attractive blossoms of the rose; the orchid which successfully copies the pheromones and genitalia of the female of a species of wasp to accomplish its own fertilization; the astonishingly minnow-like lure of the angler fish; God, Satan, Christ, Buddha, Auschwitz, cancer, and AIDS, is an immensely appealing solution to the problem of evil and pain. That Peirce had a great investment in it is shown by his uncharacteristic (and distinctly unpragmatic) cutting off of inquiry into it by insisting that to presume to define God's purpose was blasphemy.[42] Moreover, because it had provided him, since his twenties, with a desperately needed reason for his afflictions, it gave him the justification he needed to renounce his youthful atheism and to become confirmed in the spiritual safety of the Episcopal church. But, it also encouraged him to behave as he wished indifferent of consequences, because it gave him a thoroughly ambiguous standard of morality that allowed him whatever rationale he chose to give for the life of black mischief he led in the twenty years between Zina's leaving him in 1876 and the failures of all his feckless ventures, leaving him bankrupt and broken at almost sixty years of age. During those years he had squandered his fortune and reputation and was finally coming to realize that he had very likely destroyed his remaining chances for the recognition, and even the survival, of his life's work. Clearly, Peirce's life and thought were two aspects of the same sign, Peirce himself. Each aspect deeply influenced the other, sometimes with disastrous consequences for the man and his work.

The real tragedy of Peirce's life, even greater than his afflictions, was that he constructed the abstract world—the bottle—in which he found himself imprisoned. Despite his own warning that the "endless viaduct" of signs be tested at every step by what is outside its fascinating and mesmerizing capacity to include everything in its dialectial path, pragmatism, like a witch's mirror, reflected an unerringly accurate image of him in every facet. As he wrote in 1854 when he was fifteen:

'Genius is the result of thinking 'till—'till—'till Genius 'till you turn a corner and find yourself in another world. Genius is above reasoning.

and:

'Will Will. . . . ' Fill up the blank with what you will. . . . [43]

Yet, Peirce was an authentic tragic hero, not the hypocrite, degenerate, or clown he was accused of being by many of his powerful peers. The ancient Greeks would surely have accused him of hubris for his intention to discover, reveal, and come away with the secret of things—"the riddle of the Sphynx"—especially for his Prometheus-like claim that he had really escaped with the secret and was about to deliver it to humankind. And Peirce, with his thorough knowledge of Greek mythology, would have appreciated such a legendary characterization as an acute reading of his ambition and fate. In his last few years, he came to recognize in himself both the exceptional man endowed by fate with *areté* and the man who exemplified what Garrison had called the "Defective judgment in worldly affairs . . . you were born with."[44] He wore his afflictions as the badge of his daring and heroism. In pain and its relief lay much of the source of his Dandyism and rebellion (including his early atheism), of his affairs with women, of his cold rages and exaggerated sensibilities and the many nervous breakdowns of his adult life. Therein as well lay the reasons for his marriages to two women to whom he could confess these things and turn for comfort, indulgence, solace, and forgiveness, and whom he often abused, but the builder, almost the creator, of his character was not fate; it was his father.

Benjamin Peirce was brilliant, profound, facile, given to outbursts of towering rage; powerfully attractive, eloquent, and successful; a loving and overwhelming father. The one son who escaped the challenge, Herbert, became a conventionally successful bureaucrat in the Department of State. James Mills, a discreet homosexual, subordinated himself and managed, with the patronage of President Eliot, to live a useful and satisfying life as a mathematician and educator, ending his career as dean of the faculty at Harvard. The two who took up the challenge both failed. Benjamin Mills "burned the candle not only at both ends, but at every other point on its surface." He died at twenty-six, far from home, and likely of syphilis. Charles spent his life trying to surpass his father at his own subtle and demanding calling, the exploration of the abstract. He trained himself to work prodigiously around his neuralgia and left-handedness. Out of his ambition and obsession, and of his work and profound insight, came the method Peirce first called "pedestrianism," which he originally intended to be the means by which he would, step by step, outdistance his adored father and become the genius he was intended to be. Thirteen years of intense effort and refinement produced the triad proposed in "A New List of Categories," and a few years later First, Second, and Third, the dancing categories of his architectonic. Peirce's obsessive development of his categories continued essentially unbroken throughout the mounting follies and misadventures chronicled in this biography. But by 1898, he had run out of tricks and was forced to return to a ramshackle and mortgaged Arisbe, all that remained of his small store of wealth. It was at this nadir of his life that he wrote James in the spring of 1897:

> I have learned a great deal about philosophy in the last few years, because they have been very miserable and unsuccessful years,—terrible

beyond anything that the man of ordinary experience can possibly understand or conceive. . . . Much have I learned of life and the world, throwing strong lights upon philosophy in these years. Undoubtedly its tendency is to make one value the spiritual more, but not an abstract spirituality. . . . [It has] led me to rate higher than ever the individual deed as the only real meaning there is [in] the Concept, and yet at the same time to see more sharply than ever that it is not the mere arbitrary force in the deed but the life it gives to the idea that is valuable.[45]

In this letter, which describes the crux of his life, Peirce introduced the individual as a moral being distinct from the congregations of science. Peirce told James that the misery produced by the frustration of his deepest desires upon the unyielding external world resulted in a kind of mediation. According to the categories, his irresponsible individuality and the world against which he foundered could be mediated only by his conduct. Peirce finally and very painfully understood this. He spent the last fifteen years of his life, in spite of his almost constant sufferings, in self-conscious Christian atonement, working faithfully and fruitfully, with slowly improving deliberate self-control, on aspects of the semeiotic and doing his woefully inadequate best, at the same time, at the time-consuming efforts needed to take care of Juliette and to live a modest, moral life. He took solace in theism and in knowing that he had influenced such philosophers as James, Dewey, and Royce in what he believed was the right way. But he suffered the anguish and remorse of a wasted life, made especially bitter by the loneliness of having no one, except Royce in the last year of his life, with whom to share his philosophical discoveries. The picture of an angry wasp trapped in a bottle accurately expressed the view of himself that led him, in moments of weakness, to consider suicide. Peirce the pragmaticist at length clearly understood what Peirce the pragmatist had not: the method was not enough. He would have to embody, as well as he could, the highest good in his own life, moment by moment.

For the first time, he was able to perceive the individual, and therefore himself, as a moral agent who could act and evolve toward concrete reasonableness on a foundation of internal resources, as well as an external community of inquirers. He said of himself, "For long years I suffered unspeakably . . . from ignorance of how to go to work to acquire sovereignty over myself."[46] His despair and self-loathing finally drove him to change his ways, and by 1905, he was reconstructing the pragmatism of the "Illustrations" of twenty-seven years before so that it would show not only its origin in the doctrine of signs, but its dependence on ethics, the requirement for self-control. He rewrote the original maxim, under the label of pragmaticism, to embody both changes. First he showed its basis in semeiotic:

The entire intellectual purport of any symbol consists in the total of all general modes of rational conduct which, conditionally upon all the possible different circumstances and desires, would ensue upon the acceptance of the symbol.[47]

He then went on to establish what he meant by the maxim's import for ethics, "For it is to conceptions of deliberate conduct that Pragmaticism would trace the intellectual purport of symbols; and deliberate conduct is self-controlled conduct."[48] This moral reconstruction of pragmatism was the direct result of Peirce's recognition of his own folly and the remorse consequent upon it. In 1903, as one of his Lowell Lectures, he developed a triadic proposal for the pragmatistic testing of the moral content of action which in summary required that, after an action has been performed, three self-criticisms take place. The first is a comparison of the conduct with the original resolution, which was a mental formula. We have a memory of the action as an image. How does the image conform to the formula? The second self-criticism asks how the conduct accords with general intentions. The third self-criticism asks how the image of a person's conduct accords with the person's ideals of conduct. Each of these self-criticisms is accompanied by a judgment, which if favorable is felt to be pleasurable.[49]

This proposal seems a practical way to practice deliberate self-control, but it founders on the problem, ancient in its unyielding resistance to reason, of the justification for our ideals of conduct. Almost thirty years before, in "The Fixation of Belief," Peirce had rejected as justification for belief the methods of tenacity (the simple refusal to give up one's beliefs), institutional authority, and natural preferences (derived from assumptions a priori) and replaced them with the method of science. But pragmatism, even reformed as pragmaticism, provides no way to distinguish between the virtue of one consequence and another, except in terms of ever more distant and indistinct consequences, that is, in terms of habit or continuity. To the question, Why should a man choose to remain poor, when by stealing he can be rich? Peirce answered, in a farce he wrote that may have been staged at Grey Towers in 1889, that "honesty is generally a match for plausible roguery in the long run."[50] This was true, Peirce wrote in *The Monist* in 1893, because "progress comes from every individual merging his individuality in sympathy with his neighbors," that is, from a kind of evolutionary sentimentalism which is without ethical basis. Peirce had written James in 1897:

As for morality, it is not a bad thing, taking it in the true evolutionary sense. But it is not everything that evolution results in that is good. Evolution has two results. One is the realization of the dormant idea. That is good. The other is the variation of types. That is indifferent. . . . [51]

Apparently, then, ethics consists in our mutually bringing the dormant potentialities of humanity to full realization, a nineteenth-century version of the eighteenth-century vision of progress which might be called Lamarckian deism since it depends on the inheritance of acquired characteristics, a kind of habit. There is nothing in this view to prevent us from being constant liars, consistent adulterers, or persistent cads, if only we persist long enough. If we murder (an action which we currently call a moral evil) in such a way that the idea of it were to become realized in the long run in a general way—in habit or law—it would become good because it had joined the harmony of the way things have come to be in the long run. This unwanted outcome demonstrates the failure of synechism, the principle of continuity, as the foundation of ethics. For Peirce, synechism was the harmonious principle of the universe brought into being by evolutionary love, his gentle moral agent. It fails for the same reason the Swedenborgian solution to the problem of evil failed, because it cannot provide a way to distinguish good from evil. If the principle governing ethics is harmonious continuity (or generalized habit), *whatever* is, is best in the long run.

Peirce realized he had failed to find a sound basis for good conduct, and he turned in the last few years of his life to the intense study of phaneroscopy (phenomenology), the disinterested analysis of firstness considered as the "prelogical notions" of uninterpreted perception—"honest, single-minded observation of the appearances."[52] This project brought him as close as thinking can to what is beyond thought. It brought him sharply up against the question lying in wait behind *all* the thinking: How do we conduct ourselves when we are faced with what thinking will not solve? Peirce's 1907 proposal in "Guessing" was that instinct tells us how to act:

> Animals of all races rise far above the general level of their intelligence in those performances that are their proper function, such as flying and nest-building for ordinary birds; and what is man's proper function if it be not to embody general ideas in art-creations, in utilities, and above all in theoretical cognition? To give the lie to his own consciousness of divining the reasons of phenomena would be as silly in a man as it would be in a fledgling bird to refuse to trust its wings and leave the nest. . . . *If we knew* that the impulse to prefer one hypothesis to another really were analogous to the instincts of birds and wasps, it would be foolish not to give it play, within the bounds of reason; especially since we must entertain some hypothesis, or else forego all further knowledge than that which we have already gained by that very means.[53]

Peirce pointed out that the founders of modern science gave great, though not decisive, weight to instinctive judgments:

> Galileo appeals to *il lume naturale* at the most critical stages of his reasoning. Kepler, Gilbert, and Harvey—not to speak of Copernicus— substantially rely upon an inward power, not sufficient to reach the truth by itself, but yet by supplying an essential factor to the influences carrying their minds to the truth.[54]

He introduced the idea of a continuity between mind and nature as the ground of instinct by proposing that "It is certain that the only hope of retroductive [hypothetic[reasoning ever reaching the truth is that there may be some natural tendency toward an agreement between the ideas which suggest themselves to the human mind and those which are concerned in the laws of nature."[55]

Peirce came to depend entirely on instinct not only to account for the success of scientific hypotheses, but as the source of the idea of the *summum bonum* as well. For him instinct did not mean the mechanism of inherited behavior except as a degenerate form of it; it meant that Mind is embodied—is instinct—in the physical universe and in us as a part of that. In 1889, he had credited this idea in the *Century Dictionary* to his father as *Ideal-Realism,* "the opinion that nature and the mind have such a community as to impart to our guesses a tendency toward the truth, while at the same time they require the confirmation of empirical science." Peirce's idea of a universal Mind, which included "the communion of mankind" (a transfigured community of scientific investigators), displaced the earlier mathematical ground of synechism with the mystical doctrine, called the *perennial philosophy* by Leibniz to identify the ancient metaphysics that goes back two and a half millennia to Heraclitus and beyond, that Mind (the Real) is itself or through the agency of the sign both immanent and transcendent in the world of nature.[56]

For the late Peirce, who rejected the bewitching Swedenborgian solution to the problem of evil only three years before his death, matter was no longer easily domesticated as "effete mind," a pantheistic notion which contradicts Secondness conceived as "Brute Actuality," and "denies that blind force is an element of experience distinct from rationality, or logical force."[57] He proposed instead "a continuity between the characters of mind and matter, so that matter would be nothing but mind that had such indurated habits as to cause it to act with a peculiarly high degree of mechanical regularity, or routine."[58] Michael L. Raposa suggests that Peirce be called a "*panentheist,* that is, one who views the world as being included in but not exhaustive of the divine reality," a proposal that does not collapse, as pantheism does, the distinction between Mind and the universe.[59] Panentheism is a metaphysics essentially identical with mystical doctrine. The occupation of this ground placed Peirce among a great and scattered company, among them Al Ghazzali, Eckhart, Simone Weil, St. Catherine of Siena, Chuang Tzu, the author of the Diamond Sutra, Emily Dickinson, Pascal, Freeman Dyson, Gandhi, and Plato, persons who knew

> that the phenomenal world is, directly or ultimately, a manifestation of the supramundane or ultimate principle and therefore is at once both phenomenon and manifestation; that temporal existence is in some sort an index of the eternal, and that the eternal is miraculously lodged in the temporal (or vice versa), for those to see who can.[60]

The cosmological position taken by Peirce is closely similar to that of Plato (whom Peirce was then rereading) in the *Timaeus* that the universe is a "Living Being" whose

> character it was impossible to confer in full completeness on the generated thing. But he [the creator] took thought to make, as it were, a moving likeness of eternity; and, at the same time . . . he made, of eternity . . . an everlasting likeness moving according to number—that to which we have given the name Time.[61]

Peirce developed this Platonic cosmology further by describing the spontaneously created and evolving universe (tychism) as a Living Mind (objective idealism) who is embodied in the world as a system of relations represented by signs (logical realism). To borrow a mystical metaphor in the tradition of St. John of the Fourth Gospel, the man whom Peirce in his old age admired above all others, the universe is God's Utterance. As the hyphenated phrase Ideal-Realism implied as early as 1889, objective idealism, logical realism, and tychism, which Peirce had made distinct in the *Monist* series of 1891–93, were now to be taken as three characteristics of the Triune Real.

The more that Peirce's attention became drawn to the nature of the sign, the more the sign's mysterious power to embody the real became the focus of his analysis. Since "all this universe is perfused with signs, if it is not composed exclusively of signs," and all thinking is in signs that represent the real (or other signs), all our experience, if we but consider, is of the real.[62] The real is instinct in us and the rest of the universe as signs. Our way to "catch a fragment" of the thought of the Living Mind is by means of our fallible but trustworthy instinct for guessing at the real meanings of signs, whether we are biographers, scientists, poets, philosophers, or other people who want to know.[63] Hence the central place in Peirce's philosophy of the instinct of hypothetic inference.

Clearly, it was Peirce's passionate attraction to the idea of God which led him to his late formulations, all of which hinged on the realist concept of the community of mind and nature. Even his final classification of the sciences was a consequence of this enthusiasm, a fact likely to be disconcerting to most scientists and to many philosophers. As Peirce put the general point, "if we cannot in some measure understand God's mind, all science . . . must be a delusion and a snare."[64] Specifically, after setting aside the subject of aesthetics (and ethics in any sense not connected with the ideal of truth) for almost forty years as not worthy of study, he rediscovered its fundamental importance for his philosophy in the paper, started in 1903 and published in 1908, he called "A Neglected Argument for the Reality of God." There, he proposed that the "humble argument," the way of finding hypotheses he called the Pure Play of Musement that, like Schiller's concept of *Spieltrieb* follows only the "cosmical weather" of the law of liberty, would lead to a state of mind in which

> the idea of God's reality will be sure sooner or later to be found an attractive fancy, which the Muser will develop in various ways. The more he ponders it, the more it will find repose in every part of his mind, for its beauty, for its supplying an ideal of life, and for its thoroughly satisfactory explanation of his whole threefold environment. . . . [In time he] will come to be stirred to the depths of his nature by the beauty of the idea and its august practicality, even to the point of earnestly loving and adoring his strictly hypothetical God, and to that of desiring above all things to shape the whole conduct of life and all the springs of action into conformity with that hypothesis.[65]

Here, in the last decade of his afflicted life, Peirce found the highest good in "the esthetic ideal, that which we *all* love and adore, the altogether admirable, [which] has, *as ideal,* necessarily a mode of being to be called living. . . . Moreover, the human mind and the human heart have a filiation to God."[66] So powerful to Peirce was this lovely ideal he called *esthetic theism* that to muse about it gently but irresistibly transfigures our perceptions of things.[67] There, too, Peirce found the basis and justification for the ideal of a moral life and for his final classification and ordering of the normative sciences as aesthetics, followed by ethics and logic.[68] Musement, while giving play to the instinct of hypothetic inference, is also mediation and prayer, which led him at length to ask: "Where would such an idea, say as that of God, come from, if not from direct experience?" and to answer, "open your eyes—and your heart, which is also a perceptive organ—and you see him."[69] But he meant the indirect experience of God represented by the direct experience of the interpreting of signs. "As *a matter of opinion* [italics mine]," he wrote, using a mystical metaphor, "I believe that Glory shines out in everything like the sun . . . ," but the experience of that radiance escaped him.[70] As it turned out, Peirce discovered too late that his life had been, beneath both the Philosopher and the Dandy, a reckless search for the experience of the Real. I say about Peirce, borrowing Auden's words about Baudelaire, whose own recognition that God was his goad came only as syphilis cut him down:

> To the eye of nature, he was too late. As he spoke, the bird stooped and struck. But, to the eye of the spirit, we are entitled to believe he was in time—for, though the spirit needs time, an instant of it is enough.[71]

Peirce was an extraordinary and difficult man with a wayward and penetrating intelligence of great power, who perversely thought himself "exceptional" for his almost complete lack of imagination. He believed that his successes in thinking were due to persistence, and to the happy accident of hitting upon a "METHOD of thinking, which any intelligent person could master," yet his profoundly original system of relations, which he intended to be a "theory so comprehensive that, for a long time to come, the entire work of human reason . . . shall appear as the filling up of its details," was almost unintelligible to all but a very few. As a philosopher he was like Columbus, Cabot, and Magellan, the great navigators of the fifteenth and sixteenth centuries, in his deep and courageous explorations into the abstract realms of thought. But he was greater than they because, like the pioneering sixteenth-century cartographers, he also mapped out for the first time the difficult and resistant continents of Mind. As the explorers and cartographers did, Peirce had intimations of what lay beyond the work of his great predecessors, but he was the first to chart, with surprising rightness, the elements and form of a single, seamless world of thought, the infinite universe of signs and its mysterious and commonplace power to represent the Real.

Guide to the Notes

Citations to manuscripts (MS) and letters (L) followed by a reference number refer to the Charles Sanders Peirce Papers at the Houghton Library, Harvard University. The numbers follow Richard Robin's *Annotated Catalogue of the Papers of Charles S. Peirce*. References to publications from Peirce's lifetime are noted by P or O followed by a reference number. (See *A Comprehensive Bibliography and Index of the Published Works of Charles Sanders Peirce*, ed. K. Ketner et al.)

Research for this book was initially carried out in the late 1950s, before many of the resource documents were placed in their present locations. For example, the Family Correspondence from the Benjamin Peirce Papers was not placed with the Charles S. Peirce collection until 1960. An attempt was made to assign a Robin *Catalogue* number to each source item, but in a few instances that was not possible. In those cases, the reader is provided with the location of the collection.

Please refer to the list of abbreviations for further information on the scheme of abbreviation used for names, collections, and books.

Abbreviations

NAMES

ADB	Alexander Dallas Bache	HJ	Henry James
BAC	Benjamin A. Colonna	HPB	Henry Pickering Bowditch
BP	Benjamin Peirce	HPE	Helen Peirce Ellis
CAS	Charles Anthony Schott	JEH	Julius Erasmus Hilgard
CEP	Charlotte Elizabeth Peirce	JGW	Joseph G. Winlock
CJK	Cassius J. Keyser	JMB	James Mark Baldwin
CPP	Carlile P. Patterson	JMC	J. McKeen Cattell
CSP	Charles Sanders Peirce	JMP	James Mills Peirce
CWE	Charles W. Eliot	JWP	James W. Pinchot
DCG	Daniel G. Gilman	MEP	Mary E. Pinchot
EBW	Edwin Bidwell Wilson	MFP	Melusina Fay Peirce

ECP	Edward C. Pickering
FCR	Francis C. Russell
FMT	Frank M. Thorn
GAP	George Arthur Plimpton
GFB	George Ferdinand Becker
GSM	George Shattuck Morison
GWB	George W. Brown
HCL	Henry Cabot Lodge

PC	Paul Carus
SMP	Sarah Mills Peirce
SN	Simon Newcomb
SPL	Samuel P. Langley
TCM	Thomas Corwin Mendenhall
VLW	Victoria Lady Welby
WJ	William James
WPG	Wendell Phillips Garrison

BOOKS AND COLLECTIONS

Abbot	Francis Ellingwood Abbot Papers
Cattell	J. McKeen Cattell Papers
CGS	Coast and Geodetic Survey
CIW	Carnegie Institution of Washington
CP	*Collected Papers of Charles Sanders Peirce*
CSPP	Charles S. Peirce Papers
CU	Columbia University
Eliot	Charles W. Eliot Papers
Gilman	Daniel Coit Gilman Papers
HU	Harvard University
James	William James Papers
JHU	The Johns Hopkins University
Keyser	Cassius Jackson Keyser Papers
LCM	Library of Congress Manuscripts
Lodge	Henry Cabot Lodge Papers
MCCH	Milford County Court House
MD	Milford *Dispatch*
Mitarachi	Sylvia Wright Mitarachi Personal Collection
NA	National Archives
Newcomb	Simon Newcomb Papers
Pickering	Edward C. Pickering Papers
Pinchot	Pinchot Papers
PSP	*Peirce, Semeiotic, and Pragmatism: Essays by Max H. Fisch*
SI	Smithsonian Institution
W	*Writings of Charles S. Peirce: A Chronological Edition*, Volumes 1-4
Welby	Victoria Lady Welby Papers
Winlock	Joseph G. Winlock Papers

Introduction

1. Mumford, epigraph.
2. Eisele, *Studies in the Scientific*, 262.
3. Fisch, "Introductory Note," in Sebeok, *The Play of Musement*, 17.
4. Ibid., 20.
5. MS 909.
6. Apel, 192–93.
7. Alfred North Whitehead to Charles Hartshorne, 2 January 1936, as quoted in Lowe, 345.

8. Popper, 5f., as quoted in Fisch, PSP, 426.

9. Chomsky, 71, as quoted in ibid., 431.

10. Percy, "The Fateful Rift: The San Andreas Fault in the Modern Mind," 18th Jefferson Lecture, 3 May 1989; as quoted in *The Essential Peirce*, Introduction by Houser.

11. Program of *Charles Sanders Peirce Sesquicentennial International Congress, 5–10 September 1989*, HU.

12. Eisele, *Studies in the Scientific*; Fisch, *Peirce, Semeiotic, and Pragmatism*; Murphey, *The Development of Peirce's Philosophy*; *Chance, Love, and Logic*, edited by Cohen; *A History of Science*, edited by Eisele; *Writings*, edited by the Peirce Edition Project.

13. Deledalle, *Charles S. Peirce*; Walther, *Charles Sanders Peirce*, a useful biographical outline.

14. Houser, "The Fortunes and Misfortunes of the Peirce Papers," forthcoming in *Semiotics Comes of Age*, Proceedings of the 4th Congress of the International Association for Semiotic Studies (Barcelona and Perpignan, March/April 1989), vol. 3, edited by Gérard Deledalle (Berlin: Mouton de Gruyter).

15. Eisele, *The New Elements* and *A History of Science*.

16. Mumford, 53–54.

17. This conversation is reported in a letter from Mrs. Austin T. Wright, a sister of Harriet Melusina Fay Peirce (Peirce's first wife), to her daughter Sylvia. The letter is in the Personal Collection of Paul Weiss, with whose kind permission it appears here.

18. See, for example, MSS 1119, 1120.

19. Charles S. Peirce, "Illustrations of the Logic of Science. Third Paper.—How to Make Our Ideas Clear," *Popular Science Monthly* 12 (January 1878): 293 (P 119).

20. Charles S. Peirce, "Issues of Pragmaticism," *The Monist* 15 (October 1905): 481 (P 1080).

21. MS 1644.

22. CSP to CJK, 10 April 1908, Keyser, CU.

23. MS 632; Stanley Coren, *The Left-hander Syndrome* (New York: The Free Press, 1991), passim.

24. Kent, *Logic and the Classification of Science*, 3.

25. MS 1644.

26. Kent, *Logic and the Classification of Science*, 9.

27. CP 1.3–1.4.

28. CP 1.654, as quoted in Raposa, 98.

29. Archibald, 5.

30. Charles S. Peirce, "A Neglected Argument for the Reality of God," *The Hibbert Journal* 7 (October 1908): 90–112 (P 1166).

31. EBW to Paul Weiss, 22 November 1946, Weiss Personal Collection.

32. Baudelaire, 75.

33. Charles S. Peirce, "Evolutionary Love," *The Monist* 3 (January 1893): 178 (P 521), as quoted in CP 6.289; "Man's Glassy Essence," *The Monist* 3 (October 1892): 1–22 (P 480).

34. Baudelaire, 76.

35. CSP to DCG, 25 December 1879, Gilman, JHU.

36. Baudelaire, 78. Baudelaire was, in fact, suffering the first major symptoms of tertiary syphilis. E. B. Wilson suggested in 1958 that Peirce's neurological and psychological symptoms may have been caused by the same disease, which was widespread in America at the time. I find no basis for the diagnosis other than the symptoms them-

selves, which are far more likely the consequences of trigeminal neuralgia, conversion hysteria, and left-handedness.

37. L75.

38. Baudelaire, 65.

39. Ibid., 21–22.

40. Ibid., 22.

41. Melusina Fay Peirce, 122, 199–232.

42. Mitarachi.

1. Father, Son, and Melusina

1. Brooks, *The Flowering of New England*, 34.

2. Ibid., 21–45, 453–69.

3. Some helpful accounts of Peirce ancestry are King, *Benjamin Peirce: A Memorial Collection*; F. C. Peirce, *Peirce Genealogy*; Pulsifer, *Witch's Breed* and *Supplement to Witch's Breed*; R. S. Rantoul, *Historical Collections of the Essex Institute*, 161–76.

4. MSS 847, 848.

5. MS 848.

6. MS 905.

7. Lombroso, xiv–xv.

8. Archibald, 6.

9. Ibid., 5.

10. Ibid., 3–4.

11. Ibid., 12.

12. BP to CSP, 27 January 1860, Cuddeback Letter Book, Milford Historical Society, as quoted in Atkinson, 88–90.

13. Charles S. Peirce, "The Secret of Swedenborg: being an Elucidation of his Doctrine of the Divine Natural Humanity," *North American Review* 110 (April 1870): 463–68 (P 54).

14. Murphey, 16.

15. Ibid., 13–16, 294.

16. Fragment undated and unsigned, perhaps by HPE's husband, William Ellis, CSPP, HU.

17. BP to SMP, 10 September 1839, CSPP, HU.

18. "Charles Sanders Peirce," by Herbert Henry Davis Peirce, *Boston Evening Transcript*, 16 May 1914 (O 1229).

19. Mary E. Huntington to HPE, undated, as quoted in Atkinson, 134.

20. W1:1–3.

21. Atkinson, 129.

22. CEP to her Salem relatives, 12 February [1860], CSPP, HU.

23. BP to ADB, 15 January 1864, Benjamin Peirce Papers, HU.

24. MFP to BMP, 10 March 1863, as quoted in Atkinson, 130.

25. CSP to DCG, 28 February 1880, Gilman, JHU.

26. *Encyclopaedia Britannica*, 11th ed., s.v. "Neuralgia."

27. I well realize the problems in attempting to diagnose illness without the presence of the patient, but in this case, by a process of elimination, I think the conclusion justified. Because the attacks lasted all his life, the only other possible candidate is Bell's

palsy, but the occasional pain reported accompanying that disease is minor by comparison, and one of its major symptoms is the obvious sagging of one side of the face. In addition, unlike trigeminal neuralgia, which until very recently was incurable, patients with Bell's palsy often recover, but if they do not, the sagging remains. There is no evidence whatever of such sagging of Peirce's face. Two factors qualify the likelihood of trigeminal neuralgia: (a) it usually occurs in the elderly, and (b) it is sometimes accompanied by muscle spasms accompanied by a facial tic, often called *tic douloureux*. Peirce was a young man when it was first reported, and there is no evidence that he exhibited a facial tic, except that in 1876 he reported a series of nervous attacks "involving excessive sensibility & muscular contractions." (See CSP to CPP, 6 July 1876, NA, CGS, Assts. N-Z, 1876.) Peirce did not locate these contractions.

28. Carrie L. Badger to CSP, 28 November 1860, Cuddeback Letter Book, Milford Historical Society, as quoted in Atkinson, 128.

29. Fisch, PSP, 65.

30. BP to Sarah Peirce, 24 August [1845], CSPP, HU.

31. BP, undated, CSPP, HU.

32. CSP to CJK, 10 April 1908, Keyser, CU.

33. MS 632, as quoted in Kent, *Logic and the Classification of Science*, Appendix 2, 207–209.

34. Ibid.

35. Ibid., 3–4.

36. MS 296.

37. Charles S. Peirce, "The Law of Mind," *The Monist* 2 (July 1892): 533–34 (P 477).

38. MS 672.

39. BP to Sarah Peirce, 4 May 1851, CSPP, HU.

40. Atkinson, 129.

41. MS 843.

42. Fisch, PSP, 347–49.

43. *Dictionary of American Biography*, s.v. "Peirce, Charles S.," by Paul Weiss, 398–403.

44. CSP to VLW, 14 April 1909, as quoted in Hardwick, 112, and Atkinson, 133.

45. MSS 1629, 1633.

46. Mitarachi.

47. CEP to HPE, 22 May [1880], Benjamin Peirce Papers, HU.

48. Buchler, 50–51.

49. BP to SMP, 2 August 1856, CSPP, HU.

50. Martyn Paine to President Walker, 24 March 1857, Harvard University Corporation Papers, HU.

51. CP 197, 200, as quoted in Sebeok, *The Play of Musement*, 1.

52. Ibid.

53. Summary made by E. B. Wilson, 1946, now found in the Max H. Fisch Collection, Peirce Edition Project, Indiana University–Purdue University at Indianapolis.

54. MS 1629.

55. Charles S. Peirce, "Shakespearean Pronunciation," *The North American Review* 98 (April 1864): 342–69 (P 13).

56. Shakespeare, *A Midsummer Night's Dream*, V, i, 7.

57. MS 823.

58. WJ to unidentified, 16 September [1861], as quoted in Perry, vol. 1, 211.

59. Sebeok and Eco, *The Sign of Three*, 53n26.

60. MSS 917, 920–21, 1140; and Wiener, 72–75.

61. MS 339.

62. Murphey, 2–3.

63. MS 620.

64. Charles S. Peirce, "Evolutionary Love," *The Monist* 3 (January 1893): 182 (P 521).

65. Two pages torn out of a Charles S. Peirce engagement book, Mitarachi.

66. MS 1629.

67. NA, CGS, Personnel and Payroll Records, 1844–1906; Personnel Records, 1816–1881, 187.

68. CSP to ADB, 11 August 1862, NA, CGS, Assts., 1862.

69. CEP to her aunt, 6 November 1858, CSPP, HU.

70. BP to ADB, 12 October 1862, CSPP, HU.

71. SMP to BP, 11 September 1869, CSPP, HU.

72. BP to ADB, 3 and 13 March 1862, as quoted in Atkinson, 22–23.

73. Ibid., passim.

74. Ibid., 5–8.

75. Ibid., 10–11.

76. MFP to George Eliot, 2 August 1869, Beinecke Rare Book and Manuscript Library, Yale University.

77. MFP to Ralph Waldo Emerson, 5 October 1856, as quoted in Atkinson, 17.

78. W1:xxx, Introduction by Fisch.

79. Atkinson, passim.

80. CEP to BP, 3 February 1867; CEP to JMP, June 1867, CSPP, HU.

81. CEP to Benjamin Mills Peirce, 4 April 1867; CEP to Helen Mills Peirce, 18 March 1844, CSPP, HU.

82. Abbot, HU.

83. Brooks, *Indian Summer*, 260–61.

84. Wright, *Philosophical Discussions*, 234.

85. CSP to Francis Ellingwood Abbot, 17 March 1865, Abbot, HU.

86. BP to CPP, 12 February 1866, Benjamin Peirce Papers, HU.

87. Fisch and Kloesel, "Peirce and the Florentine Pragmatists," *Topoi* 1 (1982): 68–73. See also CP 8.213.

88. MS 823; published as P 32.

89. W1:xxvi, Introduction by Fisch.

90. Esposito, 42.

91. CP 5.55.

92. Buchler, 49–53.

93. Duncan Brent gives an excellent account of the point of view of the empirical mystic, especially Chapter One, "Memoir."

94. Charles S. Peirce, "Review of *The Works of George Berkeley*," *The North American Review* 113 (October 1871): 466 (P 60). See also CP 8.30.

95. CSP to CJK, 10 April 1908, Keyser, CU.

96. MS 692. See also Sebeok and Eco, *The Sign of Three*, 16.

97. W2:193–273. See also CP 5.213–.263.

98. Fisch, PSP, 325–26.

99. WJ to HPB, 24 January 1869, James, HU.

100. A. Bronson Alcott to W. T. Harris, 2 April 1868 (L 183).

101. WJ to HPB, 24 January 1869, James, HU.

102. Ibid., 29 December 1869, James, HU.

103. Fisch, PSP, 392–93.

104. MS 1036.

105. HCL, 159–61.

106. Murphey, 102.

107. Hubert Kennedy, " . . . fierce & Quixotic ally," *Harvard Magazine* 85, no. 2 (November–December 1982): 62–64.

108. Fisch, PSP, 121–22.

109. SMP to BP, 22 June 1870, CSPP, HU. See also JGW to BP, 20 June 1870, Winlock, Letters 1869–72, HU.

110. Copy of Peirce's program, Winlock, Letters Received, 1870–75. See also Itinerary, 1871, Winlock, Observatory Letters Received, HU.

111. W2:xlii, Introduction by Merrill.

112. W2:xxxiii, Introduction by Fisch.

113. NA, CGS, *Report of the Superintendent of the Coast Survey,* 1870, Benjamin Peirce report, 230; *Report of the Superintendent of the Coast Survey,* 1873 (P 76), Charles and Melusina Fay Peirce reports, 125–27.

114. CSP to JGW, 29 November 1870, Winlock, Observatory Letters Received, HU.

2. "Our Hour of Triumph Is What Brings the Void"

1. WJ to Oliver Wendell Holmes, 3 January 1868, as quoted in Perry, vol. 1, 508.

2. HJ to C. E. Norton, 24 November 1872, Norton Papers, HU.

3. John Dewey, "The Pragmatism of Peirce," in *Chance, Love, and Logic,* edited by Morris R. Cohen, 301.

4. Fisch, "Metaphysical Club," in *Studies in the Philosophy,* edited by Edward C. Moore and Richard S. Robin, 24–29.

5. WJ to Thomas Sergeant Perry, 24 August 1905, James, HU.

6. WJ to Francis Ellingwood Abbot, 23 January [1876], Abbot, HU.

7. MS 317.

8. Christine Ladd-Franklin, "Charles S. Peirce at the Johns Hopkins," *The Journal of Philosophy, Psychology, and Scientific Methods* 13 (1916): 719 (O 1243).

9. MS 325.

10. WJ to HJ, 24 November 1872, James, HU.

11. CSP to WJ, 10 November 1900, James HU. See also CP 8.253.

12. WJ to CSP, 26 November 1900, CSPP, HU. See also CP 8.253ff.

13. Fisch, "Metaphysical Club," in *Studies in the Philosophy,* edited by Edward C. Moore and Richard S. Robin, 11.

14. Perry, vol. 2, 407n6, 409.

15. Wiener, 24–26.

16. Fisch, "Metaphysical Club," in *Studies in the Philosophy,* edited by Edward C. Moore and Richard S. Robin, 3–32.

17. CP 6.482.

18. CSP to MFP, 17 December 1871, Mitarachi.

19. BP to Secretary of Treasury, 8 April 1872, NA, CGS, Appointment Division Correspondence, 1860–1891.

20. BP to CSP, 30 November 1872; CSP to BP, 28 November 1872, NA, CGS, Assts., 1866–1875.

21. Murphey, 19.

22. CSP to BP, 8 December 1871, NA, CGS, Assts., 1866–1875.

23. CSP to CWE, 2 December 1872, Eliot, HU.

24. JGW to CSP and CWE, see correspondence from 18 July 1870 through 11 June 1875; CSP to JGW, 2 February 1873, Winlock, HU.

25. WJ to HJ, 24 November 1872, James, HU.

26. Agar, 410.

27. Melusina Fay Peirce, "The Externals of Washington," *Atlantic Monthly* (December 1873): 701–16.

28. SMP to JMP, 19 May 1872, CSPP, HU.

29. Victor F. Lenzen and Robert P. Multhauf, 301–48.

30. Correspondence between CSP and CGS, 23 August 1873 through 20 October 1874, NA, CGS, Assts., 1866–1875.

31. CPP to BP, 13 April 1875, CSPP, HU.

32. SMP to CEP, [February] 1874, CSPP, HU.

33. Victor F. Lenzen and Robert P. Multhauf, 301–48.

34. SMP to CEP, 25 December 1874, CSPP, HU.

35. Atkinson, 138–39.

36. MS 771, as quoted in Fisch, PSP, 125.

37. CPP to BP, 24 May 1875, CSPP, HU.

38. CSP to SMP, 7 August 1875, as quoted in Atkinson, 131.

39. BP to CPP, 11 June 1875, NA, CGS, Private Correspondence, 1874–1877.

40. CPP to BP, 19 and 29 June 1875, CSPP, HU.

41. CSP to WJ, 21 November 1875, James, HU.

42. CSP to CPP, 23 September 1875, NA, CGS, Private Correspondence, 1874–1877.

43. JMP to CPP, 19 July 1875; BP to CPP, 19 October 1875; NA, CGS, Private Correspondence, 1874–1877.

44. MFP to CPP, 15 December 1875, NA, CGS, Private Correspondence, 1874–1877.

45. BP to CPP, 6 January 1876, NA, CGS, Private Correspondence, 1874–1877.

46. CSP to CPP, 1 October 1875, NA, CGS, Assts., 1866–1875.

47. BP to CPP, 3 February 1876, NA, CGS, Private Correspondence, 1874–1877.

48. CPP to BP, 6 February 1877, CSPP, HU.

49. CSP to WJ, 21 November 1875, James, HU.

50. HJ to WJ, 3 December 1875, James, HU.

51. WJ to HJ, 12 December 1875, James, HU.

52. HJ to WJ, 14 March 1876, James, HU.

53. Ibid., 4 July 1876, James, HU.

54. CSP to WJ, 16 December 1875, James, HU.

55. WJ to DCG, 25 November 1876, Gilman, JHU.

56. CSP to WJ, 16 December 1875, James, HU.

57. CSP to CPP, 13 January 1876, NA, CGS, Assts. N–Z, 1876.

58. Arieti, 272.

59. BP to CPP, July 1876, NA, CGS, Private Correspondence, 1874–1877.

60. CSP to CPP, 6 July 1876, NA, CGS, Assts. N–Z, 1876.

61. CSP to WJ, 1 April and 17 December 1904, James, HU.

62. CSP to BP, 29 July 1876, CSPP, HU.

63. *Fortnightly Review* 23 (1875): 788–89.

64. SMP to BP, 22 June 1870, CSPP, HU.

65. JGW to CSP, 2 February 1873, Winlock, HU.

66. CSP to CPP, 7 January 1876, NA, CGS, Private Correspondence, 1874–1877.

67. WJ to G. H. Howison, 2 April 1894, as quoted in Perry, vol. 2, 117.

68. CSP to Arthur Searle, 17 July 1875, Pickering, HU.

69. WJ to HJ, 22 May 1869, as quoted in Perry, vol. 1, 296.

70. Archibald, 2.

71. ECP to CWE, 20 January 1877, Eliot, HU.

72. CSP to ECP, 6 April 1877, Pickering, HU; CSP to CWE, 25 April 1877, Eliot, HU.

73. CWE to CSP, 27 April 1877, Eliot, HU.

74. ECP to CWE, 20 January 1877, Eliot, HU.

75. CSP to CWE, 11 May 1877, Eliot, HU.

76. Ibid., 25 May 1877, Eliot, HU.

77. CWE to CSP, 29 May 1877, Eliot, HU.

78. CSP to CWE, 26 April 1878, Eliot, HU.

79. CSP to MFP, [April] 1877, as quoted in Atkinson, 145–46.

80. SMP to JMP, 25 August 1877, CSPP, HU.

81. Melusina Fay Peirce, 5.

82. Fay, *Music Study in Germany.*

83. CP 5.393.

84. Baring-Gould, 206–58.

85. CSP to CPP, 2 April 1877, NA, CGS, Assts. H–Q, 1877.

86. CPP to BP, 21 and 28 April 1877, Benjamin Peirce Papers, HU; BP to Patterson, 16 April 1877, NA, CGS, Private Correspondence, 1874–1877.

87. CPP to BP, 14 June 1877, CSPP, HU.

88. CSP to CPP, 15 June 1877, NA, CGS, Private Correspondence, 1874–1877.

89. CSP to CPP, 28 July 1877, NA, CGS, Private Correspondence, 1874–1877.

90. CSP to WJ, 1 May 1877, James, HU.

91. CSP to CPP, 10 September 1877, NA, CGS, Assts. H–Q, 1877.

92. MS 328.

93. CSP to CPP, 21 September 1877, NA, CGS, Assts. H–Q, 1877.

94. NA, CGS, *Report of the Superintendent of the United States Coast Survey,* 1870, Appendix 21.

95. Lenzen, "Charles S. Peirce as Astronomer," in *Studies in the Philosophy,* edited by Edward C. Moore and Richard S. Robin, 41–42.

96. W2:241–42. See also Shakespeare, *Measure for Measure,* II, ii, 17.

97. Fiske, 340, as quoted in Fisch, PSP, 129.

98. CSP to CPP, 27 September 1877, NA, CGS, Assts. H–Q, 1877.

99. Ibid., 29 September 1877, CSPP, HU.

100. CPP to BP, 12 December 1877, CSPP, HU.

101. CSP to DCG, 13 January 1878, Gilman, JHU.

102. Ibid., 12 March 1878, Gilman, JHU.

103. G. B. Halsted to CSP, 14 March 1878, Gilman, JHU.

104. CSP to James Joseph Sylvester, 19 March 1878, Gilman, JHU.

105. CSP to DCG, 27 March 1878, Gilman, JHU.

106. SMP to BP, 7 August 1878, CSPP, HU.

107. CSP to CPP, 15 August 1878, NA, CGS, Assts. H–Q, 1878.

108. CPP to BP, 8 November 1878, CSPP, HU.

109. Ibid., 24 December 1878, CSPP, HU.

110. Ibid., 10 January 1879, CSPP, HU.

111. CSP to CPP, 23 May 1879, NA, CGS, Assts. L–Q, 1879.

112. W. Gibbs to CPP, 21 April 1879, NA, CGS, Assts. L–Q, 1879.

113. O. N. Rood to CPP, 11 May 1879, NA, CGS, Assts. L–Q, 1879.

114. BP to CPP, 24 May 1879, NA, CGS, Assts. L–Q, 1879.

115. CSP to CPP, 10 June 1879, NA, CGS, Assts. L–Q, 1879.

116. CSP to DCG, 6 June 1879, Gilman, JHU.

117. HJ to Henry S. Leonard, 10 February 1936, as quoted in W4:xxii, Introduction by Houser.

118. CSP to CPP, 10 June 1879, NA, CGS, Assts. L–Q, 1879.

119. W4:xiii–xiv, Introduction by Houser.

120. CPP to CSP, 8 August 1879 (L 91).

121. CSP to CPP, 9 August 1879, NA, CGS, Assts. L–Q, 1879.

122. W4:xxxviii, Introduction by Houser.

123. John Venn, "Review of *Studies in Logic*," *Mind* 8 (1883): 594–603 (O 248).

124. Christine Ladd-Franklin, "Charles S. Peirce at the Johns Hopkins," *The Journal of Philosophy, Psychology, and Scientific Methods* 13 (1916): 716–17 (O 1243).

125. Joseph Jastrow, "Charles Sanders Peirce as Teacher," *The Journal of Philosophy, Psychology, and Scientific Methods* 13 (1916): 725 (O 1244).

126. Fisch, PSP, 35–78; and W4:Introduction by Houser.

127. CSP to DCG, 25 December 1879, Gilman, JHU.

128. See, for example, ibid., 28 February 1880, Gilman, JHU.

129. BP to SMP, correspondence from 20 January to 5 February 1880, CSPP, HU.

130. Benjamin Peirce, 51–52. See also Esposito, 142.

131. Sergeant, 379–80, as quoted in W4:xx, Introduction by Houser.

132. CSP to DCG, 18 December 1880, Gilman, JHU.

133. Ibid., 4 February 1881, Gilman, JHU.

134. Ibid., 9 February 1881, Gilman, JHU.

135. James Joseph Sylvester to DCG, 28 April 1880, Gilman, JHU.

136. CSP to JEH, 1 June 1882, NA, CGS, Assts. N–R, 1882.

3. Expulsion from the Academy and the Search for a New Eden

1. Lenzen, "Charles S. Peirce as Astronomer," in *Studies in the Philosophy*, edited by Edward C. Moore and Richard S. Robin, 49.

2. NA, CGS, *Report of the Superintendent of the United States Coast Survey*, 1876, 202–337, 410–16.

3. W4:lii, Introduction by Houser.

4. Ibid., xli.

5. G. Stanley Hall, "Philosophy in the United States," *Mind* 4 (1879): 101–102 (O 144).

6. CSP to DCG, 7 February [1883], Gilman, JHU.

7. Ibid., 27 March 1883, Gilman, JHU.

8. James Joseph Sylvester to DCG, 18 April 1883, Gilman, JHU.

9. G. W. Hand to DCG, 17 April 1883, Gilman, JHU.

10. W4:lxvi, Introduction by Houser.

11. Baltimore Circuit Court Number 1, Docket 21B, 1881, 64.

12. Walther, 118–23, 167–70, passim.

13. MD, 11 October 1934.

14. Joseph Jastrow, "The Widow of Charles S. Peirce," *Science*, new series 80 (16 November 1934): 440–41 (O 1248).

15. CSP to JEH, undated report beginning on page 3, NA, CGS, Private Correspondence, 1881–1885.

16. Ibid.

17. CSP to DCG, 24 April 1883, Gilman, JHU.

18. CSP to JEH, 3 October 1883, NA, CGS, Assts. L–Q, 1883.

19. SMP to HPE, 19 September 1883, CSPP, HU.

20. Ibid., [23] November 1883, CSPP, HU.

21. CEP to HPE, [20 November 1883], CSPP, HU.

22. SMP to HPE, 27 November 1883, CSPP, HU.

23. Abbot Diary, 10 December 1892, Abbot, HU.

24. CEP to HPE, 18 December 1883, CSPP, HU.

25. Ibid., 18 March 1884, CSPP, HU.

26. Ibid., [April] 1884, CSPP, HU.

27. Ibid., 16 April 1884, CSPP, HU.

28. Ibid., 17 April 1884, CSPP, HU.

29. Ibid., [April] 1884, CSPP, HU.

30. Lester Grinspoon and James B. Bakalar, passim.

31. CSP to DCG, 15 November 1883, Gilman, JHU.

32. SN to DCG, 22 December 1883, Gilman, JHU.

33. DCG to Executive Committee, 15 November 1884, Gilman, JHU.

34. W4:lxix–lxv, Introduction by Houser.

35. Ibid., lxv.

36. Ibid., lxvn56.

37. Newcomb, passim.

38. Eisele, *Studies in the Scientific*, 57.

39. SN to CSP, 9 March 1892 (L 314).

40. CSP to DCG, 8 February 1884, Gilman, JHU.

41. Ibid., 18 February 1884, Gilman, JHU.

42. GWB to DCG, 18 February 1884, Gilman, JHU.

43. CSP to DCG, 7 March 1884, Gilman, JHU.

44. DCG to CSP, 12 April 1884, Gilman, JHU.

45. W4:lxviii–lxix, Introduction by Houser.

46. CSP to GWB, [early October] 1884, Gilman, JHU.

47. Ibid., 10 October 1884, Gilman, JHU.

48. DCG to JHU Executive Committee, 15 November 1884, Gilman, JHU.

49. GWB for the Record, 1 December 1884, Gilman, JHU.

50. W. H. Browne to DCG, 11 April 1887, Gilman, JHU.

51. CSP to FMT, 8 May 1887, NA, CGS, Assts. N–Q, 1887.

52. DCG to GWB, 12 May 1887, Gilman, JHU.

53. CSP to DCG, 30 January 1894, Gilman, JHU.

54. DCG to CSP, 6 February 1894, Gilman, JHU.

55. EBW to Paul Weiss, 22 November 1946, Weiss Personal Collection.

56. NA, CGS, Personnel Record 1881–1900; raise effective 1 January 1884.

57. CEP to JMP, 10 September 1884, CSPP, HU.

58. CEP to her cousins, 18 April 1885, CSPP, HU.

59. CSP to JEH, 5 May 1885, NA, CGS, Assts. N–Q, 1885.

60. Ibid., 1 June 1885, NA, CGS, Assts. N–Q, 1885.

61. CSP to WJ, 20 June 1885, James, HU.

62. Ibid., 24 June 1885, James, HU.

63. CSP to JEH, 29 June 1885, NA, CGS, Assts. N–Q, 1885.

64. Ibid., 30 June 1885, NA, CGS, Assts. N–Q, 1885.

65. Ibid., 1 July 1885, NA, CGS, Assts. N–Q, 1885.

66. *Washington Post*, 25 July 1885.

67. CSP to FMT, 9 August 1885, NA, CGS, Assts. H–Q, 1885.

68. Thomas G. Manning, "Peirce, the Coast Survey, and the Politics of Cleveland Democracy," *Transactions* 11 (Summer 1975): 188–93.

69. Farquahar's Report for FMT, 30 July 1885 (L 91).

70. CSP to D. E. Manning, 9 August 1885, NA, CGS, Assts. H–Q, 1885.

71. Ibid., 11 August 1885, NA, CGS, Assts. H–Q, 1885.

72. CAS to BAC, 14 August 1885, NA, CGS, Assts. H–Q, 1885.

73. CSP to BAC, 15 August 1885, NA, CGS, Assts. P–Z, 1885.

74. CSP to unidentified [probably FMT], 12 August 1885, NA, CGS, Assts. P–Z, 1885.

75. Bache, *Late Attacks upon the Coast and Geodetic Survey*.

76. BAC to CSP, 1 September 1885 (L 91).

77. FMT to CSP, 4 January 1887 (L 91).

78. CSP to WJ, 28 October 1885, James, HU.

79. Apel, 134–37.

80. See Barrow, *Theories of Everything*; Casti, *Searching for Certainty*; Coveney and Highfield, *The Arrow of Time*; Davies, *God and the New Physics*; Zee, *Fearful Symmetry*.

81. W4:546–49.

82. Ibid., 551–52.

83. Gleick, passim.

84. Prigogine and Stengers, 302–303.

85. NA, CGS, Monthly Report, November 1885.

86. CSP to FMT, 7 November 1885, NA, CGS, Assts. N–Q, 1885.

87. Abbot Diary, 13 February 1886, Abbot, HU.

88. CSP to FMT, 24 February 1886, NA, CGS, Assts. N–Q, 1886.

89. Ibid.

90. CSP to BAC, 21 April 1886, NA, CGS, Assts. and Vessels, P–W, 1886.

91. CSP to FMT, 22 March 1886, NA, CGS, Assts. N–Q, 1886.

92. Ibid., 4 June 1886, NA, CGS, Assts. N–Q, 1886.

93. Ibid., 10 August 1886, NA, CGS, Assts. N–Q, 1886.

94. FMT to CSP, 18 August 1886 (L 91).

95. CSP to FMT, 30 September 1886, NA, CGS, Assts. N–Q, 1886.

96. Ibid., 10 October 1886, NA, CGS, Assts. N–Q, 1886.

97. Ibid., 15 December 1886, NA, CGS, Assts. N–Q, 1886.

98. CSP to HCL, 30 September 1886, Lodge, Massachusetts Historical Society.

99. Thomas G. Manning, "Peirce, the Coast Survey, and the Politics of Cleveland Democracy," *Transactions* 11 (Summer 1975): 188–93.

100. FMT to CSP, 24 April 1887 (L 91).

101. CSP to BAC, 1 January 1887, NA, CGS, Assts. and Vessels M–P, 1887.

102. FMT to CSP, 4 January 1887 (L 91).

103. CSP to FMT, 28 February 1887, NA, CGS, Assts. N–Q, 1887.

104. CSP to HCL, 4 January 1887, Lodge, Massachusetts Historical Society.

105. W. L. Winchester to CSP, 22 and 27 May 1887 (L 100).

106. FMT to CSP, 3 March 1887 (L 91).

107. CSP to FMT, 22 April 1887, NA, CGS, Assts. N–Q, 1887.

108. CSP to Gifford Pinchot, [1887], CSPP, HU.

109. CSP to FMT, 9 June 1887, NA, CGS, Assts. N–Q, 1887.

110. Ibid., 29 July 1887, NA, CGS, Assts. N–Q, 1887.

111. Ibid., 29 August 1887, NA, CGS, Assts. N–Q, 1887.

112. Mrs. J. W. Pinchot Diary, Pinchot, LCM.

113. CSP to FMT, 29 September 1887, NA, CGS, Assts. N–Q, 1887.

114. CSP to A. W. Greely, draft, 27 November 1887 (L 174).

115. CSP to FMT, 29 December 1887, NA, CGS, Assts. N–Q, 1887.

116. FMT to CSP, 31 December 1887 (L 91).

117. CSP to FMT, 12 January 1888, NA, CGS, Assts. N–R, 1888.

118. House Deed Book 45, 10 May 1888, MCCH, 92.

119. Batcheler.

120. CSP to FCR, 17 September 1892 (L 387).

121. FMT to CSP, 24 January 1888 (L 91).

122. CSP to FMT, 25 January and 1 February 1888, NA, CGS, Assts. N–R, 1888.

123. Ibid., 30 March 1888, NA, CGS, Assts. N–R, 1888.

124. CAS to FMT, 2 August 1888, NA, CGS, Assts. N–R, 1888.

125. CAS to FMT, 16 August 1888 (L 91).

126. Ibid., 26 December 1888, NA, CGS, Assts. N–R, 1888.

127. CSP to FMT, 31 December 1888, NA, CGS, Assts. N–R, 1888.

128. Ibid., 30 January 1889, NA, CGS, Assts. N–R, 1888.

129. FMT to CSP, 20 February 1889 (L 91).

130. FMT to BAC, 28 May 1889, NA, CGS, Assts. M–Q, 1889.

131. CSP to FMT, 28 May 1889; and FMT to W. B. Chilton, 25 February 1889, NA, CGS, Assts. M–Q, 1889.

132. CSP to TCM, 2 December 1889, NA, CGS, Assts. M–Q, 1889.

133. Ibid., 31 July 1889, NA, CGS, Assts. M–Q, 1889.

134. Ibid., draft, [18 November 1891] (L 91).

135. Ibid., 20 November 1889, NA, CGS, Assts. M–Q, 1889.

136. SN to TCM, 28 April 1890, NA, Records of the U.S. Navy, Nautical Almanac Office, Letters Sent.

137. CSP to TCM, 22 July 1890 (L 91).

138. Victor F. Lenzen, "An Unpublished Scientific Monograph by C. S. Peirce," *Transactions* 5 (1969): 20.

139. TCM to CSP, 1 October 1890 (L 91).

140. CSP to TCM, 2 January and 15 October 1890, NA, CGS, Assts. I–Q, 1890.

141. CSP, 15 October 1890, written on the back of a CGS Circular (L 91).

142. TCM to CSP, 21 September 1891 (L 91).

4. Paradise Lost

1. MD, 9 April 1891.

2. Ibid., 12 May 1892.

3. Gifford Pinchot Diary, 1891, Pinchot, LCM.

4. E. B. Wilson, personal conversation with author regarding Henderson's conversation with J. W. Pinchot, April 1959.

5. Mrs. J. W. Pinchot Diary, 14 November 1891, Pinchot, LCM.

6. W4:544.

7. Thomas A. Sebeok and Jean Umiker-Sebeok, "You Know My Method," in Thomas A. Sebeok and Umberto Eco, 11–47.

8. PC to CSP, 2 July 1890 (L 77).

9. Ibid., 22 July 1890 (L 77).

10. Ibid., 3 August 1890 (L 77).

11. Charles S. Peirce, "The Architecture of Theories," *The Monist* 1 (January 1891): 175–76 (P 439). See also CP 6.7–.34.

12. Charles S. Peirce, "The Doctrine of Necessity Examined," *The Monist* 2 (April 1892): 334 (P 474). See also CP 6.59–.61.

13. Guth, "Speculations on the origin of matter, energy and entropy of the universe," in *Asymptotic Realms of Physics: A Festschrift in Honor of Francis Low.*

14. Charles S. Peirce, "The Law of Mind," *The Monist* 2 (July 1892): 533–59 (P 477). See also CP 6.102–.163.

15. Ibid.

16. Ibid.

17. Bohm, 172. See also *Causality and Chance in Modern Physics.*

18. E. B. Wilson to Paul Weiss, Weiss Personal Collection.

19. Charles S. Peirce, *Chance, Love, and Logic,* 253, 260–65.

20. Charles S. Peirce, "Evolutionary Love," *The Monist* 3 (January 1893): 181 (P 521). See also CP 6.287–.317.

21. G. Stanley Hall to CSP, 12 July 1890 (L 179).

22. CSP to SN, 21 December 1891, Newcomb, LCM; SN to CSP, 24 December 1891 (L 314).

23. CSP to G. F. Becker, 6 December 1891, Becker Collection, General Correspondence, 1885–1895, LCM.

24. HCL to CSP, 18 December 1891 (L 254).

25. H. S. Pritchett to JMP, 15 November 1899, CSPP, HU.

26. Josiah Royce, "Dr. Abbot's 'Way Out of Agnosticism,'" *International Journal of Ethics* (October 1890): 98–113.

27. Abbot Diary, 26 October 1887, Abbot, HU.

28. Charles S. Peirce, "Abbot Against Royce," *The Nation* 53 (12 November 1891): 372 (P 454).

29. WJ to CSP, 12 November 1891, James, HU.

30. Abbot Diary, 28 December 1888, Abbot, HU.

31. CSP to WJ, 17 November 1891, James, HU.

32. Francis Ellingwood Abbot to CSP, 15 November 1891, James, HU. Presumably Peirce sent it along to James.

33. Abbot Diary, 12 February 1886, Abbot, HU.

34. Ibid., 21 May 1892, Abbot, HU.

35. Charles S. Peirce, "Royce's World and the Individual," *The Nation* 75 (31 July 1902): 94 (P 984).

36. Abbot Diary, 31 July 1902, Abbot, HU.

37. CSP to WJ, 13 June 1907, James, HU.

38. CSP to HCL, 8 February 1892, Lodge, Massachusetts Historical Society.

39. CSP to unidentified, 10 January 1892, CSPP, HU.

40. PC to FCR, 6 February 1893, telegram (L 387).

41. CSP to Juliette Peirce, 6 December 1889, as quoted in Eisele, *Studies in the Scientific*, 325.

42. Edward C. Hegeler to CSP, 24 August 1893 (L 77).

43. Ibid., 27 February 1893 (L 77).

44. Ibid., 27 February and 2 March 1893 (L 77).

45. Ibid., 15 May 1893 (L 77).

46. Ibid., 22 June, 7, 13, and 29 July 1893 (L 77).

47. Ibid., 29 July 1893 (L 77).

48. Eisele, *Studies in the Scientific*, 323-25.

49. PC to CSP, 19 May and 10 June 1893 (L 77).

50. Ibid., 10 July 1894 (L 77).

51. Ibid., 16 July 1894 (L 77).

52. CSP to FCR, August 1894 (L 387).

53. Ibid., 5 September 1894 (L 387).

54. Ibid., 6 September 1894 (L 387).

55. Ibid., 6 September 1894, different version (L 387).

56. Ibid., 8 September 1894 (L 387).

57. Ibid.

58. Ibid., 3 November 1894 (L 387).

59. JMP to DCG, 1 October 1893, Gilman, JHU.

60. Charles S. Peirce, reviews of *What Is Meaning?* by V. Welby and *The Principles of Mathematics* by Bertrand Russell, *The Nation* 77 (15 October 1903): 308-309 (P 1028). See also CP 8.171-.175.

61. WPG to CSP (L 159).

62. Kimley Twining to CSP, 2 November 1893 (L 287).

63. *The Publishers' Weekly*, no. 1147 (20 January 1894).

64. CP, vol. 8, 282-86.

65. CSP to Father Searle, 9 August 1895 (L 397).

66. H. Holt to CSP, 2 December 1893 (L 203).

67. WJ to CSP, 24 January 1894, James, HU.

68. CSP to DeVinne Press, 27 February 1894 (L 121).

69. CSP to GAP, 25 May 1894 (L 357).

70. Ibid.

71. Eisele, *Studies in the Scientific*, 41-51.

72. Continuance Docket R, June Term, MCCH, 592.

73. MD, 26 July 1894.

74. Mrs. J. W. Pinchot Diary, entries from 16 July through 19 August 1894, Pinchot, LCM.

75. MD, 18 October 1894.

76. WPG to CSP, November 1894 (L 159).

77. W. G. Winlock to CSP, 31 December 1894, Office of the Secretary, Outgoing Correspondence, 1887-1907, 491.

78. Continuance Docket R, June Term 1894, entry for 2 February 1895, MCCH, 7.

79. Continuance Docket S, December Term 1894, entries for 18 February 1895, 24 January 1897, and 15 February 1897, MCCH.

80. E. Ginn to JMP, 14 February 1895 (L 169).

81. E. Ginn to CSP, 2 March 1895 (L 169).

82. CSP to E. Ginn, 7 March 1895 (L 169).

83. Eisele, *Studies in the Scientific,* 308–50.

84. JMP to WJ, 7 February 1895, James, HU.

85. WJ to CWE, 3 March 1895, James, HU.

86. CWE to WJ, 26 March 1895, James, HU.

87. GSM to CSP, 9 March 1895 (L 300). Correspondence continues through 1901.

88. Commonwealth vs. CSP, 20 April 1895, Docket S, October Term 1895, MCCH.

89. Commonwealth vs. CSP, June Sessions 1889, MCCH.

90. Clipping in Peirce file, Gilman, JHU.

91. Commonwealth vs. CSP, 20 April 1895, Docket S, October Term 1895, MCCH.

92. Continuance Docket S, December Term 1895, MCCH.

93. Thomas A. Sebeok and Umberto Eco, 53n26ff.

94. Brooks, *The Confident Years,* 16.

95. Ibid., 14.

96. Frank Browning and John Gerassi, 289.

97. CSP to FCR, [August 1895] (L 387).

98. CSP to T. J. Montgomery, 16 June 1892 (L 298).

99. E. R. Hewett to CSP, 28 December 1892 (L 196).

100. B. W. Payne & Sons to CSP, 22 November 1892 (L 24).

101. Charles S. Peirce, "Evolutionary Love," *The Monist* 3 (January 1893): 181–82 (P 521). See also CP 6.287–.317.

102. See, for example, MSS 1030–1035; L30, 45, 125, and 416.

103. CSP to J. F. Jameson, 8 June through 11 July 1896 (L 14).

104. WPG to CSP, 4 March 1896 (L 159).

105. CSP to FCR, 4 October 1896 (L 387).

106. Ibid., 10 October 1896 (L 387).

107. CSP to HCL, pages 2 and 4 of an undated fragment (L 254).

108. Charles S. Peirce, *Chance, Love, and Logic,* 275–76.

109. HCL to DCG, 4 January 1903, Gilman, JHU. See also L 75.

110. J. E. d'Aulby to CSP, 2 November 1896 (L 30).

111. A. Bierstadt to CSP, 5 January 1897 (L 45).

112. S. H. E. Stewart to CSP, 28 July 1898 (L 388). CSP signed release 8 August.

113. N. S. Easton to CSP, 30 July 1898 (L 125).

114. Christian J. W. Kloesel, "Charles Peirce and Honoré de Clairefont," *Versus* 49 (January–April 1988): 5–18.

115. Chapman, 94.

116. Eisele, *Studies in the Scientific,* 312.

117. CSP to FCR, 5 November 1896 (L 387).

118. Nathan Houser, ed., "The Schröder-Peirce Correspondence," *Modern Logic* 1 (Winter 1990–1991): 206–36.

119. CSP to E. Schröder, [November 1896] (L 392).

120. F. W. Frankland to CSP, 4 May 1897 (L 148).

121. WPG to CSP, 15 October 1897 (L 159).

122. J. R. Tait to CSP, 4 November 1896 (L 437).

123. Correspondence from 29 January through 17 February 1897, Becker Collection, General Correspondence, 1885–1895, LCM.

124. MD, 4 March 1897.
125. CSP to WJ, 13 March 1897, James, HU.
126. Ibid., 13 December 1897, James, HU.
127. GSM to CSP, 3 June 1897 (L 300).
128. B. E. Smith to CSP, 30 August 1897 (L 80).
129. CSP to WJ, 30 May 1897, James, HU.
130. Ibid., 15 January 1898, James, HU.
131. Ibid., 18 January 1898, James, HU.
132. Ibid., 18 December 1897, James, HU.
133. Ibid.
134. Ibid., 29 January 1898, James, HU.
135. WJ to HJ, 14 February 1898, James, HU.
136. WPG to CSP, 12 February 1898 (L 159).
137. Sara C. Bull to CWE, undated, Eliot, HU.
138. D. C. Heath Co. to CSP, 11 November 1898 (L 192).
139. Royce, *The Problem of Christianity.*
140. G. Putnam to CSP, 28 February 1898 (L 364); and JMC to CSP, 1 March 1898 (L 78).
141. CSP to G. P. Putnam's Sons, 31 March 1898 (L 78).
142. JMC to CSP, 24 May 1898 (L 78).
143. CSP to HCL, undated fragment (L 254).
144. Ibid.
145. CSP to Joseph Dick, draft fragment from 6 January 1900 (L 124).
146. WPG to Juliette Peirce, 12 October 1898 (L 159).
147. WPG to CSP, 1 November 1898 (L 169).
148. GSM to CSP, 15 December 1898 and 17 January 1899 (L 300).
149. E. J. Sommer to CSP, 14 May 1899 (L 85).
150. SN to CSP, 21 July 1899 (L 85).
151. H. S. Pritchett to HCL, 14 September 1899 (L 85).
152. H. S. Pritchett to JMP, 15 November 1899 (L 85).
153. CSP to GAP, two unfinished drafts from 18 November 1899 (L 169).
154. GAP to CSP, 24 November 1899 (L 169).
155. Ibid., 6 April 1900 (L 169).

5. Endgame

1. JMP to ECP, 27 February 1900, and ECP to JMP, 28 February 1900, Pickering, HU.
2. ECP to JMP, 16 April 1900, Pickering, HU.
3. HCL to O. H. Tittman, 20 December 1900, NA, CGS, Applications and Testimonials, 1899–1900.
4. E. D. Preston to CSP, 27 November 1900 (L 91).
5. CSP to SPL, 14 May 1900, Peirce Material II, Office of the Secretary, Incoming Correspondence, 1891–1906, SI.
6. Ibid., 23 February 1901, Peirce Material II, Office of the Secretary, Incoming Correspondence, 1891–1906, SI.
7. CSP to PC, undated fragment, [20 July 1890] (L 77).

8. WPG to CSP, 22 March 1900 (L 159).

9. Ibid., 2 April 1900 (L 159).

10. A. B. Maurice, Jr. to CSP, 18 April 1900 (L 51).

11. CSP to JMC, 9 May 1900, Cattell, LCM.

12. G. Stanley Hall to CSP, 1 June 1900 (L 179).

13. Ibid., 29 January 1901 (L 179).

14. Mighill & Co. to CSP, 2 June 1900 (L 288).

15. *Cosmopolitan* to CSP, 12 June 1900 (L 101).

16. MD, 9 August 1900.

17. GAP to CSP, 18 September 1900 (L 169).

18. WPG to CSP, 22 October 1900 (L 159).

19. CSP to JMB, 15 December 1900 (L 34).

20. F. M. Colby to CSP, 1 February 1901 (L 220).

21. GAP to CSP, 10 February 1900 (L 169).

22. Deedbook 55, 2 February 1901, MCCH, 159.

23. CP 8.253.

24. Ibid., 8.253n8.

25. Ibid., 5.13.

26. Christine Ladd-Franklin to CSP, 14 November 1900 (L 237).

27. Ibid., 9 April 1901 (L 237).

28. JMB to SN, 7 December 1900, Newcomb, LCM.

29. CSP to JMB, undated (L 34).

30. G. P. Putnam's Sons to CSP, 15 March 1901 (L 78).

31. CSP to JMC, 18 April 1901, Cattell, LCM.

32. JMC to CSP, 4 March 1903 (L 78).

33. G. P. Putnam to CSP, 21 December 1903 (L 78).

34. SPL to CSP, 3 April 1901, Office of the Secretary, Incoming Correspondence, 1891–1906, Letters Written 2 April through 27 June 1901, SI.

35. CSP to SPL, undated, [20 May 1901] (L 409).

36. Philip P. Wiener, "The Peirce-Langley Correspondence," *Proceedings of the American Philosophical Society* 91, no. 2 (1947): 201–28.

37. CSP to SPL, April 1901, Office of the Secretary, Incoming Correspondence, 1891–1906, Peirce Material I, SI.

38. GSM to CSP, 27 May 1901 (L 300).

39. CSP to JMC, 21 January 1902, Cattell, LCM.

40. GAP to DCG, 27 January 1902 (L 75).

41. CSP to President of the Carnegie Institute, 12 April 1902 (L 75).

42. M. P. Jacobi to CSP, 4 June 1902 (L 75).

43. Ibid., 12 June 1902 (L 75); J. S. Billings to M. P. Jacobi, 6 June 1902 (L 221).

44. CSP to WJ, 12 June 1902, James, HU.

45. M. Baker to CSP, 18 December 1902 (L 75).

46. CSP to Executive Committee of the Carnegie Institute, 15 July 1902 (L 75).

47. M. Baker to CSP, 30 July 1902 (L 75).

48. MD, 21 August, 9 and 16 October 1902.

49. CSP to WJ, 1 December 1902, James, HU.

50. M. Baker to CSP, 29 November 1902 (L 75).

51. CSP to JMC, 19 December 1902, Cattell, LCM.

52. JMC to JMP, 17 January 1903 (L 78).

53. JMC to C. D. Walcott, 5 January 1903 (L 75).

54. JMP to SN, 31 December 1902, Newcomb, LCM.

55. Herbert H. D. Peirce to CSP, 9 January 1903 (L 338).

56. Theodore Roosevelt to DCG, 12 January 1903 (L 75).

57. C. D. Walcott to SN, 27 February 1903, Newcomb, LCM.

58. Minutes of the Executive Committee, 13 March 1903, Carnegie Institution of Washington.

59. Carnegie Institution of Washington, from alphabetical card file for C. S. Peirce, classified misc.

60. A. Hague to WPG, 4 February 1903 (L 310).

61. WJ to CWE, 28 February 1903, Eliot, HU.

62. CSP to Christine Ladd-Franklin, 20 October 1904, in Christine Ladd-Franklin, "Charles S. Peirce at the Johns Hopkins," *The Journal of Philosophy, Psychology, and Scientific Methods* 13 (1916): 719–20 (P 1243).

63. CP 5.212, as quoted in Apel, 174.

64. Justus Buchler, "One Santayana or Two?" *The Journal of Philosophy* 51 (1954): 52–57, as quoted in Nathan Houser, "Santayana's Peirce."

65. Hardwick.

66. Kent, 4.

67. W. T. Sedgwick to CSP, 3 and 9 October 1903 (L 257).

68. William James, 4–5.

69. WPG to CSP, 18 January and 10 March 1904 (L 159).

70. CSP to SN, 15 January 1904, Newcomb, LCM.

71. CSP to WJ, 1 March 1904, James, HU.

72. CSP to JMP, 15 August 1904 (L 339).

73. CSP to VLW, 2 December 1904, as quoted in Hardwick, 43.

74. Ibid., 16 December 1904, as quoted in Hardwick, 45–46, 50.

75. CSP to WJ, 17 December 1904, James, HU.

76. CSP to VLW, 16 April 1905, as quoted in Hardwick, 52.

77. CSP to WJ, 30 July 1905, James, HU.

78. CSP to VLW, 16 April 1905, as quoted in Hardwick, 53.

79. T. S. Perry to CSP, 12 April 1905 (L 344); CSP to T. S. Perry, [20 April 1905] (L 344).

80. Charles S. Peirce, "What Pragmatism Is," *The Monist* 15 (April 1905): 178 (P 1078). See also CP 5.432.

81. Ibid. See also CP 5.436.

82. Apel, passim.

83. CSP to B. E. Smith, 7 June 1905 (L 80).

84. CSP to FCR, 3 July 1905 (L 387).

85. CSP to WJ, draft, 26 July 1905 (L 224). The final version is CSP to WJ, 30 July 1905 (L 224).

86. CSP to WJ, [23 July 1905], unsent and undated fragment numbered 11.

87. WJ to CSP, 1 August 1905, James, HU.

88. Garrison, 156–57.

89. Ibid., 58–59.

90. CSP to WJ, 1 January 1906, James, HU.

91. Ibid., 30 July 1905, James, HU.

92. C. A. Strong to WJ, 27 July 1905, James, HU.

93. CSP, [January 1906], CSPP, HU.

94. Newcomb Diary, 1906, Newcomb, LCM.

95. CSP to JMC, 8 July 1906, Cattell, LCM.

96. CSP to WJ, 31 October 1906, James, HU.

97. CSP to FCR, 28 December 1906 (L 387).

98. Rukeyser, 378.

99. WJ to HPB, 26 January 1907, James, HU.

100. WJ to MEP, undated, Family Correspondence, Pinchot, LCM.

101. CSP to WJ; see, for example, 10 March and 9 May 1907, among others, James, HU.

102. Ibid.; see, for example, 1 April 1909, James, HU.

103. Mrs. Lodge to MEP, 1 January 1907, Family Correspondence, Pinchot, LCM.

104. CSP to WJ, 13 June 1907, James, HU.

105. Mrs. H. C. Lodge to MEP, 1 February 1907, Family Correspondence, Pinchot, LCM.

106. Register of Wills, 7 September 1907, Book J, MCCH, 162.

107. CSP to SN, 31 October 1907, Newcomb, LCM.

108. Apel, 191.

109. Thomas A. Sebeok, "Indexicality," *The American Journal of Semiotics* 7, no. 4 (1990): 13.

110. Eco, 26–36, 80–86.

111. CP 6.455, as quoted in Houser, "La Structure Formelle de L'Expérience selon Peirce," 77–111.

112. MSS 205, 318, as quoted in Thomas A. Sebeok, "Indexicality," *The American Journal of Semiotics* 7, no. 4 (1990): 15.

113. CSP to W. B. Smith, 25 July 1908 (L 408).

114. CP 6.467, as quoted in Murphey, 365.

115. CP 6.502–.503

116. CP 6.492–.493.

117. Duncan Brent, epigraph.

118. CSP to FCR, 1 January 1909 (L 387).

119. CSP to WJ, 27 March 1907, James, HU.

120. Ibid., 15 December 1909, James, HU.

121. Ibid., 25 December 1909, James, HU.

122. MS 318.

123. CSP to unidentified, 4 May 1892 (L 218).

124. MSS 847, 848.

125. MS 632.

126. Royce, 184–86, as quoted in Fisch, PSP, 275.

127. Ibid.

128. CSP to F. A. Woods, 14 October 1913 (L 477).

129. *Historic Structure Report, Charles S. Peirce House,* 52–53.

130. CSP to Gifford Pinchot, 15 December 1913, Correspondence, Pinchot, LCM.

131. CSP to MEP, [7 January 1914], Family Correspondence, Pinchot, LCM.

132. MS 752.

133. J. Emerson Noll, M.D. to Gifford Pinchot, 8 September 1934, Correspondence, Pinchot, LCM.

134. Benjamin Peirce Ellis, undated, CSPP, HU, as quoted in Christian J. W. Kloesel, "Charles Peirce and Honoré de Clairefont," *Versus* 49 (January–April 1988): 16.

135. Ibid.

136. Gifford Pinchot; see, for example, 8 September to 3 December 1934, Correspondence, Pinchot, LCM.

6. The Wasp in the Bottle

1. CSP to FCR, 15 November 1904 (L 387).
2. CSP to WJ, 23 July 1905, James, HU.
3. CSP to CJK, 10 April 1908, Keyser, CU. See also Fisch, PSP, 362–74.
4. E. Schröder to CSP, 16 February 1896 (L 392).
5. Fiske, 340, as quoted in Fisch, PSP, 250.
6. L 482, as quoted in Fisch, PSP, 250.
7. CP 1.1.
8. CP 5.488.
9. Fisch, PSP, 249–60. I follow Fisch in this discussion of Peirce's views.
10. Charles S. Peirce, review of *Leibniz: The Monadology and Other Philosophical Writings*, translated by Robert Latta, *The Nation* 68 (16 March 1899): 210 (P 683).
11. Charles S. Peirce, review of *La Nouvelle Monadologie*, by Ch. Renouvier and L. Prat, *The Nation* 69 (3 August 1899): 97–98 (P 695).
12. CP 8.216.
13. Fisch, PSP, 258.
14. MS 137, as quoted in Fisch, PSP, 257.
15. CSP to FCR, 10 July 1908 (L 387).
16. W2:71.
17. CSP to WJ, 13 March 1897, James, HU.
18. Ibid., 5 June 1903, as quoted in Perry, vol. 2, 427.
19. WJ to HPB, 24 January 1869, as quoted in Henry James, 149.
20. MS 339.
21. WJ to CSP, 10 July 1903, as quoted in Perry, vol. 2, 427n7.
22. CSP to CJK, 10 April 1908, Keyser, CU.
23. MS 632.
24. MS 1565.
25. CP 4.233, 4.238. In this discussion I follow Nathan Houser, "La Structure Formelle de L'Expérience selon Peirce."
26. Hans G. Herzberger, "Peirce's Remarkable Theorem," in *Pragmatism and Purpose*, edited by Sumner, Slater, and Wilson. Robert W. Burch has provided a proof of the theorem which, so far, holds (at least for realists) in *A Peirceian Reduction Thesis and the Foundations of Topological Logic*.
27. CP 1.568–.572.
28. Charles S. Peirce, "The Architecture of Theories," *The Monist* 1 (January 1891): 175 (P 439). See also CP 6.32.
29. CP 1.357.
30. MS 904.
31. CP 1.358.
32. MS 904.
33. CP 2.85.
34. Charles S. Peirce, *The Essential Peirce*, edited by Nathan Houser and Christian Kloesel. See also CP 1.358.

35. Shakespeare, *The Merchant of Venice,* II, vi, 12.

36. Snow, 27. See also CP 5.534.

37. W2:241–42.

38. MS 330. See also CP 6.479.

39. MS 843.

40. MS 970.

41. CP 6.287, as quoted in Raposa, 89.

42. CP 8.263.

43. Mitarachi.

44. WPG to CSP 4 March 1896 (L 159).

45. CSP to WJ, 13 March 1897, James, HU.

46. MS 905.

47. Charles S. Peirce, "Issues of Pragmaticism," *The Monist* 15 (October 1905): 481 (P 1080). See also CP 5.438.

48 Ibid., 484. See also CP 5.442.

49. CP 1.591–.599.

50. MS 1562.

51. CSP to WJ, 13 March 1897, James, HU.

52. CP 1.287.

53. CP 6.476, as quoted in Raposa, 132.

54. CP 1.80.

55. Ibid., 1.81.

56. CP 8.186 for the context of the communion of mankind. Raposa in his *Peirce's Philosophy of Religion* came from a different perspective to the same formulation of Peirce's idea of Mind as both immanent and transcendent, 50–51.

57. Beverly Kent, "Peirce's Esthetics: A New Look," *Transactions* 12, no. 3 (1976): 277. See also CP 1.220.

58. CP 6.277.

59. Raposa, 51.

60. Duncan Brent, 76.

61. Plato, *Timaeus,* translated by F. M. Cornford, in Cornford, 37.

62. CP 5.448n1.

63. Ibid., 6.502.

64. Ibid., 8.168.

65. Ibid., 6.465, .467.

66. CSP to WJ, 23 July 1905, James, HU.

67. L 224, as quoted in Raposa, 110.

68. Beverly Kent, "Peirce's Esthetics: A New Look," *Transactions* 12, no. 3 (1976): 263–83. Kent gives a thoughtful account of Peirce's development of the argument which placed aesthetics as the highest of the normative sciences.

69. CP 6.493.

70. MS 310.

71. W. H. Auden, Introduction to *Intimate Journals,* 27.

BIBLIOGRAPHY

Works by Charles S. Peirce

ARTICLES

Peirce, Charles S. "A Neglected Argument for the Reality of God." *The Hibbert Journal: A Quarterly Review of Religion, Theology, and Philosophy* 7 (October 1908–July 1909): 90–112.

————. *The Monist*:
"The Architecture of Theories." 1 (January 1891): 161–176.
"The Doctrine of Necessity Examined." 2 (April 1892): 321–337.
"The Law of Mind." 2 (July 1892): 533–559.
"Man's Glassy Essence." 3 (October 1892): 1–22.
"Evolutionary Love." 3 (January 1893): 176–200.
"What Pragmatism Is." 15 (April 1905): 161–181.
"Issues of Pragmaticism." 15 (October 1905): 481–499.

————. *The Nation*:
"Abbot Against Royce." 53 (12 November 1891): 372.
Review of *Leibniz: The Monadology and Other Philosophical Writings*. Translated by Robert Latta. 68 (16 March 1899): 210.
Review of *La Nouvelle Monadologie*, by Ch. Renouvier and L. Prat. 69 (3 August 1899): 97–98.
Reviews of *What Is Meaning?* by V. Welby, and *The Principles of Mathematics*, by Bertrand Russell. 77 (15 October 1903): 308–309.

————. *The North American Review*:
"Shakespearean Pronunciation." 90 (April 1864): 342–369.
Review of *The Secret of Swedenborg: being an Elucidation of his Doctrine of the Divine Natural Humanity*, by Henry James. 110 (April 1870): 463–468.
Review of *The Works of George Berkeley, D.D., formerly Bishop of Cloyne: including many of his Writings hitherto unpublished*. Edited by Alexander Campbell Fraser. 113 (October 1871): 449–472.

————. "Illustrations of the Logic of Science. Second Paper.—How to Make Our Ideas Clear." *The Popular Science Monthly* 12 (January 1878): 286–302.

————. "An Unpublished Scientific Monograph by C. S. Peirce." Edited by Victor F.

Lenzen. *Transactions of the Charles S. Peirce Society: A Quarterly Journal in American Philosophy* 5, no. 1 (1969): 20.

EDITED VOLUMES

Peirce, Charles S. *Chance, Love, and Logic: Philosophical Essays by the Late Charles S. Peirce, the Founder of Pragmatism.* Edited by Morris R. Cohen. New York: Barnes & Noble, Inc., 1923.

————. *Collected Papers of Charles Sanders Peirce.* Edited by Charles Hartshorne and Paul Weiss. Vols. I–VI. Cambridge, Massachusetts: Harvard University Press, 1931–35.

————. *Collected Papers of Charles Sanders Peirce.* Edited by A. Burks. Vols. VII–VIII. Cambridge, Massachusetts: Harvard University Press, 1958.

————. *The Essential Peirce.* Vol. 1. Edited by Nathan Houser and Christian Kloesel. Bloomington: Indiana University Press, 1992.

————. *A History of Science: Historical Perspectives on Peirce's Logic of Science.* Edited by Carolyn Eisele. 2 vols. The Hague: Mouton Publishers, 1985.

————. *The New Elements of Mathematics by Charles S. Peirce.* Edited by Carolyn Eisele. The Hague: Mouton Publishers, 1976.

————. *Semiotic and Significs: The Correspondence between Charles S. Peirce and Victoria Lady Welby.* Edited by Charles S. Hardwick. Bloomington: Indiana University Press, 1977.

————. *Writings of Charles S. Peirce: A Chronological Edition.* Edited by the Peirce Edition Project. Projected in 30 vols. Bloomington: Indiana University Press, 1982–.

Manuscripts and Letters

Abbot, Francis Ellingwood. *Papers.* Harvard University Archives, Pusey Library, Cambridge, Massachusetts.

Becker, George Ferdinand. *Papers.* Library of Congress Manuscripts, Washington, D.C.

Carnegie Institution of Washington. Washington, D.C.

Cattell, J. McKeen. *Papers.* Library of Congress Manuscripts, Washington, D.C.

Eliot, Charles W. *Papers.* Harvard University Archives, Pusey Library, Cambridge, Massachusetts.

Eliot, George. *George Eliot and George Henry Lewes Collection.* The Beinecke Rare Book and Manuscript Library, Yale University Library, New Haven, Connecticut.

Fisch, Max H. *Max H. Fisch Collection.* Peirce Edition Project, Indiana University–Purdue University at Indianapolis, Indiana.

Gilman, Daniel Coit. *Papers.* Special Collections. Milton S. Eisenhower Library, The Johns Hopkins University.

Harvard Observatory Letters. Harvard University Archives, Pusey Library, Cambridge, Massachusetts.

Harvard University Corporation Papers. Harvard University Archives, Pusey Library, Cambridge, Massachusetts.

James, William. *Papers.* The Houghton Library, Harvard University, Cambridge, Massachusetts.

Keyser, Cassius Jackson. *Papers.* Rare Book and Manuscript Library, Columbia University, New York.

Lodge, Henry Cabot. *Papers.* Massachusetts Historical Society, Boston, Massachusetts.

Milford Historical Society. Milford, Pennsylvania.

Mitarachi, Sylvia Wright. *Papers.* Schlesinger Library, Radcliffe College, Cambridge, Massachusetts.

Newcomb, Simon. *Papers.* Library of Congress Manuscripts, Washington, D.C.

Norton, Charles Eliot. *Papers.* The Houghton Library, Harvard University, Cambridge, Massachusetts.

Peirce, Benjamin. *Papers.* The Houghton Library, Harvard University, Cambridge, Massachusetts.

Peirce, Charles S. *Papers.* The Houghton Library, Harvard University, Cambridge, Massachusetts.

Pickering, E. C. *Papers.* Harvard University Archives, Pusey Library, Cambridge, Massachusetts.

Pinchot. *Family Papers.* Library of Congress Manuscripts, Washington, D.C.

Smithsonian Institution Archives.

    RU 31, Office of the Secretary, Incoming Correspondence, 1891–1906.

    RU 34, Office of the Secretary, Outgoing Correspondence, 1887–1907.

Weiss, Paul. Personal Collection.

Winlock, Joseph G. *Papers.* Harvard University Archives, Pusey Library, Cambridge, Massachusetts.

Government Documents

Baltimore, Maryland. Circuit Court Number 1. Docket 21B. 1881.

Historic Structure Report, Charles S. Peirce House.

Milford, Pennsylvania. Milford County Court House:

    Continuance Docket R. June Term, 1894.

    Continuance Docket S. December Term, 1894.

    Continuance Docket S. December Term, 1955.

    Deedbook 55, 1901.

    Docket S. October Term, 1895.

    House Deed Book 45, 1888.

    June Sessions, 1889.

    Register of Wills, Volume J, 1913–.

U.S. National Archives. General Correspondence of Alexander Dallas Bache, Superintendent of the Coast Survey. 1844–65:

    Civil Assistants H–Z, 1862.

U.S. National Archives. Records of the Coast and Geodetic Survey. Record Group 23. Superintendent's Files (1866–1905):

    Applications and Testimonials, 1899–1900.

    Appointment Division Correspondence, 1860–1891.

    Monthly Report, 1885.

    Personnel Records 1816–1881; 1881–1900.

    Letters Received from Assistants: 1867–1875; N–Z 1875; H–Q 1877; M–Q 1878; L–Q 1879; N–R 1882; L–Q 1883; H–Q 1885; N–Q 1885; P–Z 1885; N–Q 1886; N–Q 1887; N–R 1888; M–Q 1889; I–Q 1890; N–Q 1890.

    Assistants and Naval Vessels M–P, 1887.

Private Correspondence 1874–1877: 1881–1885.

Report of the Superintendent of the United States Coast Survey 1870: 1873; 1876.

U.S. National Archives. General Records of the Department of the Navy. Record Group 45.

Articles

Auden, W. H. Introduction to *Intimate Journals,* by Charles Baudelaire. Translated by Christopher Isherwood. London: Panther Books, 1969.

Buchler, Justus. "One Santayana or Two?" *The Journal of Philosophy* 51 (1954): 52–57.

Clifford, W. K. *Fortnightly Review* 23 (1875): 788–789.

Fisch, Max H. Introduction to *Writings of Charles S. Peirce: A Chronological Edition,* vol. 1, edited by the Peirce Edition Project. Bloomington: Indiana University Press, 1982.

———. "The Decisive Year and Its Early Consequences." In the Introduction to *Writings of Charles S. Peirce: A Chronological Edition,* vol. 2, edited by the Peirce Edition Project. Bloomington: Indiana University Press, 1984.

———. "Was There a Metaphysical Club?" In *Studies in the Philosophy of Charles Sanders Peirce,* edited by Edward C. Moore and Richard S. Robin. Amherst: The University of Massachusetts Press, 1964.

———, and Kloesel, Christian J. W. "Peirce and the Florentine Pragmatists: His Letter to Calderoni and a New Edition of His Writings." *Topoi* 1 (1982): 68–73.

Hall, G. Stanley. "Philosophy in the United States." *Mind* 4 (1879): 89–105.

Herzberger, Hans G. "Peirce's Remarkable Theorem." In *Pragmatism and Purpose,* edited by L. W. Sumner, John G. Slater, and Fred Wilson. Toronto: University of Toronto Press, 1981.

Houser, Nathan. Introduction to *Writings of Charles S. Peirce: A Chronological Edition,* vol. 4, edited by the Peirce Edition Project. Bloomington: Indiana University Press, 1989.

———. "The Fortunes and Misfortunes of the Peirce Papers." Forthcoming in *Semiotics Comes of Age,* Proceedings of the 4th Congress of the International Association for Semiotic Studies (Barcelona and Perpignan, March/April 1989), vol. 3, edited by Gérard Deledalle. Berlin: Mouton de Gruyter.

———. "Santayana's Peirce." Presented to the Peirce Sesquicentennial Congress (1990). Forthcoming in Congress proceedings. Abridged version *Overheard in Seville; Bulletin of the Santayana Society,* no. 8 (1990), pp. 10–13.

———. "La Structure Formelle de L'Expérience selon Peirce." *Etudes Phénoménologiques* 9–10 (1989): 77–111.

———, ed. "The Schröder-Peirce Correspondence." *Modern Logic* 1 (Winter 1990–1991): 206–236.

Jastrow, J. "Charles S. Peirce as a Teacher." *The Journal of Philosophy, Psychology, and Scientific Methods* 13 (1916): 723–726.

———. "The Widow of Charles S. Peirce." *Science,* new series 80 (16 November 1934): 440–441.

Jevons, W. Stanley. "Recent Mathematico-Logical Memoirs." *Nature* (24 March 1881): 485–487.

Kennedy, Hubert. " . . . 'fierce & Quixotic ally.'" *Harvard Magazine* 85, no. 2 (November/December 1982): 62–64.

Kent, Beverley. "Peirce's Esthetics: A New Look." *Transactions of the Charles S. Peirce Society: A Quarterly Journal in American Philosophy* 12, no. 3 (1976): 263–283.

Kloesel, Christian J. W. "Charles Peirce and Honoré de Clairefont." *Versus* 49 (January–April 1988): 5–18.

Ladd-Franklin, Christine. "Charles S. Peirce at the Johns Hopkins." *The Journal of Philosophy, Psychology, and Scientific Methods* 13 (1916): 715–722.

Lenzen, Victor F. "Charles S. Peirce as Astronomer." In *Studies in the Philosophy of Charles Sanders Peirce*, edited by Edward C. Moore and Richard S. Robin. Amherst: The University of Massachusetts Press, 1964.

Lenzen, Victor F., and Multhauf, Robert P. "Developments of Gravity Pendulums in the 19th Century." *United States National Museum Bulletin* 240, paper 44 (1965): 301–348.

Manning, Thomas G. "Peirce, the Coast Survey, and the Politics of Cleveland Democracy." *Transactions of the Charles S. Peirce Society: A Quarterly Journal in American Philosophy* 11, no. 3 (1975): 188–193.

Merrill, Daniel D. "The 1870 Logic of Relatives Memoir." In the Introduction to *Writings of Charles S. Peirce: A Chronological Edition*, vol. 2, edited by the Peirce Edition Project. Bloomington: Indiana University Press, 1984.

Milford *Dispatch*. 9 April 1891; 12 May 1892; 26 July 1894; 16 October 1894; 4 March 1897; 9 August 1900; 21 August 1902; 9 October 1902; 16 October 1902; 11 October 1934.

Peirce, Herbert Henry Davis. "Charles Sanders Peirce." *Boston Evening Transcript*, 16 May 1914.

Peirce, Melusina Fay. *Atlantic Monthly* (December 1873): 701–716.

The Publishers' Weekly, no. 1147 (20 January 1894): 62.

Royce, Josiah. "Dr. Abbot's 'Way Out of Agnosticism.'" *International Journal of Ethics* (October 1890): 98–113.

———. "The World and the Individual." *The Nation* 75 (July 1902): 94–96.

Sebeok, Thomas A. "Indexicality." *The American Journal of Semiotics* 7, no. 4 (1990).

Sebeok, Thomas A., and Umiker-Sebeok, Jean. "You Know My Method." In *The Sign of Three: Dupin, Holmes, Peirce*, edited by Thomas A. Sebeok and Umberto Eco. Bloomington: Indiana University Press, 1983.

Venn, J. Review of *Studies of Logic*. *Mind* 8 (1883): 594–603.

Washington Post, 25 July 1885.

Wiener, Philip P. "The Peirce-Langley Correspondence and Peirce's Manuscript on Hume & the Laws of Nature." *Proceedings of the American Philosophical Society* 91, no. 2 (1947): 201–228.

Books

Agar, Herbert. *The Price of Union*. Boston: Houghton Mifflin Co., 1966.

Apel, Karl-Otto. *Charles S. Peirce: From Pragmatism to Pragmaticism*. Amherst: The University of Massachusetts Press, 1981.

Archibald, Raymond Clare. *Benjamin Peirce, 1809–1880: Bibliographical Sketch and Bibliography*. Oberlin, Ohio: The Mathematical Association of America, 1925.

Arieti, Silvan, ed. *The American Handbook of Psychiatry*. Vol. 1. New York: Basic Books, Inc., 1959.

Atkinson, Norma Pereira. "An Examination of the Life and Thought of Zina Fay Peirce, an American Reformer and Feminist." Ph.D. diss., Ball State University, 1984.

Bache, Richard A. *Late Attacks upon the Coast and Geodetic Survey.* Philadelphia: L. R. Hammersley & Co., 1884.

Baring-Gould, S. *Curious Myths of the Middle Ages.* Philadelphia: Second Series, 1868.

Barrow, John D. *Theories of Everything: The Quest for Ultimate Explanation.* Oxford: Clarendon Press, 1991.

Batcheler, Penelope Hartshorne. *Delaware Water Gap, Charles S. Peirce House.* Denver: National Park Service, Department of the Interior, 1983.

Baudelaire, Charles. *Intimate Journals.* Translated by Christopher Isherwood. London: Panther Books, 1969.

Bohm, David. *Causality and Chance in Modern Physics.* London: Routledge & Kegan Paul, 1957.

———. *Wholeness and the Implicate Order.* London: Routledge & Kegan Paul, 1980.

Brent, Duncan. *Of the Seer and the Vision.* Amsterdam: Menno Herzberger & Co., 1966.

Brooks, Van Wyck. *The Confident Years, 1885–1915.* New York: E. P. Dutton, Inc., 1952.

———. *The Flowering of New England.* New York: E. P. Dutton & Co., 1936.

———. *New England: Indian Summer, 1865–1915.* New York: E. P. Dutton & Co., 1940.

Browning, Frank, and Gerassi, John. *The American Way of Crime from Salem to Watergate.* New York: Putnam, 1980.

Buchler, Justus. *Charles Peirce's Empiricism.* New York: Octagon Books, 1966.

Burch, Robert W. *A Peirceian Reduction Thesis and the Foundations of Topological Logic.* Lubbock, Texas: Texas Tech University Press, in press.

Casti, John L. *Searching for Certainty: What Scientists Can Know about the Future.* New York: William Morrow & Co., 1990.

Chapman, John Jay. *John Jay Chapman and His Letters.* Edited by Mark A. DeWolfe Howe. Boston: Houghton Mifflin Co., 1937.

Chomsky, Noam. *Language and Responsibility.* New York: Pantheon Books, 1979.

Cornford, Francis M. *Plato's Cosmology: The Timaeus of Plato Translated with a Running Commentary.* New York: The Liberal Arts Press, 1957.

Coveney, Peter, and Highfield, Roger. *The Arrow of Time: A Voyage through Science to Solve Time's Greatest Mystery.* New York: Fawcett Columbine, 1990.

Davies, Paul. *God and the New Physics.* New York: Simon & Schuster, Inc., 1983.

Deledalle, Gérard. *Charles S. Peirce: An Intellectual Biography.* Amsterdam: John Benjamin's Publishing Co., 1990.

Dictionary of American Biography. S.v. "Peirce, Charles S.," by Paul Weiss. 1934.

Eco, Umberto. *Semiotics and the Philosophy of Language.* Bloomington: Indiana University Press, 1984.

Eisele, Carolyn. *Studies in the Scientific and Mathematical Philosophy of Charles S. Peirce: Essays by Carolyn Eisele.* Edited by Richard M. Martin. The Hague: Mouton Publishers, 1979.

Encyclopaedia Britannica. 11th ed. S.v. "Neuralgia."

Esposito, Joseph L. *Evolutionary Metaphysics: The Development of Peirce's Theory of Categories.* Athens: Ohio University Press, 1980.

Fay, Amy. *Music-Study in Germany: From the Home Correspondence of Amy Fay.* Edited by the author of "Cooperative Housekeeping." Chicago: Jansen, McClurg & Co., 1881.

Fisch, Max H. *Peirce, Semeiotic, and Pragmatism: Essays by Max H. Fisch.* Edited by

Kenneth Laine Ketner and Christian J. W. Kloesel. Bloomington: Indiana University Press, 1986.

Fiske, John. *Edward Livingstone Youmans*. New York: D. Appleton & Co., 1894.

Garrison, Wendell Phillips. *Letters and Memorials of Wendell Phillips Garrison, Literary Editor of* The Nation *1865–1906*. Boston: Houghton Mifflin, 1909.

Gleick, James. *Chaos: Making a New Science*. New York: Viking, 1987.

Grinspoon, Lester, and Bakalar, James B. *Cocaine: A Drug and Its Social Evolution*. Rev. ed. New York: Basic Books, 1985.

Guth, A. H.; Huang, K.; and Jaffe, R. L., eds. *Asymptotic Realms of Physics: A Festschrift in Honor of Francis Low*. Cambridge: Massachusetts Institute of Technology Press, 1983.

James, Henry, ed. *The Letters of William James*. 2 vols. Bombay, Calcutta, and Madras: Longmans, Green, & Co., 1920.

James, William. *Pragmatism*. New York: Meridian Books, 1955.

Kent, Beverley E. *Charles S. Peirce: Logic and the Classification of Science*. Montreal: McGill-Queens University Press, 1987.

Ketner, Kenneth Laine; Kloesel, Christian J. W.; Ransdell, Joseph M.; Fisch, Max H.; and Hardwick, Charles S., eds. *A Comprehensive Bibliography and Index of the Published Works of Charles Sanders Peirce with a Bibliography of Secondary Studies*. Greenwich, Connecticut: Johnson Associates, Inc., 1977.

King, Moses, ed. *Benjamin Peirce: A Memorial Collection*. Cambridge, Massachusetts, 1880.

Lodge, Henry Cabot. *Early Memories*. New York: Charles Scribner's Sons, 1913.

Lombroso, Cesare. *Criminal Man*. New York: Knickerbocker Press, 1911.

Lowe, Victor. *Alfred North Whitehead: The Man and His Work*. Vol. 2. Edited by J. B. Schneewind. Baltimore and London: The Johns Hopkins University Press, 1990.

Moore, Edward C., and Robin, Richard S., eds. *Studies in the Philosophy of Charles Sanders Peirce*. Amherst: The University of Massachusetts Press, 1964.

Mumford, Lewis. *Brown Decades*. New York: Dover Publications, 1955.

Murphey, Murray G. *The Development of Peirce's Philosophy*. Cambridge: Harvard University Press, 1961.

Newcomb, Simon. *The Reminiscences of an Astronomer*. Boston and New York: Houghton, Mifflin & Co., 1903.

Peirce, Benjamin. *Identity in the Physical Sciences*. Boston: Little, Brown & Co., 1881.

Peirce, Frederick C. *Peirce Genealogy*. Worcester: C. H. Hamilton Press, 1880.

Peirce, Melusina Fay. *New York: A Symphonic Study in Three Parts*. New York: Neale Publishing Co., 1918.

Perry, R. B. *The Thought and Character of William James*. 2 vols. Boston: Little, Brown & Co., 1935.

Popper, Karl. *Of Clouds and Clocks*. St. Louis: Washington University Press, 1966.

Prigogine, Ilya, and Stengers, Isabelle. *Order out of Chaos: Man's New Dialogue with Nature*. New York: Viking, 1987.

Pulsifer, Susan Nichols. *Witch's Breed: The Peirce-Nichols Family of Salem*. Cambridge, Massachusetts: Dresser, Chapman & Grimes, Inc., 1967.

————. *Supplement to Witch's Breed: The Peirce-Nichols Family of Salem*. Cambridge, Massachusetts: Dresser, Chapman & Grimes, Inc., 1967.

Rantoul, R. S. *Historical Collections of the Essex Institute*. Vol. 18. 1880.

Raposa, Michael L. *Peirce's Philosophy of Religion*. Bloomington: Indiana University Press, 1989.

Robin, Richard S. *Annotated Catalogue of the Papers of Charles S. Peirce.* Amherst: The University of Massachusetts Press, 1967.

Royce, Josiah. *The Problem of Christianity.* 2 vols. New York: Macmillan & Co., 1913.

Rucker, Darnell. *The Chicago Pragmatists.* Minneapolis: University of Minnesota Press, 1969.

Rukeyser, Muriel. *Willard Gibbs.* New York: Doubleday, Doran & Co., 1942.

Sebeok, Thomas A. *The Play of Musement.* Bloomington: Indiana University Press, 1981.

————, and Eco, Umberto, eds. *The Sign of Three: Dupin, Holmes, Peirce.* Bloomington: Indiana University Press, 1983.

Sergeant, Mrs. John T., ed. *Sketches and Reminiscences of the Radical Club.* Boston: James Osgood & Co., 1880.

Shakespeare, William. *The Workes of Shakespeare.* Edited by William George Clark and William Aldis Wright. London: Macmillan & Co., 1911.

Snow, C. P. *The Two Cultures and the Scientific Revolution.* New York: Cambridge University Press, 1959.

Walther, Elisabeth. *Charles Sanders Peirce: Leben und Werk.* Baden-Baden: Agis-Verlag, 1989.

Wiener, Philip P. *Evolution and the Founders of Pragmatism.* Cambridge: Harvard University Press, 1949.

Wright, Chauncey. *Philosophical Discussions.* In *Cambridge History of American Literature*, vol. 3. Cambridge: Harvard University Press, 1876.

Zee, A. *Fearful Symmetry: The Search for Beauty in Modern Physics.* New York: Macmillan Publishing Co., 1986.

INDEX